The Skills Balancing Act in Sub-Saharan Africa

The Skills Balancing Act in Sub-Saharan Africa

Investing in Skills for Productivity, Inclusivity, and Adaptability

Omar Arias, David K. Evans, and
Indhira Santos

A copublication of the Agence française de développement and the World Bank

ISBN (paper): 978-1-4648-1149-4
ISBN (electronic): 978-1-4648-1350-4
DOI: 10.1596/978-1-4648-1149-4
SKU: 211149

Cover photo: ©PeopleImages / istockphoto.com. Used with permission of istockphoto.com. Further permission required for reuse.

Cover design: Bill Pragluski, Critical Stages, LLC.

Library of Congress Cataloging-in-Publication Data
Names: Arias, Omar, author. | Evans, David K., 1975- author. | Santos, Indhira, author.
Title: The skills balancing act in Sub-Saharan Africa : investing in skills for productivity, inclusivity, and adaptability / by Omar Arias, David K. Evans, Indhira Santos.
Description: Washington, D.C. : World Bank, 2019. | Series: Africa development forum series | Includes bibliographical references. | Identifiers: LCCN 2019019314 (print) | LCCN 2019021656 (ebook) | ISBN 9781464813504 (electronic) | ISBN 9781464811494 (pbk.)
Subjects: LCSH: Labor supply--Africa, Sub-Saharan. | Vocational education--Africa, Sub-Saharan. | Vocational qualifications--Africa, Sub-Saharan.
Classification: LCC HD5837.A6 (ebook) | LCC HD5837.A6 A75 2019 (print) | DDC 331.1140967--dc23
LC record available at https://lccn.loc.gov/2019019314

Africa Development Forum Series

The **Africa Development Forum Series** was created in 2009 to focus on issues of significant relevance to Sub-Saharan Africa's social and economic development. Its aim is both to record the state of the art on a specific topic and to contribute to ongoing local, regional, and global policy debates. It is designed specifically to provide practitioners, scholars, and students with the most up-to-date research results while highlighting the promise, challenges, and opportunities that exist on the continent.

The series is sponsored by Agence française de développement and the World Bank. The manuscripts chosen for publication represent the highest quality in each institution and have been selected for their relevance to the development agenda. Working together with a shared sense of mission and interdisciplinary purpose, the two institutions are committed to a common search for new insights and new ways of analyzing the development realities of the Sub-Saharan Africa region.

Advisory Committee Members

Agence française de développement
- **Gaël Giraud,** Chief Economist
- **Thomas Melonio,** Executive Director, Research and Knowledge Directorate
- **Pierre Icard,** Director, Head of Knowledge Department on Sustainable Development
- **Sophie Chauvin,** Head, Edition and Publication Division
- **Hélène Djoufelkit,** Deputy Head, Economic Assessment and Public Policy Department

World Bank
- **Albert G. Zeufack,** Chief Economist, Africa Region
- **Markus P. Goldstein,** Lead Economist, Africa Region

Sub-Saharan Africa

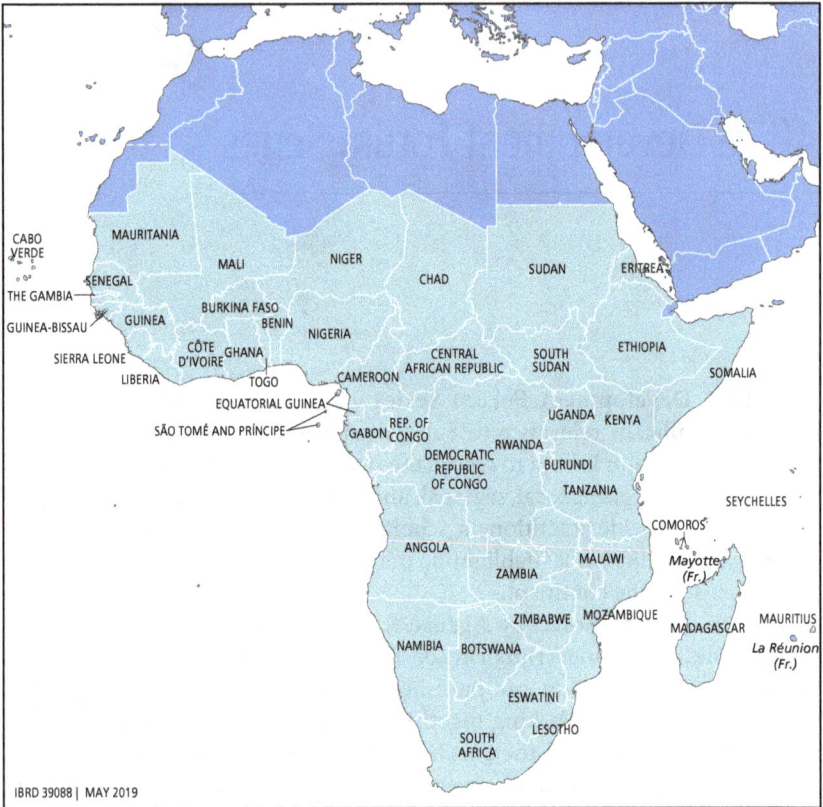

CABO VERDE
MAURITANIA
MALI
NIGER
CHAD
SUDAN
ERITREA
SENEGAL
THE GAMBIA
GUINEA-BISSAU
GUINEA
BURKINA FASO
BENIN
NIGERIA
SIERRA LEONE
CÔTE D'IVOIRE
GHANA
LIBERIA
TOGO
CAMEROON
CENTRAL AFRICAN REPUBLIC
SOUTH SUDAN
ETHIOPIA
SOMALIA
EQUATORIAL GUINEA
SÃO TOMÉ AND PRÍNCIPE
GABON
REP. OF CONGO
DEMOCRATIC REPUBLIC OF CONGO
RWANDA
BURUNDI
UGANDA
KENYA
TANZANIA
SEYCHELLES
COMOROS
ANGOLA
ZAMBIA
MALAWI
Mayotte (Fr.)
ZIMBABWE
MOZAMBIQUE
MADAGASCAR
MAURITIUS
La Réunion (Fr.)
NAMIBIA
BOTSWANA
ESWATINI
LESOTHO
SOUTH AFRICA

IBRD 39088 | MAY 2019

Titles in the Africa Development Forum Series

All books in the Africa Development Forum series are available for free at https://openknowledge.worldbank.org/handle/10986/2150.

Contents

Figures

Map

Tables

Foreword

Over the past two decades, many countries in Sub-Saharan Africa have grown their economies, lifted millions out of poverty, recovered from conflict, and greatly expanded access to education with a boost in public expenditures.

Yet the region faces enormous challenges. Countries still have a long way to go in their economic transformation, with large swaths of the population working in low-productivity jobs, often in the informal sector. Like the rest of the world, the region also faces a fast-paced reshaping of both the global and local economies: quickly evolving technological change through digital technologies and automation, increased economic competition and volatility, and a burgeoning youth population. These so-called megatrends are bringing about a fundamental shift in the historical role of manufacturing as a key driver of structural transformation and economic development. They are also rapidly changing the demand for skills and putting a high premium on those skills that ensure the adaptability and resilience of economies, the workforce, and individuals.

The World Bank recently launched the Africa Human Capital Plan to support countries as they facilitate people-driven development and accelerate more and better investments in African people, particularly women and children. Africa's human capital indicators are in a dire state; too many countries fail to ensure the acquisition of even the most basic skills among children and youth. If countries are to empower youth to thrive in a rapidly changing world of work, they will need to create an enabling environment in which children enter school well-nourished and ready to learn, in which students acquire real learning in the classroom, and in which workers participate in the job market primed for productivity. They will also need to equip them with a complex set of cognitive, social, and emotional skills.

This report examines the *Skills Balancing Act* that Sub-Saharan African countries face in their efforts to build the skills needed for more prosperous and equitable societies in a fast-changing and integrated global economy. It assesses

Sub-Saharan Africa's achievements in skills development and weighs those achievements against the challenges the region faces today and will face in the future. It argues that policy makers in the region need to make strategic and smart investments in the early years, in education and training for today's—and tomorrow's—workforce, to sustain economic transformation with equity. This will involve making trade-offs while investing in skills that promote inclusion and growth today and prosperity tomorrow.

By prioritizing universal foundational skills—cognitive and socio-emotional—of children, youth, and adults, by investing selectively in technical skills tied to growing sectors, and by implementing reforms to ensure value for money in education and training programs and safety nets, governments *can* strengthen their skills balance sheet. This report outlines what steps countries can take to do just that, building on the international evidence on programs and policy reforms that can work, many of them from countries in the region.

There are no one-size-fits-all solutions. Priorities depend on each country's context, including its state of economic transformation and the progress made with economic and institutional reforms that create the enabling environment for skills investments to pay off. The good news is that many countries in the region are already showing the way by making the necessary reforms.

The skills challenge in Sub-Saharan Africa is enormous, but it is surmountable. Countries have opportunities to invest more smartly. *The Skills Balancing Act in Sub-Saharan Africa: Investing in Skills for Productivity, Inclusivity, and Adaptability* provides a wealth of analysis and practical experiences that countries in the region can use to inform their policy making and set their own priorities and that the World Bank and other development partners can use to better support these efforts. Committed leaders, reform coalitions, and well-coordinated policies are essential to face up to the skills balancing act in Sub-Saharan Africa and unleash the potential of skills for building more prosperous and inclusive societies.

Hafez M. H. Ghanem
Vice President
Sub-Saharan Africa Region
The World Bank

Annette Dixon
Vice President
Human Development
The World Bank

Acknowledgments

The Skills Balancing Act in Sub-Saharan Africa: Investing in Skills for Productivity, Inclusivity, and Adaptability examines overarching trends that will shape Africa's economies and drive the demand for skills; it also examines skills building over the three principal stages of the life cycle. The report is the product of a team effort, co-led by Omar Arias, David K. Evans, and Indhira Santos, with a core team comprising Moussa Pouguinimpo Blimpo, Mũthoni Ngatia, Jamele Rigolini, Daniel Alonso Soto, Shobhana Sosale, and Shelby Frances Carvalho. It is structured as follows:

Chapter 1. Skills and Economic Transformation in Sub-Saharan Africa

Chapter 2. Developing Universal Foundational Skills in Sub-Saharan Africa

Chapter 3. Building Skills for the School-to-Work Transition in Sub-Saharan Africa

Chapter 4. Building Skills for Productivity through Higher Education in Sub-Saharan Africa

Chapter 5. Addressing Skills Gaps: Continuing and Remedial Education and Training for Adults and Out-of-School Youths in Sub-Saharan Africa

While the main chapters are organized around the life cycle of skills building, the overview of the report takes a cross-cutting look at five main policy questions:

- Is investment in skills in Sub-Saharan African countries meeting the needs of the economies of today and tomorrow?

- Is skills development built on solid foundations in Sub-Saharan Africa?

- Is there a good case for investing in the skills of out-of-school youths and adults in Sub-Saharan African countries?

- Are countries in the region investing adequate resources in skills?
- How can countries in the region face up to the challenges and improve the skills of their labor forces for the economies of today and tomorrow?

The authorship of the chapters is as follows: overview, Omar Arias, David K. Evans, and Indhira Santos; chapter 1, Omar Arias, with substantive contributions from Magdalena Bendini; chapter 2, Moussa Pouguinimpo Blimpo, David K. Evans, and Mūthoni Ngatia, with substantive contributions from Fei Yuan; chapter 3, Indhira Santos, Daniel Alonso Soto, and Shobhana Sosale; chapter 4, Indhira Santos and Omar Arias, with substantive contributions from Shelby Frances Carvalho, Daniel Alonso Soto, and Peter Darvas; and chapter 5, Mūthoni Ngatia and Jamele Rigolini, with substantive contributions from Valeria Perotti.

Shelby Frances Carvalho, Daniel Alonso Soto, Fei Yuan, and Magdalena Bendini contributed substantially to the analysis throughout the report. Specific background papers or technical notes were prepared by Jenny Aker and Melita Sawyer (adult education), Zirra Banu (literature review of skills studies and socioemotional skills in Africa), Jorgen Billetoft (technical and vocational education and training), Peter Darvas (higher education), Jutta Franz (apprenticeships), Valeria Perotti (training, skills, and firm productivity), Sergio Urzua (higher education), and Amarachi Utah (school-to-work transition).

The team benefited greatly from extensive consultations, discussions, and suggestions from many colleagues throughout preparation of the report.

The team is grateful for guidance, technical inputs, and support from Hafez Ghanem (vice president, Africa Region), Makhtar Diop (former vice president, Africa Region), Albert Zeufack (chief economist, Africa Region), Annette Dixon (vice president, Human Development), Francisco Ferreira (former chief economist, Africa Region), Michal Rutkowski (senior director, Social Protection and Jobs Global Practice), Jaime Saavedra (senior director, Education Global Practice), Amit Dar (strategy operations director, Human Development), Mamta Murthi (former strategy operations director, Africa Region), and Lynne Sherburne-Benz (former senior regional adviser, Africa Region) in the development of the report.

The team is particularly grateful to Luis Benveniste, Andreas Blom, Francisco Ferreira, Deon Filmer, and William Maloney—our informal advisory board—as well as the Africa Region practice managers at the time of writing, Sajitha Bashir, Halil Dundar, Meskerem Mulatu, Stefano Paternostro, and Dena Ringold, for their advice and substantive contributions to the report. The team also thanks peer reviewers Rita Almeida, Aline Coudouel, Deon Filmer, Alexandria Valerio, an anonymous reviewer, and Ana Revenga (former deputy chief economist) for their insightful and constructive advice and comments at the concept note stage or in preparation of the report.

Paul Gallagher provided excellent support to develop the key messages for the overview. Mariam Denise Brain provided excellent assistance in editing of the report. Silvia Lopez Chavez helped to develop the graphic design for the report's policy framework. Mapi Buitano, Kenneth Omondi, Rose-Claire Pakabomba, Paula Lamptey, and Ngoc-Dung Thi Tran provided invaluable logistical and administrative support. Mary Fisk and Patricia Katayama provided essential support throughout the entire publication process. Many other colleagues from the Africa Education and Social Protection teams provided valuable comments, suggestions, and generous inputs throughout development of the report. The findings, interpretations, and conclusions are those of the authors and do not necessarily reflect the views of management, the reviewers, or other colleagues consulted or engaged in the preparation of the report.

About the Authors

Omar Arias is manager for global knowledge and innovation and lead economist in the World Bank Education Global Practice. Previously, he was global lead for skills, sector manager and lead economist in the Europe and Central Asia region, sector leader of human development for Chile and the Andean countries, senior economist in the Poverty and Gender Group of the Latin American region, and research economist at the Inter-American Development Bank. He has coauthored various studies, including regional reports on skills in Africa, jobs and pensions in Europe and Central Asia, and labor informality and poverty in Latin America, as well as numerous country studies. He has peer-reviewed publications on various topics, including returns to schooling and skills, labor markets, income mobility, growth, poverty and inequality, human capital accumulation, tax evasion, and applied econometrics. He was a Fulbright scholar at the University of Illinois at Urbana-Champaign, where he obtained his master's degree and doctorate in economics.

Moussa Pouguinimpo Blimpo is a senior economist in the Office of the Chief Economist for the Africa Region (AFRCE) at the World Bank. Prior to this position, he was an assistant professor of economics and international studies at the University of Oklahoma (2012–15). He founded and led the Center for Research and Opinion Polls (CROP), a think tank based in Togo, from 2011 to 2015. His research interest focuses on a wide range of policy-relevant questions for African economies, particularly regarding education policies and human capital accumulation. He completed his PhD in economics at New York University in 2010 and spent two years as a postdoctoral fellow at Stanford University's Institute for Economic Policy Research (SIEPR).

David K. Evans is a senior fellow at the Center for Global Development. Formerly, he was a lead economist in the Chief Economist's Office for the

Africa Region of the World Bank. He is a coauthor of the World Bank's *World Development Report 2018: Learning to Realize Education's Promise.* He studies education, health, and social protection issues. He has designed and implemented impact evaluations in education, early child development, agriculture, health, and social protection in Brazil, The Gambia, Kenya, Mexico, Nigeria, Sierra Leone, and Tanzania, and he has managed education projects for the World Bank in Brazil. His recent published research articles include "What Really Works to Improve Learning in Developing Countries? An Analysis of Divergent Systematic Reviews," "Cash Transfers and Temptation Goods," and "Cash Transfers and Health: Evidence from Tanzania." He teaches economic development at the Pardee RAND Graduate School of Public Policy, and he holds a PhD in economics from Harvard University.

Mũthoni Ngatia is an economist at the Africa Gender Innovation Lab. She started at the World Bank in 2015 as a member of the Young Professionals Program; she has worked in Social Protection and Labor and, most recently, in the Office of the Chief Economist for Africa. Prior to joining the World Bank, she was an assistant professor of economics at Tufts University. Her research has looked at how social networks affect individuals' behavior in low- and middle-income countries. She has an AB in applied mathematics and economics from Harvard University and a PhD in economics from Yale University.

Jamele Rigolini is lead economist in the World Bank's Social Protection and Jobs Global Practice. His areas of expertise include human development, poverty, social protection, and jobs and skills. Prior to joining the World Bank, he was an assistant professor of economics at the University of Warwick (United Kingdom) and also worked for the Inter-American Development Bank, the International Union for Conservation of Nature, and McKinsey & Co. At the World Bank, he spent four years in the East Asia and Pacific's Social Protection Unit; he moved to the Office of the Chief Economist of the Latin America and Caribbean region, where he managed the yearly intersectoral flagship reports and maintained a close dialogue with other international organizations, Latin American academics, and think tanks. From 2013 to 2016, he was the Human Development Program leader for the Andean countries (Bolivia, Chile, Ecuador, Peru, and the República Bolivariana de Venezuela). He holds a diploma in physics from the Swiss Federal Institute of Technology (ETH) in Zürich and a PhD in economics from New York University. In addition to his policy work, he remains active in research and has published in leading academic journals, including the *Journal of Public Economics, Journal of Development Economics, Economics & Politics, Economic Letters,* and *World Development.*

Indhira Santos is a senior economist at the World Bank, where she works on labor markets, skills, and social protection. She was a primary author of the *World Development Report 2019: The Changing Nature of Work* and the *World Development Report 2016: Digital Dividends.* She is currently working in the Africa Region and has also worked in the Europe and Central Asia and South Asia regions, after coming to the World Bank as a Young Professional in 2009. Prior to joining the World Bank, she was a research fellow at Bruegel, a European policy think tank in Brussels, from 2007 to 2009. She has also worked for the Economic Research Center of the Pontificia Universidad Católica Madre y Maestra (PUCMM) and the Ministry of Finance of the Dominican Republic. She was a Fulbright scholar at Harvard University, where she obtained her PhD in public policy and a master's in public administration in international development.

Shobhana Sosale is a staff member in the Education Global Practice at the World Bank. She is a development practitioner with more than 20 years of experience in education and skills development. She analyzes and publishes on topics linking political economy and cross-sectoral issues in education, social protection, private sector development, and finance. She has designed, implemented, and managed education and skills development projects and programs across countries in Africa, East Asia, Europe and Central Asia, and South Asia. She has published widely in education and related fields. Before joining the World Bank, she was involved in research on small and medium enterprise development at the Indian Institute of Management in Bangalore.

Daniel Alonso Soto is a labor economist in the Skills and Employability Division at the Organisation for Economic Co-operation and Development (OECD). Before this position, from 2011 to 2017, he worked for the World Bank and for the Inter-American Development Bank. Prior to joining these international institutions, he was an associate professor of economics at the University of Oviedo. Reflecting his passionate interest in public policy evaluation, his research focuses on a wide range of topics related to education and labor markets, particularly school-to-work transition and human capital accumulation issues. He holds a master's degree in economics and finance and a PhD in applied economics from the University of Navarra, with visiting research fellowships at the London School of Economics, the University of Michigan, and the University Carlos III of Madrid.

Abbreviations

ACE	Africa Center of Excellence
ASET	applied science, engineering, and technology
ECD	early child development
EPAG	Economic Empowerment of Adolescent Girls and Young Women
GDP	gross domestic product
GISDC	Ghana Industrial Skills Development Center
ICT	information and communication technology
ILO	International Labour Organization
ISCED	International Standard Classification of Education
ISTARN	Informal Sector Training and Resources Network
MECESUP	Higher Education Quality Improvement Program
MITD	Mauritius Institute of Training and Development
NGO	nongovernmental organization
NQF	national qualification framework
NVTI	National Vocational Training Institute
OECD	Organisation for Economic Co-operation and Development
OJT	on-the-job training
PASEC	Programme d'Analyse des Systèmes Educatifs de la CONFEMEN
PASET	Partnership for Applied Sciences, Engineering, and Technology
PISA	Program for International Student Assessment
PPP	public-private partnership
R&D	research and development

RTQF	Rwanda TVET qualifications framework
SABER	Systems Approach for Better Education Results
SABER-WfD	Systems Approach for Better Education Results Workforce Development
STEM	science, technology, engineering, and mathematics
STEP	Skills Towards Employability and Productivity
STEP-B	Science and Technology Education Post-Basic Program
tfgP	Feel Good Project
TVET	technical and vocational education and training
UNESCO	United Nations Educational, Scientific, and Cultural Organization
VETA	Vocational Education and Training Authority
VWFA	visual word form area
WfD	Workforce Development

Executive Summary

Sub-Saharan Africa's growing working-age population constitutes a major opportunity to reduce poverty and increase shared prosperity. But the region's workforce is the least skilled in the world, constraining economic prospects. Countries in Sub-Saharan Africa have invested heavily in skills building, with public expenditure on education increasing sevenfold over the past 30 years. More children are in school today than ever before. Yet in half the countries in the region, fewer than two in every three children complete primary school; even fewer reach and complete higher levels of education.

For children in school, learning outcomes have been persistently poor, leading to huge gaps in basic cognitive skills—literacy and numeracy—among children, young people, and adults. The literacy rate of the adult population is below 50 percent in many countries, and functional literacy and numeracy are even lower.

Achieving significant progress in building skills is possible in Sub-Saharan Africa, but it will require enacting systemwide change. Small-scale programs and local reforms often fail to achieve the desired impacts at scale. Achieving more equitable access, quality, relevance, and efficiency in skills building cannot hinge just on scaling up "best practices." There is a need to pay attention to the governance environment in which skills programs take place. Multiple agencies at the central and local levels are involved in skills development strategies, making skills "everyone's problem, but no one's responsibility." Lack of coordination and weak capacity can result in inefficiencies, duplication of efforts, or, perhaps worse, lack of attention to important issues. Therefore, to achieve broad and sustained results, policies and reforms need to tackle the politics of policies, build capacity for evidence-based policies, and create incentives to align the behaviors of all stakeholders with the pursuit of national skills development goals.

In their policy choices, countries will face trade-offs—often stark ones—that will have distributional impacts and a bearing on their development path. This is the challenge of the skills balancing act in Sub-Saharan Africa.

Policy Framework for Skills Investments in Sub-Saharan Africa

The portfolio of potential skills investments that countries in the region can make should aim to achieve three policy goals: (a) accelerate overall productivity growth (prosperous economies), (b) promote economic inclusion (inclusive societies), and (c) ensure the adaptability of the workforce in the 21st century (resilient economies and individuals). Countries in the region face hard choices when considering skills investments to achieve these goals.

A smart skills development strategy requires figuring out which skills are needed, for what, who needs them, and how they can be developed at the right time and in the right way. Figure ES.1 illustrates a framework aimed at guiding skills priorities for education and training policies and investments in the region. The figure encapsulates three main guiding principles.

First, skills investments need to reckon with two main potential trade-offs. The first is between investing in skills with greater potential to maximize economywide productivity gains, such as technical skills for economic activities with high growth potential that can catalyze economic transformation by reallocating productive resources and tapping new technologies, and investing in skills aimed at economic inclusion, such as skills for improving livelihoods and earnings opportunities, especially for the poor. The second potential trade-off is between investing in the skills needed by the out-of-school young and adult population for today's largely agrarian and self-employment-based economies and investing in the skills needed by future cohorts of workers for tomorrow's transforming economies to ensure their adaptability to employment changes in their working lives and resilience in navigating the fast-changing world of work.

Second, a balanced skills portfolio requires investing cost-effectively over the life cycle in the multiplicity of skills needed in modernizing economies. These skills include, broadly, (a) *foundational cognitive skills* (for example, literacy and numeracy), (b) *foundational socioemotional skills* (for example, related to managing one's self and relating with others, such as self-regulation, perseverance, curiosity, empathy, and tolerance), and (c) *technical or job-specific skills* (for example, vocational and professional qualifications and digital and management skills). These skills are important for new cohorts of workers—those of school age and youths still in education—and for the current stock of youths, teens, and older adults already outside the formal education system. A balanced skills portfolio encompasses a range of investments in building foundational, cognitive, and socioemotional skills for infants, toddlers, and teenagers and technical skills for youths and adults and investments in reinforcing skills through on-the-job training, labor training, and education programs.

In making these investments, policy makers should consider that skills formation is a lifelong process in which skills beget skills. Figure ES.1 shows the optimal stages for acquiring different skills over the life span, highlighting how and when the skills that are most appropriate to each stage are acquired.

Figure ES.1 **Policy Framework for Skills Policy Priorities in Sub-Saharan Africa**

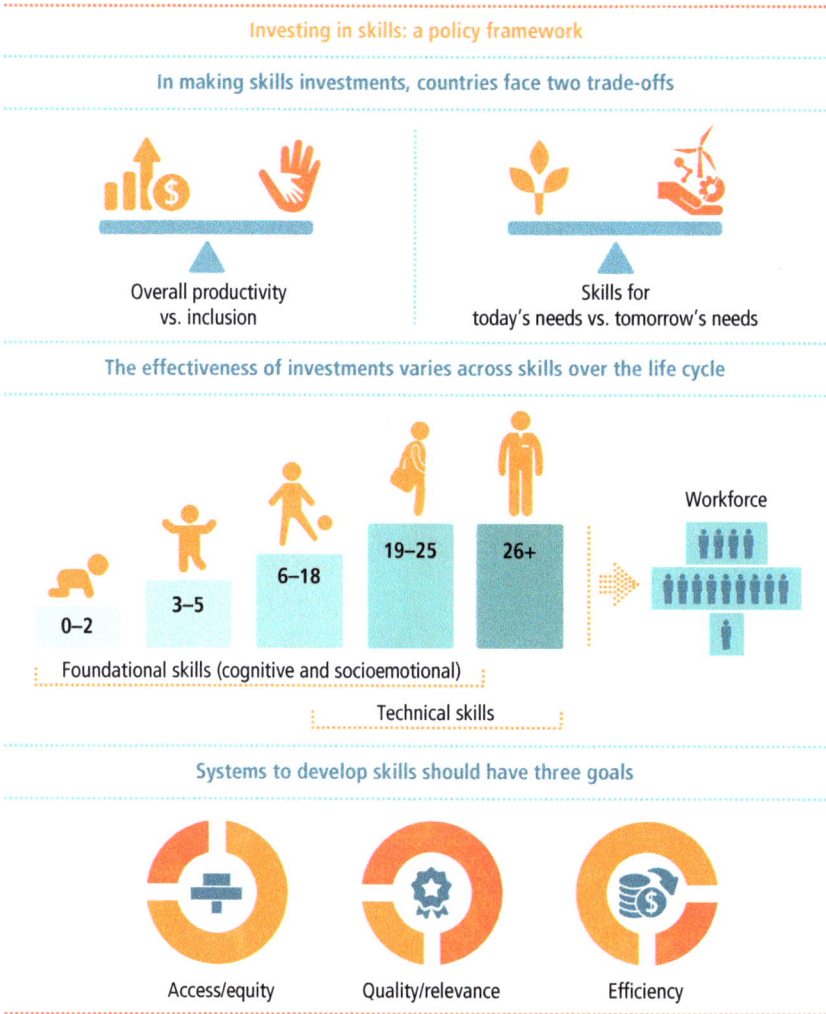

Investing in skills: a policy framework

In making skills investments, countries face two trade-offs

Overall productivity
vs. inclusion

Skills for
today's needs vs. tomorrow's needs

The effectiveness of investments varies across skills over the life cycle

0–2

3–5

6–18

19–25

26+

Workforce

Foundational skills (cognitive and socioemotional)

Technical skills

Systems to develop skills should have three goals

Access/equity

Quality/relevance

Efficiency

Human capital formation is a time-dependent process. Investments in the early years are crucial, because this is when neural connections flourish and are pruned and solidified.

Cognitive and socioemotional development is highly influenced by maternal and child health and nutrition, especially during the first 1,000 days of life, and by the quality of nurturing environments during infancy and childhood. Although basic cognitive skills are well set by the teen years, schooling can provide subject knowledge and tools that enhance these abilities, as well as socioemotional skills that remain malleable through adolescence and the early adult years. Foundational skills determine a person's "readiness to learn" in basic education, postsecondary schooling, training, and on the job. Although it is more cost-effective to invest earlier, brain plasticity and malleability through adulthood mean that later investments can remedy foundational skills gaps among the current stock of workers. Such investments are especially important for the most vulnerable individuals, who fall out of the education system early on and fail to acquire critical foundational skills. These investments can bring positive intergenerational effects; that is, literate mothers are more likely to raise healthier children with stronger foundational skills.

The third guiding principle is that, to provide the right skills, at the right time, and in the right way, education and training systems need to ensure equity, quality, and efficiency. Investments and policy reforms need to provide wide access to opportunities for skills acquisition (*equitable access*), learning that builds skills to meet labor market demand (*quality and relevance*), and value-for-money in the financing and provision of education and training to minimize waste of resources (*efficiency*).

Facing the Skills Balancing Act: Focus on Foundational Skills

Foundational skills—investments in the early years as well as basic literacy and numeracy—circumvent one of the big trade-offs: universal foundational skills increase economic growth and promote inclusion. Countries should prioritize building universal foundational skills for today's and tomorrow's workers. This effort begins with investments to promote equality of opportunities and school readiness, including through investments in maternal health, child nutrition, and early stimulation during the first 1,000 days of life and the early years. It requires countries to continue to improve access to basic education and decisive actions to close large and persisting learning gaps, through improvements in schooling quality. It also demands interventions, such as second-chance and adult literacy programs, to support those who missed out on critical foundational skills building.

Countries should, first and foremost, step up smart investments in the early years of individuals' lives to eradicate chronic child malnutrition and promote healthy childhood development. Stunting rates in Sub-Saharan Africa are among the highest in the world, and countries inside and outside the region are showing the way to fight child stunting (Galasso et al. 2016).

At the next level of basic skills, the expansion of access to primary and secondary education needs to go hand in hand with ensuring effective teaching in schools. This is a simple yet powerful lesson for countries in Sub-Saharan Africa. Many countries in other regions of the world, including richer economies, which expanded access without assuring effective teaching and thus school quality, have failed to produce learning and skills. A focus on quality will no doubt be challenging, given existing gaps in physical infrastructure and pressure from increasing demand for secondary education. Countries will have to find simultaneous ways to build more high schools and improve the quality of education provided by becoming more efficient in the use of resources.

In continuing to expand access, Sub-Saharan African countries can find lessons from successes in enrolling and keeping children in school within and outside the region. Countries in the region with the biggest gains in enrollment boast free education. The elimination of tuition fees marked major increases in enrollment in Kenya, Malawi, and Uganda, with smaller jumps in Cameroon, Tanzania, and Zambia. Ethiopia, Lesotho, and Malawi have leveraged cash transfer programs targeted to poor families as part of a strategy to increase enrollment and to offset other indirect costs, including the opportunity cost of schooling; the results have been overwhelmingly positive. These positive impacts hold for unconditional and conditional programs, although evidence from Burkina Faso suggests that the children who are most vulnerable to dropout—girls overall and boys who are doing less well in school—may benefit from conditional transfers.

Targeted financial assistance and complementary low-cost interventions can help to keep boys and girls in schools. Enrollment in and completion of secondary education are also deterred by high opportunity costs to studying or, for girls, by teenage marriage or pregnancy. Targeted assistance may be effective. In Ghana, scholarships for students who were admitted to secondary school but could not immediately enroll—usually because of lack of funds—doubled the rate of high school completion, improved math and language learning scores, increased the odds of enrolling in tertiary education by 30 percent, and reduced the number of children among girls by age 25 (Duflo, Dupas, and Kremer 2017).

Involving the Private Sector

Many countries struggle to find the fiscal space to cope with the wave of students transitioning to secondary school. Access remains inequitable. Public-private partnerships (PPPs) can help to crowd in resources to address the infrastructure and service needs in secondary education. PPPs in education could potentially leverage public financing aimed at improving equity of access through the delivery of all or part of secondary education infrastructure or services to low-income households. A study of a PPP in Uganda, where the government offered a per student subsidy to participating low-cost private secondary schools, found that the subsidy helped schools to absorb large numbers of eligible students, equally among girls and boys, and that student performance in participating schools improved (Barrera-Osorio et al. 2016).

Private schools have been part of the landscape of African education for many years. Ultimately, what matters is that the state guarantees access to quality education for all children and youths. In environments where public provision is scarce, private schools can fill a substantial gap, but governments have to play a strong regulatory role and empower families to make informed decisions regarding their children's education. Governments and parents should hold all schools (public and private) accountable for results.

Getting Families Involved

Parental participation and empowerment can be useful in ensuring quality standards in schools. Yet, too often, parental decisions are based on incomplete information. For example, parents may demand early education in English or French rather than their mother tongue, even though literacy occurs more rapidly if it is begun in the mother tongue, as was recently seen in Kenya (Piper, Schroeder, and Trudell 2016). Evidence from Madagascar shows that parents often underestimate the returns to schooling (Nguyen 2008). Yet, when given relevant information, most parents make the best decisions for their children. Information campaigns can help to increase parental engagement and empowerment.

Keeping Children Engaged by Providing Better Schooling

Most critically, effective teaching in classrooms is central to keeping children in school longer and assuring that they learn and acquire skills. In recent years, a large body of evidence from school interventions in low- and middle-income countries clearly points to more effective teaching through improved pedagogy as the most impactful way to improve learning (Evans and Popova 2016). A pedagogical approach with proven results is helping teachers to teach to the level of the child. In many countries, an ambitious and inflexible curriculum leaves many students behind. Interventions that help teachers to target their teaching to the diverse learning needs of students in the classroom have been highly effective. In Ghana, supplementing teachers with community assistants to help the weakest students has led to sizable gains in literacy and numeracy, especially when it is done after school (Duflo and Kiessel 2012). Further, in Ghana, training teachers to teach students in small groups, targeted to their learning level, boosted their literacy skills (Duflo and Kiessel 2012). In rural

Kenya, separating primary students into groups based on their initial ability led to sizable gains in math and language for both high and low achievers, allowing teachers to teach at a level more appropriate to children's needs (Duflo, Dupas, and Kremer 2011).

Using Technology to Improve Learning

Technology-aided instruction has the potential to improve learning when it is used to aid teachers and give students an individualized learning experience. There has been much hype on the potential for new technologies to facilitate leap-frogging in education in low- and middle-income countries and to achieve advances such as those that medical technology has delivered for health. But the evidence so far is sobering and demonstrates that technology works best when it is used to complement teachers rather than replace them. Hardware-focused interventions that provide computers at home or at school have had little impact on learning outcomes. Interventions that rely on technology-enabled instruction to improve pedagogy and allow students to learn at their own pace have worked better. Recently, interventions that use technology to give students a dynamic learning experience seem to deliver much bigger impacts on learning.

Taken together, this evidence suggests that, when embracing the promise of technology-aided instruction, countries in the region should move with caution. Realizing the potential of technology-based education will depend on the details of the specific intervention and the extent to which it alleviates binding constraints on learning. Careful planning and assessment are needed. Technology can fulfill its promise if it is assessed with an eye toward cost-effectiveness and a careful assessment of what country systems can implement.

Improving Teachers' Ability to Teach

Given the prominent role of teachers in learning, much effort is needed to have better teachers in schools. Many teachers in the region do not command the minimum subject knowledge they are expected to teach and do not sufficiently use the pedagogical practices associated with more learning. Since it is much more difficult and costly to skill up or retrain a workforce of unprepared teachers, high-performing education systems, such as those in Finland and Singapore, have highly selective teacher education programs in which few applicants are accepted. Analysis of the requirements for entry into teacher training programs in many Sub-Saharan African countries suggests that standards are very low. Countries around the world have experimented with different ways to attract better candidates to the teaching profession, including creating special incentives for top students to go into teaching in Chile or raising the standards of entry into teacher training colleges in Peru. Improving the standards of entry into the profession itself can potentially improve outcomes.

Strengthening Socioemotional Skills

Another opportunity to leapfrog can come from incorporating socioemotional skills into the goals and teaching practices of schools, institutions, and programs. A related area of policy priority is ensuring that preschool and basic education (general and vocational) curricula and pedagogic practice pay adequate attention to the critical development of socioemotional skills. These skills can be taught as part of the regular school curricula through specific activities, goals, and pedagogic support that have been proven effective. The experience with related reforms and interventions in the world can offer useful lessons, such as recent innovations in several countries, including Colombia, North Macedonia, Peru, the United States, and Vietnam.

An area warranting policy reform is postponing early tracking into technical and vocational education and training (TVET) in secondary education to allow youths to acquire stronger foundational skills. Some educational systems still track students into vocational and technical streams too early (in lower-secondary school) at the expense of foundational skills. Early tracking into vocational and technical schools inhibits the acquisition of strong foundational skills, limiting the adaptability and lifetime earnings of TVET graduates. In the short to medium term, delayed tracking needs to be accompanied by strengthening the foundational skills in TVET schools and institutions and broadening the narrow focus on technical and vocational skills.

Building Foundational Skills among the Current Stock of Workers

Finally, strengthening foundational skills among out-of-school youths and adults has been a blind spot in the region, especially in agriculture and the informal economy. Given the deficiencies in basic literacy, numeracy, and socioemotional skills of current workers, remedial programs aimed at addressing these gaps can play an important role in improving people's livelihoods and productivity. Although adult literacy programs have had a mixed record of impacts, recent innovative programs hold promise. The Project Alphabetisation de Base par Cellulaire is a mobile phone–based literacy and numeracy program in rural Niger that—by tapping into people's intrinsic motivations—has managed to boost literacy and numeracy among adults (Aker, Ksoll, and Lybbert 2012). There is also great potential in incorporating adult literacy and socioemotional interventions into agricultural extension and cash transfer programs, as is being done in Brazil's Bolsa Familia and Mexico's Prospera cash transfer programs.

Facing the Skills Balancing Act: Invest in the Technical Skills of Youth and Adults

Investing in the technical skills of youths and adults requires improving the equity, efficiency, and relevance of TVET and higher education. In most countries in the region, these two subsectors remain small, creating opportunities to leapfrog by establishing early the institutional and policy frameworks that can ensure more equity, efficiency, and relevance and drawing lessons from countries that have already expanded these systems.

Responding to Social and Equity Concerns in the Provision of Technical Skills

For TVET and higher education, the most important goal for achieving equity is to ensure school readiness. Readiness means imparting strong foundational skills for all in early childhood and basic education, especially among children and youths from disadvantaged backgrounds. For disadvantaged youths close to entering tertiary education, bridge and remedial programs in secondary school or at the beginning of tertiary can help to level the playing field and improve readiness. In Namibia, for example, the Pathways Program at the University of Namibia targets students from the marginalized Owambo ethnic group, with a focus on preparing them to study science and engineering at the tertiary level. In addition, bridge programs can tackle gaps in socioemotional skills that are considered key for success in TVET or tertiary studies.

Addressing Financial Constraints

Improving equity requires paying attention to other financial and nonfinancial constraints that keep many from acquiring quality technical skills. For upper-secondary and tertiary TVET and higher education, public financing should be targeted through needs-based scholarships and subsidized student loans. In lower-secondary TVET, if it exists, the same kind of public financing that is used for general secondary education will create opportunities for youths to gain skills that will deliver the highest returns for them. In other words, if a country has a policy of free lower-secondary education, then financing TVET at that level will allow more differentiated skills. On average, there is less cost sharing in Africa at the tertiary level than in other regions, but some countries have tried to move progressively away from free higher education and toward cost-sharing arrangements. Malawi, Uganda, and Zambia have shifted some costs, including living expenses, to students. Botswana, Ethiopia, and Lesotho have implemented deferred cost-sharing programs in which students repay tuition incrementally after graduation. Kenya, Mauritania, Mauritius, Namibia, Rwanda, South Africa, and Tanzania have implemented means-tested support.

Beyond the formal education system, improving equity in out-of-school and on-the-job training requires a strong focus on the informal sector through informal apprenticeships, labor programs aimed at disadvantaged youths, and on-the-job training in micro and small firms, especially in rural areas.

Improving Governance and Financing in TVET and Higher Education

Regulation and quality assurance can contribute to improving efficiency (and quality) in tertiary education and training. Over the past decade, many Sub-Saharan African countries have set up agencies to conduct assessments and accreditation of tertiary institutions, but capacity is limited. Quality assurance mechanisms range from simple licensing of institutions by the ministry responsible for tertiary education to comprehensive systemwide program accreditation and national qualification frameworks. By 2012, 21 African countries had already established quality assurance agencies, and a dozen other countries were at relatively advanced stages of doing so. These agencies are performing some basic quality control, having closed or prevented the opening of some low-quality programs.

Most critically, public funding of TVET and higher education institutions in the region needs to be linked gradually to performance or performance-enhancing reforms. Most financing of public TVET and higher education in the region is done on a historical basis, based on inputs (number of staff or salaries), enrollment (cost per student, as in the case of higher education in Kenya and Rwanda), or normative unit costs (student-teacher ratios and prescribed unit costs by discipline, as in Ghana and Nigeria's higher education). These financing mechanisms create few incentives for cost saving, innovation, improved quality, or improved labor market relevance for students. To create such incentives, the ambitious approach is to direct the bulk of public financing through a performance-based system. Experience in Africa and elsewhere with performance-based mechanisms offers possible stepping stones. These mechanisms include, for example, paying for performance in higher education in Mali and in the regional centers of excellence and focusing initially on performance-enhancing reforms, as in Chile.

Fostering Economic Relevance and Demand-Driven Provision of TVET

Given the large informal sector in the region and rapid changes in skills demand, there is a need to rethink the public sector's role in technical and vocational education and training. Staying relevant requires an agility and flexibility that publicly provided TVET and higher education struggle to attain. Partnering with the private sector—including on training provision—will be critical, as countries inside and outside the region increasingly recognize.

TVET needs to be geared more toward preparing workers for nonwage employment outside the manufacturing sector. This effort begins with course offerings, which only recently started incorporating entrepreneurship and core business skills training that are directly relevant for self-employment, management of small enterprises, and services. For example, these skills encompass costing, pricing, preparing financial statements, keeping business records, project management, marketing, sales, and preparing business plans, among others. Promising programs, such as Educate! in Rwanda and Uganda, are introducing entrepreneurship, work readiness skills, and experiential applied teaching methodologies in secondary schools. Tanzania is developing new TVET curricula with a focus on skills for self-employment.

There is also a need to address inflexible course times that make it difficult to combine training and work, lack of practical training, and high costs that make education inaccessible or irrelevant for workers in the informal sector. Better incorporating the views and skills needs of the informal sector in public TVET—for example, by linking to existing organizations of informal workers and enterprises—can be a way forward. TVET institutions in Kenya are often associated with business centers through which consultancies are provided to small-scale entrepreneurs. Graduates of youth polytechnics are encouraged to form business groups, and these groups then approach credit providers.

Making TVET relevant to the needs of catalytic sectors requires building gradual but sustained engagement with employers at the local level. In Tanzania, for example, the private sector is increasingly playing an advisory role in TVET through the Tanzania National Business Council; the Association of Tanzania Employers occasionally helps to define strategic priorities.

The private sector is a critical partner for improving teacher quality and offering opportunities for on-the-job training, whether in the formal or informal sector. TVET teacher education is largely university based, and in-service continuous training is generally lacking. Exceptions are the dedicated Vocational Teachers Training College in Tanzania and the Normal Schools for Teachers of Technical Education in Cameroon. Relatively few teachers in public institutions have industrial experience, in part because of the requirements for a teaching certificate. Countries could explore more aggressive options for twinning arrangements with private firms and other countries to upgrade the skills of TVET teachers, allowing the local recruitment of people with relevant skills but without teaching certificates. This additional support could be combined with stronger incentives to perform, including publishing examination results.

Fostering Demand-Driven and Active Learning Approaches in Higher Education

Improving the labor market relevance of higher education will require aligning teaching and research activities at public and private universities with market signals. Governments can offer incentives to set up and strengthen industry-university links—for example, by bringing in intermediaries or providing matching funds.

Adopting more active learning practices and a "careers" approach to skills development in higher education starts with the design of curricula. University programs need to combine academic subjects with more hands-on experiences that deliver the multiplicity of skills (technical, cognitive, and socioemotional) necessary to perform the jobs that youths are expected to take upon graduation. This task-based approach recognizes that what matters is whether workers have the skills to perform the tasks of a job and not just a diploma. Moreover, institutions need to pursue work-based learning opportunities more aggressively through apprenticeships or internships. Many countries in the region have or are in the process of generating national apprenticeship and internship frameworks, with a view to enhancing the workplace experience of youths, including university graduates. This effort is to be encouraged, and the international evidence suggests that—when well designed—these frameworks can indeed improve employability.

Given that fast transformation of the economies of countries in Sub-Saharan Africa will require a new generation of entrepreneurs, strengthening entrepreneurship education in universities both directly and indirectly needs to be a priority. Several universities in Africa have established incubation centers—for example, allowing and encouraging students to try out new ideas and take them to market.

There is an important role for regional cooperation and international partnerships with recognized universities in the region and the world. Today's digital technologies make this easier. For example, the Massachusetts Institute of Technology and a consortium of 15 other top universities has started to offer micro-masters programs that require only one full semester on campus in the United States. Targeted scholarship programs that include requirements for returning to the home country can also be helpful, particularly for students in science, technology, engineering, and mathematics (STEM) fields.

Improving the Efficiency and Relevance of Skills Building for Out-of-School Youths and Adults

On-the-Job Training

Laying the basis for building and upgrading the skills of out-of-school youths and adults can be achieved by addressing market and coordination failures that prevent firms (especially small, informal enterprises) from offering on-the-job training and incentivizing them to do so. On-the-job training is an important channel through which workers upgrade their skills during their working life. It is also a vehicle for helping firms to adopt new technologies and new business practices. But the incidence of on-the-job training in much of the region is lower than expected for countries' income levels. It is essential to create the right incentives for firms to train their workers.

Apprenticeships

Given how ubiquitous informal apprenticeships are in the informal sector, it is important to make them more productive. Recent reforms to improve informal apprenticeships usually include measures to improve the quality of training, such as the use of dual training principles (that is, classroom and on-the-job training), training of master craftspersons, and upgrading of technology; measures to improve working conditions and inclusion in informal sector training (promotion of gender equality and occupational health and safety); and measures to establish mechanisms for certification of informally trained artisans, improve the recognition of existing (traditional) certification systems, and institutionalize or improve quality assurance with the involvement of local business associations. Despite these attempts, few reforms have been formally evaluated. In addition, attempts at giving structure to informal apprenticeships and bringing them closer to formal ones have failed to pick up scale. The objective of policy interventions should not be to make informal apprenticeships look like formal ones. The policy objective should be to improve the learning process of apprentices.

Self-Employment and Entrepreneurship

Given that most Sub-Saharan Africans are not in wage employment and, even when they are, do not remain so for long, labor market training programs aimed at improving employability and supporting self-employment are essential. Training programs can remedy the technical or job-specific skills gap of out-of-school youths and adults and build basic cognitive and socio-emotional skills. Although such programs are growing rapidly, the global evidence from rigorous evaluations is mixed regarding the effectiveness of these short-term programs.

Training programs supporting self-employment and small-scale entrepreneurship are among the most widespread remedial training programs in Africa. The programs take various forms, from public works with a training component supporting entrepreneurship to programs promoting small-scale entrepreneurship and improvements in the productivity of small-scale entrepreneurs. Recent programs in Kenya and South Africa, which have been rigorously evaluated, show that training in specific business skills can lead to higher profits and sustainability for businesses and gains in employment and earnings for employees (Anderson, Chandy, and Zia 2016; McKenzie and Puerto 2017). In Togo, training for entrepreneurs to improve business practices as well as socioemotional skills aimed at helping entrepreneurs to become more proactive and resilient to obstacles led to higher sales and profits (Campos et al. 2017). In a successful program in Uganda, youth groups received grants that they could use to obtain vocational training or to start a business, leading to substantial increases in business assets and earnings (Blattman, Fiala, and Martinez 2014).

Facing the Skills Balancing Act: Enact Systemwide Change and Make Skills Building Everyone's Business

Achieving substantial progress in skills building in Sub-Saharan Africa will require enacting systemwide change, not just scaling up "best practices." There is a need to pay attention to the governance environment in which scaling up takes place. To achieve broad and sustained results, policies and reforms need to establish credible commitment, support coordination, and promote cooperation among all actors. To this end, it is important to tackle the politics of skills policies and create incentives to align the behaviors of all stakeholders to the pursuit of national skills development goals.

The international experience from both successful and failed attempts to reform governance points to three broad avenues for enacting systemwide change:

1. *Use information and other metrics* of system performance to generate *commitment* and buy-in for reforms, empower stakeholders to hold governments and providers accountable for results, and guide and adapt policy decisions, which requires collecting household-level data, conducting robust national student assessments, establishing management information systems, and participating in international student tests.

2. *Shift incentives* to align the interests and behaviors of all stakeholders to *cooperate* toward the achievement of skills-building outcomes.

3. *Strengthen the capacity* of government agencies, particularly ministries of health, education, labor, and social development, to pursue nationwide, coordinated, evidence-based policies.

Metrics on system performance can be used to guide policy development and to identify, refine, and adapt successful local solutions. Data from national surveys and student assessments can be used to track progress in tracer indicators and final outcomes that are relevant both to skills formation—from child health to learning to skills formation—and to returns to these skills. Such data are ultimately the basis for building and using evidence to guide the cycle of policy design, implementation, feedback for improvement, and innovation and to indicate whether policies are enacting systemwide change in skills formation.

Several countries have disseminated information on poor performance to mobilize public opinion and get politicians and others to commit to improving results. Information on standards for outcomes and service delivery can empower parents and users to hold providers accountable for results. Simple standards and goals for child development, student learning, and other skills outcomes can allow parents to know how well their children are doing compared with the expected standards and make them more likely to hold providers and local or even central authorities accountable for the quality of services. In Uganda, a newspaper campaign designed to inform local primary schools about their entitlement to grants led to an increase in the flow of funds to schools and accelerated the expansion of school enrollment.

There are limits, however. Important aspects of service delivery, such as teacher contracts and pay, are generally managed centrally and depend on system-level incentives. For instance, short-term contracts for teachers are often used to increase the local accountability of teachers. However, a nationwide reform of this type in Kenya was undermined partly by a power struggle between government and teachers unions.

Countries in Sub-Saharan Africa should also strive to build coalitions for achieving skills results at scale. In addition to tilting public opinion through information regarding system performance, countries can create coalitions to foster cooperation and shift the balance of power in favor of good policies and reforms. Cooperation also requires recognizing the multiple, often competing, and evolving interests of stakeholders. For instance, although many health personnel, teachers, and other social service providers are truly devoted to serving their clientele—mothers, children, and youths—insufficient resources and lack of support can undermine morale and distract their attention from achieving results. Policies that combine resources and pedagogical support for teachers with reforms and mechanisms to improve their accountability for delivering learning, such as teacher evaluations or performance pay, may have a better chance of buy-in.

Conclusions

Although countries in Sub-Saharan Africa can learn much from regional and global experiences to leapfrog their skills development, there are few institutional shortcuts. The institutional underpinning of skills strategies in the region may find practices to emulate and pitfalls to avoid in other world experiences; however, the strategies must be homegrown to be attuned to the political realities of each country. Just like investment priorities, they should reflect each country's context. In most policy choices, countries will face trade-offs—often stark ones—that will have distributional impacts and a bearing on their development path. Committed leaders, reform coalitions, and well-coordinated policies are essential for taking on the skills balancing act in Sub-Saharan Africa.

References

Aker, Jenny C., Christopher Ksoll, and Travis J. Lybbert. 2012. "Can Mobile Phones Improve Learning? Evidence from a Field Experiment in Niger." *American Economic Journal: Applied Economics* 4 (4): 94–120.

Anderson, Stephen J., Rajesh Chandy, and Bilal Zia. 2016. "Pathways to Profits: Identifying Separate Channels of Small Firm Growth through Business Training." Policy Research Working Paper 7774, World Bank, Washington, DC.

Barrera-Osorio, Felipe, Pierre de Galbert, James Habyarimana, and Shwetlena Sabarwal. 2016. "Impact of Public-Private Partnerships on Private School Performance: Evidence from a Randomized Controlled Trial in Uganda." Policy Research Working Paper 7905, World Bank, Washington, DC.

Blattman, Christopher, Nathan Fiala, and Sebastian Martinez. 2014. "Generating Skilled Self-Employment in Developing Countries: Experimental Evidence from Uganda." *Quarterly Journal of Economics* 129 (2): 697–752.

Campos, Francisco, Michael Frese, Markus Goldstein, Leonardo Iacovone, Hillary Johnson, David McKenzie, and Mona Mensmann. 2017. "Teaching Personal Initiative Beats Traditional Training in Boosting Small Business in West Africa." *Science* 357 (6357): 1287–90.

Duflo, Esther, Pascaline Dupas, and Michael Kremer. 2011. "Peer Effects, Teacher Incentives, and the Impact of Tracking: Evidence from a Randomized Evaluation in Kenya." *American Economic Review* 101 (5): 1739–74.

———. 2017. "The Impact of Free Secondary Education: Experimental Evidence from Ghana." Working Paper, Massachusetts Institute of Technology, Cambridge, MA.

Duflo, Annie, and Jessica Kiessel. 2012. "Teacher Community Assistant Initiative (TCAI)." Policy Brief 4004, International Growth Centre, London.

Evans, David K., and Anna Popova. 2016. "What Really Works to Improve Learning in Developing Countries? An Analysis of Divergent Findings in Systematic Reviews." *World Bank Research Observer* 31 (2): 242–70.

Galasso, Emanuela, and Adam Wagstaff, with Sophie Naudeau and Meera Shekar. 2016. "The Economic Costs of Stunting and How to Reduce Them." Policy Research Note 5, World Bank, Washington, DC.

McKenzie, David, and Susana Puerto. 2017. "Growing Markets through Business Training for Female Entrepreneurs: A Market-Level Randomized Experiment in Kenya." Policy Research Working Paper 7993, World Bank, Washington, DC.

Nguyen, Trang. 2008. "Information, Role Models, and Perceived Returns to Education: Experimental Evidence from Madagascar." Economics Department, Massachusetts Institute of Technology, Cambridge, MA.

Piper, Benjamin, Leila Schroeder, and Barbara Trudell. 2016. "Oral Reading Fluency and Comprehension in Kenya: Reading Acquisition in a Multilingual Environment." *Journal of Research in Reading* 39 (2): 133–52.

Overview

Omar Arias, David K. Evans, and Indhira Santos

Summary

Sub-Saharan Africa is home to the 10 youngest countries in the world. The working-age population is growing, creating a major opportunity to reduce poverty and increase shared prosperity. But the region's workforce is the least skilled in the world, constraining economic prospects. Thus, building the skills—foundational cognitive, socioemotional, and technical—of today's workers and those of future generations will be vital for realizing the development potential of the region. Despite economic growth, declining poverty, and investments in skills building, too many students in too many countries in Sub-Saharan Africa are not acquiring the foundational skills they need to thrive and prosper in an increasingly competitive global economy.

Countries in Sub-Saharan Africa have invested heavily in skills building, with public expenditure on education increasing sevenfold over the past 30 years. On average, education absorbs about 18 percent of total public spending and 5 percent of gross domestic product (GDP), the largest spending ratios among low- and middle-income regions. There is, of course, variation across countries, in the range of about 11–28 percent of total government spending and 2–15 percent of GDP. In addition to public resources, households contribute around 25 percent of total national education expenditure.

More children are in school today than ever before. Over the past half-century, primary completion rates have more than doubled, while lower-secondary completion rates have increased more than fivefold. Yet in half the countries in the region, fewer than two in every three children complete primary school. In most countries, far less than 50 percent complete secondary education, and barely 5 percent make it to higher education. Although gender gaps in both primary and secondary school have narrowed in most African nations, significantly more girls than boys are out of school. In some countries, fewer than three girls are in school for every four boys.

For children in school, learning outcomes have been persistently poor, leading to huge gaps in basic cognitive skills—literacy and numeracy—among children, young people, and adults. The literacy rate of the adult population is below 50 percent in many countries, and functional literacy and numeracy are even lower. Even at recent rates of progress, in the decades to come, the region will continue to fall behind other regions in the world in educational attainment at all levels. In addition, child stunting rates remain stubbornly high, leading to adverse impacts on all future skills investments.

Countries' skills-building efforts have to strive to make spending smarter in order to ensure greater efficiency and better outcomes. But smart investing in skills is difficult. Sub-Saharan African countries face two difficult choices in balancing their skills portfolio: striking the right balance between investing in overall productivity growth and inclusion, on the one hand, and between investing in the skills of the workforce of today and of tomorrow, on the other hand.

One investment that results in growth and inclusion is investment in strong foundational skills for all. Sub-Saharan African countries can close significant gaps in education and training if they prioritize universal foundational skills by tackling child stunting and building the literacy, numeracy, and socioemotional skills of children, youths, and adults. This strategy requires focusing on investments in the early years and inputs that matter most for the quality of education; specifically, it requires investing in effective teaching, not merely hiring more teachers or building more buildings. It requires providing training that draws on the latest evidence and creating incentives for the best to become teachers. Particular attention needs to be paid to ensuring equal access to quality services for the poor and to closing gender gaps, especially in high-inequality contexts. It also requires supporting youths and adults who have missed out on foundational skills. Such support would include interventions that build basic literacy and socioemotional skills among individuals employed in farm and nonfarm rural activities and in low-productivity urban self-employment. The expansion of basic education in the region calls for renewed public-private partnerships (PPPs), with a strong regulatory role for the state.

In skills training, countries have to be selective and ruthlessly demand driven. For productivity growth, support should target demand-driven technical and vocational education and training (TVET), higher education, entrepreneurship, and business training programs tied to catalytic sectors. Such support should incentivize more on-the-job training, especially in smaller firms. Special attention should be paid to science, technology, engineering, and mathematics (STEM) fields, focusing on the transfer and adoption of technology in economies with an enabling policy environment for these skills investments to pay off. Economic inclusion requires investing in labor market training programs focused on serving disadvantaged youths and improving the skills of workers in low-productivity activities in urban areas (for example, through informal apprenticeships) and rural areas (for example, in comprehensive livelihood programs and agricultural extension services). For adaptability, reforms should be introduced in secondary and tertiary education to delay the tracking of students into technical and vocational education streams, at least until the upper-secondary level. In addition, education systems should create effective pathways between academic and technical tracks and introduce more active and work-based learning practices.

In designing and implementing this skills agenda, countries should engage multiple actors. Families can invest in and nurture children's cognitive and socioemotional development by providing quality care and parenting and by engaging with schools to hold them accountable for effective service delivery. The private sector can provide services to enhance access and quality, invest in on-the-job training, work with education and training providers to ensure that programs are aligned with their needs, and engage in national social dialogue to prioritize skills development and reforms to create a policy-enabling environment for skills investments to pay off.

Achieving significant progress in building skills is possible in Sub-Saharan Africa, but it will require enacting systemwide change. Small-scale programs and local reforms often fail to achieve the desired impacts at scale. Achieving more equitable access, quality, relevance, and efficiency in skills building cannot hinge on just scaling up "best practices." There is a need to pay attention to the governance environment in which skills programs take place. Multiple agencies at the central and local levels are involved in skills development strategies, making skills "everyone's problem, but no one's responsibility." Lack of coordination and weak capacity can result in inefficiencies, duplication of efforts, or, perhaps worse, lack of attention to important issues. Therefore, to achieve broad and sustained results, policies and reforms need to tackle the politics of policies, build capacity for evidence-based policies, and create incentives to align the behaviors of all stakeholders to the pursuit of national skills development goals.

In their policy choices, countries will face trade-offs—often stark ones—that will have distributional impacts and a bearing on their development path. This is the core of the skills balancing act in Sub-Saharan Africa.

Challenges and Opportunities for Skills Building in Sub-Saharan Africa

In the past 20 years, decades after independence and recovery from conflict in several countries, Sub-Saharan African countries have grown rapidly, reduced the incidence of poverty, and boosted access to education. The region has lifted millions out of poverty and put an unprecedented number of children through school. More than two-thirds of children now complete primary school, up from just over half in 1990, and completion of lower-secondary education nearly doubled in the same period. In several countries, access to tertiary education has begun to expand. The region increased its public expenditure on education sevenfold between 1984 and 2014.

Thus, Sub-Saharan Africa is on the right track. But to accelerate its social and economic transformation in the next 20 years, the region must overcome its skills crisis by making strategic and smart investments in early child development (ECD) and in education and training. Despite progress, in half the countries of Sub-Saharan Africa, fewer than two in every three children complete primary school. In most countries, far less than 50 percent complete secondary education, and barely 5 percent of the working-age population make it to higher education. Learning outcomes have been so poor for so long that a learning crisis has led to huge gaps in basic cognitive skills (literacy and numeracy) among children, youths, and out-of-school adults, with important gender gaps. To overcome this crisis, countries need smart investments to continue expanding access to and improving the quality and relevance of skills building. This effort is vital if the region is to avoid the fate of continuing to fall behind other regions in the world 20 years from now, blunting its competitive edge and its chances to take advantage of the demographic window of opportunity.

The challenge of skills development in Sub-Saharan Africa historically shares many similarities with the challenges faced by other regions of the world when at similar levels of development. To reap the demographic dividend, the region needs to invest appropriately in the skills of today's children and those of future cohorts. Meanwhile, the region needs to invest in the skills of youths and adults to spur economic growth and economic transformation from agrarian to industrial and service-based economies. To meet these challenges, countries in the region will need to overcome significant institutional weakness in the skills-building system.

At the same time, in some important ways, the skills development challenge in Sub-Saharan Africa is unique. Countries are undergoing economic transformation while facing a more challenging environment than other regions of the world faced at similar stages of development in the 19th and 20th centuries. The region needs to build skills from the bottom up at a time of stiff economic competition. The workforce—both of today and of tomorrow—needs a wider set of foundational cognitive, socioemotional, and technical skills to succeed in a radically more demanding world that puts a premium on the adaptability of individuals and systems. At the same time, countries are pressed to meet the mounting aspirations of their youth. When young people are denied opportunities for a better future, the unskilled, discontented, and disconnected are easy prey for those seeking to spread anger, fear, and radicalization.

In addition to the challenges, Sub-Saharan African countries also have opportunities to invest smarter and build skills rapidly. Countries can apply the expanding body of rigorous evidence on what can work in skills building; they can leverage the use of new technologies and social programs, such as cash transfers for service delivery; and, finally, they can tap the opportunities from regional cooperation to achieve farther-reaching progress with economies of scale and lower costs.

Policy Framework for Skills Investments in Sub-Saharan Africa

The portfolio of potential investments that countries in the region can make should aim to achieve three policy goals: (a) accelerate overall productivity growth (prosperous economies), (b) promote economic inclusion (inclusive societies), and (c) ensure the adaptability of the workforce in the 21st century (resilient economies and individuals). Countries in the region face hard choices when considering skills investments to achieve these goals.

A smart skills development strategy requires figuring out which skills are needed, for what, who needs them, and how they can be developed at the right time and in the right way. Figure O.1 illustrates a framework aimed at guiding priorities for education and training skills policies and investments in the region. The figure encapsulates three main guiding principles.

First, skills investments need to reckon with two main potential trade-offs. The first is between investing in skills with greater potential to maximize economywide productivity gains, such as technical skills for economic activities with high growth potential that can catalyze economic transformation by reallocating productive resources and tapping new technologies, and investing in skills aimed at economic inclusion, such as skills for improving livelihoods and earnings opportunities, especially for the poor. The second potential trade-off is between investing in the skills needed by the out-of-school young and adult population for today's largely agrarian and self-employment-based economies and investing in the skills needed by future cohorts of workers for tomorrow's transforming economies to ensure their adaptability to employment changes in their working lives and their resilience in navigating the fast-changing world of work.

Second, a balanced skills portfolio requires investing cost-effectively over the life cycle in the multiplicity of skills needed in modernizing economies. These skills include, broadly, (a) *foundational cognitive skills* (for example, literacy and numeracy), (b) *foundational socioemotional skills* (for example, related to managing one's self and relating with others, such as self-regulation, perseverance, curiosity, empathy, and tolerance), and (c) *technical or job-specific skills* (for example, vocational and professional qualifications and digital and management skills). These skills are important for new cohorts of workers—those of school age and youths still in education—and for the current stock of youths, teens, and older adults already outside the formal education system. A balanced skills

Figure O.1 Policy Framework for Skills Policy Priorities in Sub-Saharan Africa

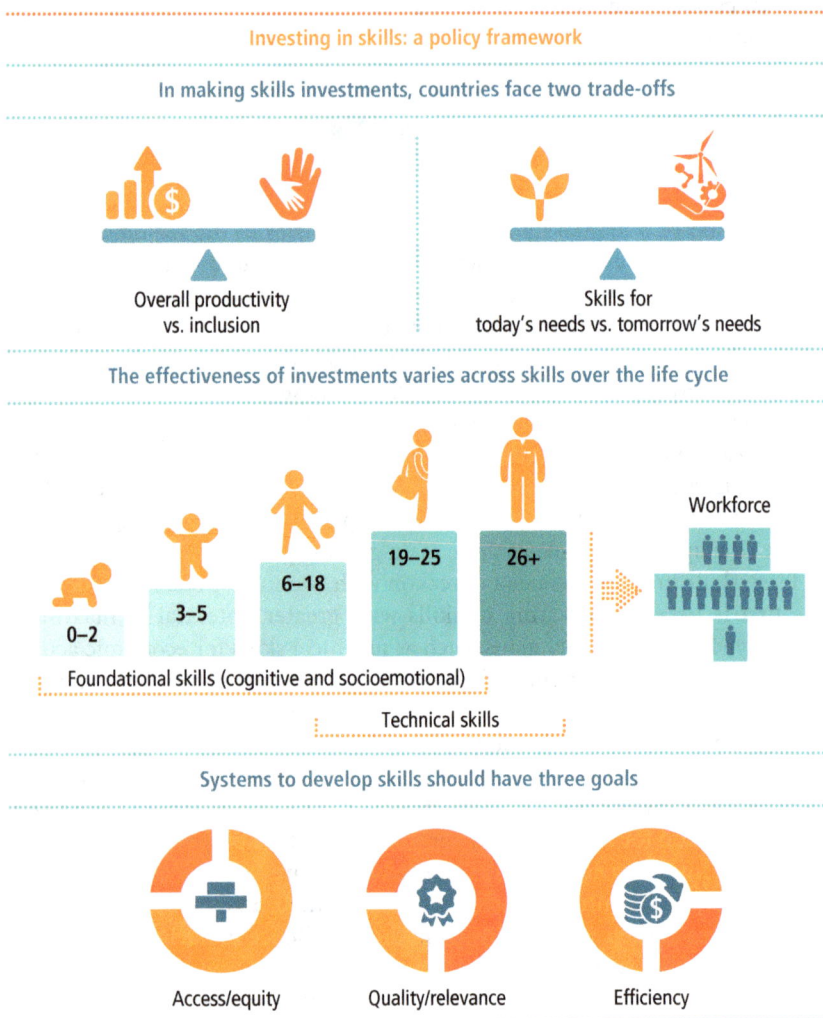

Investing in skills: a policy framework

In making skills investments, countries face two trade-offs

Overall productivity
vs. inclusion

Skills for
today's needs vs. tomorrow's needs

The effectiveness of investments varies across skills over the life cycle

0–2

3–5

6–18

19–25

26+

Workforce

Foundational skills (cognitive and socioemotional)

Technical skills

Systems to develop skills should have three goals

Access/equity

Quality/relevance

Efficiency

portfolio encompasses a range of investments in building foundational, cognitive, and socioemotional skills for infants, toddlers, children, and teenagers and technical skills for youths and adults and in reinforcing skills through on-the-job training, labor training, and education programs.

In making these investments, policy makers should consider that skills formation is a lifelong process in which skills beget skills. Figure O.1 shows the optimal stages for acquiring different skills over the life span, highlighting how and when the skills that are most appropriate to each stage are acquired. Human capital formation is a time-dependent process. For families who are unable to engage in human capital formation at the right time, the prime opportunity is gone. Investments in the early years are crucial, because this is when neural connections flourish and are pruned and solidified.

Cognitive and socioemotional development is highly influenced by maternal and child health and nutrition, especially during the first 1,000 days of life, and by the quality of nurturing environments during infancy and childhood. Although basic cognitive skills are well set by the teen years, schooling can provide subject knowledge and tools that enhance these abilities, as well as socioemotional skills that remain malleable through adolescence and the early adult years. Foundational skills determine a person's "readiness to learn" in basic education, postsecondary schooling, training, and on the job. Although it is more cost-effective to invest earlier, brain plasticity and malleability in adulthood mean that later investments can remedy foundational skills gaps among the current stock of workers. Such investments are especially important for the most vulnerable individuals, who fall out of the education system early on and fail to acquire critical foundational skills. These investments can bring positive intergenerational effects; that is, literate mothers are more likely to raise healthier children with stronger foundational skills.

The third guiding principle is that, to provide the right skills, at the right time, and in the right way, education and training systems need to ensure equity, quality, and efficiency. Investments and policy reforms need to provide wide access to opportunities for skills acquisition (*equitable access*), learning that builds skills to meet labor market demand (*quality and relevance*), and value-for-money in the financing and provision of education and training to minimize waste of resources (*efficiency*).

Armed with these guiding principles, countries need to rally multiple actors in skills development. A coalition of investors—families, government, and the private sector, including employers and private providers of training—is vital to making the most of investments in ECD, education, and training. Members of the coalition have distinctive and complementary roles. *Families* can actively invest in and nurture children's cognitive and socioemotional development by providing quality prenatal and child care and parenting and by holding schools accountable for effective service delivery. The *private sector* can participate effectively in service provision to enhance access and quality; invest in on-the-job-training to build skills; engage with education and training providers to ensure that programs are aligned with the sector's needs; and engage in national social dialogue to prioritize skills development and reforms to create a policy-enabling environment for skills investments to pay off.

The *public sector* has a crucial role to play in ensuring equity and addressing market and coordination failures. It does this through investments and complementary policies that ensure individuals' readiness (foundational skills), opportunities, and incentives for skills acquisition. That is, the public sector should ensure equality of opportunities and an environment conducive to realizing the potential returns to investments in skills (both public and private). This role includes tackling the political economy of reforms, fostering cooperation, commitment, and coordination of stakeholders through strategic leadership, social dialogue, and adequate incentives, and supporting the most vulnerable individuals who fail to acquire critical foundational skills.

The Skills Balancing Act

Four cross-cutting questions encapsulate the main policy issues regarding investments in skills in Sub-Saharan Africa:

- Are investments in skills meeting the needs of the economies of today and tomorrow?
- Is current skills development built on a solid foundation?
- Is there a good case for investing in the skills of out-of-school youths and adults?
- Are countries in the region investing adequate resources in skills?

In answering these questions, governments in Sub-Saharan Africa face a difficult balancing act in making hard choices among pressing and competing skills investments. To manage the trade-offs and enable skills investments to pay off, priorities should be tailored to the country context, particularly the skills level, state of economic transformation, and policy environment. The balancing act is a matter of allocating scarce public resources.

Are Investments in Skills in Sub-Saharan Africa Meeting the Needs of the Economies of Today and Tomorrow?

The short answer is, "Often not," for three reasons.

The first reason is that, in most countries, the formal education and training system largely caters to wage employment in the very small formal sector. To be sure, a key role of skills investments in the region is to meet the skills needs of catalytic sectors that will enable economic transformation. This effort is vital for Sub-Saharan Africa to move workers from low-productivity sectors, like subsistence agriculture, to higher-value jobs, including modern agriculture. High-skill jobs in leading economic activities not only raise earnings, but also indirectly create additional jobs. However, skills investments need to reckon with the reality of today's economies, which rely heavily on subsistence agriculture and informal employment—mostly in self-employment and in small firms in the services sector—to provide jobs and livelihoods. Skills policies need to improve the earnings and livelihoods of the large population who will likely remain in agriculture and informal jobs for decades to come.

On average, across countries in Sub-Saharan Africa, 8 of every 10 jobs are in agriculture or nonfarm household enterprises, most often in services. In some countries, such as The Gambia, Ghana, and South Africa, manufacturing and services already are or are becoming important sources of jobs. However, as shown in figure O.2, labor has moved out of agriculture more slowly in most of Sub-Saharan Africa than in the rest of the world, and projections show that, even in optimistic scenarios, the share of nonwage informal employment is likely to change very slowly (Filmer and Fox 2014). Most nonwage informal jobs are low-productivity jobs that provide low earnings.

Formal education and training systems in the region often fail to prepare workers adequately for the jobs they are most likely to have. Agricultural extension programs that incorporate skills training often do not pay attention to remedying deficits in the foundational (basic literacy, numeracy, and socioemotional) skills of farmers, even though these skills are at least as important as technical skills for the adoption of new technologies and more productive agricultural practices. Entrepreneurship education in secondary schooling is nascent, although programs such as Educate! in Rwanda and Uganda can be a model in this area. Training programs for the self-employed remain limited in scope and suffer from significant design and implementation issues. Recent innovations in programs that combine multiple skills training with cash transfers show promise.

Formal and informal apprenticeships have not achieved their potential. In many countries in the region, ongoing reforms in apprenticeship frameworks are aiming to expand access to these opportunities by providing more incentives to the private sector to take on apprentices, strengthening partnerships with employers (including in the management of such schemes), complementing on-the-job training with classroom training (including in foundational skills), more clearly recognizing the skills gained, and combining apprenticeships with more comprehensive support that aids the transition to higher-productivity self-employment or wage work.

The second reason why investments are not meeting the needs of economies is misalignments in programs that invest in skills for the small formal sector. As countries in the region grow richer over time, firms are increasingly reporting that the lack of skills is a constraint to their growth and productivity (figure O.3). Productive and export-oriented firms are feeling the pinch from a shortage of skills the most. As documented by Perotti (2017), skills are also becoming more binding, as other constraints to firms' operations, particularly access to finance,

Figure 0.2 Sectoral Distribution of Employment in Sub-Saharan Africa

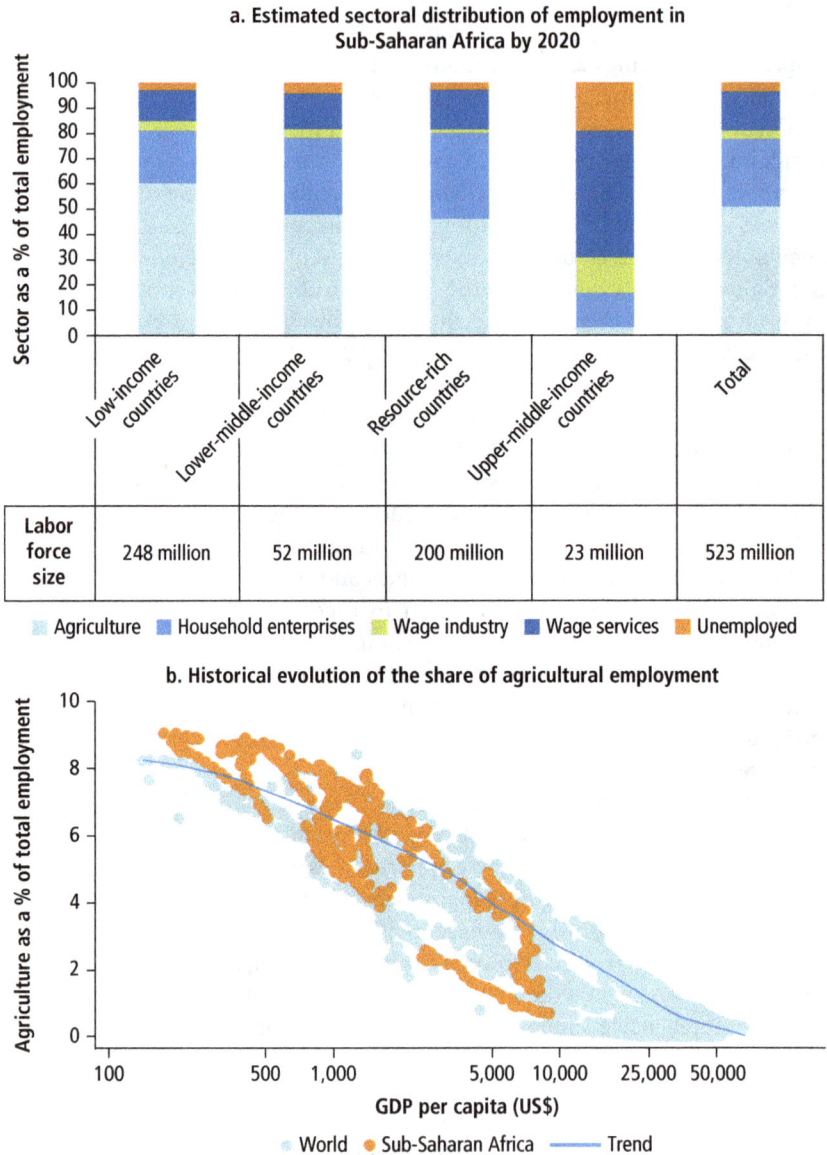

a. Estimated sectoral distribution of employment in Sub-Saharan Africa by 2020

	Low-income countries	Lower-middle-income countries	Resource-rich countries	Upper-middle-income countries	Total
Labor force size	248 million	52 million	200 million	23 million	523 million

Legend: Agriculture — Household enterprises — Wage industry — Wage services — Unemployed

b. Historical evolution of the share of agricultural employment

Agriculture as a % of total employment (y-axis); GDP per capita (US$) (x-axis)

Legend: World — Sub-Saharan Africa — Trend

Sources: For panel a, Filmer and Fox 2014. For panel b, data from the Groningen Growth and Development Centre 10-Sector Database.

Figure O.3 Share of Firms Rating Skills as a Greater-than-Average Constraint Compared with 14 Other Business Environment Factors in Sub-Saharan Africa and the World, by Size of Firm and GDP per Capita

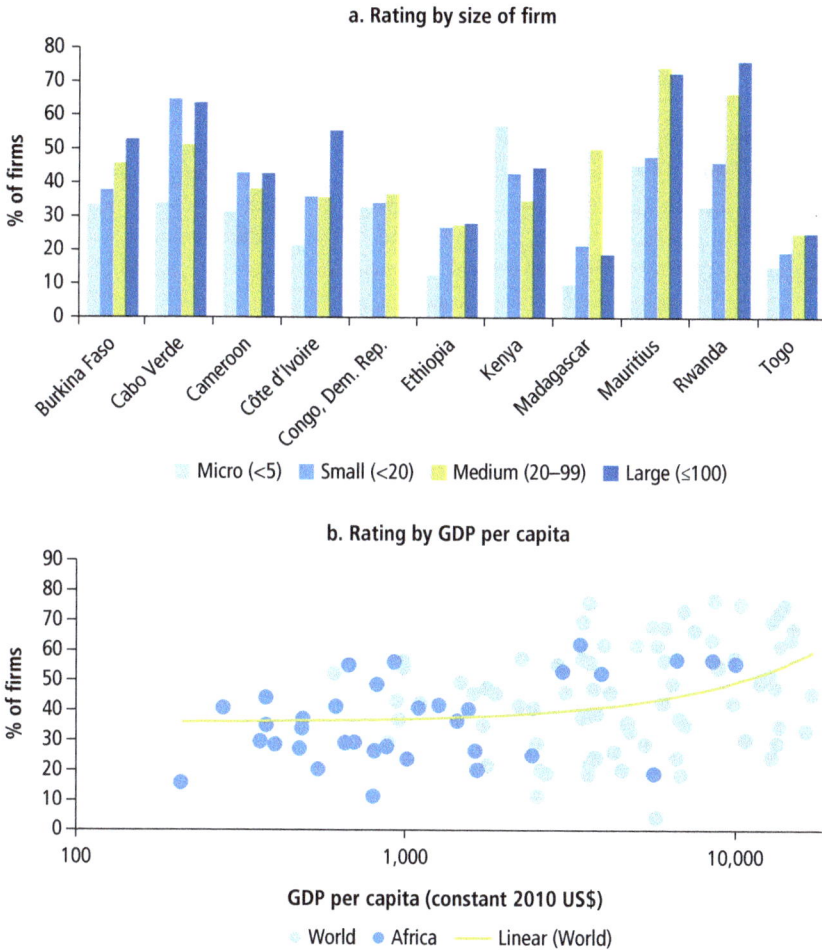

a. Rating by size of firm

Micro (<5)   Small (<20)   Medium (20–99)   Large (≤100)

b. Rating by GDP per capita

GDP per capita (constant 2010 US$)

World   Africa   — Linear (World)

Source: Perotti 2017, based on World Bank Enterprise Surveys.
Note: Both panels employ data from the standard Enterprise Surveys covering largely formal firms, excluding microenterprises. Panel b also includes data for microfirms from specialized Enterprise Surveys for Sub-Saharan Africa. The indicator measures the % of firms that rate skills (on a scale of 1 = not important to 5 = important) above the average rating that the same firm gives to all of the constraints surveyed.

are addressed. Moreover, as in many other low- and middle-income economies, employers in the region are increasingly requiring workers to have a multiplicity of skills, including literacy, numeracy, socioemotional skills, and technical skills. For example, more than half of the formal and informal large and small firms surveyed by the School-to-Work Transition Surveys in Benin, Liberia, Malawi, and Zambia reported that technical, interpersonal, and higher-order cognitive skills (problem solving, decision making) are very or extremely important for them.

Although some degree of skills mismatch is natural and unavoidable in any growing and restructuring economy, many graduates from technical, vocational, and general education pursue fields for which labor demand is weak. Although average returns to education, especially higher education, are high and, in some cases, increasing, there is a lot of variation across and within fields of study. Often, investments in TVET or higher education do not pay off for many students (figure O.4). TVET does seem to pay off for students with the weakest prospects in the labor market and the slimmest chances of reaching the high-quality universities for which returns to education are the highest. That said, although TVET can help in the school-to-work transition and confers a positive earnings premium on average, there is a lot of variation across students, fields, and institutions. This variation in returns to postsecondary education may result from students' lack of readiness (due to weak foundational skills), as well as the low quality of and misalignment with labor market needs of technical and vocational education at the upper-secondary and tertiary levels. Just above a quarter of the region's university students are enrolled in programs in the applied sciences, engineering, and technology, with a lower fraction among women. The region has only 92 scientific researchers per 1 million people, compared with the global average of more than 1,000.

At a deeper level, these gaps stem from institutional weaknesses. TVET and higher education often have poor links to labor demand, lack diverse pathways that can allow students to build skills cumulatively, and have financing and accountability mechanisms that are not tied to results. Figure O.5 shows how a subset of countries in the region (Cameroon, Chad, Tanzania, and Uganda) score on internationally comparable institutional assessments of formal workforce development systems (composed mostly of TVET, but also labor market programs). The region often lags other low- and middle-income regions and high-performing countries in the early stages of development of their TVET systems. Similar institutional weaknesses pervade higher education.

The third reason why investments are not meeting the needs of economies is that the nature of work is changing, sometimes too rapidly for education and training systems to adapt. Countries in Sub-Saharan Africa, like the rest of the world, face three megatrends that are reshaping the global economy, rapidly

Figure O.4 Relative Returns to TVET and Higher Education in Ghana and Kenya

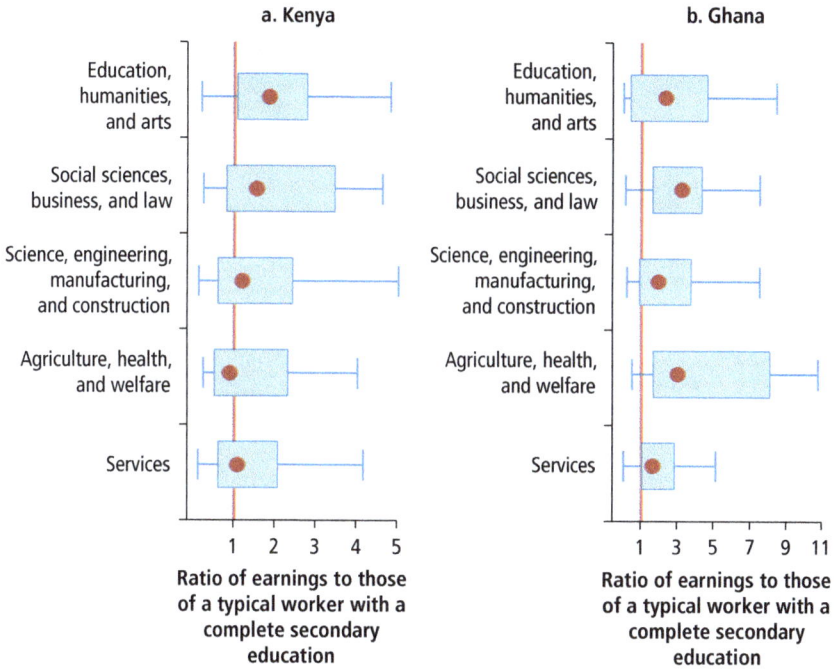

Source: Based on World Bank Skills Towards Employability and Productivity (STEP) Surveys.
Note: The figure shows the ratio of earnings from various TVET fields and university education to the earnings of typical individuals with complete secondary education across the distribution. The red dot represents the median of the distribution. The lower end of the box represents the 25th percentile, and the upper end represents the 75th percentile. The lines outside the box represent the ratio for the highest and lowest values of earnings excluding outliers. TVET = technical and vocational education and training.

changing the demand for skills, and posing opportunities and challenges for skills policies: population shifts, global integration, and technological change (with the shrinking role of manufacturing as a source of employment and a force of economic transformation).

The first trend pertains to population shifts. Most countries in Sub-Saharan Africa are entering or have entered the demographic transition with the "dependency ratio" (the fraction of the population that is too young or too old to work) declining and giving rise to the potential "demographic dividend." Changes in fertility in most of the region are favorable to human capital accumulation. In almost every country today, fertility rates are falling and families are having fewer children. Lower fertility can free up resources, as the workforce grows faster than the dependent population, raising per capita

Figure O.5 Workforce Development Performance across Specific Policy Goals, by Region

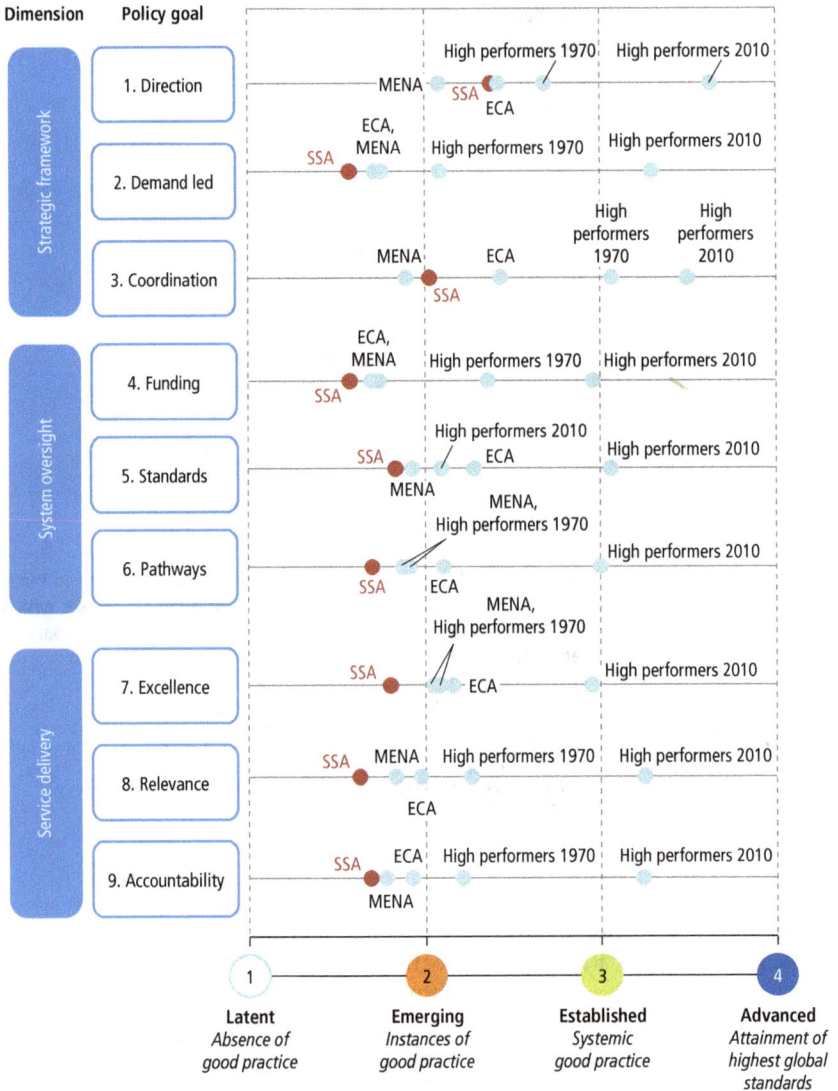

Source: Based on World Bank Systems Approach for Better Education Results Workforce Development (SABER-WfD) Ratings and Data database.
Note: 1 = latent; 2 = emerging; 3 = established; 4 = advanced; TVET = technical and vocational education and training; ECA (Europe and Central Asia) refers to average values for Armenia, Bulgaria, Georgia, North Macedonia, Moldova, Tajikistan, Turkey, and Ukraine, SSA (Sub-Saharan Africa) refers to average values for Burundi, Cameroon, Chad, Tanzania, and Uganda. MENA (Middle East and North Africa) refers to average values for Egypt, Arab Rep.; Iraq; Jordan; Morocco; Tunisia; West Bank and Gaza; and Yemen, Rep. High performers 1970 = Ireland (1980), Korea, Rep. (1970), and Singapore (1970); High performers 2010 = Chile (2011), Ireland (2000), Korea, Rep. (2010), Malaysia (2010), and Singapore (2010).

incomes and the capacity of families to invest in the skills of their offspring. This demographic dividend is accompanied by urbanization. Across the region, more than one-third of the population already live in urban areas, facilitating service delivery (figure O.6).

Altogether, more resources potentially are available to invest in the early years and in quality basic education, and the costs of making these investments are lower. Demographic forces offer many countries in the region a unique "window of opportunity" to harness the potential of a significant increase in their nation's young population to generate greater productivity, increase prosperity, and reduce poverty. Although the demographic transition in Southern African countries is more advanced, they still have a decade or so to take advantage of the heightened potential payoff to skills investments during the transition. At the same time, countries in the region will need to secure resources

Figure O.6 **Megatrends That Shape Skills Demand in Sub-Saharan Africa**

a. Urbanization by GDP per capita

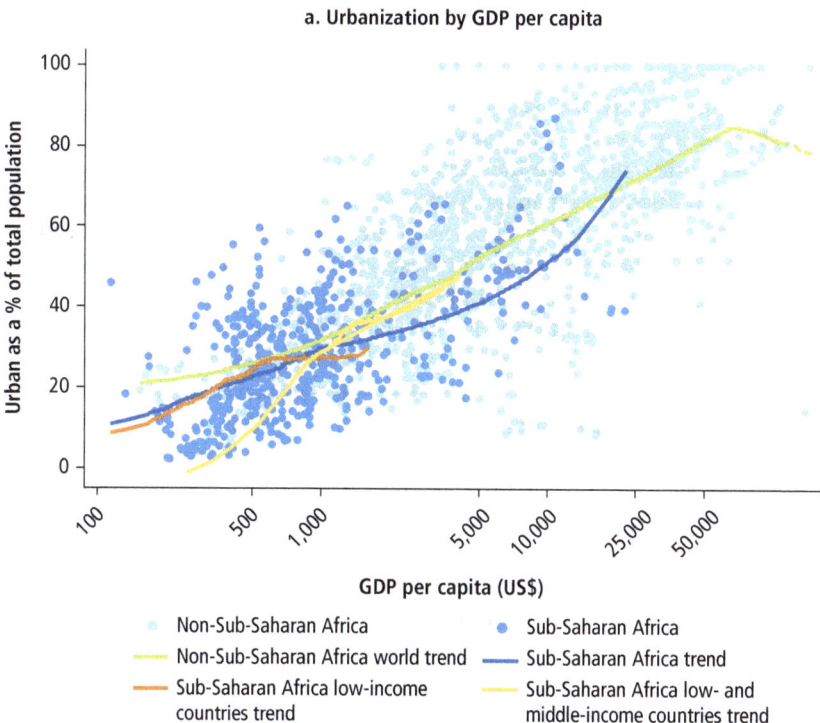

(continued next page)

Figure O.6 (continued)

b. Peak in share of employment in manufacturing, by year and GDP per capita

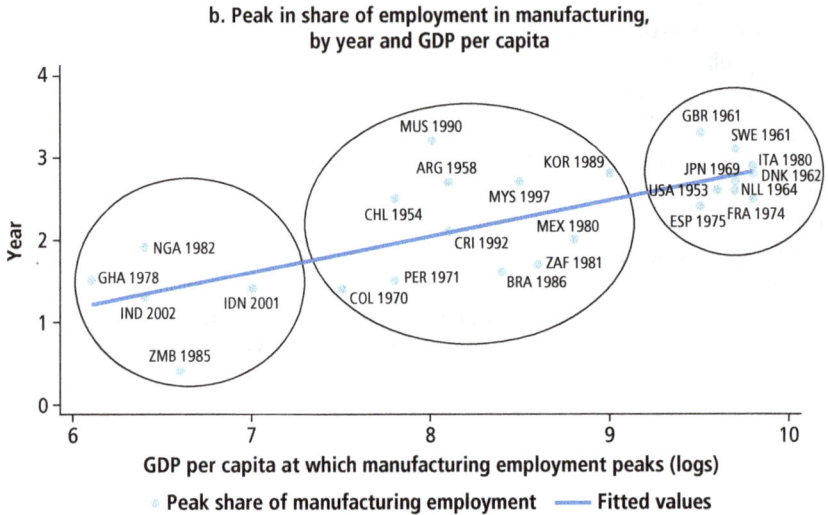

Sources: For panel a, based on World Development Indicators database and household surveys. For panel b, Rodrik 2016.

to expand the supply of basic education and secondary schools and to ensure access to quality schooling for the growing student population.

The second trend is the increasingly interconnected nature of the global economy. Production in manufacturing and services takes place in interlocked global value chains, in which China and other East Asian economies have managed to capture the lion's share of investments in export-oriented industries. This trend goes hand in hand with increased economic competition.

Finally, the third trend is the impact of digital technologies and robots and the rapidly changing world of work. Technology increases the demand for skills, including more advanced skills (World Bank 2019). Even if automation does not lead directly to the destruction of routine jobs in Sub-Saharan Africa, many of these jobs may disappear in countries like China before African economies can capture the related industries through lower labor costs. Moreover, just as critically, even when jobs are not destroyed, these technologies change the types of skills that are needed at work.

These last two trends combined bring about the challenge of premature deindustrialization. As shown in figure O.6, panel a, drawing on the work of Rodrik (2016), over the past two decades, manufacturing has had a shrinking role as a force of transformation to pull labor from agriculture in the region. Increasingly, services—often from informal self-employment and microenterprises—are the engine for transformation and job creation. Limited jobs will be created in the formal sector, especially in manufacturing, over the decades to come. More individuals will need to be prepared to create their own job.

Policy makers should factor in these regional megatrends when establishing priorities for managing the trade-offs in skills investments. First, the trends will raise the educational and social mobility aspirations of families and individuals, especially youths. Second, the trends will change the types of skills that are in demand. Demand for high-level nonroutine cognitive and socioemotional skills will grow; demand for the skills required for many routine low- and medium-skill jobs will fall. And third, the trends will accelerate the speed of change and put a premium on the adaptability of individuals and systems.

At the same time, these changes will bring opportunities for countries to step up progress in skills formation. As countries go through the demographic transition, the share of younger people in the working-age population will rise faster, and younger workers will replace older and less educated workers at a faster pace. Most countries have only recently set out on this path and can still reap most of these benefits. Furthermore, countries in the region can apply the expanding body of rigorous evidence regarding what can work in skills building and learn from the successes and failures of other countries and regions. They can leverage the use of new technologies and the advantages of service delivery in more urban societies, as well as a wider net of social programs, such as cash transfers. Low- and middle-income countries have a higher life expectancy than today's high-income countries reached at comparable stages of development, thanks to improvements in health technology, such as vaccinations and antibiotics (Deaton 2013). Recent applications of new technologies could extend the significant gains in school enrollment to learning outcomes. And finally, the region can tap the opportunities from regional cooperation and approaches to common problems to achieve farther-reaching progress with economies of scale and lower costs.

Patience is required, since skills investments, especially in new cohorts, have a long maturity and take time to bear fruit. It will take nearly two decades for investments in the skills of today's children to translate into a more productive labor force and higher national and family incomes. Because of slow progress in the past, in many countries, up to 30 percent of prime-age and older adults failed to acquire a minimum set of foundational skills. This situation puts those families at higher risk of poverty, which hinders the opportunities of their children. These families would have to wait a decade or more before any schooling bequests to their young children can lift family incomes significantly. In many countries, the demographic window of opportunity is opening; in others, it has been open for some time. For some, that window is closing. Given the importance that governments, employers, and families in the region place on education and training, this is not an opportunity to be missed.

Is Skills Development Built on a Solid Foundation in Sub-Saharan Africa?

In most countries in Sub-Saharan Africa, it is not, for several reasons.

In recent decades, the region has made big strides in enrollment in basic (especially primary) education, which should be celebrated. In 1950, more than three-quarters of children in Sub-Saharan Africa did not attend school. By 2010, that figure had fallen to less than a third. According to the United Nations Educational, Scientific, and Cultural Organization (UNESCO 2016), in the majority of countries, more than 80 percent of primary-age children are enrolled in school today. Burundi is a standout performer, having more than doubled the proportion of primary-age children enrolled in school, from less than 41 percent in 2000 to 96 percent in 2014. Burkina Faso, Guinea, Niger, and Mozambique boosted their primary enrollment ratios by 30–36 percentage points; Ghana, Lesotho, Mali, Senegal, and Zambia increased theirs by about 22–26 percentage points.

Yet, access to basic education remains incomplete. Inequities in access to education persist among children across demographic and socioeconomic groups and regions within countries. Although the number of out-of-school children in the region has fallen over the past two decades, 31 million primary-age children and nearly 57 million adolescents and youths of secondary-school age, many of them girls, were not attending school in 2014 (UNESCO 2016). Although more than 8 of every 10 school-age children were enrolled in primary school, only two of every three adolescents were enrolled in lower-secondary school. In Nigeria, the region's most populous country, nearly 9 million children are not attending school; many of them live in the conflict-affected Northeast region.

Thus, achieving universal basic education remains elusive. Overall, about 55 percent of children complete primary education and less than one in three children complete lower-secondary education. The overall rate of primary-school completion is much lower in Sub-Saharan Africa than in Asia and the Pacific, Latin America and the Caribbean, and other regions. There is significant variation within Africa, of course. Botswana, Cabo Verde, Ghana, Kenya, the Seychelles, and South Africa are close to achieving universal completion of primary education. But in Burkina Faso, Burundi, Guinea, Mozambique, and Niger—countries with the greatest recent progress in enrollment—fewer than 50 percent of students complete primary education.

The low rate of school completion stems from a combination of inadequate physical access, repetition, family income constraints, and social norms biased against girls. In several countries, many children still lack adequate access to primary school. In Lesotho, Malawi, Mali, and Rwanda, half or more of children live more than 2 kilometers from the nearest primary school and must walk at least a half hour each way. High repetition rates persist in primary school and often extend to higher grades. In countries like Benin, Burundi, Côte d'Ivoire, Lesotho, Rwanda, and Togo, 15–25 percent or more of children repeat a grade in primary school. Although the vast majority of African nations do not charge formal tuition fees in compulsory basic education, the region still has the highest number of countries that do charge tuition fees, including Guinea, Somalia, South Africa, Zambia, and Zimbabwe. These fees, together with other indirect costs (for books, uniforms, and so forth), can amount to a significant burden for the poorest families. Finally, enrollment figures mask significant numbers of overage students, an important factor that is linked to school leaving, especially at the lower- and upper-secondary education levels, due to a combination of late entry and repetition. UNESCO (2016) estimates that the region has the countries with the highest proportions of overage primary school students, with more than one-third of students overage. Across the region, early marriage, teenage pregnancy, and other social norms lead to early school leaving by many girls.

Secondary enrollment and completion rates are still low, particularly among girls, although they are growing. By 2014, overall only 40 percent of youths in the region were enrolled in upper-secondary school, and only 15 percent completed it. Growing primary completion rates and population growth have been increasing the demand for secondary education across the continent. The pressure is mounting. Between 1990 and 2010, the cohort of children ages 5–14 years grew 65 percent in the region. Countries will need to ramp up construction of new secondary schools and assure that they are well staffed and resourced. Gender disparities in secondary schooling remain widespread; for example, most countries have not yet achieved gender parity. In the Central African Republic and Chad, both recently affected by conflict and violence, nearly half as many girls as boys were enrolled in secondary school in 2012; in contrast, in Lesotho, 71 boys were enrolled for every 100 girls.

Sub-Saharan Africa's advances have not been rapid enough to keep up with global progress on educational attainment, particularly in other low- and middle-income countries. The desirable structure of educational attainment resembles a diamond, with a majority of the population completing basic and high school education and building foundational skills and a fraction of the population reaching tertiary (university or tertiary TVET) education, which will increase progressively as countries become richer. As shown in figure O.7, this is the current structure in most countries in East Asia and Pacific, a region that in 1950 looked like Sub-Saharan Africa today. Despite recent progress, today Sub-Saharan Africa still has an education pyramid with a wide base of low-educated adults.

Figure 0.7 Educational Pyramids in Sub-Saharan Africa and Other Regions, 1950 and 2010

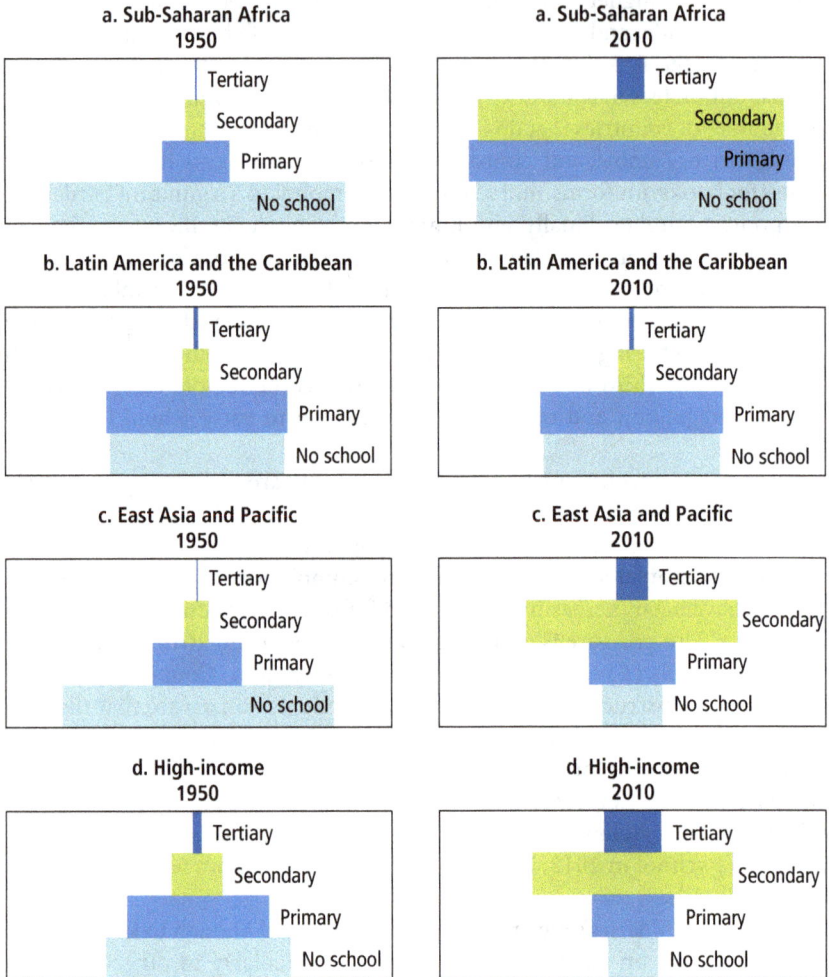

a. Sub-Saharan Africa
1950

Tertiary
Secondary
Primary
No school

a. Sub-Saharan Africa
2010

Tertiary
Secondary
Primary
No school

b. Latin America and the Caribbean
1950

Tertiary
Secondary
Primary
No school

b. Latin America and the Caribbean
2010

Tertiary
Secondary
Primary
No school

c. East Asia and Pacific
1950

Tertiary
Secondary
Primary
No school

c. East Asia and Pacific
2010

Tertiary
Secondary
Primary
No school

d. High-income
1950

Tertiary
Secondary
Primary
No school

d. High-income
2010

Tertiary
Secondary
Primary
No school

Source: Based on the data set of Barro and Lee 2013 (online update February 4, 2016).
Note: The graphs show the percentage of the adult population (ages 25–65) reaching each level of education (incomplete or complete).

Sub-Saharan Africa risks falling even further behind in educational attainment in the decades to come. Under current trends, UNESCO (2016) projects that by 2030, about 3 of every 4 children will complete the full cycle of primary, 6 in 10 will complete lower-secondary, and 4 in 10 will finish upper-secondary education. UNESCO projects that only eight countries in the region would achieve universal lower-secondary completion by 2030 if they expanded at the fastest rate of progress ever observed in the region. This projection suggests that the speed of educational progress required to meet the Sustainable Development Goal target of universal foundational skills would be unprecedented. Worryingly, with recent rates of progress in education, the region would continue to diverge from Asia and Latin America over the next couple of decades in the completion rates of primary, secondary, and tertiary education of the adult population (figure O.8).

There is considerable variation across countries in the region. Well-performing countries, such as Ghana and South Africa, have an educational structure today that is beginning to resemble that of East Asian economies. In contrast, in countries like Mali and Niger, around 70 percent of young adults ages 20–24 have no formal education.

Moreover, even when countries succeed in enrolling more children and keeping them in school, most students fail to acquire even the most basic foundational skills. As children reach the end of basic education, more than half cannot carry out basic reading or math tasks. According to recent student assessments, more than half of second-grade students in Ghana, Malawi, Mali, Uganda, and Zambia cannot read a single word. This finding compares with

Figure O.8 Projected Gap in Educational Attainment of the Workforce in Sub-Saharan Africa and Other Regions

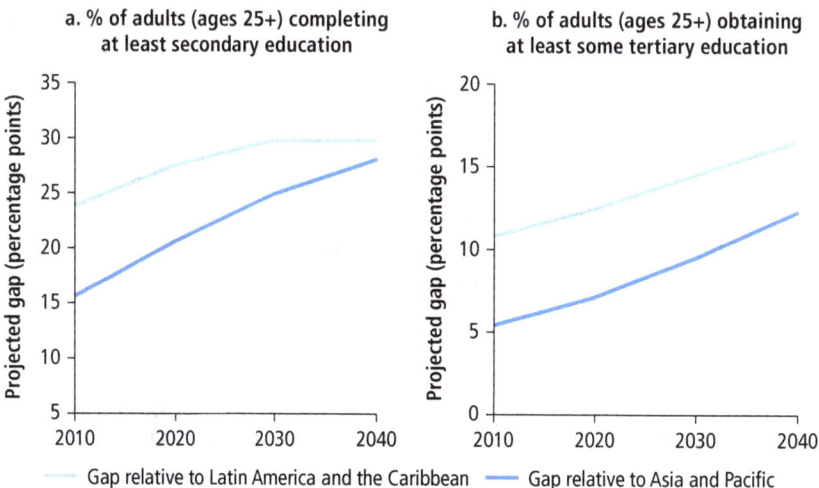

a. % of adults (ages 25+) completing at least secondary education

b. % of adults (ages 25+) obtaining at least some tertiary education

Gap relative to Latin America and the Caribbean — Gap relative to Asia and Pacific

Source: Based on data set of Barro and Lee 2013 (online update February 4, 2016).
Note: The gap is based on simple averages across countries (not population weighted). Asia includes both South and East Asia.

just 1 in 10 in Jordan, a third in Morocco, and less than 4 in 10 in Nepal. Kenyan children ages seven years and younger in the North East (one of the poorest regions) are eight times more likely to be unable to read letters than their peers in Nairobi. Even countries like Botswana, Ghana, and South Africa perform worse than all other participating countries on international student assessments (such as the Trends in International Mathematics and Science Study). When adults in Ghana and Kenya recently participated in the World Bank Skills Towards Employability and Productivity (STEP) Surveys, which measure the functional literacy of urban adults, they performed far worse than adults in other low- and middle-income countries. In Kenya, less than 1 percent of tertiary-educated adults who completed the reading skills test achieved a level 4 or 5 in proficiency (for example, synthetizing or integrating information from multiple texts). More than a quarter were at level 1 or below, meaning that they could not enter personal information into a document or identify a single piece of information from a simple text.

These deficits in basic foundational skills start very early in life. Chronic malnutrition (stunting) rates in many countries hinder readiness to learn even before children enter the education system. Across the region, more than a third of children under five are stunted. The prevalence of under-five child stunting is significantly higher in low-income and fragile states, reaching nearly 40 percent. Even in upper-middle-income countries, the child stunting rate is just under 25 percent, which is still dramatically high (figure O.9, panel a). Stunting is associated with lower levels of schooling, cognitive ability, and earnings later in life. Furthermore, access to preschool and other ECD services is low and highly unequal. As a result, by age five, children from better-off families are twice as likely to demonstrate certain cognitive skills than those from poor families. Nevertheless, some countries in the region are among the most successful countries in the world in reducing stunting. Kenya reduced its stunting rate from 40 to 26 percent (a one-third reduction) over 15 years; Ethiopia lowered its rate by 10 percentage points in a decade. Malawi, Senegal, and Tanzania also made progress, albeit at a slower pace (figure O.9, panel b).

The gaps in investments in the early years are compounded by the low quality of schooling in basic education, as revealed by teacher absenteeism and deficiencies in subject knowledge. Effective teaching—the most critical determinant of learning—is lacking in many countries in the region. Data from the Service Delivery Indicators program, based on nationally representative surveys of primary schools in Kenya, Mozambique, Nigeria, Senegal, Tanzania, Togo, and Uganda, reveal that too many teachers do not even show up to schools, and, even if they do, too many are unprepared and lack the proper support. On average, across the seven countries, teachers were absent from the classroom—when a visitor appeared unannounced to check during class time—more than 40 percent of the time. In Mozambique, when time lost

Figure 0.9 **Child Stunting Rates in Sub-Saharan Africa**

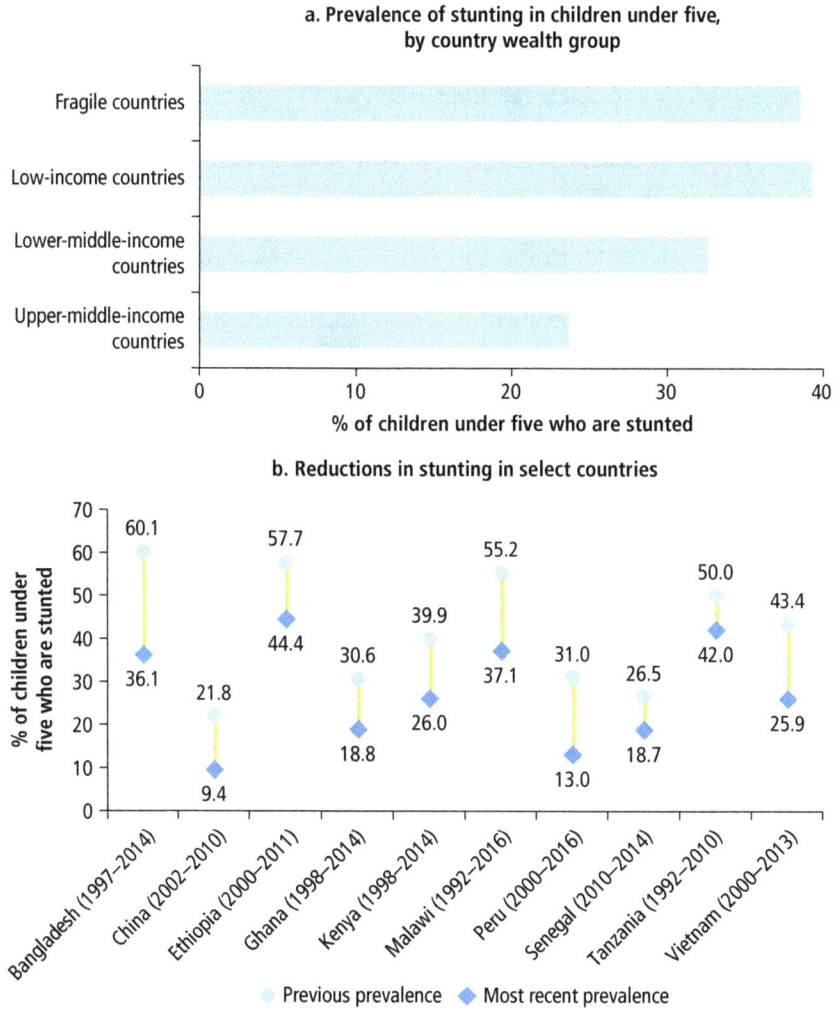

**a. Prevalence of stunting in children under five,
by country wealth group**

b. Reductions in stunting in select countries

○ Previous prevalence   ◆ Most recent prevalence

Sources: For panel a, based on data from the latest wave of USAID Demographic and Health Surveys in the past 10 years (from 2007 to 2017) for Sub-Saharan African countries and economies except Angola, Botswana, Cabo Verde, the Central African Republic, Djibouti, Equatorial Guinea, Eritrea, Guinea-Bissau, Mauritania, Mauritius, Réunion, the Seychelles, Somalia, South Africa, and Sudan. For panel b, Shekar et al. 2016 and, for Peru, Marini, Rokx, and Gallagher 2017.

within a lesson is also taken into account, students experienced an average of just 1 hour and 40 minutes of daily effective teaching time. Moreover, in recent tests of teachers in these countries, on average, one in every three teachers failed to demonstrate the minimum knowledge of the math content they are required to teach, reaching as low as 50 percent in some countries. Even in South Africa, nearly 80 percent of sixth-grade math teachers did not have a complete understanding of the sixth-grade math curriculum (Venkat and Spaull 2015).

The Service Delivery Indicators data (http://datatopics.worldbank.org/sdi) from classroom observations also reveal weaknesses in the pedagogical approaches deployed in teacher instruction. Across countries, around 30 percent of classroom time was spent writing on the blackboard or lecturing or reading to students, 30 percent was devoted to interacting with students, 22 percent was spent asking students questions and listening to responses, and 6 percent was devoted to testing. Most of the questions asked students to recite memorized information. Only 43 percent of teachers summarized the lesson at the end of class. About 6 of every 10 teachers used positive reinforcement (like smiling at students), and 3 in 10 used negative reinforcement in their interactions. All in all, observers identified a lot of room to incorporate pedagogical practices shown to be positively associated with learning outcomes.

Teachers in Sub-Saharan Africa teach in challenging environments. They often work far from their home and receive little instructional and pedagogical support. Salaries are often delayed and lower than salaries of comparably trained professionals. However, in most systems, teachers are neither held accountable for poor performance nor rewarded for good performance, including recognition and the opportunity to mentor others. The failure of education systems to provide support and incentives for teachers is likely a proximate cause of the failure of schools to deliver the levels of learning that are necessary for children to acquire strong foundational skills.

Not surprising, the huge gaps in ECD and learning in basic education hinder equitable access and readiness to acquire postsecondary skills. In many countries, students are tracked to vocational education too early (in lower-secondary school) and miss the opportunity to acquire the foundational skills needed to navigate their lives in a rapidly changing world of work. Youths from disadvantaged families, particularly with low-educated parents, have few opportunities to pursue tertiary education, especially at the university level. In addition, even those who make the transition to higher education frequently have weak foundational skills and tend to perform poorly. For instance, a study of South African high school graduates finds that those who do worse on the final high school graduation test have lower chances of progressing to university and, even if they do, are more likely to drop out before completing (van Broekhuizen 2016). Weak foundational skills hinder access to and success in STEM, applied sciences, and pedagogical fields, from which the next generation of engineers, doctors, and better-prepared teachers will emerge.

Again, skills beget skills. Skills developed early in life are the foundation for the development of other skills throughout life. Solid foundational skills—literacy, numeracy, and socioemotional—determine a child's readiness to learn throughout education and into adult life. Only by ensuring that everyone—rich or poor, girl or boy, from the capital city or a rural area—has this foundation can inequalities throughout the education and training system be effectively addressed.

Is There a Good Case for Investing in the Skills of Out-of-School Youths and Adults in Sub-Saharan Africa?

Yes, although programs to improve the skills of this population have a mixed record of impacts. These investments need to be carefully crafted, cost-effective, and well leveraged. There are two main reasons why countries in the region need to invest smartly in out-of-school young and older adults.

First, the legacy of low access and poor quality of basic education means that the basic skills deficit among out-of-school youths and adults is too large to be ignored. According to UNESCO (2015), more than two-thirds of the working-age population in Sub-Saharan Africa has left the formal education system without completing primary education. In 2008, about 40 percent of adults, more than 160 million, and 50 percent of adult women were illiterate, defined as being unable to read or write in any language. Literacy rates in the region are much more varied, ranging from less than 50 percent (West and Central Africa) to more than 90 percent (South Africa). The functional literacy rate—the ability to apply literacy skills to tasks at work and in daily life—is likely to be even lower, as suggested by data from functional literacy assessments in countries like Ghana and Kenya. In any case, the stock of unskilled workers is very large, and many unskilled workers still have long working lives ahead of them because they never entered school or dropped out of the school system very early. Moreover, given that improving child development outcomes, rates of completion, and the quality of basic and upper-secondary education will take time, the relative size of the pool of youths and adults lacking basic skills will shrink gradually at best over the next few decades.

The second reason to invest in out-of-school young and older adults is because investments in their foundational and technical skills can bring important economic and social benefits. These skills can improve livelihoods, enable mobility out of low-productivity jobs, improve productivity in existing jobs, and enhance social cohesion, since jobs are more than just incomes. A recent cross-country study by Valerio et al. (2016) finds that the returns to literacy are highest in Ghana and Kenya, the two African countries included in the study (figure O.10, panel a). The majority of the working population in Africa will likely remain in

Figure O.10 Foundational Skills, Earnings, and Productivity in Sub-Saharan Africa

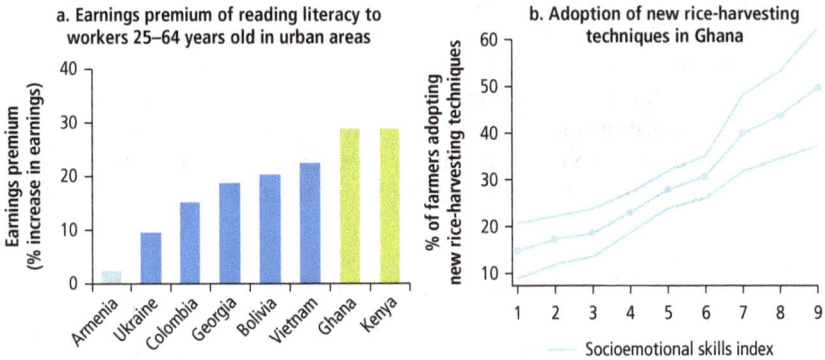

a. Earnings premium of reading literacy to workers 25–64 years old in urban areas

b. Adoption of new rice-harvesting techniques in Ghana

Sources: For panel a, Valerio et al. 2016, based on World Bank Skills Towards Employability and Productivity (STEP) Surveys. For panel b, Ali, Bowen, and Deininger 2017.
Note: In panel b, the socioemotional skills index includes measures of work centrality, tenacity, achievement, power motivation, locus of control, impulsiveness, polychronicity, optimism, organization, and trust. The higher the index, the stronger are the socioemotional skills.

agriculture and informal employment for the next few decades. Farmers with stronger cognitive and socioemotional skills (such as future orientation and persistence) have been shown to be more likely to adopt more productive technologies in rice production in Ghana (figure O.10, panel b) and tobacco, an export-oriented cash crop, in Malawi. In Kenya, these skills have been shown to raise productivity in maize production and to reinforce technical skills.

Training in vocational, socioemotional, and entrepreneurship or management skills, often bundled with other forms of support or workplace experience, has led to improvements in countries like Ethiopia, Kenya, Liberia, South Africa, and Togo. Moreover, improvements in adult skills can have direct and indirect positive effects on intergenerational human capital. Parental literacy, particularly of mothers, and improvement in adults' incomes can enhance children's skills development by improving child health, early stimulation, and the learning environment at home.

Many programs that aim to build skills among youths and adults fail; those that succeed tend to have modest impacts. The impacts of remedial adult education and training programs should be gauged against what they are set to accomplish, which is partially redressing gaps in skills that formal education failed to provide. Although adults learn in many ways—through work, training, apprenticeships, or social interactions—remedying large deficits in foundational skills later in life is more difficult and costly. Not surprising, then, the impacts of well-designed programs tend to be on a par with the returns to a year of schooling, but many also fail (McKenzie and Puerto 2017).

There are lessons about how to make the most of investments in these programs and to mitigate the trade-offs between these investments and investments in the skills of new cohorts. Skills programs for out-of-school youths and adults can be made more cost-effective if they are tailored to the needs, constraints, and incentives of the target population and the contexts of local labor markets. Programs that are paired with social and productive inclusion or agricultural extension programs can be delivered at a lower cost per. Skills programs for out-of-school youths and adults can also be made more efficient and effective by harnessing the power of new digital technologies. The key is to apply the lessons learned from successful and promising programs and to evaluate new programs before scaling them up.

Are Countries in the Region Investing Adequate Resources in Skills?

For the most part, countries' levels of spending are commensurate with what they can afford and what can be expected, but there is ample room to leverage current investments. Given that skills-building efforts need to expand, all countries have to improve the efficiency of public spending and crowd in more private investment. Figure O.11 compares average spending in Sub-Saharan African countries with other low- and middle-income regions.

Figure O.11 Spending on Education as a Share of GDP and Total Spending, by Region

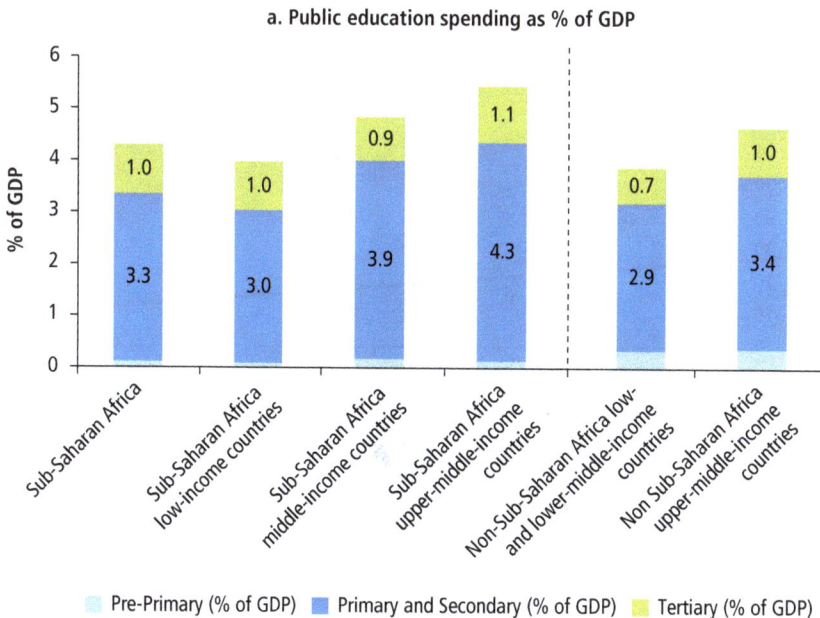

a. Public education spending as % of GDP

Pre-Primary (% of GDP)   Primary and Secondary (% of GDP)   Tertiary (% of GDP)

(continued next page)

Figure O.11 (continued)

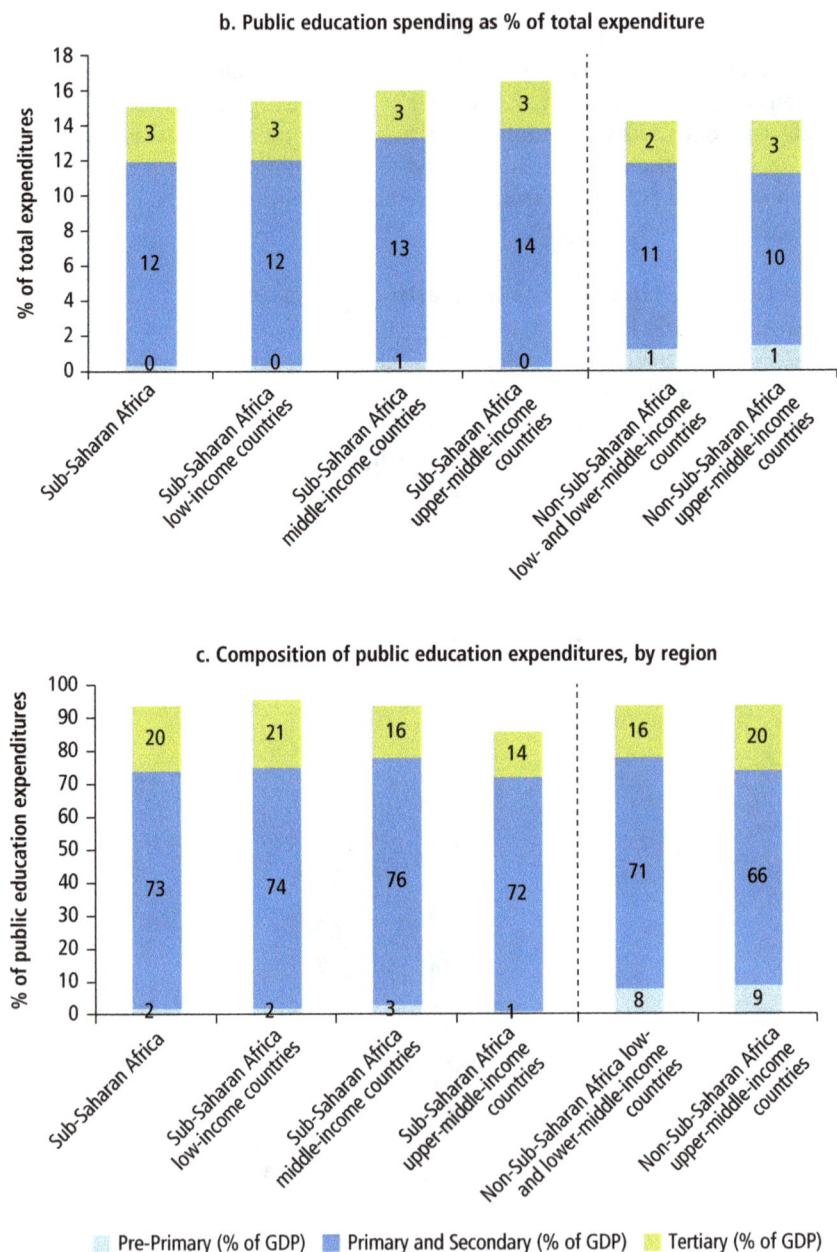

b. Public education spending as % of total expenditure

c. Composition of public education expenditures, by region

Pre-Primary (% of GDP)   Primary and Secondary (% of GDP)   Tertiary (% of GDP)

Source: World Development Indicators Database.
Note: Values are the average from the three most recent available years (2010–15).

On average, Sub-Saharan Africa already devotes significant public resources to education. This conclusion has been reached by recent detailed analyses of public spending in the region, such as UNESCO (2011) and Global Education Commission (2016). A country's effort on education and the priority it gives to the sector can be gauged by the level of public education expenditure as a percentage of total government expenditure and as a percentage of GDP. These indicators fail to account for private investments in education and other skills training by families and enterprises; however, the public sector plays a major role in providing education and training services, and these measures, though incomplete, allow international comparisons. The internationally recommended targets are for governments to invest 15–20 percent of total public expenditure and 4–6 percent of GDP on education. On average, countries in Sub-Saharan Africa allocate about 18 percent of total public spending and 5 percent of GDP to education, the highest spending ratios among low- and middle-income regions. There is variation across countries, with a range of about 11–28 percent of total government spending and of 2–15 percent of GDP. In addition to public resources, households contribute around 25 percent of total national education expenditure (UNESCO 2011).

The region had the greatest increase in spending among low- and middle-income regions over the past decade. Real public spending rose, on average, about 6 percent per year; it rose 0.7 percentage point of GDP among countries with available data. This expansion of education expenditure allowed countries to maintain or even increase expenditure per pupil while they expanded enrollment in basic and even tertiary education. Currently, spending per student in basic education is commensurate with the levels of other low-income countries.

Thus, it is unrealistic to expect most countries to increase dramatically their public investment in skills; instead, countries should seek to improve efficiency. All countries should make the most of current spending, by improving the targeting of resources to foundational skills and families in greater need and establishing stronger accountability mechanisms, such as better financial management and reliable education management information systems to cut waste and reduce the costs of inputs and infrastructure spending. Of great importance is to scale up effective interventions to enable and compel teachers to spend their time teaching by tackling the systemic causes of absenteeism. There are some exceptions: for example, some natural resource–rich countries in the region can afford and need to increase their education spending (in terms of GDP per capita and overall public expenditure), while also improving efficiency.

Moreover, countries need to reallocate public education expenditure to prioritize foundational skills and disadvantaged groups. Although the region already devotes most public spending to basic education, resources devoted to preprimary education account for just about 0.3 percent of education spending. Countries with high child stunting rates also need to step up investments in effective interventions, such as prenatal care and cash transfers tied to health and nutrition services. To create room for this additional spending, countries can reduce higher education subsidies for the well-off by implementing selective cost recovery, expanding student loan programs—when the conditions for their success are met—and using social impact bonds. Public spending on postsecondary technical and vocational education and higher education can be targeted to disadvantaged groups based on merit and giving greater weight to fields of study with potentially greater externalities for growth and productivity, such as STEM and agricultural technicians.

Finally, countries need to crowd in private sector investments and leverage other public spending for skills building. Workplace learning and on-the-job training are an important source of skills formation. On average, about 30 percent of formal sector firms in Sub-Saharan Africa provide on-the-job training, compared with 35 percent of firms in the rest of the world. The region's incidence of firm training is comparable to that in South Asia, higher than in the Middle East and North Africa, but lower than in East Asia and the Pacific, Europe and Central Asia, or Latin America and the Caribbean. The percentage of firms offering training varies from 9 percent in Sudan to as high as 55 percent in Rwanda. On-the-job training in micro and small firms, often informal, is even more challenging. The potential reasons for the lower incidence of on-the-job training are multiple and likely vary across countries. Improvements in infrastructure, the business environment, and governance could lead to increases in on-the-job training. To the extent that market failures, such as firm credit constraints, are important, public sector interventions may have a role to play in incentivizing on-the-job training, such as tax and spending incentives.

Facing the Skills Balancing Act: How Can Countries in Sub-Saharan Africa Improve the Skills of Their Labor Force for Today and Tomorrow?

More and better skills can help to create more productive, inclusive, and adaptable economies in Sub-Saharan Africa. Guided by the previously discussed policy framework, the report highlights four strategic directions for policies and reforms aimed at helping Sub-Saharan African countries to meet the challenges of improving the skills of their workforce to transform their economies while preparing for a rapidly changing world of work:

1. Set priorities for skills investments tailored to the country context and policy reforms to create the enabling environment for investments to pay off by (a) prioritizing the universal foundational skills (cognitive and socioemotional) of children, youths, and adults, (b) investing selectively in the technical skills of youths and adults through TVET, higher education, and on-the-job training tied to growing sectors and economic inclusion, and (c) striving for equity, quality, and efficiency in skills-building systems.

2. Focus on investments in the early years, provide inputs that matter most for quality (for example, effective teachers, not only buildings), and provide support for youths and adults who have missed out on basic skills.

3. Invest selectively in technical skills for youths and adults, giving greater attention to skills for growing sectors (through market-driven TVET and higher education, incentives for on-the-job training, and entrepreneurship support) and skills for disadvantaged youths and adults (including through remedial education, informal apprenticeships, and self-employment support), while implementing reforms to ensure demand-driven content and value-for-money in education and training programs.

4. Harness the roles of all stakeholders—public and private sectors and families—and seize the potential of learning and other performance metrics to enact systemwide change, guide policy and spending decisions, and achieve more responsive and adaptive education and training systems.

Make Difficult Choices to Set Priorities

Investing in the foundational skills of children, youths, and adults is the most effective strategy to enhance productivity growth, inclusion, and adaptability simultaneously. Therefore, all countries should prioritize building universal foundational skills for today's and tomorrow's workers. This effort is more pressing in countries with low basic educational attainment and poor learning outcomes among children and youths.

When it comes to other priorities, more than other regions in the past, Sub-Saharan Africa must strike the right balance between competing priorities. Figure O.12 illustrates how, armed with the policy framework outlined here, countries can balance competing priorities in skills investments according to their initial context, namely, their skills base, state of economic transformation, and policy environment, as proxied by income per capita, educational attainment of the adult population, and ranking in the World Bank Doing Business indicators (http://www.doingbusiness.org), respectively. Given a high overlap between countries' skills base and state of economic transformation, figure O.12 combines these two dimensions into one.

Figure O.12 Skills Challenges in Sub-Saharan Africa, by Countries' Stage of Economic Transformation and Policy Environment

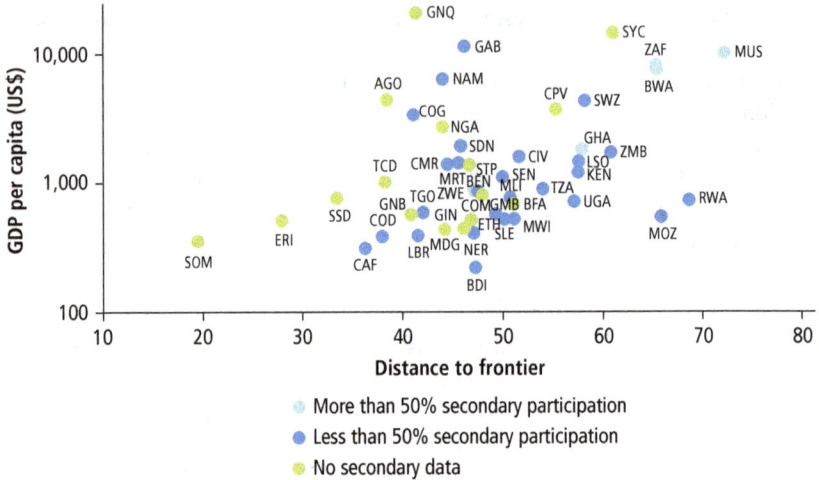

Sources: Based on World Development Indicators database for GDP per capita (most recent year, constant US$) and World Bank Doing Business 2015 data for distance to frontier.

As an illustration of skills priorities, consider five broad groups of countries, each with its own challenges in skills development. There will, of course, be significant variation within these groups, and every country will need to judge the most essential investments in skills for its people:

1. *More advanced in transformation and a policy environment more conducive to reaping the returns to skills* (for example, Botswana, Mauritius, the Seychelles, and South Africa). These upper-middle and high-income countries have made the most strides in reallocating labor out of agriculture and into more productive activities and in implementing reforms to improve the business environment for the private sector, relative to the rest of the region. They are better placed to reap the rewards of investing more in postsecondary technical skills through TVET, higher education, and on-the-job training, although they should continue to implement policy reforms to improve their global competitiveness standing. They also should invest in skills for disadvantaged youths and adults, including through remedial education, informal apprenticeships, and self-employment support. As they expand access to postsecondary education and training, they could benefit from leveraging the role of the private sector in the provision of education and training and ensure its market-driven relevance.

2. *Transforming and a less conducive policy environment* (for example, Ghana and Namibia). These countries have made progress in moving labor out of agriculture and growing their economies, but they are still lagging in economic and regulatory reforms. Although they need to continue investing in postsecondary technical skills for growing sectors to aid economic transformation, they also need to ramp up their reform efforts to ensure that these investments pay off. At the same time, they need to invest in skills for the inclusion of disadvantaged youths and adults, including remedial education, informal apprenticeships, and self-employment.

3. *Natural resource rich and a less conducive policy environment* (for example, Angola, Cameroon, the Republic of Congo, Gabon, Mauritania, and Nigeria). These countries are rich in natural resources, yet their economies are less diversified. For the most part, they lag in reforms. They can afford to invest in postsecondary technical skills tied to the needs of natural resource and related sectors through industry-led training and PPPs for specialized training abroad and to tap into the derived rents to diversify their economies, provided they also enact policy reforms to create a business environment conducive to transformation and diversification. They also need to invest in skills for disadvantaged youths and adults.

4. *Lagging in transformation and a more conducive policy environment* (for example, Mozambique and Rwanda). These countries have made more efforts to improve their business environment, although they lag in their economic transformation. They can invest selectively in postsecondary technical skills tied closely to catalytic (growth potential) sectors, while deepening policy reforms to promote transformation and leveraging partnerships with the private sector. This group also needs to devote greater attention to the skills of youths and adults geared toward improving earnings and livelihoods in low-productivity sectors.

5. *Lagging in transformation and a less conducive policy environment* (for example, the Central African Republic, the Democratic Republic of Congo, Guinea-Bissau, and Somalia). These countries have a substantial pending policy agenda for creating a business environment that can spur private investment, reward and incentivize skills investments, and achieve sustained economic growth and productive transformation. More than other countries, they need to give greater weight to investing in supporting livelihoods for inclusion and social cohesion, including through support for agriculture, self-employment, and informal apprenticeships. They need to implement policy reforms to ignite economic transformation before they can step up investment in postsecondary technical skills; they could benefit from PPPs to leverage private provision, including in basic education.

Most countries in the region fall somewhere along the continuum between these five groups. Rapidly transforming economies need to pay more attention to the adaptability and reskilling of their workforces. Countries that have good policies will reap higher returns from investing in tertiary and other skills that galvanize economic dynamism. Low-income settings affected by fragility and conflict will reap a premium from skills to improve livelihoods and to avoid poverty traps that may hinder economic growth.

In pursuing their priorities, policy makers need to guide their investments over the life cycle of individuals according to the three traditional objectives of education and training systems: investments and policy reforms need to pursue *equity* to achieve wide access to opportunities for skills acquisition, *quality* and relevance to provide education that meets appropriate standards and responds to labor market demand, and *efficiency* to ensure that education and training financing and provision deliver value-for-money.

When it comes to public spending, the message is clear: ensure more value-for-money. Countries should aim to sustain current levels of investment in skills and strive to make spending smarter to ensure greater efficiency and integration with other social policies. Some countries may need to increase spending, reprioritize public spending across sectors, increase their tax effort, and tap more external resources. All countries will be able to increase the absolute level of spending in skills as they grow their economies. For all, however, the imperative is to make the most of their current spending efforts, including rebalancing their skills investment portfolio by redirecting current spending, for example, from subsidies for the well-off in tertiary education to early child education and nutrition.

Given the complexities of the skills agenda, countries should actively harness the contributions of multiple actors in their skills strategies. As highlighted here, the various actors involved in skills building have distinctive and complementary roles to play. Families can invest in and nurture children's cognitive and socioemotional development by providing quality care and parenting and by holding schools accountable for effective service delivery. The private sector can participate effectively in service provision by enhancing access and quality, investing in on-the-job training to build skills, engaging with education and training providers to ensure that programs are aligned with their needs, and actively engaging in national social dialogue to prioritize skills development and reforms to create a policy-enabling environment for skills investments to pay off. The public sector has a crucial role to play in pursuing equity and addressing market failures through investments and complementary policies to ensure individuals' readiness (foundational skills), opportunities (equitable access), and incentives (complementary enabling and regulatory policies, information on returns) and to realize the potential returns from skills investments. Governments should also tackle the political economy of reforms by fostering cooperation, commitment, and coordination of stakeholders through strategic leadership, social dialogue, and adequate incentives (World Bank 2017b).

Focus on Foundational Skills

Foundational skills—investments in the early years as well as basic literacy and numeracy—circumvent one of the big trade-offs: universal foundational skills increase economic growth and promote inclusion. Countries should prioritize building universal foundational skills for today's and tomorrow's workers. This effort begins with investments to promote equality of opportunities and school readiness, including through investments in maternal health, child nutrition, and early stimulation during the first 1,000 days of life and the early years. It requires countries to continue to improve access to basic education and to take decisive actions to close large and persisting learning gaps, through improvements in schooling quality. It also demands interventions, such as second-chance and adult literacy programs, to support individuals lacking critical foundational skills.

School Readiness

Countries should, first and foremost, step up smart investments in the early years of individuals' lives to eradicate chronic child malnutrition and promote healthy childhood development. Stunting rates in Sub-Saharan Africa are among the highest in the world, and countries inside and outside the region are showing the way to fight child stunting (Galasso et al. 2016). Peru and Senegal provide useful lessons.

Peru used a multiprong approach to halve child stunting rates in just a decade, from 33 to 14 percent. This success was broadly a result of three mutually reinforcing factors: (a) political commitment at the highest level, (b) targeted and results-oriented financing to implement evidence-based policies, and (c) changing behaviors for lasting results. Time-bound and concrete targets established at the presidential level rallied coordination and cooperation across agencies and levels of government. Regular data collection and dissemination helped to garner and sustain political support across different government administrations. To strengthen key health and nutrition services, results-based financing targeted municipalities that were most in need in tandem with conditional cash transfers for poor families with children, tied to regular child growth monitoring and other health and nutrition services. To promote healthy child growth, a major media campaign made stunting visible and empowered parents to change behaviors and parenting care practices (Shekar et al. 2016).

Senegal lowered child stunting rates to among the lowest rates in the region. The government created a special initiative within the Prime Minister's Office to fight malnutrition and coordinate efforts across sectors. The initiative used a multisector, community-focused program targeted to children under five, pregnant or lactating women, and mothers in vulnerable families. It promoted regular child growth monitoring, breastfeeding, and nutrition education on child feeding and care practices. It also distributed and promoted the use of vitamin A and iron supplements and included community-level food security activities (Shekar et al. 2016).

The large-scale delivery of ECD, including preschool programs, requires careful attention to implementation, using adaptive learning to adjust to the country context. Some countries have recently announced or are considering universalizing preprimary education, including Burkina Faso, Ethiopia, Ghana, Kenya, Liberia, Malawi, Nigeria, Sierra Leone, Tanzania, and Uganda. Achieving this goal will require finding cost-effective models for delivering quality services at scale. In a given context, the realities of government and community capacity may favor a community-based model, a center-based model, or a mixed approach, such as community organizing of parents.

Even the right ECD program design will not deliver results if countries do not get the implementation right. Programs inside and outside Sub-Saharan Africa that prove ineffective often have an overly ambitious design that fails to factor in implementation challenges, like ensuring adequate staffing. Testing and evaluating approaches that combine local and global knowledge and experiences with adaptive implementation at scale can improve the odds of success. In The Gambia, the government tested and evaluated two approaches to integrating a new ECD curriculum into the formal school system—an informal arrangement using community volunteers and an additional classroom in existing primary schools to serve children ages 3–6 (Blimpo et al. 2017). The results of the evaluation favored the latter, in combination with actions to improve take-up rates, address staffing challenges, and implement quality assurance and monitoring. In Mozambique, an evaluation of a community-based preschool program that yielded positive results led to a successful scale-up of the program (Martinez, Naudeau, and Pereira 2013).

In center-based ECD delivery, teacher quality and classroom practices—more than infrastructure—are paramount. A recent evaluation of an ECD school-based program in Ecuador finds that, measured by classroom observations, better teachers lead to the most significant learning gains in children's language, math, and self-regulation (Araujo et al. 2016). In Colombia, far costlier center-based ECD services failed to deliver impacts on child development outcomes compared with a home visits program, giving misguided priority to shiny infrastructure over effective instructors (Attanasio et al. 2015).

Effective Teaching

The expansion of access to primary and secondary education needs to go hand in hand with ensuring effective teaching in schools. This is a simple yet powerful lesson for countries in Sub-Saharan Africa seeking to leapfrog progress in skills building. Many countries in other regions of the world, including richer economies, expanded access without assuring effective teaching and school quality and, as a result, failed to produce learning and skills. A focus on quality will no doubt be challenging, given existing gaps in physical infrastructure and pressure from increasing demand for secondary education. Countries will have to find simultaneous ways to build more high schools and to improve the quality of education by becoming more efficient in the use of resources.

In continuing to expand access, Sub-Saharan African countries can find lessons from successes in enrolling and keeping children in school within and outside the region. The countries in the region with the biggest gains in enrollment boast free education. The elimination of tuition fees marked major increases in enrollment in Kenya, Malawi, and Uganda, with smaller jumps in Cameroon, Tanzania, and Zambia. Ethiopia, Lesotho, and Malawi have leveraged cash transfer programs targeted to poor families as part of a strategy to increase enrollment and offset other indirect costs, including the opportunity cost of schooling; the results have been overwhelmingly positive. These positive impacts hold for unconditional and conditional programs, although evidence from Burkina Faso suggests that children who are the most vulnerable to dropout—girls overall and boys who are doing less well in school—may benefit from conditional transfers. Conditional cash transfers in Malawi more than tripled girls' school attendance, in addition to reducing early marriage (Baird et al. 2010; Baird, McIntosh, and Özler 2011). The Cycle to School Program in Bihar, India, improved access without constructing additional schools (Muralidharan and Prakash 2017). It provided all girls ages 14 and 15 who enrolled in ninth grade with funds to buy a bicycle and increased their probability of being enrolled in or having completed ninth grade by 30 percent, closing the access gap with boys by 40 percent.

Targeted financial assistance and complementary low-cost interventions can help to keep boys and girls in school. Enrollment and completion of secondary education is also deterred by a higher opportunity cost to studying or, for girls, by teenage marriage or pregnancy. Targeted assistance may be effective. In Ghana, scholarships for students who were admitted to secondary school but could not immediately enroll—usually because of lack of funds—doubled the rate of high school completion, improved math and language learning scores, increased the odds of enrolling in tertiary education by 30 percent, and reduced the number of children among girls by age 25 (Duflo, Dupas, and Kremer 2017).

Private Sector Involvement

Many countries struggle to find the fiscal space to cope with the wave of students transiting to secondary school. Access remains inequitable. PPPs can help to address the infrastructure and service needs in secondary education.

PPPs in education could potentially leverage public financing aimed at improving equity of access through the delivery of all or part of secondary education infrastructure or services to low-income households. A study of a PPP in Uganda, where the government offered a per student subsidy to participating low-cost private secondary schools, found that the subsidy helped schools to absorb large numbers of eligible students, equally among girls and boys, and that student performance in participating schools improved (Barrera-Osorio et al. 2016).

Private schools have been part of the landscape of African education for many years. One in every six students in Sub-Saharan Africa attends private primary schools. However, recent developments have brought private provision of education to the headlines, including the emergence of chains of for-profit schools and moves by some governments to provide public resources to private schools for some provision (PPPs). Ultimately, what matters is that the state guarantees access to quality education for all children and youths. In environments where public provision is scarce, private schools can fill a substantial gap, but governments have a strong role to play in regulating education and empowering families to make informed school decisions. Governments should hold all schools (public and private) accountable for results. In countries with weak regulatory capacity, policy makers must ask themselves whether effective regulation would be more manageable than direct provision.

Family Involvement
Parental participation and empowerment can be useful in ensuring quality standards in schools. Yet, too often, parental decisions are based on incomplete information. For example, parents may demand early education in English or French rather than their mother tongue, even though literacy occurs more rapidly if it is begun in the mother tongue, as was recently found in Kenya (Piper, Schroeder, and Trudell 2016).

Families and adolescents may be unaware of or misperceive the value of education. Low-cost interventions may address these information gaps. In Madagascar, such an intervention provided parents and students with accurate data on the returns to education and led to improved attendance and learning (Nguyen 2008). Other interventions that indirectly improve the perceived gains from education—for example, by facilitating job search assistance and intermediation or by affecting relevant social norms through, for example, legislating quotas for female political leadership, as in India—have also increased school enrollment and attainment.[1] Other potentially helpful interventions include addressing the issue of safety for girls attending schools and improving relevance to the labor market, for example, by introducing entrepreneurship courses and socioemotional skills in secondary school.

Child Engagement
Effective teaching in classrooms is central to keeping children in school longer and assuring that they learn and acquire skills. In recent years, a large body of evidence from school interventions in low- and middle-income countries clearly points to more effective teaching through improved pedagogy as the most impactful way to improve learning (Evans and Popova 2016). A pedagogical approach with proven results is helping teachers to teach to the level of the child. In many countries, an ambitious and inflexible curriculum leaves many students behind. Interventions that help teachers to target their teaching to the diverse learning needs of students in the classroom have been highly effective. In Ghana, supplementing teachers with community assistants to help the weakest students has led to sizable gains in literacy and numeracy, especially when it is done after school (Duflo and Kiessel 2012). Also in Ghana, training teachers to teach students in small groups, targeted to their learning level, boosted literacy (Duflo and Kiessel 2012). In rural Kenya, separating primary students into groups based on their initial ability led to sizable gains in math and language for both high and low achievers, allowing teachers to teach at a level more appropriate to children's needs (Duflo, Dupas, and Kremer 2011).

Role of Technology
Technology-aided instruction has the potential to improve learning when it is used to aid teachers and give students an individualized learning experience. There has been much hype on the potential for new technologies to facilitate leapfrogging in education in low- and middle-income countries and to achieve advances such as those that medical technology has delivered for health. But the evidence so far is sobering and demonstrates that technology works best when it is used to complement rather than replace teachers. Hardware-focused interventions that provide computers at home or at school have had little impact on learning outcomes. Interventions that rely on technology-enabled instruction to improve pedagogy and allow students to learn at their own pace have worked better. Recently, interventions that use technology to give students a dynamic learning experience seem to deliver much bigger impacts on learning.

Taken together, this evidence suggests that, when embracing the promise of technology-aided instruction, countries in the region should move with caution. Realizing the potential of technology-based education will depend on the details of the specific intervention and the extent to which it alleviates binding constraints on learning. Careful planning and assessment are needed. Technology can fulfill its promise if it is assessed with an eye toward cost-effectiveness and a careful assessment of what country systems can implement.

Better Teachers
Given the prominent role of teachers in learning, much effort is needed to have better teachers in schools. Many teachers in the region do not command the

minimum subject knowledge they are expected to teach and do not sufficiently use the pedagogical practices associated with more learning. Since it is much more difficult and costly to skill up or retrain a workforce of unprepared teachers, high-performing education systems, such as those in Finland and Singapore, have highly selective teacher education programs in which only a few applicants are accepted. Analysis of the requirements for entry into teacher training programs in many Sub-Saharan African countries suggests that standards are very low. Countries around the world have experimented with different ways to attract better candidates into the teaching profession, including creating special incentives for top students to go into teaching in Chile or raising the standards of entry into teacher training colleges in Peru. Improving the standards of entry into the profession itself can potentially improve outcomes.

Socioemotional Skills

Another opportunity to leapfrog can come from incorporating socioemotional skills into the goals and teaching practices of schools, institutions, and programs. A related area of policy priority is ensuring that preschool and basic education (general and vocational) curricula and pedagogic practice pay adequate attention to the critical development of socioemotional skills. These skills can be taught as part of the regular school curricula through specific activities, goals, and pedagogic support. The experience with related reforms and interventions in the world can offer useful lessons, such as recent innovations in several countries, including Colombia, North Macedonia, Peru, the United States, and Vietnam.

An area warranting policy reform is postponing early tracking into TVET in secondary education to allow youths to acquire stronger foundational skills. Some educational systems still track students into vocational and technical streams too early (in lower-secondary education) at the expense of foundational skills. Early tracking into vocational and technical schools inhibits the acquisition of strong foundational skills, limiting the adaptability and lifetime earnings of TVET graduates. In the short to medium term, delayed tracking needs to be accompanied by strengthening the foundational skills in TVET schools and institutions and broadening the narrow focus on technical and vocational skills.

Foundational Skills for the Current Stock of Workers

Finally, strengthening foundational skills among out-of-school youths and adults has been a blind spot in the region, especially in agriculture and the informal economy. Given the deficiencies in basic literacy, numeracy, and socioemotional skills in current workers, remedial programs aimed at addressing these gaps can play an important role in improving people's livelihoods and productivity. Although adult literacy programs have had a mixed record of impacts, recent innovative programs hold promise. The Project Alphabetisation de Base par Cellulaire is a mobile phone–based literacy and numeracy program in rural Niger that—by tapping into people's intrinsic motivations—managed to boost literacy and numeracy among adults (Aker, Ksoll, and Lybbert 2012). There is also great potential in incorporating adult literacy and socioemotional interventions into agricultural extension and cash transfer programs, as is being done in the context of Brazil's Bolsa Familia and Mexico's Prospera cash transfer programs.

Invest in the Technical Skills of Youths and Adults

Investing in the technical skills of youths and adults requires improving the equity, efficiency, and relevance of TVET and higher education. In most countries in the region, these two subsectors remain small, creating opportunities to leapfrog by establishing early the institutional and policy frameworks that can ensure more equity, efficiency, and relevance and drawing lessons from countries that have already expanded these systems.

Social and Equity Concerns in the Provision of Technical Skills

For TVET and higher education, the most important goal for achieving equity is to ensure school readiness. This means imparting strong foundational skills for all in early childhood and basic education, especially among children and youths from disadvantaged backgrounds. For disadvantaged youths close to entering tertiary education, bridge and remedial programs in secondary school or at the beginning of tertiary can help to level the playing field. In Namibia, for example, the Pathways Program at the University of Namibia targets students from the marginalized Owambo ethnic group, with a focus on preparing them to study science and engineering at the tertiary level. In addition, these bridge programs can tackle gaps in socioemotional skills that are considered key for success in TVET or tertiary studies.

Improving equity requires addressing financial and nonfinancial constraints that keep many from acquiring quality technical skills. For upper-secondary and tertiary TVET and higher education, public financing should be targeted through needs-based scholarships and subsidized student loans. In lower-secondary TVET, if it exists, the same kind of public financing that is used for general secondary education will create opportunities for youths to gain skills that will deliver the highest returns for them. In other words, if a country has a policy of free lower-secondary education, then financing TVET at that level will allow more differentiated skills. On average, there is less cost sharing in Africa at the tertiary level than in other regions, but some countries have tried to move progressively away from free higher education and toward cost-sharing arrangements. Malawi, Uganda, and Zambia have shifted some costs, including living expenses, to students. Botswana, Ethiopia, and Lesotho have implemented deferred cost-sharing programs in which students repay tuition incrementally after graduation. Kenya, Mauritania, Mauritius, Namibia, Rwanda, South Africa, and Tanzania have implemented means-tested support.

There are also several examples of promising loan schemes in the region. For example, Ghana's Student Loan Trust carries sufficient interest and has established strong administrative and loan default policies, thus minimizing government loss and improving cost sharing. Some countries, including Botswana, Ethiopia, and South Africa, have created alternatives to loan repayment in the form of public service as teachers (Ethiopia) or specialization in a field facing a shortage of skilled labor (Botswana).

Beyond the formal education system, improving equity in out-of-school and on-the-job training requires a strong focus on the informal sector through informal apprenticeships, labor programs aimed at disadvantaged youths, and on-the-job training in micro and small firms, especially in rural areas.

Information and support could be particularly important when trying to address gender biases in the selection of fields of study and occupation (box O.1). Men across Africa tend to earn more than women. They also work in distinct sectors. In Ethiopia, male-dominated sectors include furniture making, manufacturing, and electricity. In Uganda, they include carpentry, electrical work, and metal work. Ugandan women who work in male-dominated sectors earn as much as men and three times more than women in female-dominated sectors. What leads women to enroll in training for male-dominated sectors? In Ethiopia, knowing someone in the sector makes a big difference. In Uganda, women who have a male role model in the sector are much more likely to make the move (Buehren and van Salisbury 2017; Campos et al. 2015).

BOX O.1

Strengthening Strategic Sectors through Training

In Nigeria, the government wanted to increase the workforce in information technology and call centers. Through a two-month training program, the government certified university graduates in these areas. As a result, graduates were more than 25 percent more likely to enter the information technology and call center sectors. The impact was especially large for women, as there was an initial bias against women working in these sectors. The impact demonstrates that exposure through training can overturn biases and increase opportunities for women.

Source: Croke, Goldstein, and Holla 2017.

Better Governance and Financing for Efficiency and Results in TVET and Higher Education

Regulation and quality assurance can contribute to improving efficiency (and quality) in tertiary education and training. Over the past decade, many Sub-Saharan African countries have set up agencies to conduct assessments and accreditation of tertiary institutions, but capacity is limited. Quality assurance mechanisms range from simple licensing of institutions by the ministry responsible for tertiary education to comprehensive systemwide program accreditation and national qualification frameworks. By 2012, 21 African countries had already established quality assurance agencies, and a dozen other countries were at relatively advanced stages of doing so. These agencies are performing some basic quality control, having closed or prevented the opening of some low-quality programs. Yet, many countries in the region are still aiming to develop full national qualification frameworks. This effort might be premature. Many of these agencies lack the capacity to implement their mandates more fully, which requires defined standards of quality and performance and the capacity to assess whether those standards are being met. Since building complex quality assurance frameworks can take time, countries can focus first on building simple but solid fundamentals that instill market discipline.

Most critically, public funding of TVET and higher education institutions in the region needs to be linked gradually to performance or performance-enhancing reforms. Most financing of public TVET and higher education in the region is done on a historical basis, based on inputs (number of staff or salaries), enrollment (cost per student, as in the case of higher education in Kenya and Rwanda), or normative unit costs (student-teacher ratios and prescribed unit costs by discipline, as in higher education in Ghana and Nigeria). These financing mechanisms create few incentives for cost saving, innovation, improved quality, and improved labor market relevance for students. To create such incentives, the ambitious approach is to direct the bulk of public financing through a performance-based system. Early experimentation with performance-based mechanisms in Africa offers possible stepping stones. These mechanisms include, for example, paying for performance in higher education, as in Mali and regional centers of excellence, and focusing initially on performance-enhancing reforms, as in Chile. Competitive innovation funds—such as, for example, the Teaching and Learning Innovation Fund in Ghana or the Quality Innovation Fund in Mozambique—can be used to steer promising reforms and innovations to increase access to tertiary education, improve the quality of teaching, or improve the management of institutions. These and other mechanisms can help countries to move gradually toward financing-for-results reforms that could apply to universities and TVET institutions.

Countries need to pay attention to prerequisite factors for the success of performance-financing reforms. A challenge is to define quantitative and transparent indicators and collect the data required to measure them. There is also a risk of "creaming"—that is, that service providers will have an incentive to exclude youths and adults who are difficult to train or transition into jobs. To counter this risk, contracts can provide premiums for priority target groups, as in the centers of excellence or the Employment Fund in Nepal. An alternative or complement would be to use a voucher system that allows individuals to choose and directly pay training providers (whether public or private). Such a voucher program was used in Western Kenya and resulted in a significant increase in access to public and private TVET among youths (Hicks et al. 2011).

For public universities, promoting innovation in programs, curricula, teaching methods, and partnerships requires greater autonomy. Insufficient autonomy to select the staff they need and design their academic programs makes it more difficult for universities to serve the needs of the labor market and the economy. For greater chances of success, reforms to achieve greater autonomy should be combined with performance-financing and governance arrangements that strengthen accountability across-the-board. Providing students with relevant information and support so that they can choose among institutions and fields of study can help to strengthen accountability for results.

Economic Relevance and Demand-Driven Provision of TVET

Given the large informal sector in the region and rapid changes in skills demand, there is a need to rethink the public sector's role in TVET. Staying relevant requires an agility and flexibility that publicly provided TVET and higher education struggle to attain. Partnering with the private sector—including on training provision—will be critical, as countries inside and outside the region increasingly recognize.

TVET needs to be geared more toward preparing workers for nonwage employment outside of the manufacturing sector. This begins with course offerings, which only recently started incorporating training in entrepreneurship and core business skills that are directly relevant for self-employment, management of small enterprises, and services. For example, these skills encompass costing, pricing, preparing financial statements, keeping business records, project management, marketing, sales, and preparing business plans, among others. Promising programs, such as Educate! in Rwanda and Uganda, are introducing entrepreneurship, work readiness skills, and experiential applied teaching methodologies in secondary schools. Tanzania is developing new TVET curricula with a focus on skills for self-employment.

There is also a need to address inflexible course times that make it difficult to combine training and work, lack of practical training, and high costs that make education inaccessible or irrelevant for workers in the informal sector. Better incorporating the views and skills needs of the informal sector in public TVET—for example, by linking to existing organizations of informal workers and enterprises—can be a way forward. TVET institutions in Kenya are often associated with business centers through which consultancies are provided to small-scale entrepreneurs. Graduates of youth polytechnics are encouraged to form business groups, and these groups then approach credit providers.

Making TVET relevant to the needs of catalytic sectors requires building gradual but sustained engagement with employers at the local level. In Tanzania, for example, the private sector is increasingly playing an advisory role in TVET through the Tanzania National Business Council; the Association of Tanzania Employers occasionally helps to define strategic priorities.

Several PPPs are now underway in the region to introduce job-related training designed to meet the short-term needs of employers. In Ghana, since 2005, the Industrial Skills Development Center has provided training in mechanical, electrical, and process engineering through a governance arrangement that includes industry representatives on its decision-making board and an impressive list of partner firms. South Africa's Middelburg Higher Technical School has established successful partnerships with companies like Toyota Motor Company that invest in the school, provide workplace training, and consider graduates for employment. Although these initiatives need to be assessed, they incorporate some of the lessons from successful or promising new models of TVET training, particularly the benefits of a close involvement of employers and alignment with their needs.

The private sector is a critical partner for improving teacher quality and offering opportunities for on-the-job training, whether in the formal or informal sector. TVET teacher education is largely university based; in-service continuous training is generally lacking. Exceptions are the dedicated Vocational Teachers Training College in Tanzania and the Normal Schools for Teachers of Technical Education in Cameroon. Relatively few teachers in public institutions have industrial experience, in part because of the requirements for a teaching certificate. Countries could explore more aggressive options for twinning arrangements with private firms and other countries to upgrade the skills of TVET teachers, allowing the local recruitment of people with relevant skills but without teaching certificates. This additional support can be combined with stronger incentives to perform, including publishing examination results.

Demand-Driven and Active Learning Approaches in Higher Education

Improving the labor market relevance of higher education will require aligning teaching and research activities at public and private universities with market signals. Governments can offer incentives to set up and strengthen industry-university links—for example, by bringing in intermediaries or providing matching funds.

Adopting more active learning practices and a "careers" approach to skills development in higher education starts with the design of curricula. University programs need to combine academic subjects with more hands-on experiences that deliver the multiplicity of skills (technical, cognitive, and socioemotional) necessary to perform jobs that youths are expected to take upon graduation. This task-based approach recognizes that what matters is whether workers have the skills to perform the tasks of a job and not just a diploma. Moreover, institutions need to pursue work-based learning opportunities more aggressively through apprenticeships or internships. Many countries in the region have or are in the process of generating national apprenticeship and internship frameworks, with a view to enhancing the workplace experience of youths, including university graduates. This approach is to be encouraged, and the international evidence suggests that—when well designed— these frameworks can indeed improve employability.

Given that fast transformation of the economies of countries in Sub-Saharan Africa will require a new generation of entrepreneurs, directly and indirectly strengthening entrepreneurship education in universities must be a priority. Several universities in Africa have established incubation centers, for example, allowing and encouraging students to try out new ideas and take them to the market.

There is an important role for regional cooperation and international partnerships with recognized universities in the region and the world. Today's digital technologies make this easier. For example, the Massachusetts Institute of Technology and a consortium of 15 other top universities has started to offer micro-masters programs that require only one full semester on campus in the United States. Targeted scholarship programs that include requirements for returning to the home country can also be helpful, particularly for students in STEM fields. The Partnership for Applied Science, Engineering, and Technology is a recent African-led initiative to leverage the knowledge and experiences of countries in Asia and Latin America, including Brazil, China, India, and the Republic of Korea, by bringing together governments, the private sector, and other partners to improve the capacity of universities and research centers in applied science, engineering, and technology (ASET) fields. The initiative provides regional scholarships and innovation funds, benchmarking and strategic planning in ASET fields, regional quality assurance mechanisms, large-scale data collection and research, and soon TVET centers of excellence.

Efficiency and Relevance of Skills Building for Out-of-School Youths and Adults

On-the-Job Training

Laying the basis for remedying and upgrading the skills of out-of-school youths and adults can be achieved by addressing market and coordination failures that prevent firms (especially small, informal enterprises) from offering on-the-job training and incentivizing them to do so. On-the-job training is an important channel through which workers upgrade their skills during their working life. It is also a vehicle that can help firms to adopt new technologies and new business practices. But in much of the region, the incidence of on-the-job training is lower than expected for countries' income levels. It is essential to create the right incentives for firms to train their workers.

Apprenticeships

Given how ubiquitous informal apprenticeships are in the informal sector, it is important to make them more productive. Recent reforms to improve informal apprenticeships often include measures to improve the quality of training, such as the use of dual training principles (that is, classroom and on-the-job training), training of master craftspersons, and upgrading of technology; measures to improve working conditions and inclusion in informal sector training (promotion of gender equality and occupational health and safety); and measures to establish mechanisms for certification of informally trained artisans, improve the recognition of existing (traditional) certification systems, and institutionalize or improve quality assurance with the involvement of local business associations. Despite these attempts, few reforms have been formally evaluated. In addition, attempts to give structure to informal apprenticeships and bring them closer to formal ones have failed to pick up scale. The objective of policy interventions should not be to make informal apprenticeships look like formal ones. The policy objective should be to improve the learning process of apprentices.

Self-Employment and Entrepreneurship

Given that most Sub-Saharan Africans are not in wage employment and, even when they are, do not remain so for long, labor market training programs aimed at improving employability and supporting self-employment are essential. Training programs can remedy the technical or job-specific skills gaps of out-of-school youths and adults and build basic cognitive and socioemotional skills. Although such programs are growing rapidly, the global evidence from rigorous evaluations is mixed regarding the effectiveness of these short-term programs.

Training programs supporting self-employment and small-scale entrepreneurship are among the most widespread remedial training programs in Africa. The programs take various forms, from public works with a training component supporting entrepreneurship to programs promoting small-scale entrepreneurship and improvements in the productivity of small-scale entrepreneurs. Recent programs in Kenya and South Africa, which have been rigorously evaluated, have shown that training in specific business skills can lead to higher profits and sustainability for businesses and gains in employment and earnings for employees (Anderson, Chandy, and Zia 2016; McKenzie and Puerto 2017). In Togo, training for entrepreneurs to improve business practices as well as socioemotional skills aimed at helping entrepreneurs to become more proactive and resilient to obstacles led to higher sales and profits (box O.2). In a successful program in Uganda, youth groups received grants that they could use to obtain vocational training or to start a business, leading to substantial increases in business assets and earnings (Blattman, Fiala, and Martinez 2014).

BOX O.2

Training in Personal Initiative

Business owners perform best when they have not only standard business skills, but also socioemotional skills, such as personal initiative. In Togo, a set of microenterprise owners participated in one of two training programs—a leading business training program (on accounting, marketing, human resource management, and formalization) or a program that sought to increase personal initiative and entrepreneurial behaviors (goal setting, planning and feedback, innovation, and self-starting behavior). Both trainings were brief: three half-day sessions over four weeks. Over the subsequent two years, profits increased 30 percent for those participating in the personal initiative training; profits increased by a much smaller, statistically insignificant amount for those who received the traditional training.

Source: Campos et al. 2017.

Enact Systemwide Change and Make Skills Building Everyone's Business

Achieving substantial progress in skills building in Sub-Saharan Africa will require enacting systemwide change. As elaborated in *World Development Report 2017: Governance and the Law* (World Bank 2017a), many successful small-scale programs and local reforms, such as those mentioned in the preceding discussion, fail to achieve the desired impacts at scale. Achieving more equitable access, quality, relevance, and efficiency in skills-building systems cannot hinge on just scaling up "best practices." There is need to pay attention to the governance environment in which scaling up takes place. To achieve broad and sustained results, policies and reforms need to establish credible commitment, support coordination, and promote cooperation among all actors. To this end, it is important to tackle the politics of skills policies and create the incentives to align the behaviors of all stakeholders to the pursuit of national skills development goals.

The international experience from the successful and failed attempts to reform governance points to three broad avenues for enacting systemwide change:

- *Use information and other metrics* of system performance to generate commitment and buy-in for reforms, empower stakeholders to hold governments and providers accountable for results, and guide and adapt policy decisions, which requires collecting household-level data, conducting robust national student assessments, establishing management information systems, and participating in international student tests.

- *Shift incentives* to align the interests and behaviors of all stakeholders to *cooperate* toward the achievement of skills-building outcomes.

- *Strengthen the capacity* of government agencies, particularly ministries of health, education, labor, and social development, for pursuing nationwide, coordinated, evidence-based policies.

Metrics on system performance can be used to guide policy development and identify, refine, and adapt successful local solutions. Data from national surveys and student assessments can be used to track progress in tracer indicators and final outcomes that are relevant to skills formation—from child health to learning to skills formation—and returns to skills. Such data are ultimately the basis for building and using evidence to guide the cycle of policy design, implementation, feedback for improvement, and innovation and to indicate whether policies are enacting systemwide change in skills formation.

Several countries have disseminated information on poor performance to mobilize public opinion and get politicians and others to commit to improving results. Information on performance standards for outcomes and service delivery can empower parents and users to hold providers accountable for results. Simple standards and goals for child development, student learning, and other skills outcomes can allow parents to know how well their children are doing compared with the expected standards and make them more likely to hold providers and local or even central authorities accountable for the quality of services. In Uganda, a newspaper campaign designed to inform local primary schools about their entitlement to grants led to an increase in the flow of funds to schools and accelerated the expansion of school enrollment. These approaches are all examples of enabling the "short route" to accountability.

There are limits, however, to how much can be achieved via the local "short route" to accountability. Important aspects of service delivery, such as teacher contracts and pay, are generally managed centrally and depend on system-level incentives. For instance, short-term contracts for teachers are often used to increase the local accountability of teachers. However, in Kenya a nationwide reform of this type was undermined partly by a power struggle between government and teachers unions.

Countries in Sub-Saharan Africa should also strive to build coalitions for achieving skills results at scale. In addition to tilting public opinion through information regarding system performance, countries can create coalitions to foster cooperation and shift the balance of power in favor of good policies and reforms. Cooperation also requires recognizing the multiple, often competing, and evolving interests of stakeholders. For instance, although many health personnel, teachers, and other social service providers are truly devoted to serving their clientele—mothers, children, and youths—insufficient resources and lack of support can undermine morale and detract their attention from achieving results. Policies that combine resources and pedagogical support for teachers with reforms and mechanisms to improve their accountability for delivering learning, such as teacher evaluations or performance pay, may have a better chance of buy-in.

Skills development is a multisector endeavor that requires coordinated policies. Broadly construed, skills are "everyone's problem, but no one's responsibility," as is commonly said of nutrition policies. Multiple agencies at the central and local levels are involved in skills development strategies. Lack of coordination can result in inefficiencies, duplication of efforts, or, perhaps worse yet, lack of attention to important issues. Inadequate investments in child development hinder the ability of schools to produce learning, regardless of the quality of teachers and infrastructure. Countries have attempted various ways to address the coordination problem, from entrusting one ministry (for example, social development) with coordination to elevating this mandate to a unit or team under the president or prime minister's watch. Others have used the national budget, for instance, through results-oriented financing, as a key instrument to ensure that the required programs and interventions are well aligned. Again, no one formula can guarantee success.

Countries need to invest in building technical capacity to design, implement, and assess policies and reforms in relevant line ministries. Central government agencies, such as ministries of education and labor, face severe weaknesses in evidence-based policy formulation, budget planning and execution, information systems, management, and evaluation capacity. These capacity constraints make it very difficult to pursue policy initiatives that can foster commitment, cooperation, and coordination to enact systemwide changes that improve the quality of services. Resources and careful attention to long-term capacity building are also essential.

Conclusions

Although countries in Sub-Saharan Africa can learn much from regional and global experiences to leapfrog their skills development, there are hardly any institutional shortcuts. The institutional underpinning of skills strategies in the region may find approaches to emulate and pitfalls to avoid in other regions; however, the strategies must be homegrown to be attuned to the political realities of each country. Just like investment priorities, they should reflect each country's context. In most policy choices, countries will face trade-offs—often stark ones—that will have distributional impacts and a bearing on their development path. Committed leaders, reform coalitions, and well-coordinated policies are essential for taking on the skills balancing act in Sub-Saharan Africa.

Note

1. For evidence on job-recruiting services, see Jensen 2012; for evidence on female leadership, see Beaman et al. 2012.

References

Aker, Jenny C., Christopher Ksoll, and Travis J. Lybbert. 2012. "Can Mobile Phones Improve Learning? Evidence from a Field Experiment in Niger." *American Economic Journal: Applied Economics* 4 (4): 94–120.

Ali, Daniel Ayalew, Derick Bowen, and Klaus W. Deininger. 2017. "Personality Traits, Technology Adoption, and Technical Efficiency: Evidence from Smallholder Rice Farms in Ghana." Policy Research Working Paper 7959, World Bank, Washington, DC.

Anderson, Stephen J., Rajesh Chandy, and Bilal Zia. 2016. "Pathways to Profits: Identifying Separate Channels of Small Firm Growth through Business Training." Policy Research Working Paper 7774, World Bank, Washington, DC.

Araujo, M. Caridad, Pedro Carneiro, Yyannú Cruz-Aguayo, and Norbert Schady. 2016. "Teacher Quality and Learning Outcomes in Kindergarten." *Quarterly Journal of Economics* 131 (3): 1415–53.

Attanasio, Orazio, Sarah Cattan, Emla Fitzsimons, Costas Meghir, and Marta Rubio-Codina. 2015. "Estimating the Production Function for Human Capital: Results from a Randomized Control Trial in Colombia." NBER Working Paper 20965, National Bureau of Economic Research, Cambridge, MA.

Baird, Sarah, Ephraim Chirwa, Craig McIntosh, and Berk Özler. 2010. "The Short-Term Impacts of a Schooling Conditional Cash Transfer Program on the Sexual Behavior of Young Women." *Health Economics* 19 (S1): 55–68.

Baird, Sarah, Craig McIntosh, and Berk Özler. 2011. "Cash or Condition? Evidence from a Cash Transfer Experiment." *Quarterly Journal of Economics* 126 (4): 1709–53.

Barrera-Osorio, Felipe, Pierre de Galbert, James Habyarimana, and Shwetlena Sabarwal. 2016. "Impact of Public-Private Partnerships on Private School Performance: Evidence from a Randomized Controlled Trial in Uganda." Policy Research Working Paper 7905, World Bank, Washington, DC.

Barro, Robert, and Jong-Wha Lee. 2013. "A New Data Set of Educational Attainment in the World, 1950–2010." *Journal of Development Economics* 104 (C): 184–98.

Beaman, Lori, Esther Duflo, Rohini Pande, and Petia Topalova. 2012. "Female Leadership Raises Aspirations and Educational Attainment for Girls: A Policy Experiment in India." *Science* 335 (6068): 582–86.

Blattman, Christopher, Nathan Fiala, and Sebastian Martinez. 2014. "Generating Skilled Self-Employment in Developing Countries: Experimental Evidence from Uganda." *Quarterly Journal of Economics* 129 (2): 697–752.

Blimpo, Moussa P., Pedro Carneiro, Pamela Jervis Ortiz, and Todd Pugatch. 2017. "Scaling Up Children's School Readiness in The Gambia: Lessons from an Experimental Study." RISE Annual Conference, Washington, DC.

Buehren, Niklas, and Taylor van Salisbury. 2017. "Female Enrollment in Male-Dominated Vocational Training Courses: Preferences and Prospects." Gender Innovation Lab Policy Brief, World Bank, Washington, DC.

Campos, Francisco, Michael Frese, Markus Goldstein, Leonardo Iacovone, Hillary C. Johnson, David McKenzie, and Mona Mensmann. 2017. "Teaching Personal Initiative Beats Traditional Training in Boosting Business in West Africa." *Science* 357 (September 22): 1287–90.

Campos, Francisco, Markus Goldstein, Laura McGorman, Ana Maria Boudet, and Obert Pimhidzai. 2015. "Breaking the Metal Ceiling: Female Entrepreneurs Who Succeed in Male-Dominated Sectors." Policy Research Working Paper 7503, World Bank, Washington, DC.

Croke, Kevin, Markus Goldstein, and Alaka Holla. 2017. "Can Job Training Decrease Women's Self-Defeating Biases? Experimental Evidence from Nigeria." Policy Research Working Paper 8141, World Bank, Washington, DC.

Deaton, Angus. 2013. *Great Escape: Health, Wealth, and the Origins of Inequality.* Princeton, NJ: Princeton University Press.

Duflo, Esther, Pascaline Dupas, and Michael Kremer. 2011. "Peer Effects, Teacher Incentives, and the Impact of Tracking: Evidence from a Randomized Evaluation in Kenya." *American Economic Review* 101 (5): 1739–74.

———. 2017. "The Impact of Free Secondary Education: Experimental Evidence from Ghana." Working Paper, Massachusetts Institute of Technology, Cambridge, MA.

Duflo, Annie, and Jessica Kiessel. 2012. "Teacher Community Assistant Initiative (TCAI)." Policy Brief 4004, International Growth Centre, London.

Evans, David K., and Anna Popova. 2016. "What Really Works to Improve Learning in Developing Countries? An Analysis of Divergent Findings in Systematic Reviews." *World Bank Research Observer* 31 (2): 242–70.

Filmer, Deon, and Louise Fox. 2014. *Youth Employment in Sub-Saharan Africa.* Africa Development Series. Washington, DC: World Bank.

Galasso, Emanuela, and Adam Wagstaff, with Sophie Naudeau and Meera Shekar. 2016. "The Economic Costs of Stunting and How to Reduce Them." Policy Research Note 5, World Bank, Washington, DC.

Global Education Commission. 2016. "The Learning Generation: Investing in Education for a Changing World." International Commission on Financing Global Education Opportunity, New York.

Groningen Growth and Development Centre. Various years. 10-Sector Database. Groningen, the Netherlands: University of Groningen, Faculty of Economics and Business, Groningen Growth and Development Centre.

Hicks, Joan Hamory, Michael Kremer, Issac Mbiti, and Edward Miguel. 2011. "Vocational Education Voucher Delivery and Labor Market Returns: A Randomized Evaluation among Kenyan Youth." Report for the Spanish Impact Evaluation Fund, World Bank, Washington, DC.

Jensen, Robert. 2012. "Do Labor Market Opportunities Affect Young Women's Work and Family Decisions? Experimental Evidence from India." *Quarterly Journal of Economics* 127 (2): 753–92.

Marini, Alessandra, Claudia Rokx, and Paul Gallagher. 2017. "Standing Tall: Peru's Success in Overcoming Its Stunting Crisis." Working Paper, World Bank, Washington, DC.

Martinez, Sebastian, Sophie Naudeau, and Vitor Pereira. 2013. "The Promise of Preschool in Africa: A Randomized Impact Evaluation of Early Childhood Development in Rural Mozambique." Working paper, World Bank, Washington, DC; Save the Children, New York.

McKenzie, David, and Susana Puerto. 2017. "Growing Markets through Business Training for Female Entrepreneurs: A Market-Level Randomized Experiment in Kenya." Policy Research Working Paper 7993, World Bank, Washington, DC.

Muralidharan, Karthik, and Nishith Prakash. 2017. "Cycling to School: Increasing Secondary School Enrollment for Girls in India." *American Economic Journal: Applied Economics* 9 (3): 321–50.

Nguyen, Trang. 2008. "Information, Role Models, and Perceived Returns to Education: Experimental Evidence from Madagascar." Economics Department, Massachusetts Institute of Technology, Cambridge, MA.

Perotti, Valeria. 2017. "Training, Skills, and Firm Productivity in Formal African Firms." Background paper for this report, World Bank, Washington, DC.

Piper, Benjamin, Leila Schroeder, and Barbara Trudell. 2016. "Oral Reading Fluency and Comprehension in Kenya: Reading Acquisition in a Multilingual Environment." *Journal of Research in Reading* 39 (2): 133–52.

Rodrik, Dani. 2016. "Premature Deindustrialization." *Journal of Economic Growth* 21 (1): 1–33.

Shekar, Meera, Jakub Kakietek, Julia Dayton Eberwein, and Dylan Walters. 2016. *An Investment Framework for Nutrition: Reaching the Global Targets for Stunting, Anemia, Breastfeeding, and Wasting.* Vol. 2: *Main Report.* Washington, DC: World Bank.

UNESCO (United Nations Educational, Scientific, and Cultural Organization). 2011. "Financing Education in Sub-Saharan Africa—Meeting the Challenges of Expansion, Equity and Quality." UNESCO, Montreal.

———. 2015. "EFA Global Monitoring Report 2015. Regional Overview: Sub-Saharan Africa." UNESCO, Paris.

———. 2016. *Global Education Monitoring Report—Education for People and Planet: Creating Sustainable Futures for All.* Paris: UNESCO.

USAID (U.S. Agency for International Development). Various years. Demographic and Health Survey database. Washington, DC: USAID. https://dhsprogram.com/.

Valerio, Alexandria, Maria Laura Sanchez Puerta, Namrata Tognatta, and Sebastian Monroy-Taborda. 2016. "Are There Skills Payoffs in Low- and Middle-Income Countries? Empirical Evidence Using STEP Data." Policy Research Working Paper 7879, World Bank, Washington, DC.

van Broekhuizen, Hendrik. 2016. "Graduate Unemployment and Higher Education Institutions in South Africa." Stellenbosch Economics Working Paper 08/16, Department of Economics, University of Stellenbosch, Matielan, South Africa.

Venkat, Hamsa, and Nic Spaull. 2015. "What Do We Know about Primary Teachers' Mathematical Content Knowledge in South Africa? An Analysis of SACMEQ 2007." *International Journal of Educational Development* 41 (March): 121–30.

World Bank. 2017a. *World Development Report 2017: Governance and the Law.* Washington, DC: World Bank Group. https://openknowledge.worldbank.org /handle/10986/6001.

———. 2017b. *World Development Report 2018: Learning to Realize Education's Promise.* Washington, DC: World Bank.

———. 2019. *World Development Report 2019: The Changing Nature of Work.* Washington, DC: World Bank Group.

———. Various years. Enterprise Survey database. Washington, DC: World Bank. http://www.enterprisesurveys.org.

———. Various years. SABER-WfD Ratings and Data. Washington, DC: World Bank. http://saber.worldbank.org/index.cfm?indx=8&pd=7&sub=1.

———. Various years. Skills Towards Employability and Productivity (STEP) Survey. Washington, DC: World Bank.

———. Various years. World Development Indicators database. Washington, DC: World Bank.

Chapter 1

Skills and Economic Transformation in Sub-Saharan Africa

Omar Arias

Over the past two decades, Sub-Saharan Africa has achieved strong economic growth, reduced poverty, and dramatically improved access to education. Yet economic transformation, poverty reduction, and skill levels remain far below those in other regions. To accelerate economic transformation and poverty reduction in the 21st century, Sub-Saharan Africa needs to make smart investments in skills development. This effort requires investing in multiple skills aligned with three policy goals (productivity growth, inclusion, and adaptability), carrying out the policy reforms to make these investments pay off, while factoring in the megatrends that will continue to shape the region's economic transformation.

  Skills investments need to reckon with two fundamental trade-offs across policy goals: the first entails investing in skills to meet the needs of catalytic sectors that can maximize productivity growth, while investing in skills to improve the livelihoods of the poor; the second entails investing in the current stock of workers to remedy the accumulated skills gaps, while investing in new cohorts to prepare them and the economy to compete in and adapt to a global economy and rapidly changing world of work. In reckoning with these trade-offs, countries need (a) to manage the expansion of skills-building systems by assuring equity in coverage as well as quality, relevance, and efficiency of skills investments and (b) to set policy priorities tailored to the initial conditions and enabling policy environment.

Introduction

Human capital is essential to accelerate and sustain inclusive economic growth in Sub-Saharan Africa. In its exhaustive review of studies and historical experience, the Commission on Growth and Development concludes, "No country has sustained rapid growth without keeping up impressive rates of public investment in [infrastructure,] education, and health."[1] Investments in education and health that lead to learning and enhanced human capacities crystalize in a workforce with adequate skills. Recent studies show that what matters to growth is not educational attainment per se but rather ensuring that individuals develop valuable skills (see Hanushek and Woessmann 2009). When complemented with reforms to foster a more vibrant private sector, including an enabling business environment and integration in global markets, a skilled workforce enables firms to move up in value chains, adapt to economic changes, adopt new technologies, and spur innovation. In Sub-Saharan Africa, skills are crucial to countries' economic transformation of moving labor out of low-productivity activities—mostly in subsistence agriculture and nonfarm self-employment—and into activities that have higher productivity and greater potential to enable workers to earn more in their current employment. It is not surprising that the skills agenda is a high priority for governments, employers, and, most important, families and individuals throughout the region.

Although similar to other regions in some respects, Sub-Saharan Africa faces a unique skills development challenge. Throughout history and across regions, countries have invested in skills to reap demographic dividends and facilitate economic transformation, while grappling with institutional weaknesses in their skills-building systems. In addition, Sub-Saharan Africa is faced with a world that is radically more demanding, a global economy that is far more integrated and competitive, and swift changes in technology and business that require a wider set of skills. Like most countries, Sub-Saharan Africa struggles to ensure that children, youth, and adults alike acquire the skills that employers need today but also the skills that individuals need to navigate a labor market in constant flux. However, countries in the region are still grappling with expanding access to basic education, ensuring that learning confers new cohorts with basic skills, and tackling the substantial accumulated skills deficits of the out-of-school population. Moreover, rising aspirations after decades of independence, recovery from armed conflicts in many cases, and entrenched inequalities add urgency to the promise that a good education and training are the ticket to better lives. Tackling the youth employment challenge is central to realizing the promise of the demographic dividend in the region (Filmer and Fox 2014).

For Sub-Saharan Africa, skills investments need to reckon with the needs of economies in the near term and in the future. African economies of today are unlikely to reflect the economies of 10, 20, or 30 years from now. Skills investments have a long-term maturity. Skills investments in Africa should enable the process of economic transformation and prepare new cohorts for the types of jobs that will be available, while also catering to today's highly informal economies and the prevalence of earning opportunities in household enterprises and subsistence family farming. Although the bulk of employment in the region is likely to remain informal for decades to come (Filmer and Fox 2014), the nature of work is likely to change significantly (across and within economic sectors and occupations).

This first chapter of the report frames the analysis of skills priorities in the context of structural transformation in the region. It offers a backdrop and framework to reflect on the report's guiding question: How can Sub-Saharan Africa invest most effectively and develop skills to enhance inclusive growth and reduce poverty over the next 10 years and beyond? To this aim, the chapter examines three main questions: Which skills are needed for the current and future workforce in Sub-Saharan African countries? Do current and future forces of economic transformation in Sub-Saharan Africa call for skills strategies that depart from historical experience and the path of other low- and middle-income economies? Are the levels and patterns of investment adequate to face up to the region's skills challenge? Rather than giving sweeping answers to these questions, the chapter offers a framework and guiding principles for countries in the region to establish priorities suited to their unique context.

This chapter adopts a historical and forward-looking perspective to derive a framework for guiding smart skills investments in Africa. It does this in five steps. First, the chapter discusses the range of skills important in modern economies and how these are acquired throughout the life cycle and get embedded in the current stock and future cohort of workers. Second, it examines the current demand for skills as revealed and priced by employers and labor markets as well as the importance attached to them by individuals and their families. Third, it argues that skills investments in the region should be forward looking and factor in global megatrends that are shaping structural transformation, labor markets, and demand for skills. Fourth, the chapter looks back at the region's historical progress in access to education and skills acquisition, compares it with the paths of other regions, and reflects on plausible trajectories for future improvements. Finally, the chapter presents a policy framework and elements of a country typology to guide skills investments and priorities for the region and to provide a unifying thread for the report. These elements are used to derive strategic implications for policies, pointing to the role of key actors in skills building: families and individuals, government (central and local), and the private sector (both employers and service providers).

Skills for Africa: Which Skills, When to Develop Them, and for Whom

Which Skills

Many skills are needed to participate productively in modernizing economies. The report defines skills broadly to include (a) foundational cognitive, socio-emotional, and digital skills, (b) technical or job-specific skills, and (c) so-called "higher-order skills."

Foundational cognitive skills comprise functional literacy and numeracy (that is, the ability to write, read, and comprehend text as well as perform basic math operations) that are the foundation for learning and subject knowledge acquisition.[2] They have been the traditional focus of school curricula and assessments of student learning and academic achievement. Foundational socioemotional skills refer to the beliefs, attitudes, and behaviors that allow individuals to manage themselves and their relationships with others, including by regulating emotions, setting goals, accomplishing tasks, and dealing with frustration and conflict. They go by different names such as soft skills, life skills, noncognitive skills, and personality traits and comprise factors such as beliefs about intelligence, self-regulation, perseverance, pro-social behavior, empathy, and curiosity. There is growing evidence regarding their importance for success in school and work and for other life outcomes and regarding interventions to teach them in and out of school (box 1.1). As digital technologies are ever more prevalent in our daily lives, digital literacy is becoming another foundational skill. Basic information and communication technology (ICT) skills are essential for the effective use of digital devices and associated tools (from computers to mobile devices, e-mail, and consumer or business software) to face the challenges and tap the opportunities that emergent technologies pose for the way in which we communicate and learn at school, at work, and in life more generally.

Technical or job-specific skills are skills required to perform specific tasks in a job. In this report, they encompass occupational, vocational, and professional knowledge and qualifications as well as management skills.

Finally, the higher-order skills refer to the capacity of individuals to tackle open-ended problems in novel situations through critical thinking, problem solving, and self-regulating their own learning. Although there is less consensus about how these skills can be taught, they build on solid foundational skills and, when relevant, also technical skills (box 1.2).

Skills Beget Skills

A cross-disciplinary body of evidence from neuroscience, epigenetics, psychology, and economics, popularized by Nobel Prize winner James Heckman and coauthors, demonstrates that skills formation is a cumulative life-cycle process

BOX 1.1

The Importance of Socioemotional Skills

A growing body of empirical evidence, particularly from the fields of psychology, sociology, and economics, is highlighting the key role of socioemotional skills in predicting health, academic, labor, and other life outcomes, in some cases being at least as important as cognitive skills (see the review by Kautz et al. 2014). Socioemotional skills such as self-regulation, grit, and resilience can influence academic performance by, for instance, influencing education choices and facilitating tasks such as studying and working as well as by influencing economic and social achievement beyond adolescence (Heckman, Stixrud, and Urzua 2006; Roberts et al. 2007).

In addition to being important in their own right, these skills are relevant because they enable and complement cognitive skills. Socioemotional and cognitive skills are highly interdependent and foster one another in the development of learning abilities (Cunha et al. 2006).

Equally important from a policy standpoint, a growing number of studies are testing and evaluating ways to develop these skills from childhood and into adolescence and early adulthood. Like most dimensions of human development, socioemotional skills are the result of the interplay between nature and nurture: children are born with a genetic blueprint that interacts with their social environments and experiences over the life course to determine the expression of that blueprint (Center on the Developing Child 2016). A growing number of studies are showing that these skills can be developed through interventions.

Existing research in this area is limited largely to the United States and a few other Organisation for Economic Co-operation and Development (OECD) countries. However, as discussed in chapter 2, emerging evidence from low- and middle-income countries is yielding a picture similar to that of high-income countries. The World Bank's Skills Towards Employability and Productivity (STEP) Surveys have documented correlational evidence between socioemotional skills and education and labor market outcomes. As discussed in chapter 2, emerging findings from experimental studies in countries like North Macedonia, Peru, and Turkey are offering rigorous evidence on how these skills can be developed through interventions in schools.

with dynamic complementarities (see, for example, Cunha et al. 2006). Skills formation can be thought of as climbing a ladder starting very early in life: as individuals age, they build on the learning in each step to move up to the next step. Cognitive and socioemotional skills complement and reinforce each other. In fact, the so-called executive function skills encompass a combination of cognitive and socioemotional functioning that has been shown to define "readiness to learn" in school, training, and on the job. For instance,

---

BOX 1.2

Developing Higher-Order Skills

Many employers and educators point out that teaching basic (foundational) and technical skills is no longer sufficient for the demands of an increasingly complex workplace. Workers are expected to solve open-ended problems that involve novel situations, which require so-called higher-order skills such as critical thinking and problem solving. Higher-order skills are associated with metacognitive skills defined as "thinking about thinking" and "learning about learning" involving cognitive processes that allow individuals to self-regulate their own learning by recognizing what they understand or not about a given problem and how they can fill their learning gaps in a systematic (sequential, iterative) fashion.

These metacognitive skills are often related to the top three levels of Bloom's taxonomy for learning (Bloom, Canning, and Chan 2006), the most widely used framework for teaching higher-order thinking skills (figure B1.2.1). Higher-order skills include analyzing, evaluating, and creating and are thought to involve the use of logic and reasoning, judgment, problem solving, and creative thinking. Lower-order thinking skills pertain to the lower three levels of Bloom's taxonomy: remembering (facts), understanding (patterns), and applying information (to solve problems).

Figure B1.2.1 A Revision of Bloom's Taxonomy of Learning

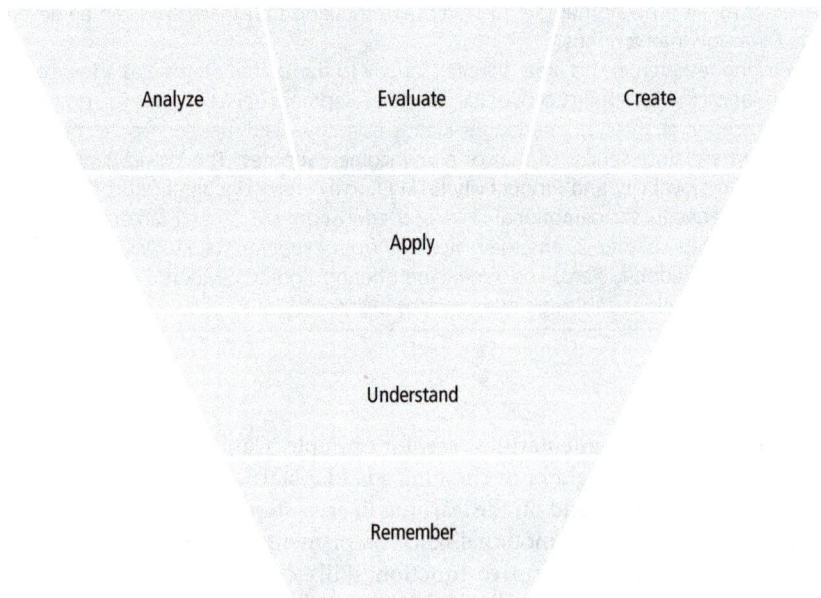

Analyze	Evaluate	Create

Apply

Understand

Remember

Source: Based on Anderson and Krathwohl 2001.

as discussed in chapter 2, a child's math learning outcomes are influenced by beliefs about whether intelligence and specifically "math ability" is fixed or can be developed as well as by the ability to stay on task and tolerate frustration. Foundational skills are essential for a "well-educated" labor force that can adapt in the rapidly changing labor markets of the 21st century global economy.

When to Develop Them

Figure 1.1 illustrates when and how skills are acquired, noting that there are optimal stages for developing different skills over the life span. As explained later, this report is structured around the major stages of skills building in the life cycle.

Different periods are sensitive to the formation of these multiple skills. Heritability and environmental influences both determine how skills are developed over the life course.[3] In particular, the malleability of the brain (called neuroplasticity) is greatest during the first years of life and later in adolescence, when neural connections flourish, are pruned, and solidify. This development of the brain's capacity is highly influenced by maternal and child health and nutrition starting in the womb and continuing through the first years of life— especially during the first 1,000 days of life, known as the nutrition window of opportunity (for a recent review of studies, see Galasso et al. 2017). The quality of nurturing environments during infancy through adolescence further shapes foundational cognitive and socioemotional learning. Child abuse, neglect, or extreme stress can be particularly damaging.

While basic cognitive abilities are well set by the teen years, schooling provides subject knowledge and tools that enhance the use of these abilities to undertake tasks and solve new problems. Socioemotional skills continue to develop and remain malleable through adolescence and early adult years; as discussed throughout the report, some can potentially be taught cost-effectively with interventions (Kautz et al. 2014). Technical skills are acquired through technical and vocational schooling and training (whether formal or informal, on the job or in the classroom), and job-specific skills are built through work experience.

The learning that takes place outside of school is an important source of skills formation. In the United States, this postschool learning accounts for as much as one-third to one-half of all skills formation (Heckman, Lochner, and Taber 1998). The contribution of informal learning, particularly on the job, is often neglected due to misconceptions about adult learning and the scarcity of relevant data. Recent advances in neuroscience and newly collected data on adult skills are challenging these misconceptions. Because of neuroplasticity, the brain continues to change beyond middle age, and although some cognitive functions (such as working memory and mental speed) start to decline as early as age 40, compensation and reorganization of neural pathways can allow a

Figure 1.1 Flow and Stock of Skills Development over the Life Cycle

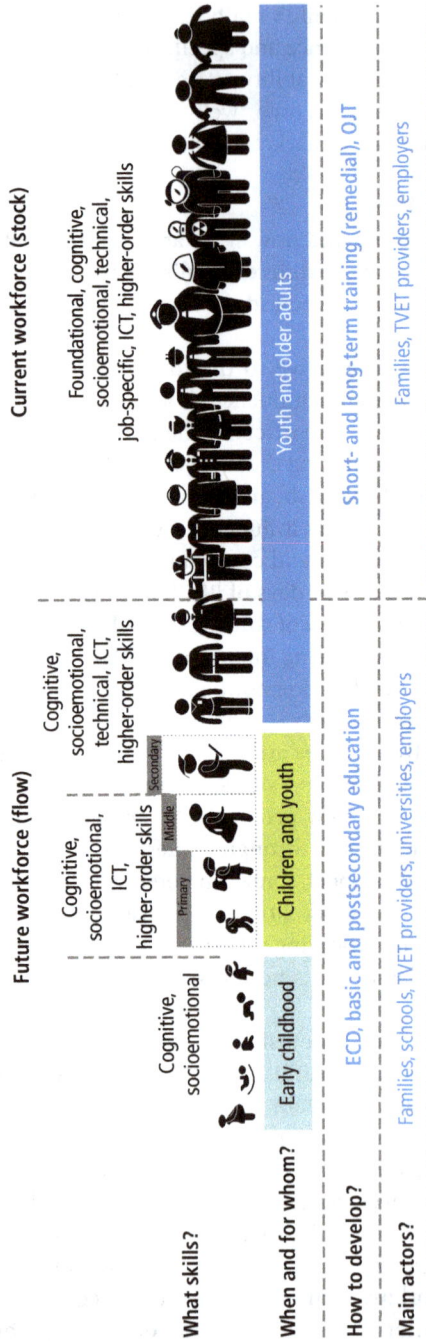

	Future workforce (flow)	Current workforce (stock)
What skills?	Cognitive, socioemotional	Cognitive, socioemotional, ICT, higher-order skills	Cognitive, socioemotional, technical, ICT, higher-order skills	Foundational, cognitive, socioemotional, technical, job-specific, ICT, higher-order skills
When and for whom?	Early childhood	Children and youth	Youth and older adults
How to develop?	ECD, basic and postsecondary education	Short- and long-term training (remedial), OJT
Main actors?	Families, schools, TVET providers, universities, employers	Families, TVET providers, employers

(Primary, Middle, Secondary)

Source: Elaboration by Alexandria Valerio, Viviana Venegas, and Omar Arias.
Note: ECD = early child development; ICT = information and communication technology; OJT = on-the-job training; TVET = technical and vocational education and training.

person to maintain high overall functional performance. Factors such as emotional regulation and conscientiousness tend to increase beyond middle age, and the brain gets better at using prior experiences and knowledge to take shortcuts to find solutions (see the review in Center on the Developing Child 2016; Roberts, Wood, and Caspi 2008).

As discussed in chapter 5, new insights into how the adult brain learns can be incorporated into adult education and training programs (formal or informal) to make them more impactful and cost-effective. The experience and social learning accumulated through wage or self-employment, including in agriculture, can also contribute to skills acquisition.

For Whom to Develop Them

Skills acquisition of individuals gets embedded in the human capital of a country's workforce. The number of years of education is an imperfect measure of skills. The productivity content of an individual's education level depends on the quality of family and school formation during infancy, childhood, adolescence, and adulthood. The workforce comprises individuals—young, middle age, and older adults—who never attended, dropped out, or never went through the education system and who have continued to acquire or erode their skills at different times (spanning decades) and contexts. It feeds from the flow of new cohorts of individuals of school age and youth who are still in school or training.

As a result, the stock of workers embodies highly diverse pathways of skills acquisition. As discussed later on, of particular concern in Sub-Saharan Africa is the large share of the population who never acquired (and continue to fail to acquire) essential foundational skills. As discussed in chapter 5, without minimum foundational skills, technical skills training alone often fails to address skills gaps or to increase the employability of workers.

Skills policies in Sub-Saharan Africa need to devote attention to these multiple skills for three main reasons. First, as discussed further below, both foundational and technical skills matter for productive transformation and the long-term growth of the economy. Second, they matter for social mobility, as there are significant gaps in skills between Africans coming from better-off and worse-off families, and those who only stay in school for a few years have few opportunities to remedy the gaps in their foundational skills. Gaps in foundational skills are particularly troublesome since they hinder higher educational attainment and prevent individuals from being able to adapt to a constantly changing economic environment where narrow skills can be rendered obsolete. Chapters 2 through 4 examine these issues. And third, as discussed next, both families and labor markets in Sub-Saharan Africa put a high value on education and skills, and employers complain about the lack of both foundational and technical skills among workers.

Skills Wanted: The Demand for Skills in Sub-Saharan Africa Today

Skills Shortages as Perceived by Employers

Many enterprises in Sub-Saharan Africa report the lack of skills to be a greater-than-average obstacle to their business. Figures 1.2 through 1.4 present data from the World Bank Enterprise Surveys (http://www.enterprisesurveys.org) on the importance of skills as a constraint for business (analyzed by Perotti 2017 for this report). These data are based on representative samples of formal (mostly larger) firms in manufacturing, services, and construction in Sub-Saharan Africa and low- and middle-income countries in other regions as well as samples of informal firms (largely microenterprises) from specialized surveys in the region. The indicator measures the percentage of firms rating skills as a greater obstacle than the average rating they give to all of the other 14 business environment factors surveyed. On average, about one-third of firms in the region report skills as a greater-than-average constraint, albeit with some variation across countries. Larger firms are more likely to report skills as a greater-than-average obstacle, with percentages as high as 50–70 percent in several countries (figure 1.2, panel a). Even among microenterprises, the percentage of firms rating skills as a greater-than-average obstacle is as high as 30 percent or more in most countries. The indicator of relative severity suggests that worldwide skills are considered a greater-than-average obstacle as countries develop (figure 1.2, panel b). The indicator for the region is roughly at par with that of other low-income economies and reaches 50 percent above the world trend in Sub-Saharan middle-income economies.

Firms in the region increasingly cite difficulty finding workers with adequate skills as economies grow. Consistent with the worldwide trend, as Sub-Saharan economies have grown, more firms have reported skills as being a greater-than-average obstacle in recent years (figure 1.3). This trend has been marked in countries like Ghana, Rwanda, Senegal, and Tanzania. The positive relationship observed worldwide and within the region between the level of development of an economy and the importance given to the skills obstacle suggests that skills gaps, while already an issue in Sub-Saharan Africa, will become increasingly more binding as countries develop. In fact, more detailed analysis of the firm data indicates that firms that are more integrated with external markets (exporting, foreign-owned, or both) and that hire more workers cite skills as relatively more binding (Perotti 2017).

As other constraints to business growth become less binding, employers increasingly feel the pinch of skills gaps. As shown in figure 1.4, firms in Sub-Saharan Africa typically consider skills as one of the most important of the 15 obstacles surveyed; electricity, infrastructure, governance, taxes, and access to finance rank higher. The data using country-level averages for 111 low- and

Figure 1.2 **Share of Firms Rating Workforce Skills as a Greater-than-Average Constraint Compared with 14 Other Business Environment Factors in Sub-Saharan Africa and the World, by Size of Firm and GDP per Capita**

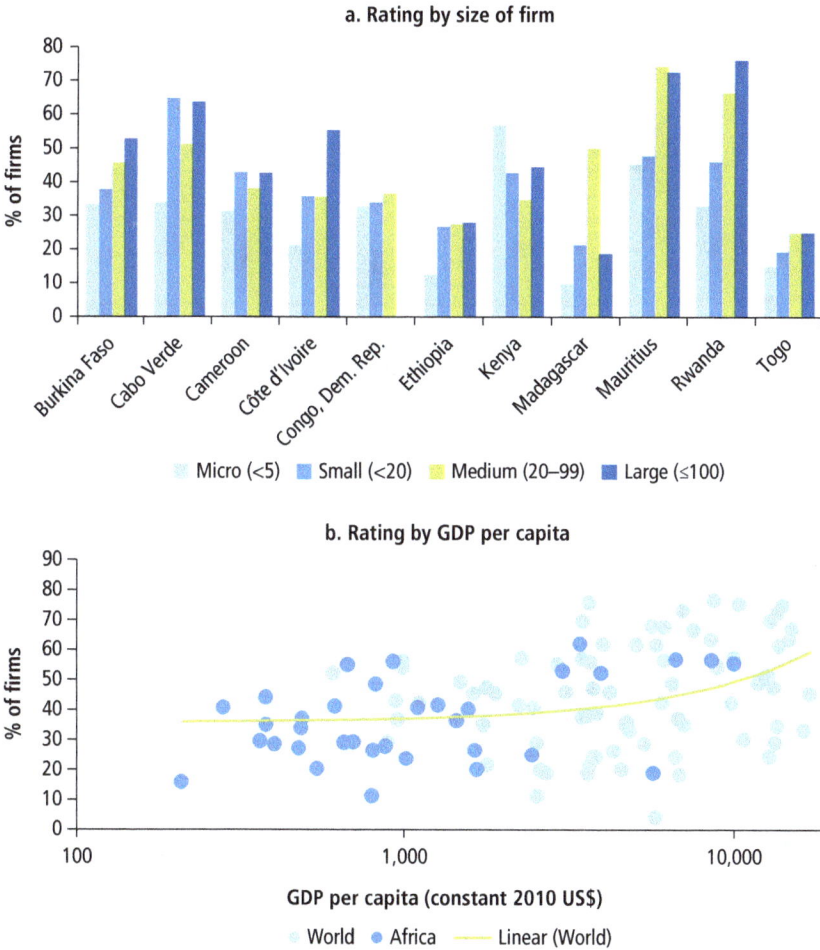

a. Rating by size of firm

Micro (<5)   Small (<20)   Medium (20–99)   Large (≤100)

b. Rating by GDP per capita

GDP per capita (constant 2010 US$)

World   Africa   —— Linear (World)

Source: Perotti 2017, based on World Bank Enterprise Surveys.
Note: Both panels employ data from the standard Enterprise Surveys covering largely formal firms, excluding microenterprises. Panel b also includes data for microfirms from specialized Enterprise Surveys for Sub-Saharan Africa. The indicator measures the % of firms that rate skills (on a scale of 1 = not important to 5 = important) above the average rating that they give to all of the other 14 constraints surveyed.

Figure 1.3 **Share of Firms Rating Workforce Skills as a Greater-than-Average Constraint Compared with 14 Other Business Environment Factors in Sub-Saharan Africa, by GDP per Capita**

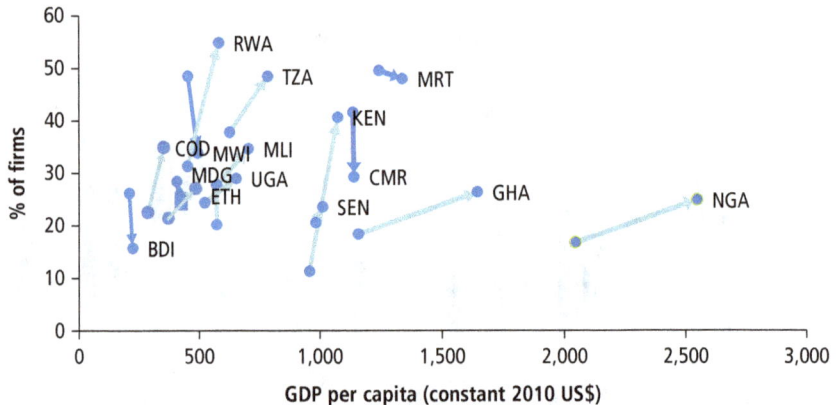

Source: Perotti 2017, based on World Bank Enterprise Surveys (covering largely formal firms, excluding microenterprises).
Note: The arrows indicate trends in overall firms' rating responses as economies develop. BDI = Burundi; CMR = Cameroon; COD = Democratic Republic of Congo; ETH = Ethiopia; GHA = Ghana; KEN = Kenya; MDG = Madagascar; MLI = Mali; MRT = Mauritania; MWI = Malawi; NGA = Nigeria; RWA = Rwanda; SEN = Senegal; TZA = Tanzania; UGA = Uganda.

middle-income economies reveals a worldwide and regional trend for firms to perceive skills as being a relatively more important obstacle when more immediate factors of the business environment—access to finance, in particular—are relatively less important. This inverse relationship between the severity of skills deficits and access to finance as constraints remains even after controlling for a country's average educational attainment and gross domestic product (GDP) per capita and when considering all obstacles jointly (Perotti 2017). In contrast, there is no systematic correlation between the percentage of firms that rate skills as a relatively more severe obstacle and the percentage of firms that rate other business environment factors as more severe than average.

There is no cross-country correlation between the severity of the indicator for skills deficits and a country's share of the adult labor force with low educational attainment. This lack of correlation is consistent with firms' valuing school quality that ultimately produces skills more than educational quantity. Also, as discussed in chapter 5, manufacturing firms (for which these data are available) are more likely to provide training themselves when they identify skills as a greater-than-average obstacle (Perotti 2017); such training can complement the skills lacking from formal education. In sum, even though this evidence does not allow any causal interpretation, it suggests that firms in Sub-Saharan Africa will see skills gaps as more binding to their business as they and their economies grow and modernize.

Figure 1.4 **Share of Firms Rating Workforce Skills and Other Business Environment Factors as a Greater-than-Average Constraint in Sub-Saharan Africa and the World**

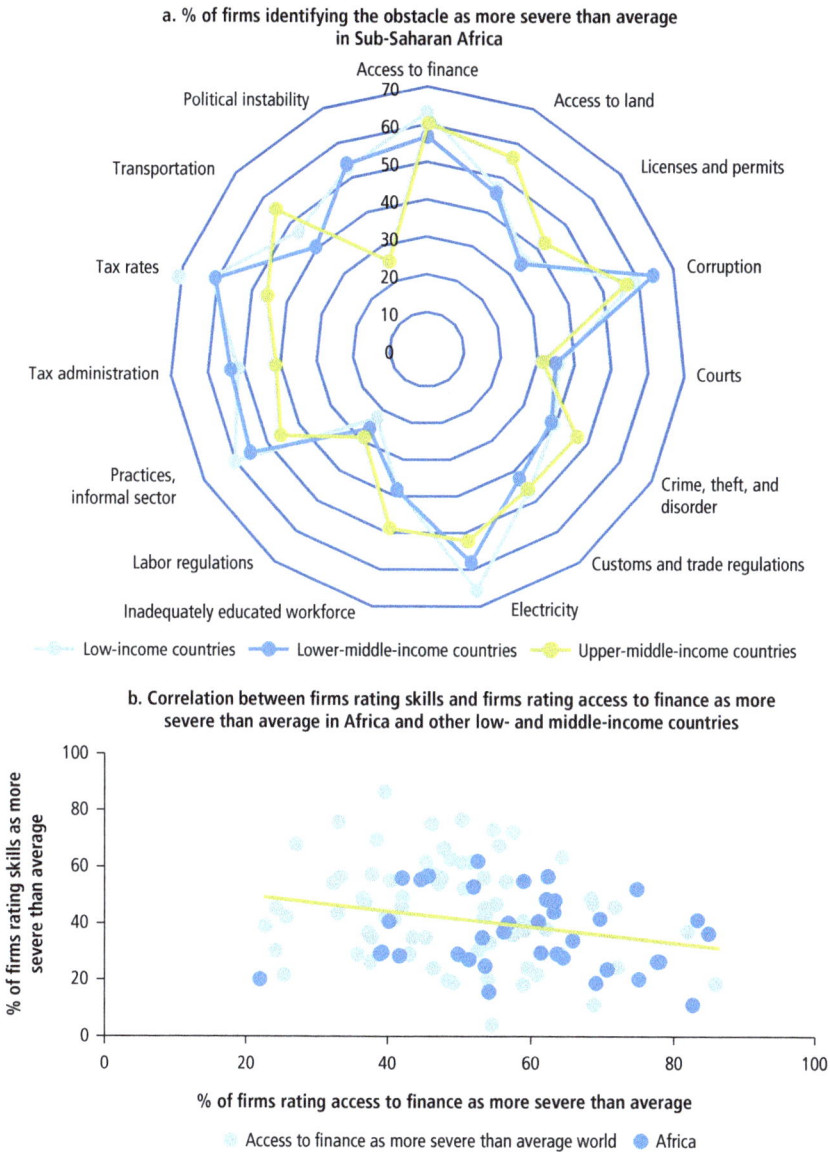

a. % of firms identifying the obstacle as more severe than average in Sub-Saharan Africa

- - - Low-income countries   —●— Lower-middle-income countries   —●— Upper-middle-income countries

b. Correlation between firms rating skills and firms rating access to finance as more severe than average in Africa and other low- and middle-income countries

% of firms rating skills as more severe than average

% of firms rating access to finance as more severe than average

○ Access to finance as more severe than average world   ● Africa

Source: Perotti 2017, based on World Bank Enterprise Surveys.
Note: Both panels use data from the standard Enterprise Surveys covering largely formal firms, excluding microenterprises. Panel b includes data for microfirms from specialized Enterprise Surveys for Sub-Saharan Africa; world = low- and middle-income countries in other regions.

When employers complain that workers do not have the right skills, they are reflecting on more than just education credentials or technical qualifications. As discussed in Filmer and Fox (2014), employers in the region, like elsewhere, value a multiplicity of skills, both foundational and technical. This is also found in recent employer surveys that delve more deeply into which skills are scarce or most valued. Figure 1.5 depicts data from the International Labour Organization (ILO) School-to-Work Transition Surveys, which ask employers in four countries which skills are scarce or most valued. The findings clearly indicate that employers in these countries see foundational cognitive and socioemotional skills as being at least as important as technical skills. Similar evidence from employer surveys in OECD countries and other low- and middle-income economies points to the importance of foundational cognitive and socioemotional skills in addition to technical skills in firms' hiring decisions (Cunningham and Villaseñor 2014). Several studies using new labor force data have found that these skills carry significant earnings returns in labor markets of both high-income and low- and middle-income economies.[4] Moreover, when employers complain about gaps in skills, they are reflecting on the perceived shortage of foundational and technical skills among new entrants and the adult work force.[5] Skills gaps can take many forms, from gaps in foundational (cognitive and

Figure 1.5 Share of Employers Rating the Skill as Important or Very Important in Benin, Liberia, Malawi, and Zambia

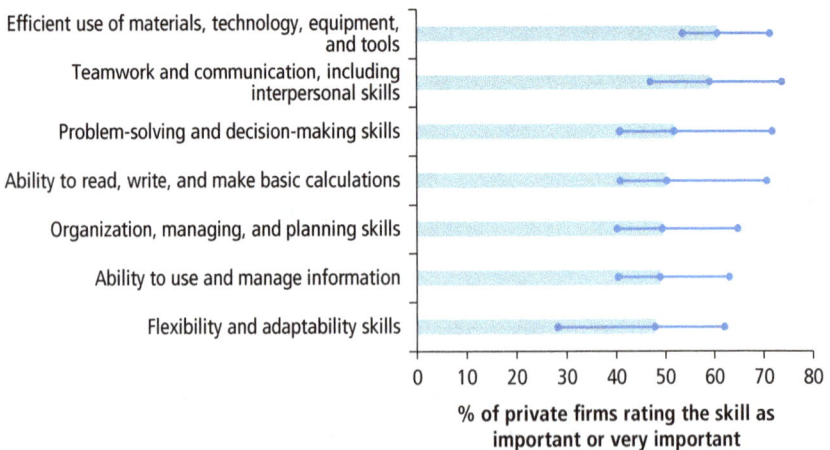

Source: Estimates based on International Labour Organization School-to-Work Transition Surveys of employers (circa 2014).
Note: The lines with dots represent the average, minimum, and maximum values in the sample of countries excluding outliers.

socioemotional) skills to gaps in technical skills, and can affect both current and future workers. Technical skills are not the sole factor increasing employability.

These employer perceptions should be interpreted with caution. The interpretation of the data on demand for skills needs to be tempered given that investments in skills have a long-term maturity. The African economies of today are unlikely to reflect the African economies of 10 or 20 years from now. Moreover, the expectation that the education system should deliver workers who are ready to work, specifically young recruits, is unreasonable, as much of the learning happens on the job. Trainability of applicants seems a more attainable minimum requirement. As discussed in chapter 5, firms should be encouraged to invest in worker skills. Technological change can be expected to reinforce this trend, as the required skills will consequently change and the education and training system is slow to adapt. Skills investments in Africa need to reckon with today's highly informal economies and subsistence family farming. They need to support the process of economic transformation and be attuned to the types of jobs that will be available for new cohorts of Africans.

Returns to Education and Skills in Labor Markets

Returns to education, as indicators of the pricing of skills, are high in the region. In a comprehensive global analysis of the private returns to education, as measured by higher individual hourly earnings in wage employment, Montenegro and Patrinos (2014) find that the average returns to a year of schooling are highest in Sub-Saharan Africa (12.4 percent versus a global average of 9.7 percent) and, following the global trend, are higher for women (14.5 percent) than for men (11.3 percent). In their sample of 139 countries, the five economies with the highest average returns are all from the region: Burundi, Ethiopia, Namibia, Rwanda, and South Africa. The average marginal returns are higher in Sub-Saharan Africa than in other regions at all levels of education, being highest for tertiary (21.0 vs. 14.6 percent) and primary (14.4 vs. 11.5 percent) than for secondary (10.6 vs. 6.8 percent) education. That is, on average, an individual who completes an additional year of tertiary education enjoys 21 percent higher earnings than a person who only achieves a secondary education. An individual who completes an additional year of primary education enjoys 14.4 percent higher earnings than an individual who has no schooling.

Average returns to schooling vary with countries' economic transformation and progress and the educational attainment of new cohorts. Figure 1.6 plots the most recent estimates (circa 2010) from Montenegro and Patrinos (2014) of average returns to schooling in Sub-Saharan countries against the educational attainment of the age cohort 25–29 (as a measure of progress in educational expansion) and an indicator capturing contextual dimensions of a country's economic development deemed relevant to skills investments—namely, income per capita, economic structure, link to external markets, urbanization, and demographic transition (see the note to figure 1.6 for details). Both indicators are normalized (with mean 0 and standard deviation 1), so the higher the number, the more a country has advanced in its economic transformation (for example, grew richer, became less reliant on low-productivity agriculture, became more open and urbanized) or the more it has expanded access to education for young cohorts.

Figure 1.6 **Average Returns to Education for Wage Employment in Sub-Saharan Africa, circa 2010**

a. Average returns to education, by countries' initial level of development

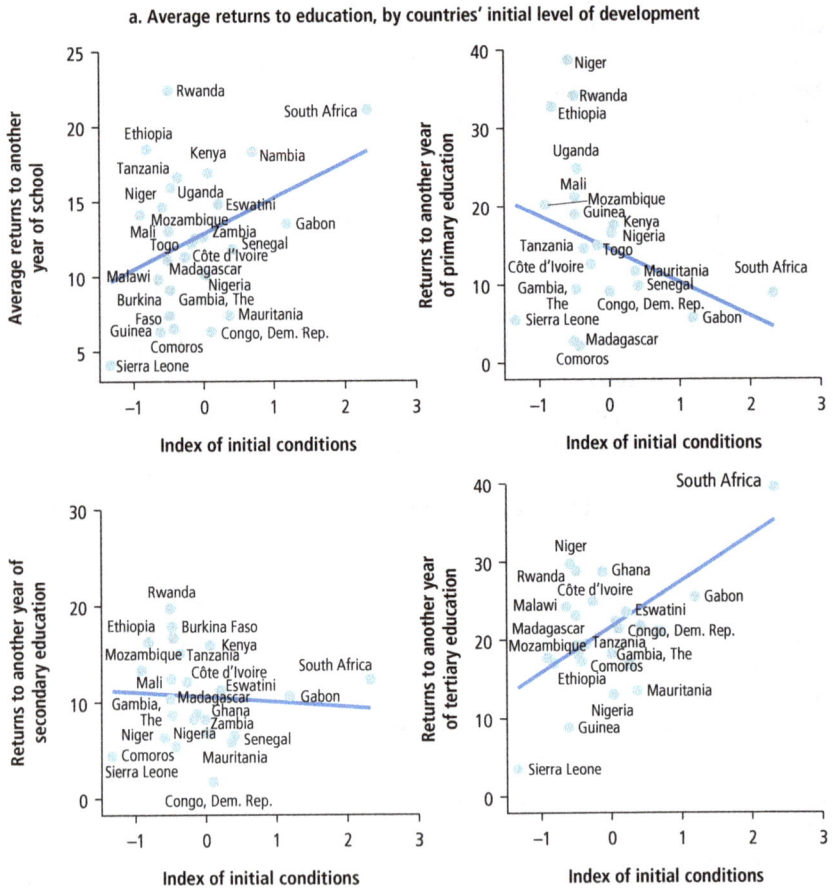

(continued next page)

Figure 1.6 (continued)

b. Average returns to education, by labor force's educational attainment

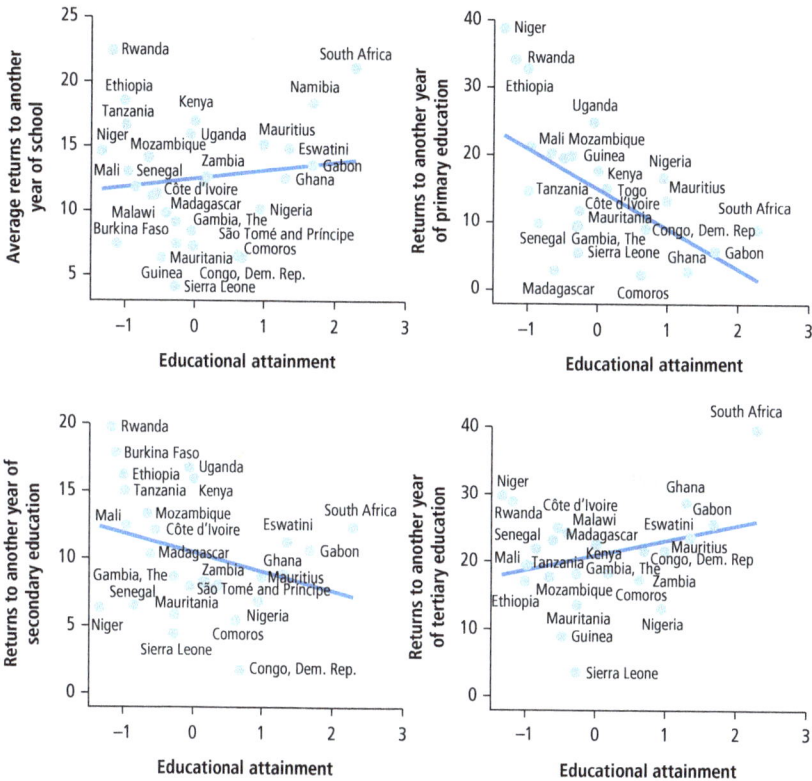

Source: Based on Montenegro and Patrinos 2014 estimates using labor surveys.
Note: The index of initial conditions is an indicator capturing contextual dimensions of a country's economic development deemed relevant to skills investments—namely, income per capita, economic structure (for example, share of value added and productivity in agriculture), link to external markets (for example, openness to trade and foreign investment), urbanization, and demographic transition (dependency ratio). Educational attainment is measured by the percentage of the population ages 25–29 with at least a complete primary education (some secondary and beyond).

Average returns to an additional year of education range from about 5 to 20 percent and tend to be higher in faster-transforming economies. This positive association is driven by higher returns to tertiary education (reaching or exceeding 20 percent) and lower returns to primary and secondary education (near an average of 10 percent) as economies transform and grow richer. A similar pattern, although less marked, is observed for the relationship between average returns by level of education and countries' educational attainment of young cohorts. The panels show a high dispersion in returns to education, which, as discussed later in the chapter, is related partly to differences across countries in the enabling policy environment for investments in skills to pay off.

Average returns to schooling tend to be lower for the self-employed and informal wage workers, although they are generally positive and economically significant. The results discussed only apply to wage work (and thus to a small fraction of employment in the region) since the data in Montenegro and Patrinos (2014) do not include self-employed (farm or nonfarm) or informal sector workers. However, Van der Sluis, van Praag, and Vijverberg (2005) conducted a systematic review of more than 100 empirical studies of the effect of education on performance in self-employment and entrepreneurship in low- and middle-income economies (one-third from Africa) and find that an additional year of schooling leads to an average 5.5 percent higher self-employment earnings, with higher returns for women and for workers in more agricultural countries. Country studies in the region often find lower private returns to education for the self-employed than for wage workers, for example, in Ghana, Kenya, Nigeria, and Tanzania, although returns are found to be similar for both types of workers in South Africa and Uganda (for Ghana and Tanzania, see Rankin, Sandeful, and Teal 2010; for Kenya, see World Bank 2016a; for Uganda, see Kavuma, Morrissey, and Upward 2015; for South Africa, see Koch and Ntege 2008; for Nigeria, see Uwaifo Oyelere 2008). Among wage workers, returns to schooling tend to be higher for those in formal jobs, including in the public sector. Yet the earnings premium to education for workers in self-employment is positive and economically significant. These results should be interpreted with caution, as the factors that drive the type of employment of an individual— the actual skills he or she possesses—generally also correlate with his or her potential earnings in any given job.

The earnings returns to schooling reflect in large part a payoff to the cognitive, socioemotional, and technical skills that more educated individuals acquire or possess. A recent study by Valerio et al. (2016) uses data with measures of reading literacy and other foundational socioemotional skills to estimate the earnings returns to these skills in several low- and middle-income countries. The data cover both wage and self-employed workers in urban areas. As figure 1.7 shows, the returns to literacy are very significant, particularly in Ghana and Kenya, the two African countries included in the study, where, on average, workers scoring 1 standard deviation above the mean measure of literacy enjoy hourly earnings about 30 percent higher. There are also positive returns to socioemotional (in Kenya) and technical skills that go beyond the level of education of individuals. The results in Valerio et al. (2016) imply that the average returns to schooling are reduced by about half after accounting for measured skills. This is consistent with findings from other international studies that a significant portion of the returns to schooling reflects the fact that education goes hand in hand with the acquisition of foundational and technical skills that enhance labor productivity (for example, Bowles, Gintis, and Osborne 2001; Heckman, Stixrud, and Urzua 2006).

The skills acquired through work experience also carry a significant payoff. Returns to actual years of work experience, which capture on-the-job skills acquisition of both specific technical as well as socioemotional skills, are positive and larger in low- and middle-income economies (Montenegro and Patrinos 2014). Given the low levels of schooling, on-the-job learning may be a relatively more important source of skills acquisition in low- and middle-income countries than in high-income countries. Figure 1.7 (panel b) illustrates the results from Montenegro and Patrinos (2014) showing a strong positive association between the returns to schooling and the returns to work experience. Returns to work experience for an individual tend to have an inverted U-shape. Earnings increase at a declining rate starting at about 2–4 percent, on average, for the first years of work experience up to the prime-age years (depending on the country and type of employment), after which earnings decline with each year of work experience. Work experience has also been found to correlate with the performance of small firms. For instance, Gokcekus, Anyane-Ntow, and Richmond (2001) find that, in addition to schooling, on-the-job training of an entrepreneur is associated positively with higher technical efficiency in a sample of microenterprise manufacturers of wood products in Ghana. This again underscores the potential contribution of on-the-job learning that takes places outside of school. This important source of skills formation should

Figure 1.7 Contribution of Literacy Skills and On-the-Job Learning to Earnings in Sub-Saharan Africa

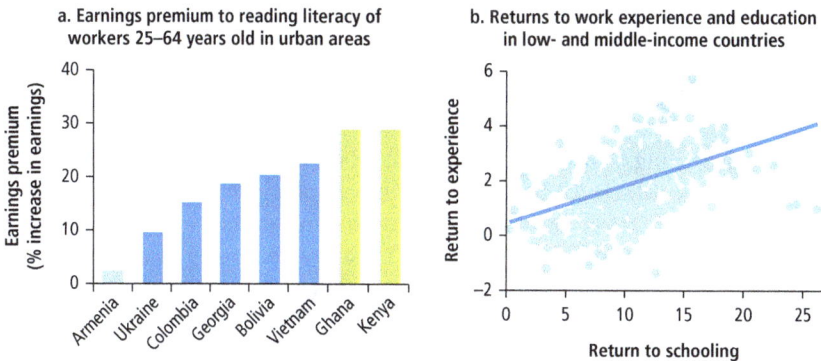

a. Earnings premium to reading literacy of workers 25–64 years old in urban areas

b. Returns to work experience and education in low- and middle-income countries

Sources: For panel a, Valerio et al. 2016, based on World Bank Skills Towards Employability and Productivity (STEP) Surveys (http://microdata.worldbank.org/index.php/catalog/step/about). For panel b, Montenegro and Patrinos 2014.

not be neglected. Chapter 5 discusses results from interventions that use cash grants and training to improve employment opportunities, which could build skills through on-the-job learning.

Socioemotional skills are important for entrepreneurship. Klinger, Khwaja, and del Carpio (2013) analyze data from 1,580 small business owners with loans from banks and microfinance institutions in Colombia, Kenya, Peru, and South Africa and find that entrepreneurs' business profits and repayment behavior are strongly correlated with their individual personality traits, which are often taken as proxies of socioemotional skills. For instance, conscientiousness, need for autonomy, persistence, achievement orientation, and honesty help to predict who is more likely to enter or perform better as an entrepreneur. De Mel, McKenzie, and Woodruff (2008) conclude that finance is not the sole constraint to growth of microenterprises in Sri Lanka. Their results support using reliable measures of socioemotional skills to screen prospective entrepreneurs for enterprise financing support. Also, to the extent that some of these skills (such as goals orientation) can be taught, they should be part of entrepreneurship training programs.

Contribution of Education and Skills to Productivity and Incomes in Agriculture

Education has been found to be a key determinant of the adoption of new technologies in agriculture. Recent literature has focused on how learning and risk aversion in the presence of credit and insurance market failures matter for the decision of farmers to adopt technologies and the outcomes of doing so. Farmers with more education are found to be more adept at learning about new technologies and adopting them (Foster and Rosenzweig 1995). This relationship probably reflects the fact that cognitive skills such as literacy and numeracy allow individuals to acquire and process information quickly not only on the availability of new technologies but also on their benefits and how to apply them in a given setting (Huffman 2001). Chapter 5 discusses some promising interventions to develop basic literacy among out-of-school youths and adults.

Social learning, which requires skills to relate to and communicate well with others, is an underappreciated factor for the technology adoption of smallholders in Sub-Saharan Africa. Farmers learn from their neighbors or from individuals in their network about the effect of adopting a new technology and then decide whether to do so (Conley and Udry 2010). Measures of individuals' social network are the strongest predictors of the adoption of key new technologies by U.S. farmers in the 20th century (Skinner and Staiger 2005). Social networks are found to be more important among Ethiopian farmers for the adoption of new technologies and harvest methods, such as fertilizer and improved seeds, than learning from extension agents (Krishnan and Patnam 2014; Liverpool-Tasie and Winter-Nelson 2012).

Other socioemotional skills related to goals (future) orientation, industriousness, flexibility, and perseverance are also potentially important for farmers' technological adoption. Farmers' ability to exercise their agency to decide what crops and production methods to adopt, to persist on effort, and to tolerate risks are considered central to understanding agricultural performance (de Janvry, Sadoulet, and Suri 2016). Several recent studies in Sub-Saharan Africa illustrate these relationships. Abay, Blalock, and Berhane (2017) analyze data from a survey of 7,500 Ethiopian rural farm households and find that farmers who reveal an internal locus of control (that is, who believe they have power over events and outcomes in their lives) are more likely to adopt new production methods, including the use of fertilizers, improved seeds, and irrigation. Laajaj and Macours (2017) surveyed 900 farmers in western Kenya and measured a wide range of technical (knowledge of best harvesting techniques), cognitive (for example, literacy, numeracy), and socioemotional (for example, the big-five personality factors) skills. While showing the difficulties of obtaining reliable measures of many of these skills in rural settings, their best estimates suggest that all of these skills are equally and independently correlated with farmers' productivity.

Figure 1.8 illustrates the results from two other studies. Frese et al. (2017) find that among 500 farm household couples in Malawi, female socioemotional skills related to perseverance, work centrality, and optimism are significantly associated with the adoption of tobacco (panel a), a profitable crop that is produced exclusively for export markets. Controlling for a number of socioeconomic and farm characteristics, a 1-standard-deviation increase in women's socioemotional skills is associated with a one-third higher probability of harvesting tobacco coupled with the use of productive inputs such as fertilizer and agricultural advice services.

In another study, Ali, Bowen, and Deininger (2017) use data from 1,200 rice farmers in Ghana to show that several socioemotional skills—related to individuals' motivation and approach to work tasks—are strong predictors of the adoption of transplanting, a more effective harvesting technique that is offered to Ghanaian farmers as part of the technology package in local extension programs but that few farmers adopt. Figure 1.8 (panel b) illustrates their results: the percentage of farmers predicted to adopt the technique is 34 percentage points higher for those who score among the top 10 percent in measured socioemotional skills compared with those who score in the bottom 10 percent. The effects are twice as large as those of the farmer's level of education, experience, and cognitive ability. These socioemotional skills also correlate with higher returns from adoption and technical efficiency in rice production. Farmers who score higher in polychronicity (flexibility to juggle multiple tasks) and optimism (belief that uncertain events will turn out well) are more likely to adopt

Figure 1.8 Correlation between Socioemotional Skills and Farm Productivity in Sub-Saharan Africa

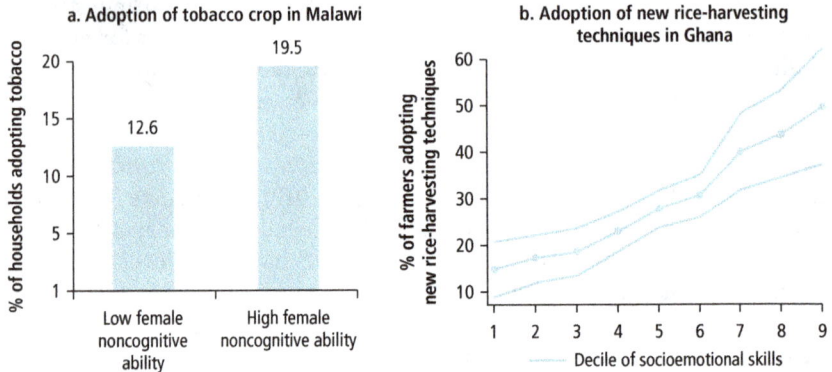

a. Adoption of tobacco crop in Malawi

b. Adoption of new rice-harvesting techniques in Ghana

Source: For panel a, Frese et al. 2017. For panel b, Ali, Bowen, and Deininger 2017.
Note: In panel a, low noncognitive ability refers to women who score below the median score of measured socioemotional skills (perseverance, work centrality, and optimism) and vice versa. In panel b, socioemotional skills include measures of work centrality, tenacity, achievement, power motivation, locus of control, impulsiveness, polychronicity, optimism, organization, and trust.

transplanting, while those scoring higher in polychronicity and work centrality (importance attached to work) achieve more production efficiency. A higher achievement orientation (inclination to act in pursuit of goals) and power motivation (inclination to plan, control, or influence others) correlates with higher benefits from adoption.

A greater focus on socioemotional skills can help to accelerate agricultural innovation. While these studies largely document correlations, they underscore the need to factor socioemotional skills into training and agricultural support programs in the region. These skills can help farmers to respond flexibly to new opportunities and to tolerate risks and ambiguity, learn from errors, persist in the pursuit of tasks in the face of obstacles, put themselves in unfamiliar situations, and navigate social interactions. These skills have received limited attention in agricultural support programs. They could be used to identify individuals most likely to adopt and disseminate technologies; such individuals could become peer agents of change in order to speed up the diffusion process. Chapter 5 discusses some interventions that try to develop socioemotional skills among youths and emerging results from rigorous evaluations.

Perceived Value of Education and Children's Foundational Skills

Sub-Saharan Africans put a high value on education, although views on the importance of education vary across the region, as well as views on whether school prepares children and youths well for work. In a 2013 Gallup survey of

32 Sub-Saharan African countries (Dago and Ray 2014), when people were asked to choose the most important factor that determines success in life, 40 percent cited education, 30 percent chose networks and connections, about 20 percent picked intelligence, and 10 percent said work ethics. However, beliefs differed significantly across the region. More Anglophone Africans (59 percent) believe in the importance of education than Francophone Africans (23 percent), while more Francophone Africans (49 percent) see networks and family connections as key to success. Across the region, nearly two-thirds of respondents said that they believe that schools (at the secondary level) do a good job of preparing students for the world of work, with responses ranging from 86 percent in Rwanda to 38 percent in Tanzania.

Sub-Saharan Africans differ from citizens in other regions in the value they attach to children's socioemotional qualities. Figure 1.9 shows data from the World Values Surveys (http://www.worldvaluessurvey.org/wvs.jsp) on the value that people around the world attach to the cultivation of socioemotional qualities in children (see also box 1.3). Some differences stand out. Overall, Sub-Saharan Africans value hard work[6] and obedience relatively more and value responsibility, independence, and, to a lesser extent, tolerance relatively less

Figure 1.9 Average Valuation of Children's Socioemotional Qualities in Sub-Saharan Africa and Other Regions

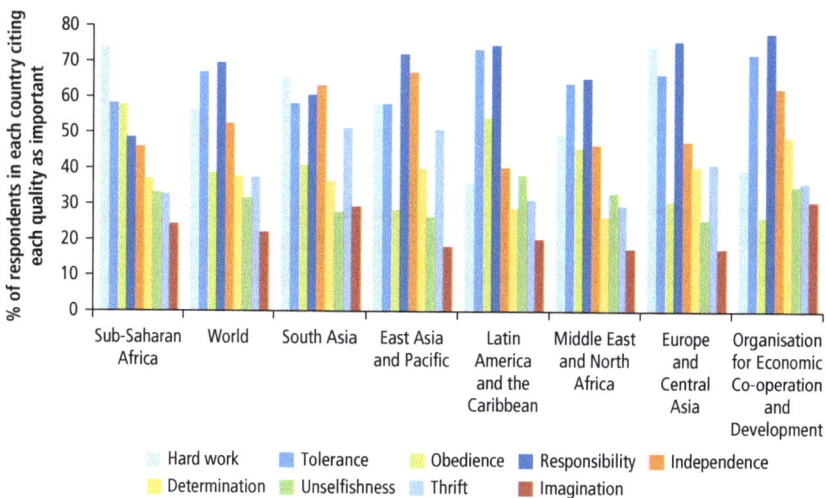

Source: Calculations based on Berkeley Center's World Values Surveys, most recent year.
Note: The following question was asked: "Here is a list of qualities that children can be encouraged to learn at home. Which, if any, do you consider to be especially important? Please choose up to five." The figure plots the average across countries in each region of the percentage of respondents citing a given quality.

BOX 1.3

Values Attached to Children's Socioemotional Qualities: The World Values Surveys

The World Values Surveys (http://www.worldvaluessurvey.org/wvs.jsp) is a global research project that collects data on people's values and beliefs in countries around the world, often spanning one to two decades. The analysis in this report uses data from the project for 89 countries for the most recent year, including 11 Sub-Saharan African countries: Burkina Faso, Ethiopia, Ghana, Mali, Nigeria, Rwanda, South Africa, Tanzania, Uganda, Zambia, and Zimbabwe. The countries' samples are said to be nationally representative, covering approximately 1,000 individuals ages 15 or older.

The results in the chapter pertain to the following question: "Here is a list of qualities that children can be encouraged to learn at home. Which, if any, do you consider to be especially important? Please choose up to five." The question was presented to respondents along with the following list of qualities: hard work, responsibility, determination and perseverance, independence, tolerance and respect for other people, imagination, obedience, unselfishness, thrift and saving money and things, self-expression, and religious faith. Because of data limitations or scope of the analysis, the last three qualities are not considered.

than other citizens of the world. These differences are particularly marked compared with citizens in East Asia and Pacific or high-income countries. For instance, about a third of Sub-Saharan African respondents ranked determination (akin to perseverance or grit, a skill said to be essential for long-term achievement) among the top five important qualities, far below the ranking of respondents in East Asia and Pacific and OECD countries.

Most of the differences in the valuation of children's socioemotional qualities reflect differences in the country context rather than differences in the socioeconomic characteristics of the population. The differences in the importance attached to socioemotional qualities of children may be a result of differences in socioeconomic and demographic characteristics of the respondents, such as level of income, education, age, and others. For instance, more educated individuals may attach a higher value to qualities such as determination and less importance to others like obedience. These valuations may change along with the development level of countries. Figure 1.9 shows the results of an exercise to pinpoint the role of these factors. It plots the predicted percentage of respondents in each country who cite each socioemotional quality as important against income per capita, after parceling out population differences in demographic and socioeconomic characteristics.

There are two main findings. First, country-level factors are very dominant, and differences in the valuation of children's socioemotional qualities are only weakly related to a population's characteristics. For instance, while individuals who are more educated and report higher socioeconomic status across the spectrum of countries are less likely to cite obedience as one of the five most important qualities, the relationship is weak. Second, the relationship between the valuation of children's socioemotional qualities and a country's GDP per capita varies (figure 1.10). As countries become richer, they are significantly less likely to view hard work and obedience as one of the five most important qualities. Most Sub-Saharan African countries fit into this pattern, with the exception of Ethiopia, where survey respondents tend to attach less importance to these qualities than expected for the country's income level. The association of other qualities with a country's income level is weaker. Individuals in richer economies are more likely to cite children's responsibility and, to a lesser extent, tolerance as important. The importance attached to other qualities is not related to a country's income level (results not reported).

Cultural factors are likely behind the variation in the valuation of children's socioemotional qualities. The sociological and anthropological literature suggests that history, religion, and geographic location inform a country's culture and traditions, exerting an important influence on what its people value (Amos 2013; Banda 2014; Kağıtçıbaşı 2007). Traditional societies with closely knit family relationships or collective cultures that are more likely to rely on material and emotional interdependence may place a higher value on obedience, whereas postindustrial Western societies, which tend to be more individualistic and to be characterized by familial relationships that are more independent both materially as well as emotionally, may place a higher value on independence. These factors may be behind some of the cross-country differences in valuation.[7] For instance, the valuation of socioemotional qualities for Burkina Faso and Mali (in Francophone Africa), on the one hand, and Ghana and Nigeria (in Anglophone Africa), on the other, tends to be similar for most qualities. These countries are not only close to each other geographically, and share some common historical and cultural traits. Likewise, the patterns of valuation in South Africa, Uganda, Zambia, and Zimbabwe (all Anglophone and geographically proximate) are also similar for most socioemotional qualities. In the case of South Africa, these similarities exist despite a much higher income per capita. Rwanda and Tanzania, in Eastern Africa, also display comparable valuation of most socioemotional qualities. Meanwhile, survey respondents in Ethiopia tend to attach a much higher importance to independence and lower importance to obedience and hard work than other Sub-Saharan African and low-income countries in the sample. This may be related to Ethiopia's distinctive historical, religious, and cultural heritage.

Figure 1.10 **Relationship between the Valuation of Children's Socioemotional Qualities and Countries' Level of Development**

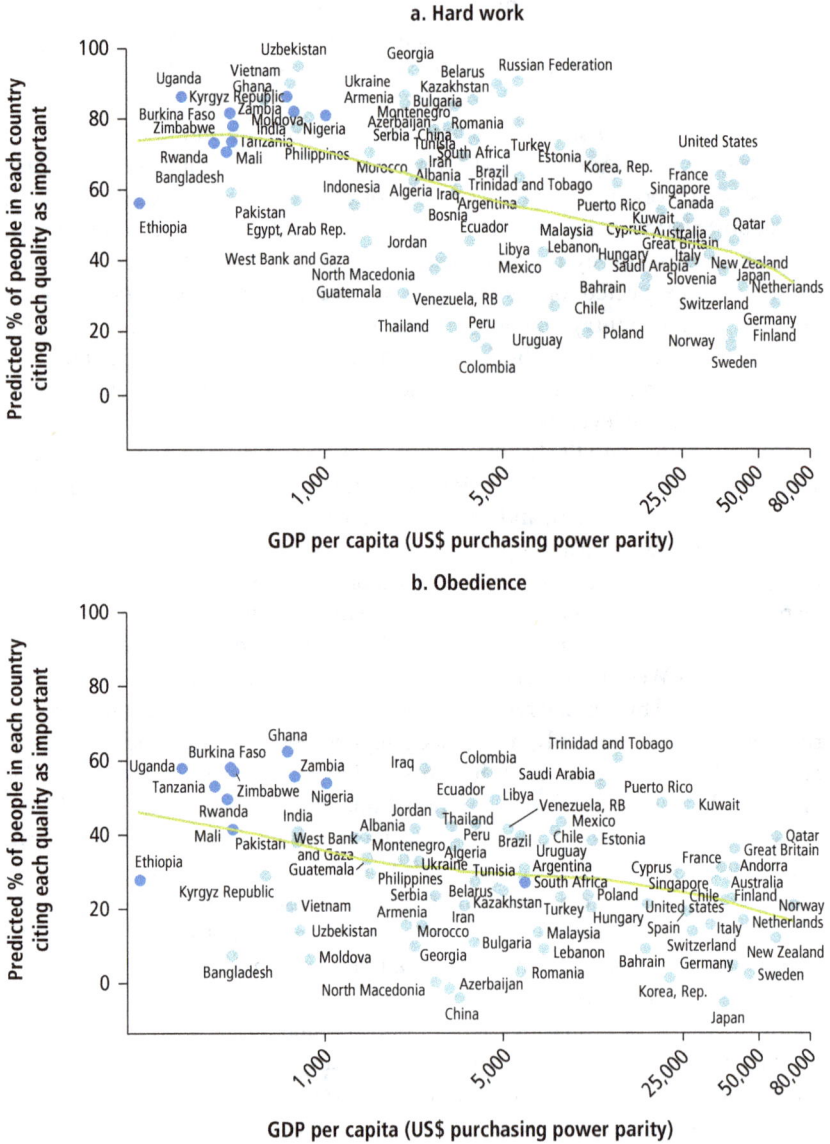

a. Hard work

b. Obedience

(continued next page)

Figure 1.10 (continued)

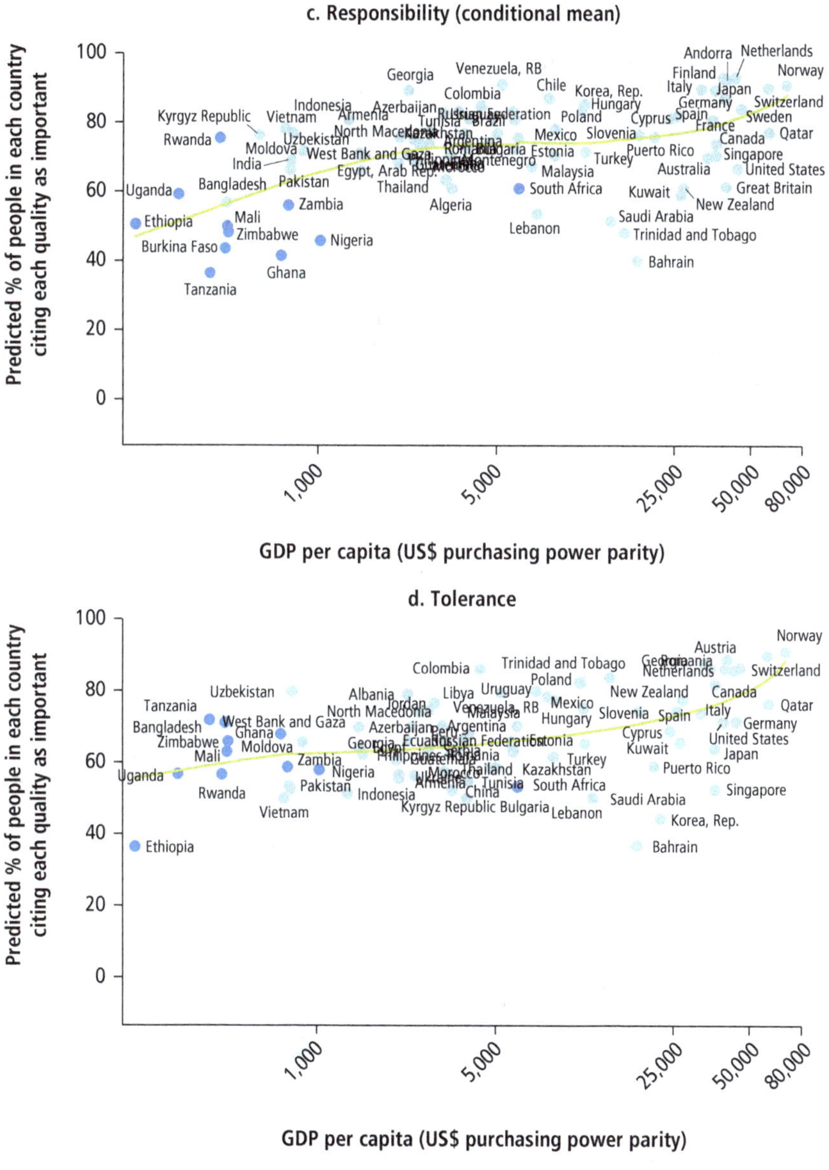

c. Responsibility (conditional mean)
Predicted % of people in each country citing each quality as important
100
80
60
40
20
0
1,000
5,000
25,000
50,000
80,000
GDP per capita (US$ purchasing power parity)
d. Tolerance
Predicted % of people in each country citing each quality as important
100
80
60
40
20
0
1,000
5,000
25,000
50,000
80,000
GDP per capita (US$ purchasing power parity)

Source: Estimates based on Berkeley Center's World Values Surveys, most recent year.
Note: Panels plot coefficients of the country fixed effects from an ordinary least squares regression of the probability of citing a specific quality among the five most important, controlling for several individual characteristics, including age, number of children, marital status, education level, and self-reported income and wealth status.

Some of the socioemotional qualities may have an instrumental value in economic outcomes. For instance, studies in both high-income and low- and middle-income economies have found the need for autonomy (independence) to be associated with entrepreneurial dispositions (Andreas and Frese 2007; de Mel, McKenzie, and Woodruff 2008; Klinger, Khwaja, and del Carpio 2013; Leutner et al. 2014). Cultivating such a skill may have payoffs that run against skills such as obedience. As noted before, other socioemotional skills are predictive of entrepreneurship performance. Some socioemotional skills such as self-regulation and social skills will arguably become more important in the context of a fast-changing and integrated world where self-learning and social interactions in diverse teams at work are ever more prevalent.

Policies can be used to encourage families and steer societal norms to nurture socioemotional qualities. Figure 1.11 illustrates the policy levers. Interactions with parents, caregivers, and educators as well as child-rearing practices and investments at home and school play a crucial role in children's socioemotional development (National Research Council and Institute of Medicine 2000). Parents, caregivers, and educators' beliefs and values influence which skills they are more likely to prioritize and, in turn, influence investments (both nonmonetary and monetary) in children's skills development. The value that parents and educators assign to socioemotional qualities, in turn,

Figure 1.11 Families and Socioemotional Skills: Policy Levers

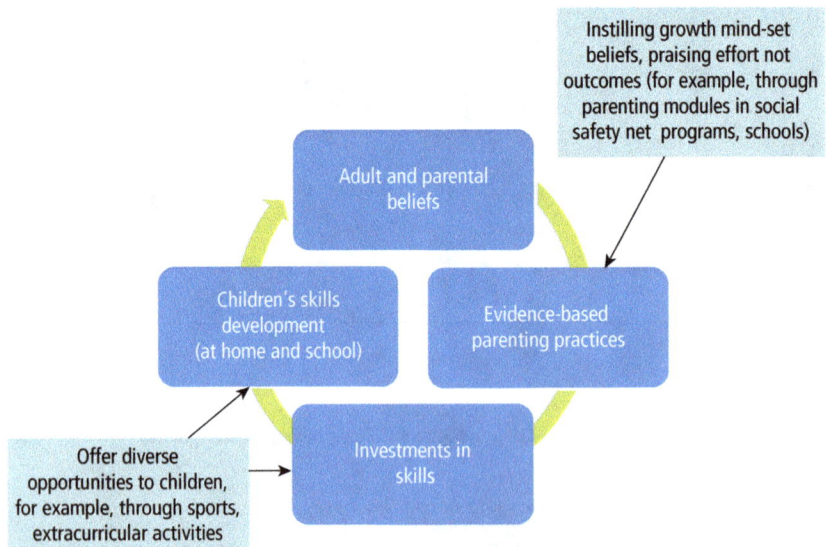

is influenced by societal values, which are themselves a by-product of cultural and socioeconomic contexts (Kağıtçıbaşı 2007). The process of skills development is self-reinforcing both within and across generations, because positive child outcomes encourage further investments and because stronger foundations are likely to have a positive effect on beliefs, practices, and investments when these children become parents (Cunha et al. 2006). The link between answers to the World Values Survey (http://www.worldvaluessurvey.org/wvs .jsp) and child-rearing practices has not been established. More research is warranted on how adult valuation of socioemotional qualities translates into the cultivation of skills at home and in school.

The success of initiatives to support effective parenting in Sub-Saharan Africa hinges on recognizing that child-rearing practices vary across the region's multicultural and heterogeneous societies and are linked to values and traditions. Although some socioemotional skills have an instrumental value, they do not necessarily have a higher intrinsic value independent of the context in which children grow up. It is important to document and build on existing practices of how communities care for and raise children and then to work with community leaders to understand the intrinsic value of some parenting practices and redirect them to others that the evidence supports as being more favorable to child socioemotional development (Garcia, Pence, and Evans 2008; Pence and Shafer 2006). For instance, to the extent that parents who prioritize obedience want their children to be "well behaved," they can learn about ways to foster children's own socioemotional self-regulation that can nurture children's self-regulated behaviors while encouraging their sense of autonomy. As discussed in chapter 2, a growing body of evidence suggests that parents, caregivers, and educators can learn about evidence-based child-rearing and parenting practices (such as praising effort, not intelligence), and such learning can be accomplished through parenting modules in social safety nets or through interventions in schools and extracurricular activities.

Skills and Economic Transformation in Sub-Saharan Africa

Policy makers in Sub-Saharan Africa need to invest in skills being mindful of the impacts of key global and regional megatrends that are bound to shape the region's economic transformation. African countries, like the rest of the world, face three megatrends that are reshaping the global economy, rapidly changing the demand for skills, and posing both opportunities and challenges for skills policies. These trends are population shifts (the promise of the region's demographic dividend and urbanization), the integration into potentially shifting global value chains, and new technologies (digitalization and, more broadly, technological and organizational change). These forces will shape the types of jobs available as well as the demand and the opportunities for skills acquisition, especially for new cohorts of Sub-Saharan Africans.

Population Shifts

The demographic dividend offers many countries in the region a unique opportunity to translate the human capital accumulation of young cohorts into a more productive labor force. As examined in detail in a recent report on Sub-Saharan Africa's demographic transition (Canning, Raja, and Yazbeck 2015), Africa is the region in the world with the greatest potential to reap a demographic dividend. As the share of younger cohorts in the working-age population rises and lower fertility rates leave more resources to invest in children's cognitive and socioemotional development and quality education, unskilled workers can become a lower share of the workforce. However, the larger cohorts of children entering and progressing through the education system pose a major challenge to the overall financing of educational expansion and the assurance of quality.

Urbanization, another population trend, has an important bearing on skills formation in Sub-Saharan Africa. The region is urbanizing quickly (figure 1.12), and more than one-third of the population already lives in urban areas. Continued mobility of labor to urban areas can improve the allocation of resources, facilitate a better match between workers and jobs, and ignite the forces of agglomeration that are critical for productivity growth (Lall, Henderson, and Venables 2017).

Studies in several countries point to potential spillovers that trigger a multiplier effect, whereby highly skilled jobs in leading economic activities raise local employment and income levels, mainly by increasing the demand for services. Estimates from Sweden and the United States show that one additional high-skill job in leading sectors indirectly generates between three and five jobs (Moretti 2012; Moretti and Thulin 2013). The size of the employment multiplier depends on several factors, including whether the workforce has the required skills for the jobs that can be created indirectly, as this affects the elasticity of the local labor supply. Furthermore, Moretti (2004) finds that firms' productivity growth in the United States was significantly higher in cities where the share of college graduates had increased more; productivity spillovers across industries were larger when firms were linked economically through value chains, inputs, or technology. Finally, U.S. historical evidence shows that the growth of urban centers is associated with an increase in jobs that use interpersonal skills more intensely (Bacolod, Blum, and Strange 2009). Skills policies across rural and urban areas in the region need to enable and adapt to these forces of urban agglomeration.

Figure 1.12 Urbanization in Sub-Saharan Africa and the Rest of the World, by GDP per Capita

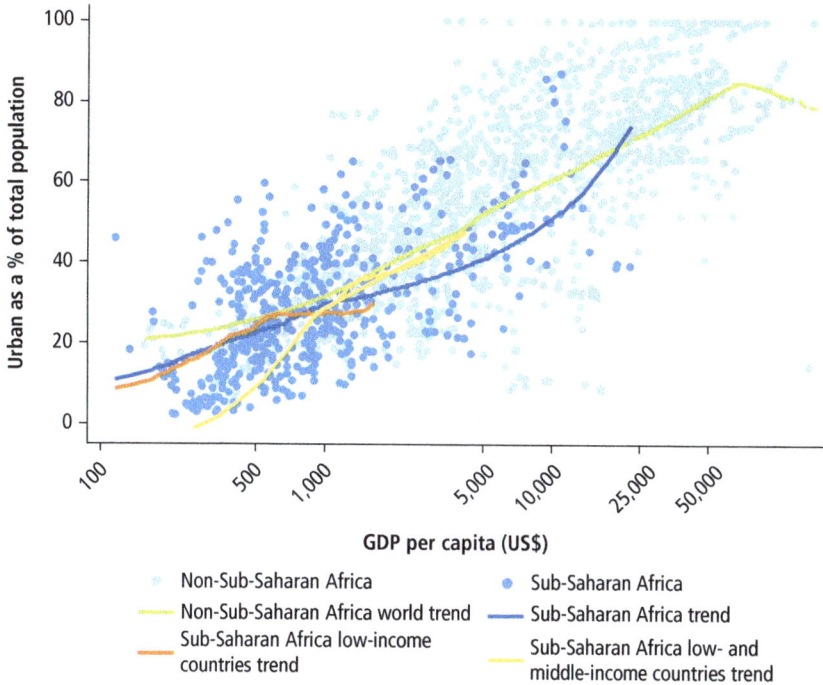

Source: Estimates based on World Development Indicators database and household surveys.

Integration with the Global Economy

The second trend is the increasingly interconnected nature of the global economy. Production in both manufacturing and services takes place in interlocked global value chains, in which China and other East Asian economies have managed to capture a lion's share of investments in export-oriented industries. This trend goes hand in hand with increased economic competition. In several countries, further integration into international product markets during the 2000s—including the commodities exports boom—is driving a steady shift in value added and employment toward export-based activities and services. Coupled with the global change in demand for skills, the creation and destruction of jobs will affect the demand for skills as firms modernize and turnover in declining sectors (for example, agriculture) gives way to expanding sectors (particularly services). This process may create mismatches in the supply of and demand for skills, which could be exacerbated as export-led growth gains importance and firms tap into newly developed higher-value-added and export-intensive activities.

New Technologies

The third trend is the impact of digital technologies and robots and the rapidly changing world of work. The demand for skills is being shaped by three factors: (a) the spread of ICTs and other non-ICT technologies associated with skill-biased technological change; (b) the move to more flexible forms of organizational and workplace practices associated with skill-biased organizational change; and (c) the relocation of all or some of the tasks involved in the production of goods and services to countries with lower unit labor costs associated with outsourcing or off-shoring, also known as "trade in tasks." New technologies risk destroying more jobs than they create, at least in the near term. In high-income and in some low- and middle-income economies, as there is a higher penetration of digital technologies, jobs involve less routine (repetitive) and manual tasks that can be easily automated and require more nonroutine tasks. "Jobs polarization" in the form of faster rising employment in high- and low-skill occupations and stagnation or decline in middle-skill has been documented in high-income countries and in some low- and middle-income economies.

Sub-Saharan Africa is not immune to the impacts of automation. There is some evidence of automation of routine tasks in middle-skill jobs in some low- and middle-income economies (figure 1.13). The *World Development Report 2016: Digital Dividends* estimates that—from a technological standpoint—in countries like Nigeria and South Africa, more than 40 percent of today's jobs may be at risk of being significantly transformed or replaced altogether by digital technologies over the next two to three decades (World Bank 2016b). Even if automation does not directly lead to the destruction of routine jobs in Sub-Saharan Africa, many of these jobs may disappear in countries like China before African economies can capture the related industries through lower labor costs. Just as critically, even when jobs are not destroyed, these technologies change the skills that are needed for work. With the cost of digital technologies falling exponentially, it is important for investments in the skills of tomorrow's cohorts of workers to be consistent over the long term with the key labor competencies needed in a dynamic labor market. This shifts the focus toward the tasks that workers actually do in a job and the set of skills required to complete these tasks. There is evidence from OECD and other low- and middle-income economies that, in a constantly changing economic environment, many jobs have become less routine and more interactive, with implications for skills requirements.

Opportunities and Challenges Created by Economic Transformation

These last two trends combined bring about the challenge of premature deindustrialization. This process involves a shrinking of manufacturing as a

Figure 1.13 Impact of Digital Technologies on the Skills Intensity of Employment in Select Countries

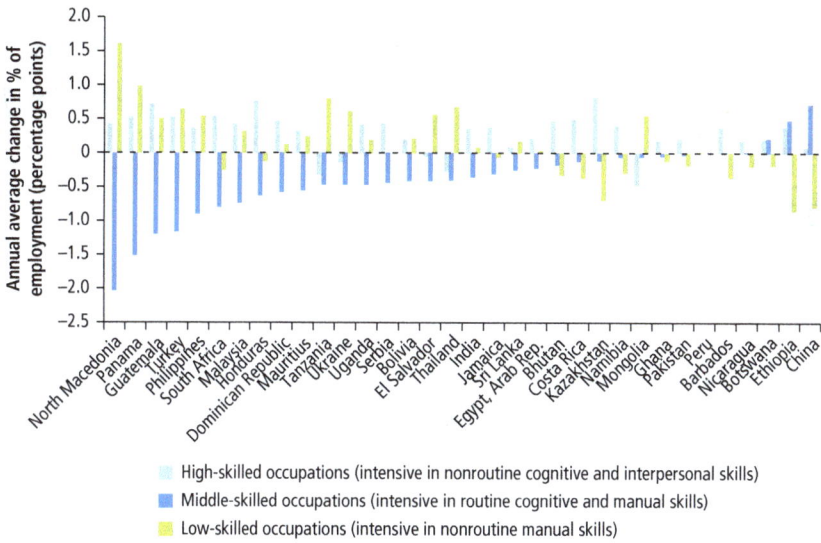

High-skilled occupations (intensive in nonroutine cognitive and interpersonal skills)

Middle-skilled occupations (intensive in routine cognitive and manual skills)

Low-skilled occupations (intensive in nonroutine manual skills)

Source: World Bank 2016b.

force of transformation to pull labor from agriculture (Rodrik 2016), as shown in figure 1.14. Increasingly, the engine for transformation and job creation in the region will come from services, often from informal self-employment and microenterprises. Jobs in the formal sector—and in manufacturing, in particular—will likely be limited over the next decades to come. More individuals will need to be prepared to create their own jobs, largely in the services sector. Education and training policies are thus pressed to find a balance so that workers have the skills suited to today's economic realities, those that are needed to enable economic transformation, and those that will allow them to adapt in fast-changing labor markets.

Despite growing urbanization, agricultural employment continues to be the largest source of employment and driver of poverty in the region. As the recent regional report on youth employment (Filmer and Fox 2014) argues, the economic transformation of most countries in the region is likely to be gradual so that employment in agriculture and other subsistence household enterprises will continue to be substantial (figure 1.15). Three-quarters of the poor are located in rural areas, and the vast majority rely on agriculture for their livelihoods. The *World Development Report 2008* found that GDP growth in agriculture is at least twice as effective in reducing poverty as nonagricultural growth (World Bank 2007). Higher agricultural productivity not only is a source

Figure 1.14 Peak in Share of Employment in Manufacturing, by Year and GDP per Capita

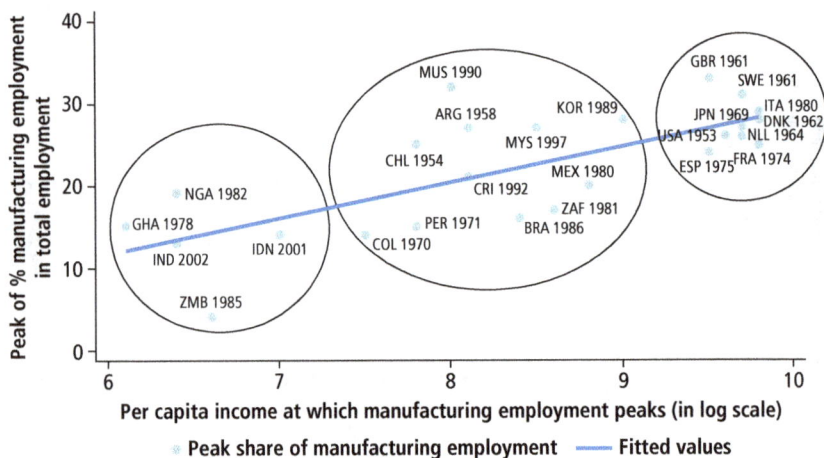

Source: Rodrik 2016.

of economic growth but also catalyzes the development of related industries—accounting, in some cases, for about a third of GDP—and the broader nonfarm economy. The links between agriculture and industry illustrate the importance of agricultural growth. Productivity growth in agriculture keeps food prices from rising, resulting in low wages that contribute to the competitiveness of nonagricultural sectors. Agricultural growth also generates multiplier effects on the rest of the economy.

The most successful development stories generally involve a transformation of agriculture. Many pathways are available to the rural poor, including employment in the rural nonfarm economy, movement toward higher-value agricultural activities, and rural-urban migration. Fostering a vibrant nonfarm economy, with investments in supporting skills, is at the center of any strategy. Ethiopia and Ghana are showing the way in the region.

The skills of the workforce will influence how these trends play out for the region's economic transformation. Meeting skills requirements in catalytic sectors is crucial for economic transformation in Sub-Saharan Africa. Economic transformation can ignite the forces of agglomeration critical for productivity growth and trigger a multiplier effect whereby higher-paying jobs in leading sectors can boost employment and income levels in other sectors linked through value chains or pure consumption spillovers. The global trends in technology and trade also create opportunities for higher productivity, including in agriculture, nonfarm self-employment, and household enterprises, either through

Figure 1.15 Share of Agricultural Employment and Sectoral Distribution of Employment in Sub-Saharan Africa and the World

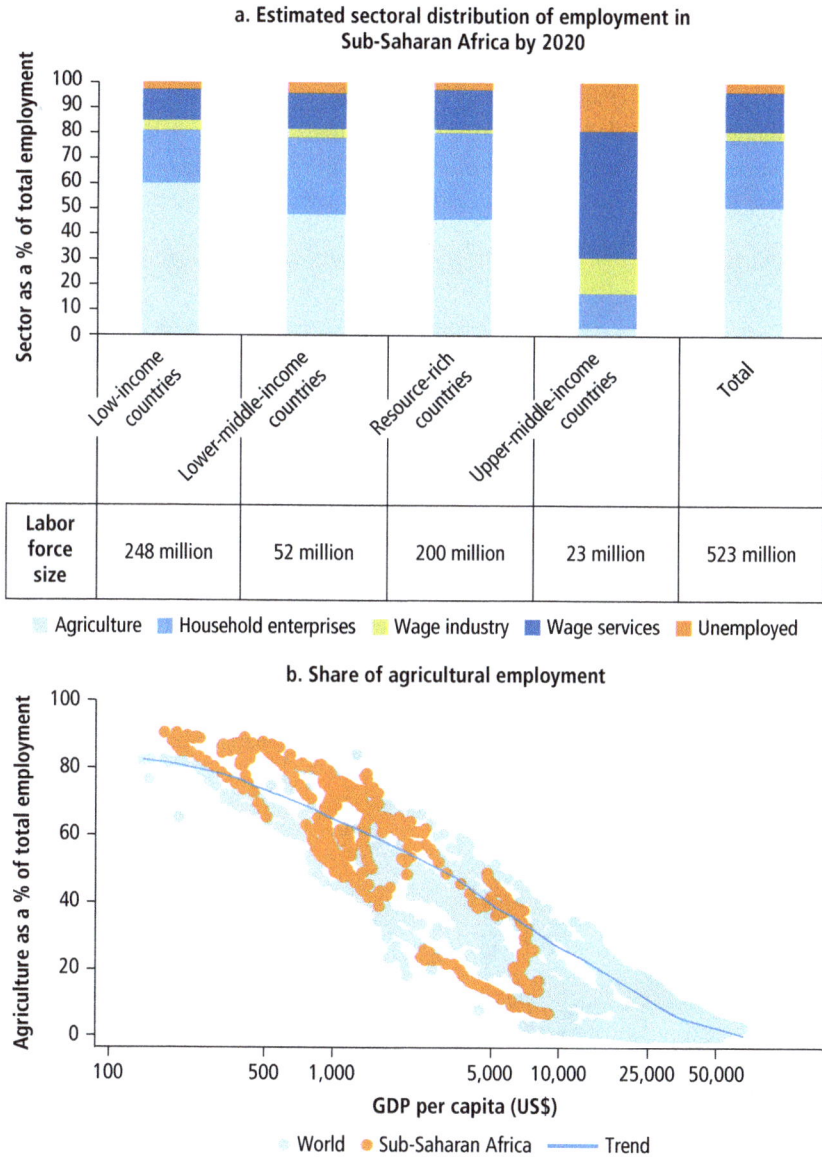

a. Estimated sectoral distribution of employment in Sub-Saharan Africa by 2020

	Low-income countries	Lower-middle-income countries	Resource-rich countries	Upper-middle-income countries	Total
Labor force size	248 million	52 million	200 million	23 million	523 million

Agriculture   Household enterprises   Wage industry   Wage services   Unemployed

b. Share of agricultural employment

World   Sub-Saharan Africa   Trend

Sources: For panel a, Filmer and Fox 2014. For panel b, data from the Groningen Growth and Development Centre 10-Sector Database.

outsourcing or through the use of digital work platforms. These opportunities have implications for skills requirements (World Bank 2016b). A labor force equipped with the required skills can engage faster with these technologies, allowing citizens to access new jobs (box 1.4). Consider a farmer scaling up production, diversifying into more profitable crops, or moving to nonfarm self-employment in rural areas or in the city. He needs to learn how to adopt new, more efficient harvesting techniques, how to sell his products, or how to acquire new vocational skills to make the most of his labor services. In order to acquire and use these technical skills, he needs a minimum level of literacy, numeracy,

---

BOX 1.4

Jobs, Tasks, and Changes in Demand for Skills in the Digital Global Economy

The rapid pace of changes in technology and in business organization and trade over the last two decades has spurred an active debate about the key labor competencies needed in a dynamic labor market. The skills content of jobs is heavily determined by the technologies used in production processes. As technology evolves, new occupations appear, and the required skill mix is changing constantly. The production and occupational structures of most high-income economies have undergone a steady shift in value added and employment toward knowledge-intensive activities and services (for example, finance, hospitality, retail). The ensuing changes in the demand for skills have been attributed primarily to three forces: (a) the spread of information and communication technologies, known as skill-biased technological change, (b) changes to more flexible forms of organizational and workplace practices, known as skill-biased organizational change, and (c) the relocation of all or some of the tasks involved in the production of goods and services to countries with lower unit labor costs, known as outsourcing or offshoring.

This process has led labor economists to go beyond the common use of educational attainment and experience as crude proxies of skills to adopt a task approach to skills and jobs. This approach focuses on the tasks that workers actually do in a job and on the set of skills required to complete these tasks. The earliest example of this task-based approach is the seminal study of Autor, Levy, and Murnane (2003). They measure the average task content of jobs and the associated skill requirements in order to uncover how changes in the U.S. occupational structure induce shifts in the demand for skills: new technologies reduce the demand for routine cognitive and manual tasks that can be easily automated and increase the demand for nonroutine tasks. New occupations with high content of analytical and interpersonal skills are becoming more prevalent, while occupations that are intensive in repetitive tasks are increasingly being performed by computers. Acemoglu and Autor (2011) connect this process to the literature on "trade in tasks" and technological change and derive implications for

(continued next page)

Box 1.4 (continued)

employment, skills demand, and earnings. One implication is a process of "jobs polar-ization" in the form of faster-rising employment in high- and low-skill occupations and stagnation or decline in middle-skill occupations, which is well-documented in numer-ous high-income countries, including most of Western Europe (Goos and Manning 2007; Goos, Manning, and Salomons 2009; Handel 2012).

In a more recent study, Autor and Handel (2013) extend the approach to measure task demands within an occupation as well across occupations. They collect data for a representative sample of U.S. workers on three broad tasks: cognitive, routine, and manual. Their findings illustrate the power of the tasks approach to understanding the labor market dynamics affecting skills demand. For instance, 24 percent of salary work-ers in their sample use higher-level math in their job, 37 percent regularly read docu-ments longer than six pages, and 29 percent predominantly manage or supervise others. Although education is a strong determinant of the task content of jobs, broad occupational categories are correlated more strongly with how frequently tasks are performed on the job than with worker's education level, and tasks remain significant predictors of wages after controlling for education and other worker characteristics.

This literature is enriching the understanding of the consequences of technological change and economic development for labor demand and skills policy and can enhance the design of education and training programs.

---

interpersonal skills (to learn from others), planning, resilience, and persistence to orient and sustain efforts in the face of failures in the transition. Solid foun-dational and technical skills are needed for individuals to engage in self-employment or wage jobs in dynamic economic sectors that can absorb rural labor and catalyze productive transformations.

Sub-Saharan African countries are not alone in facing these trends. Throughout the world, education and training systems are being challenged to ensure that workers are equipped with the skills that will allow them to adapt in rapidly changing labor markets. Some degree of skills mismatch is natural and unavoidable in every growing and restructuring economy due to adjustment costs and the delayed response of national educational systems. Especially in the context of fast-changing technology, changes in the skill structure of the labor supply tend to lag those of labor demand, even in a well-performing labor market. Retraining is often difficult for displaced groups because the skill requirements of newly created jobs differ significantly from those of the jobs that were destroyed.

In order to provide an overall framework for the more detailed analysis of the report, the next section examines the extent to which the opportunities for skills acquisition in the region have been keeping up with the needs of today and preparing for the challenges and opportunities of tomorrow.

The Progress in Skills Development in Sub-Saharan Africa

While the region has made big strides in enrollment in basic education in recent decades, the important goal of universal basic education remains elusive. In 1950, more than three-quarters of children in Sub-Saharan Africa did not go to school. By 2010, that figure had fallen to less than a third. According to UNESCO (2016), in the majority of countries, more than 80 percent of primary-age children are enrolled in school today. Yet, access to basic education remains incomplete. Although the number of out-of-school children in the region has fallen over the last couple of decades, 31 million primary-age children and nearly 57 million adolescents and youth of secondary-age were not attending school around 2014 (UNESCO 2016). More than 8 of every 10 primary-age children were enrolled in primary school, and 2 of every 3 adolescents were enrolled in lower-secondary school. But only about 55 percent of children complete primary education and less than 1 in 3 children complete lower-secondary education. Secondary enrollment and completion rates are still low, although growing. By 2014, overall only 4 of every 10 youths in the region were enrolled in upper-secondary school, and only 15 percent completed it. The overall rate of completion of primary school is much lower than in East Asia and Pacific, Latin America and the Caribbean, and other regions.

Educational Attainment

Advances in educational attainment in Sub-Saharan Africa have not been rapid enough to keep up with progress in other low- and middle-income regions. The region has fallen far behind the rest of the world in the educational achievement of its population. Figure 1.16 shows educational pyramids for Sub-Saharan Africa and other regions, and high-income economies. The desirable structure of educational attainment resembles a diamond, with a majority of the population completing basic education and building foundational skills and a smaller fraction of the population reaching tertiary education—university or tertiary technical and vocational education and training (TVET)—which will increase progressively as countries become richer. This is the pattern in most countries in East Asia and Pacific, a region that in 1950 looked like Sub-Saharan Africa today. Despite recent progress, Sub-Saharan Africa still has an educational pyramid with a wide base of low-educated adult population.

Sub-Saharan Africa risks falling even farther behind in educational attainment in the decades to come. Given current trends, UNESCO (2016) projects that by 2030 about 3 out of every 4 children will complete the full cycle of primary education, 6 out of 10 will complete lower-secondary school, and 4 out of 10 will finish upper-secondary school. It projects that only 8 countries in the region will achieve universal lower-secondary completion by 2030 if they expand at the fastest rate of progress ever observed in the region. This suggests

Figure 1.16 Evolution of Educational Pyramids in Sub-Saharan Africa and Other Regions, 1950 and 2010

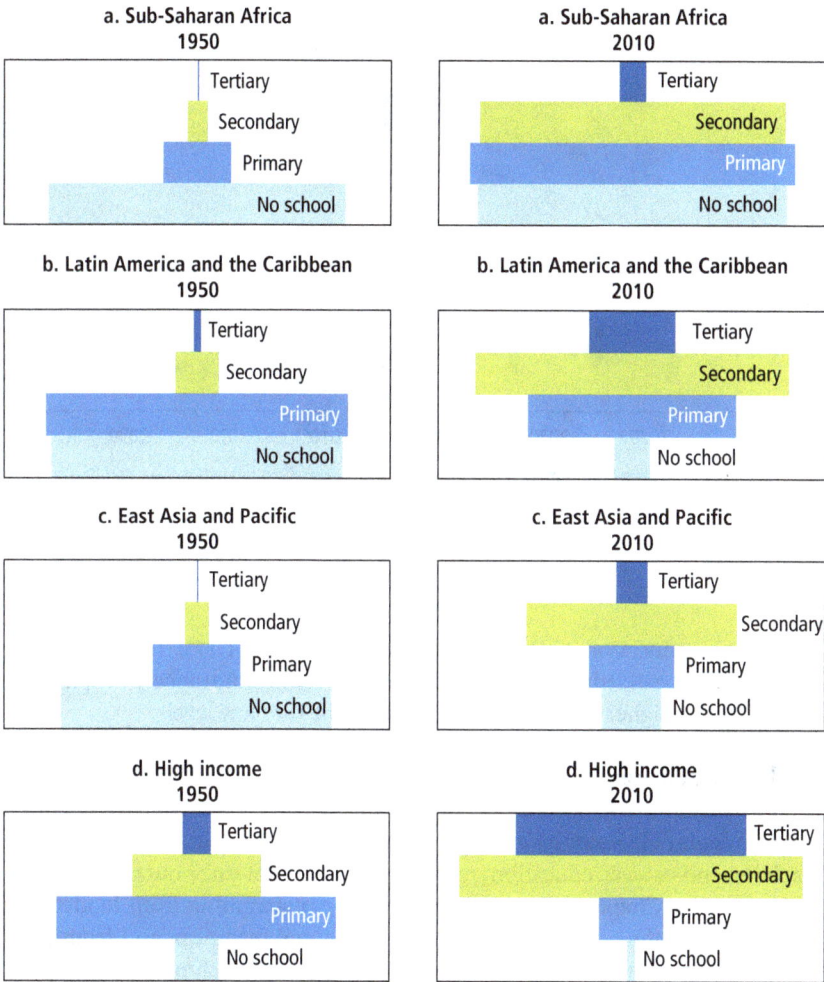

a. Sub-Saharan Africa 1950

Tertiary
Secondary
Primary
No school

a. Sub-Saharan Africa 2010

Tertiary
Secondary
Primary
No school

b. Latin America and the Caribbean 1950

Tertiary
Secondary
Primary
No school

b. Latin America and the Caribbean 2010

Tertiary
Secondary
Primary
No school

c. East Asia and Pacific 1950

Tertiary
Secondary
Primary
No school

c. East Asia and Pacific 2010

Tertiary
Secondary
Primary
No school

d. High income 1950

Tertiary
Secondary
Primary
No school

d. High income 2010

Tertiary
Secondary
Primary
No school

Source: Based on the data set of Barro and Lee 2013 (online update February 4, 2016).
Note: The graphs show the percentage of adults (ages 25–65) reaching each level of education (incomplete or complete).

that the speed of educational progress required to meet the Sustainable Development Goal of universal foundational skills will have to be unprecedented. Worryingly, at recent rates of educational progress, the region will continue to diverge from East Asia and Pacific and Latin America and the Caribbean over the next couple of decades in terms of completion rates of primary, secondary,

Figure 1.17 Projected Gap in Educational Attainment of the Workforce in Sub-Saharan Africa and Other Regions

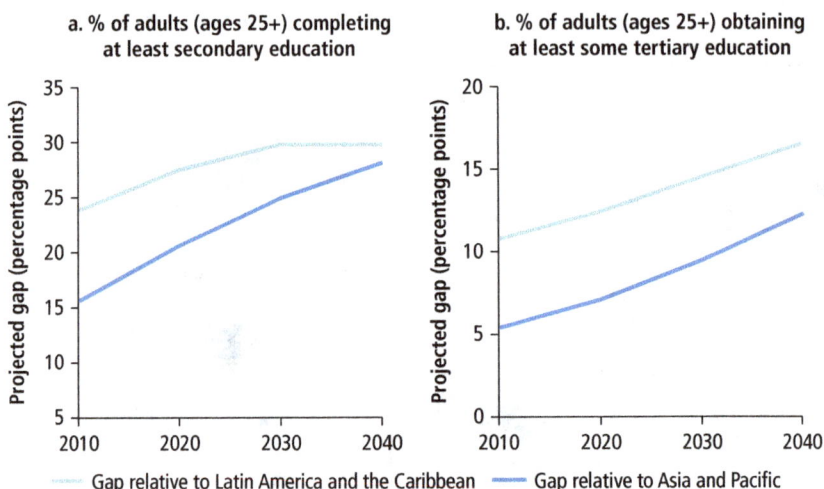

a. % of adults (ages 25+) completing at least secondary education

b. % of adults (ages 25+) obtaining at least some tertiary education

Gap relative to Latin America and the Caribbean ——— Gap relative to Asia and Pacific

Source: Based on data set of Barro and Lee 2013 (online update February 4, 2016).
Note: The gap is based on simple averages across countries (not population weighted). Asia includes both South (for example, India) and East (for example, China) Asia.

and tertiary education of the adult population (figure 1.17). The historically large gaps in basic education progress are the main hindrance to expanding enrollment in higher education from the current very low levels.

Skills Acquisition

Even when countries succeed in enrolling and keeping more children in school, most students fail to acquire even the most basic foundational skills. As children reach the end of basic education, more than half cannot carry out basic reading or math tasks. Chapter 2 analyzes the challenges stemming from inadequate investments in the early years, which hinder school readiness, and from poor educational quality, with big gaps in ensuring effective teaching.

The pressure is mounting. The growth of primary completion rates and population have been increasing the demand for secondary education across the continent. Between 1990 and 2010, the cohort of children ages 5–14 grew 65 percent in the region. Countries will need to construct new secondary schools, to ensure that they are well staffed and resourced, and to ensure that they actually produce learning. The next section examines the efforts of countries in the region to invest in skills, to satisfy the needs arising from the continuing expansion of education, and to tackle gaps in the skills of youths and adults already out of the school system.

Public Spending on Education in Sub-Saharan Africa

Countries in the region have made tremendous efforts over the last decade to step up their investments in education. Figure 1.18 presents a series of comparisons of public spending on education in Sub-Saharan African countries with the rest of the world. These investments are incomplete indicators of investments in skills: they do not cover investments in the early years of child development or in labor market training and agricultural support programs, and they do not account for private investments in education and other skills training by families and enterprises. Spending data on these areas are very sparse and not readily available on a comparable basis for most countries in the region. However, public education spending generally accounts for the bulk of investments in skills formation in countries where the public sector plays a major role in providing education and training services, as is the case in the region. A country's effort and priority given to education are gauged by the level of public education expenditure as a percentage of GDP and as a percentage of total government expenditure. Commonly used international benchmarks call for governments to invest 15–20 percent of total public expenditure and 4–6 percent of GDP on education.

Figure 1.18 Average Public Spending on Education in Sub-Saharan Africa and Other Regions

a. Education spending as % of GDP

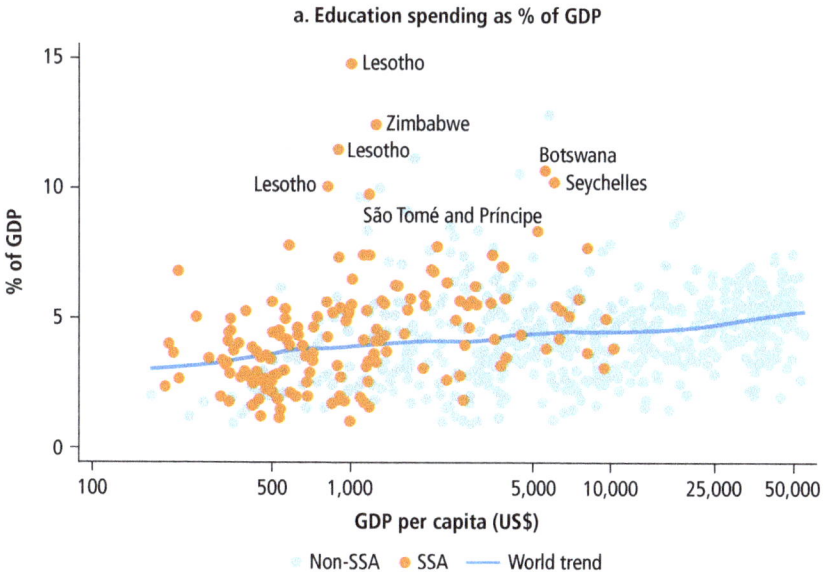

(continued next page)

Figure 1.18 (continued)

b. Education spending as % of total spending, 1995–2015

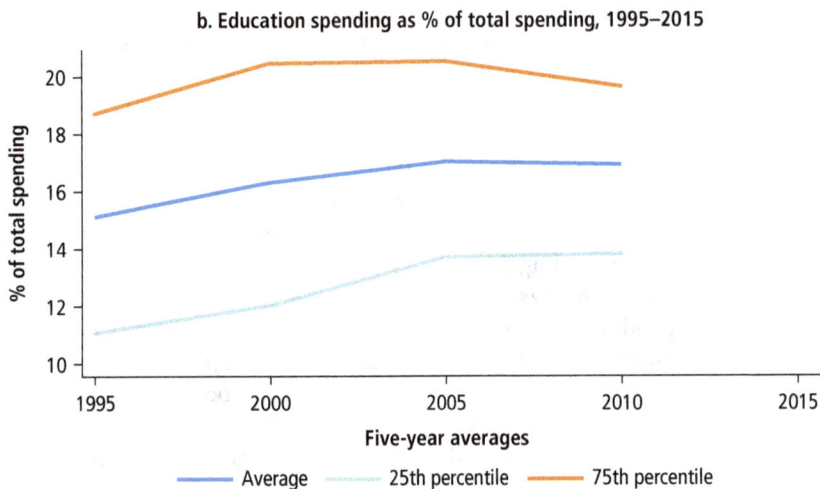

c. Education spending, by level of education

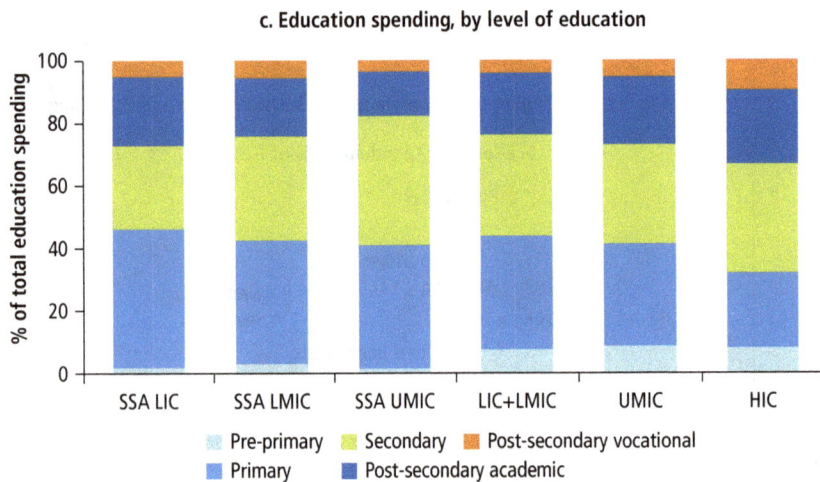

(continued next page)

Figure 1.18 (continued)

d. Education spending per student on tertiary education

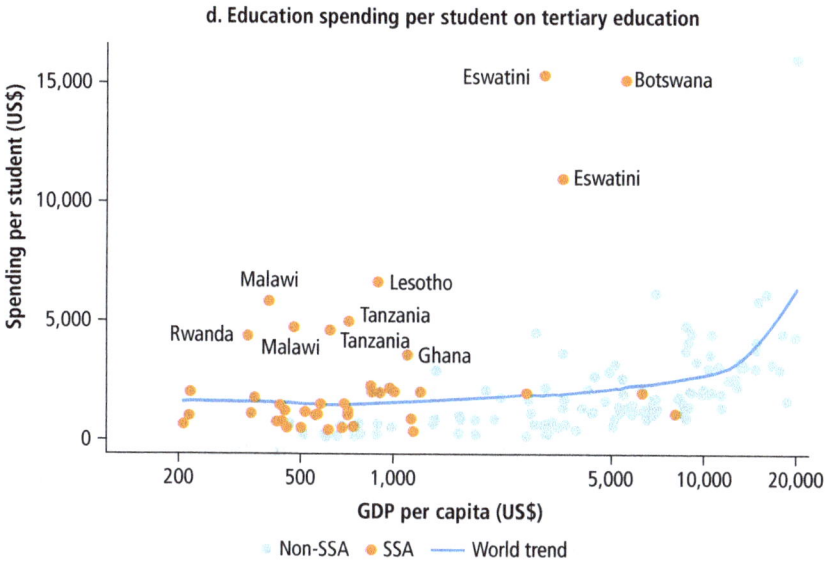

Source: Estimates based on United Nations data.
Note: HIC = high-income countries; LIC = low-income countries; LMIC = lower-middle-income countries; SSA = Sub-Saharan Africa; UMIC = upper-middle-income countries. Panels a and d use all available data during 1990–2015 (since 1970 for spending as percentage of GDP), so some countries have multiple data points. The evolution of public spending is based on the average of the latest three points in time over the last decade.

For the most part, countries' level of spending is commensurate with what is affordable and what can be expected. Overall, Sub-Saharan Africa already devotes significant public resources to education. On average, Sub-Saharan African countries allocate about 18 percent of total public spending and 5 percent of GDP to education, higher than the spending ratios in other low- and middle-income regions. That is, countries in the region devote a relatively high proportion of resources to education, despite their low GDP per capita and competing demands for infrastructure and public services that also are important for economic growth and well-being. This has been shown by detailed analyses of public spending in the region, such as UNESCO (2011) and the Global Education Commission (2017).

The region increased spending the most among low- and middle-income regions over the last decade. Real public spending rose, on average, by about 6 percent a year and by 0.7 percentage point of GDP among countries with available data during the last decade. This expansion of education expenditure allowed countries to maintain or even increase the expenditure per pupil while they were expanding enrollment in basic and even tertiary education. Currently, spending per student on basic education is commensurate with the levels in other low-income countries.

There is, of course, variation in spending efforts across countries. As evident in figure 1.18, the average figures mask heterogeneity in public spending across countries. Public education spending ranges from about 11 to 28 percent of total government spending and from as low as 2 to as much as 15 percent of GDP. Some natural-resource-rich countries can afford and need to step up their education spending (in terms of GDP per capita and overall public expenditure), while also improving efficiency. Several lower-income countries still have room to step up spending and will likely have to leverage external support and public-private partnerships (PPPs) to close the gaps in service provision, including in primary and secondary education.

For most countries, it is unrealistic to count exclusively on increased public investment in skills. Given that skills-building efforts need to expand, all countries need to improve the efficiency of public spending. As discussed throughout the report, countries need to establish stronger accountability mechanisms, such as better financial management and reliable education management information systems to cut waste and reduce the costs of inputs and infrastructure spending. As discussed in chapter 2 of this report, of great importance are efforts to scale up effective interventions to enable teachers to spend their time in effective teaching and tackle the systemic causes of absenteeism. To address the huge skills gaps of the out-of-school youth and adult population, discussed in chapter 5, there is also room to leverage current investments in cash transfer programs and training imparted through agricultural extension services.

Moreover, there is room to reallocate public education expenditures to prioritize foundational skills and disadvantaged groups. Countries can improve the targeting of resources to foundational skills and families in greater need. Although the region already devotes most public spending to basic education, resources devoted to preprimary education account for just about 0.3 percent of education spending (figure 1.18). As discussed in chapter 2, many countries have too high child stunting rates and need to step up investments in effective interventions such as prenatal care and cash transfers tied to health and nutrition services. In order to create room for this additional spending, chapter 4 argues that countries can reduce higher education subsidies for the well-off, implement selective cost recovery, expand student loan programs when the conditions for their success are met, and leverage social impact bonds. Public spending on postsecondary technical and vocational education and higher education can be targeted to disadvantaged groups on the basis of merit and give greater weight to fields of study with potentially greater externalities for growth and productivity such as science, technology, engineering, and mathematics as well as agriculture.

Finally, countries need to crowd in private sector investments for skills building. PPPs can help to crowd in resources to address infrastructure and service needs, particularly to expand secondary education. Private provision of education has made headlines in recent years, including the emergence of chains of for-profit schools and the provision, by some governments, of public resources to private schools through PPPs. As discussed in chapter 2, what matters the most is that the state guarantees access to quality education for all children and youths. In environments where public provision is severely constrained, private schools can help fill the gap but need to have proper oversight to ensure that they achieve learning results. As noted, workplace learning and on-the-job training (OJT) are an important source of skills formation. Chapter 5 finds that firms in Sub-Saharan Africa tend to invest less in OJT than firms in other regions. The potential reasons for the lower incidence of OJT are multiple and likely vary across countries. Improvements in infrastructure, the business environment, and governance could lead to increases in OJT. To the extent that market failures, such as the credit constraints of firms, are important, there may be a role for public sector interventions aimed at incentivizing on-the-job training through tax and spending incentives.

Skills Priorities for Sub-Saharan Africa: A Framework and Country Typology

Based on the preceding discussion, the chapter now proposes a policy framework and country typology to provide a unifying thread across the chapters of the report and to distill skills priorities for education and training policies in the region. A smart skills development strategy requires figuring out which skills are needed, for what, who needs them, and how they can be developed at the right time and in the right way. Figure 1.19 illustrates the framework aimed at guiding priorities for investments and policies to build skills through early child development (ECD) and through education and training. It illustrates the interrelationship across overarching policy goals of skills policies, the link between these goals and the traditional objectives of the education and training system, and the role of the various actors involved in skills building, namely, families, government, and the private sector (both employers and private providers). It encapsulates three main considerations.

The first guiding principle is that there are three main aims of policies and investments in skills. The first goal is accelerating productivity growth and economic transformation by reallocating productive resources and tapping

Figure 1.19 A Framework for Skills Policy Priorities in Sub-Saharan Africa

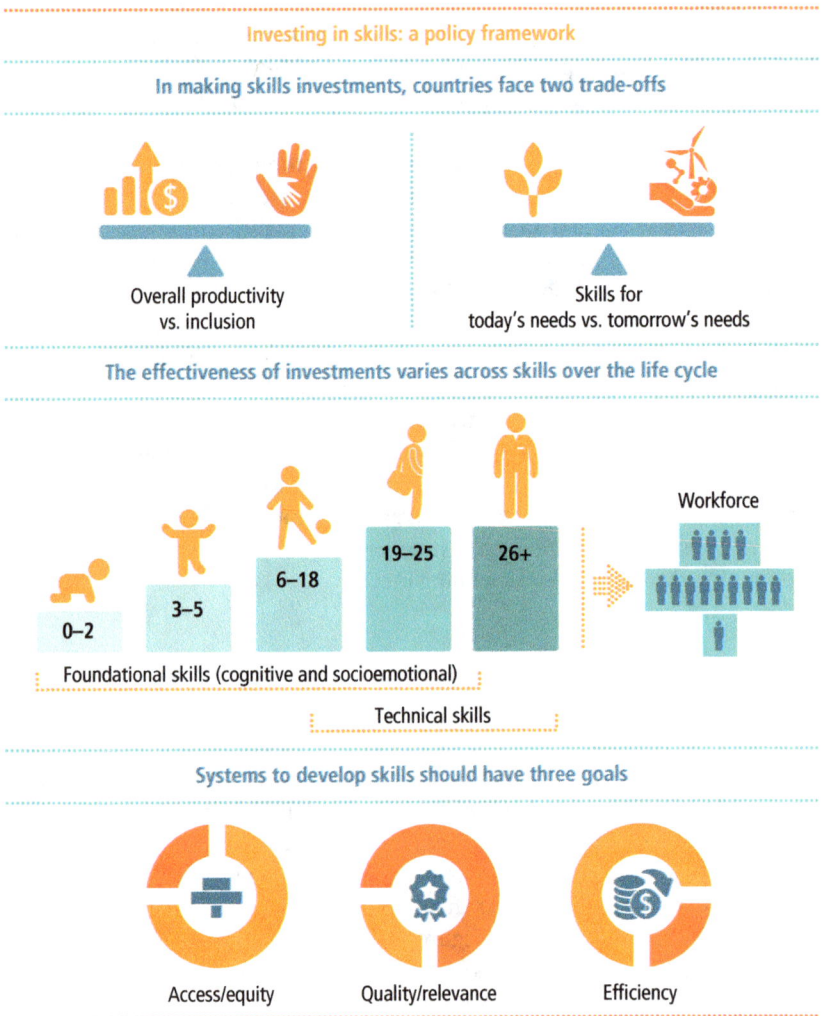

Investing in skills: a policy framework

In making skills investments, countries face two trade-offs

Overall productivity
vs. inclusion

Skills for
today's needs vs. tomorrow's needs

The effectiveness of investments varies across skills over the life cycle

0–2

3–5

6–18

19–25

26+

Workforce

Foundational skills (cognitive and socioemotional)

Technical skills

Systems to develop skills should have three goals

Access/equity

Quality/relevance

Efficiency

new technologies. The second goal is enhancing social inclusion through employability and earnings opportunities, particularly for the poor. And the third goal is ensuring the adaptability and resilience of individuals and the workforce to navigate economic and job changes in fast-changing labor markets.

In pursuing these goals, policy makers need to reckon with two potential trade-offs in skills investments. The first trade-off is between investments in skills with greater potential to maximize productivity gains and grow the economy and investments in skills aimed at economic inclusion through livelihoods. That is, the trade-off is between investing in skills needed for leading sectors in transforming economies and investing in skills that cater to the needs of today's largely agrarian, self-employment-based economies. The second trade-off is between investing in skills that are needed today and investing in skills that will be needed in the future. That is, there is a trade-off between investing in skills for new cohorts (today's children) and investing in skills for the current stock of workers (the out-of-school young and adult population); there is also a trade-off between investing in skills that may help individuals to transition faster into the jobs of today and investing in skills that may help them to adapt in a rapidly changing world of work. These trade-offs are related but distinct and will be a consideration in many, but not all, decisions regarding skills investments.

The first trade-off involves determining the focus of skills investments for the current working-age population, that is, among youths and adults. On the one hand, there is a need to meet the skills needs of catalytic sectors—through secondary or tertiary TVET as well as higher education—as these sectors are crucial for achieving economic growth and for igniting economic transformation driven by productivity growth through intersectoral labor relocation (for example, out of agriculture). This investment can boost higher-paying jobs in leading sectors and trigger a multiplier effect on employment and incomes in other sectors linked through value chains or consumption spillovers. At the same time, since this transformation will be gradual, many workers still need skills—provided through adult education and training and other labor programs—that are tied to employment and earnings opportunities in agriculture and nonfarm self-employment and household enterprises.

The second trade-off recognizes that, although it is always more cost-effective to invest earlier, within a given resource envelope, there is a need to strike a balance between investing in new cohorts and investing in the current stock of workers. On the one hand, there is a balance to strike between investments in ECD and the basic education of today's children and investments in upper-secondary and postsecondary education and training of today's youths and adults already outside the education system. On the other hand, both among new cohorts and the current working-age population, investments need to strike a balance between focusing on foundational skills needed for further learning and more adaptable working lives and focusing on narrower technical and vocational skills that facilitate the school-to-work transition but may quickly become obsolete. This trade-off is relevant in deciding when to track students into vocational tracks in lower-secondary or upper-secondary education, as well as how much programs for youths and adults should remedy gaps in foundational literacy, numeracy, and socio-emotional skills.

The second consideration is that multiple skills are needed to achieve balanced policy goals in modernizing economies. As discussed before, these skills include broadly (a) foundational cognitive, socioemotional, and digital skills and (b) technical or job-specific skills, including management skills. These skills are important for both new cohorts of future workers (those of school age and youths still in the education system) and the current stock of young, middle-age, and older adults already outside the formal education system. A balanced skills portfolio, therefore, encompasses investing in foundational, cognitive, and socioemotional skills for infants, toddlers, and teenagers and in technical skills for youths and adults; it also encompasses the reinforcement of skills through on-the-job training, labor training, and education programs for youths and adults.

Finally, the third consideration is that policy makers need to prioritize skills investments over the life cycle of individuals guided by the three traditional objectives of education and training systems. That is, in managing the potential trade-offs across policy goals, investments and policy reforms need to pursue *equity* for assuring wide access to opportunities for skills acquisition, *quality* for assuring learning and relevance by meeting appropriate standards and responding to labor market demand, and *efficiency* for assuring the financing and provision of education and training that deliver value for money.

Governments in Sub-Saharan Africa have to make hard choices among pressing and competing skills investments and should set priorities tailored to the country context. Education and training policies in Sub-Saharan Africa are, therefore, pressed to strike a balance among skills attuned to today's economic realities, those needed to enable these economic transformations, and those needed for workers to adapt flexibly in a fast-changing world of work. Priorities will depend on a country's initial skill levels, state of economic transformation, and policy environment. In order to guide more specific policy priorities, the report operationalizes these dimensions as follows: current skill levels (percentage of the working-age population with at least some secondary education), state of economic transformation (current income per capita, share of employment in agriculture, and importance of natural resources), and the enabling environment for reaping the returns to skills investments (investment climate as proxied by the World Bank Doing Business database). Figure 1.20 illustrates these dimensions for countries in the region, using the country's GDP per capita as a proxy for the state of economic transformation because it correlates highly with the share of employment in agriculture for which data are not available for all countries.

For illustrating skills priorities, the report distinguishes between five groups of countries:

- *Advanced in transformation and reformers* (for example, Botswana, Mauritius, the Seychelles, South Africa). These are the upper-middle to high-income

Figure 1.20 Skills Challenges in Sub-Saharan Africa, Educational Achievement, by Countries' Stage of Economic Transformation and Policy Environment

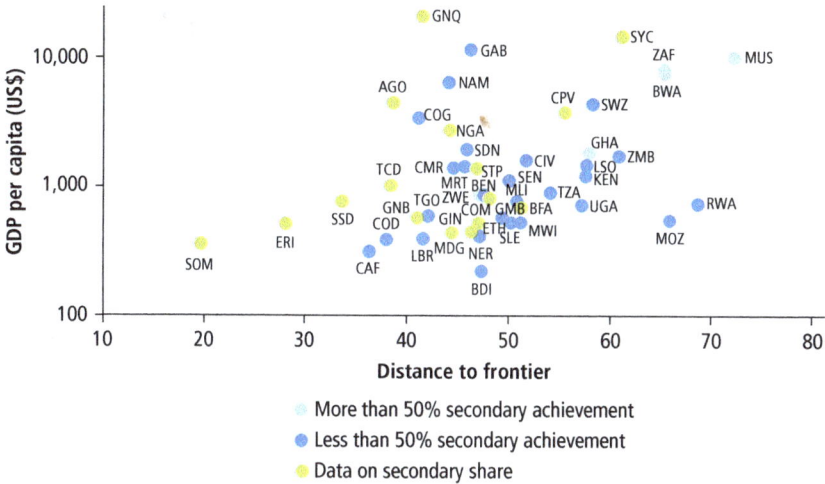

Source: Estimates based on World Development Indicators database for GDP per capita (most recent year, constant US$) and World Bank Doing Business 2015 data for distance to frontier (best business environment).

countries in the region that have made the most strides in reallocating labor out of agriculture and into more productive activities and in implementing reforms to improve the business environment for the private sector. These countries are better placed to reap the returns to investing in postsecondary technical skills through TVET, higher education, and OJT.

- *Transforming but lagging in reforms* (for example, Ghana, Namibia). These countries have made progress in moving labor out of agriculture and growing their economies, but they need to ramp up their economic and regulatory reform efforts as they continue to invest in postsecondary technical skills.

- *Natural-resource-rich and lagging in reforms* (for example, Angola, Cameroon, the Republic of Congo, Gabon, Mauritania, Nigeria). These countries comprise the natural-resource-rich economies in the region, which, while richer, are less diversified. For the most part, they also lag in reforms. They can afford to invest in postsecondary technical skills tied to the needs of natural resource and related sectors and use the derived rents to diversify their economies.

- *Lagging in transformation but reformers* (for example, Mozambique, Rwanda). These countries have made significant efforts to improve their business environment, although they lag in their economic transformation. They can carry out selective investments in postsecondary technical skills closely tied to catalytic (growth potential) sectors and leverage partnerships with the private sector, but they still need to devote great attention to improving the skills of youths and adults to improving earnings and livelihoods in low-productivity sectors.

• *Lagging in both transformation and reforms* (for example, the Central African Republic, the Democratic Republic of Congo, Guinea-Bissau, Somalia). These countries have a substantial pending policy agenda in terms of creating a business environment that can spur private investment, reward and incentivize skills investments, and achieve sustained economic growth and productive transformation. More than in other countries, they can prioritize investing in supporting livelihoods for inclusion and social cohesion.

The country groups are meant to illustrate policy priorities along a continuum. Rather than box countries in rigid categories, the country typology is meant to illustrate key strategic directions for priorities in the region. Rapidly transforming economies need to pay more attention to the adaptability and reskilling of the workforce. Countries that have good business-enabling environments will reap higher returns from investing in tertiary and other skills that galvanize economic dynamism. Low-income countries affected by fragility and conflict will realize a premium from skills to improve livelihoods and avoid poverty traps that may hinder economic growth. Countries that start off with low basic education attainment (and low foundational skills) among young cohorts face large opportunity costs from investing in tertiary and adult skills.

In managing the trade-offs in skills investments, countries should leverage the strengths and resources of multiple actors. Coalitions of investors—namely, families, government, and the private sector, both employers and private providers—are vital to making the most of investments in the early years, in education, and in training. The various actors have distinct and complementary roles. Families can actively invest in and nurture children's cognitive and socioemotional development by providing quality care and parenting and by holding schools accountable for effective service delivery. The private sector can participate effectively in service provision to enhance access and quality, invest in OJT to build skills, engage with education and training providers to ensure that programs are aligned with their needs, and actively engage in national social dialogue to prioritize skills development and reforms to create an enabling policy environment for skills investments to pay off. Skills formation is plagued by many market and coordination failures (Almeida, Behrman, and Robalino 2012). The public sector has a crucial role to play in ensuring equity and addressing these market and coordination failures through investments and complementary policies that ensure individuals' Readiness (foundational skills), Opportunities (equitable access), and Incentives (complementary enabling and regulatory policies, information on returns) to materialize the ROI for skills investments and support the most vulnerable individuals who fail to acquire critical foundational skills.

Achieving substantial progress in skills building in Sub-Saharan Africa will require enacting systemwide change. As elaborated in *World Development Report 2017: Governance and the Law* (World Bank 2017), many successful small-scale programs and local reforms fail to achieve the desired impacts at scale. Achieving more equitable access, quality, relevance, and efficiency in skills-building systems cannot hinge on just scaling up "best practices." There is a need to pay attention to the governance environment in which scaling-up takes place. Skills development is a multisectoral endeavor and requires coordinated policies. Broadly construed, skills are "everyone's problem, but no one's responsibility," as is commonly said of nutrition policies. Multiple agencies at the central and local levels are involved in skills development strategies. Therefore, to achieve broad and sustained results, policies and reforms need to establish credible commitment, support coordination, and promote cooperation among all actors. To this end, they must tackle the politics of policies and create the incentives to align the behavior of all stakeholders to the pursuit of national skills development goals.

The rest of the report examines skills building over the three stages in the life cycle as follows:

- *Chapter 2.* Developing Universal Foundational Skills
- *Chapter 3.* Building Skills for the School-to-Work Transition
- *Chapter 4.* Building Skills for Productivity through Higher Education
- *Chapter 5.* Addressing the Skills Gaps of Out-of-School Youths and Adults through Continuous and Remedial Education and Training.

Each chapter addresses a set of specific questions, drawing on original analysis and synthesis of existing studies in order to explore (a) how the skills appropriate to each stage of the life cycle are acquired and the market and institutional failures affecting skills formation; (b) what systems are needed for individuals to access these skills (family investments, private sector institutions, schools, and other public programs); (c) how those systems can be strengthened; and (d) how the most vulnerable individuals, who fall outside the standard systems and have missed critical building blocks in skills acquisition, can be supported.

Notes

1. The other components of growth strategies highlighted are investments in infrastructure and policies to promote macroeconomic stability, allocative efficiency, exports, innovation, and inclusion (Commission on Growth and Development 2008).
2. Cognitive skills are related more generally to measures of general intelligence or IQ tests, which assess verbal, mathematical, spatial, visual or perceptual, memory, speed, logical reasoning, and pattern recognition abilities. A distinction is made between crystalized intelligence, which is acquired knowledge, information, and concepts and their application, and fluid intelligence, which is "raw" reasoning, problem solving, and learning ability, independent of previously acquired knowledge.
3. A solid body of evidence from biology (epigenetics), neuroscience, psychology, and education supports a consensus that the "nature" vs. "nurture" distinction is obsolete and vindicates the power of public intervention to influence cognitive and socioemotional abilities (Cunha et al. 2006; National Research Council and Institute of Medicine 2000).
4. For a literature review, see Borghans, Meijers, and ter Weel (2008); for Europe, see Brunnelo and Schlotter (2011); for the United States, see Heckman, Stixrud, and Urzua (2006); for Latin America, see Cunningham, Acosta, and Muller (2016).
5. The questions on skills constraints in firm surveys generally do not specify to employers which segment of the labor force to focus on when answering.
6. The results are consistent with the 2013 Gallup survey, which also found that Sub-Saharan Africans—more than respondents in any other region—attach more importance to hard work in achieving success in life (Dago and Ray 2014).
7. For African countries for which data are available for multiple rounds of the World Values Surveys (http://www.worldvaluessurvey.org/wvs.jsp) (Ghana, Nigeria, Rwanda, South Africa, and Zimbabwe), the revealed valuations of child qualities remain stable over time.

References

Abay, Kibrom A., Garrick Blalock, and Guush Berhane. 2017. "Locus of Control and Technology Adoption in Sub-Saharan Africa: Evidence from Ethiopia." IFPRI Working Paper, International Food Policy Research Institute, Washington, DC.

Acemoglu, Daron, and David Autor. 2011. "Skills, Tasks, and Technologies: Implications for Employment and Earnings." In *Handbook of Labor Economics*. Amsterdam: Elsevier.

Ali, Daniel Ayalew, Derick Bowen, and Klaus Deininger. 2017. "Personality Traits, Technology Adoption, and Technical Efficiency: Evidence from Smallholder Rice Farms in Ghana." Policy Research Working Paper 7959, Washington, DC, World Bank.

Almeida, Rita, Jere Behrman, and David Robalino. 2012. *The Right Skills for the Job? Rethinking Training Policies for Workers*. Washington, DC: World Bank.

Amos, Patricia Mawusi. 2013. "Parenting and Culture: Evidence from Some African Communities." In *Parenting in South American and African Contexts*, edited by Maria Lucia Seidl-de-Moura, ch. 4. London: IntechOpen. doi:10.5772/56967.

Anderson, Lorin W., and David R. Krathwohl, eds. 2001. *A Taxonomy for Learning, Teaching, and Assessing: A Revision of Bloom's Taxonomy of Educational Objectives.* New York: Pearson, Allyn & Bacon.

Andreas, Rauch, and Michael Frese. 2007. "Let's Put the Person Back into Entrepreneurship Research: A Meta-Analysis on the Relationship between Business Owners' Personality Traits, Business Creation, and Success." *European Journal of Work and Organizational Psychology* 16 (4): 353–85.

Autor, David, and Michael J. Handel. 2013. "Putting Tasks to the Test: Human Capital, Job Tasks, and Wages." *Journal of Labor Economics* 31 (2, pt. 2): S59–S96.

Autor, David, Frank Levy, and Richard Murnane. 2003. "The Skill Content of Recent Technological Change: An Empirical Exploration." *Quarterly Journal of Economics* 118 (4): 1279–333.

Bacolod, Marigee, Bernardo Blum, and William C. Strange. 2009. "Skills and the City." *Journal of Urban Economics* 65 (2): 127–35.

Banda, Charles. 2014. "African Family Values in a Globalised World: The Speed and Intensity of Change in Post-Colonial Africa." *Development in Practice* 24 (5–6): 648–55. doi:10.1080/09614524.2014.939060.

Barro, Robert, and Jong-Wha Lee. 2013. "A New Data Set of Educational Attainment in the World, 1950–2010." *Journal of Development Economics* 104 (C): 184–98.

Bloom, David, David Canning, Kevin Chan, and Dara Lee Luca. 2014. "Higher Education and Economic Development in Africa." *International Journal of African Higher Education* 1 (1): 23–57. http://ent.arp.harvard.edu/AfricaHigherEducation/Reports/BloomAndCanning.pdf.

Borghans, Lex, Huub Meijers, and Bas ter Weel. 2008. "The Role of Noncognitive Skills in Explaining Cognitive Test Scores." *Economic Inquiry* 46 (1): 2–12.

Bowles, Samuel, Herbert Gintis, and Melissa Osborne. 2001. "The Determinants of Earnings: A Behavioral Approach." *Journal of Economic Literature* 39 (4): 1137–76.

Brunello, Giorgio, and Martin Schlotter. 2011. "Non Cognitive Skills and Personality Traits: Labour Market Relevance and Their Development in Education and Training Systems." IZA Discussion Paper 5743, Institute of Labor Economics, Bonn, May.

Canning, David, Sangeeta Raja, and Abdo Yazbeck. 2015. *Africa's Demographic Transition: Dividend or Disaster?* Africa Development Forum; Washington, DC: World Bank; Paris: Agence Française de Développement.

Center on the Developing Child. 2016. "Building Core Capabilities for Life: The Science behind the Skills Adults Need to Succeed in Parenting and in the Workplace." Center on the Developing Child, Harvard University, Cambridge, MA. www.developingchild.harvard.edu.

Commission on Growth and Development. 2008. *The Growth Report: Strategies for Sustained Growth and Inclusive Development.* Washington, DC: World Bank. https://openknowledge.worldbank.org/handle/10986/6507.

Conley, Timothy G., and Christopher R. Udry. 2010. "Learning about a New Technology: Pineapple in Ghana." *American Economic Review* 100 (1): 35–69.

Cunha, Flavio, James J. Heckman, Lance J. Lochner, and Dimitriy V. Masterov. 2006. "Interpreting the Evidence on Life Cycle Skill Formation." In *Handbook of the Economics of Education,* edited by Eric A. Hanushek and Frank Welch, 697–812. Amsterdam: North-Holland Elsevier.

Cunningham, Wendy, Pablo Acosta, and Noël Muller. 2016. *Minds and Behaviors at Work: Boosting Socioemotional Skills for Latin America's Workforce.* Directions in Development—Human Development. Washington, DC: World Bank.

Cunningham, Wendy, and Paula Villaseñor. 2014. "Employer Voices, Employer Demands, and Implications for Public Skills Development Policy." Policy Research Working Paper 6853, World Bank, Washington, DC.

Dago, Achille, and Julie Ray. 2014. "Belief in Work Ethic Strong across Africa." Gallup, August 1. https://news.gallup.com/poll/174263/belief-work-ethic-strong-across -africa.aspx.

de Janvry, Alain, Elisabeth Sadoulet, and Tavneet Suri. 2016. "Field Experiments in Developing Country Agriculture." In *Handbook of Economic Field Experiments.* Vol. 1, edited by Abhijit Banerjee and Esther Duflo. Amsterdam: Elsevier.

de Mel, Suresh, David McKenzie, and Christopher Woodruff. 2008. "Returns to Capital in Microenterprises: Evidence from a Field Experiment." *Quarterly Journal of Economics* 123 (4): 1329–72.

Filmer, Deon, and Louise Fox. 2014. *Youth Employment in Sub-Saharan Africa.* Washington, DC: World Bank.

Foster, Andrew, and Mark Rosenzweig. 1995. "Learning by Doing and Learning from Others: Human Capital and Technical Change in Agriculture." *Journal of Political Economy* 103 (December): 1176–209.

Frese, Michael, Markus Goldstein, Talip Kilic, and Joao Montalvao. 2017. "Female Noncognitive Skills and Cash Crop Adoption: Evidence from Rural Malawi." Working Paper 8095, World Bank, Washington, DC, October. https://editorialexpress.com/cgi -bin/conference/download.cgi?db_name=CSAE2016&paper_id=1077.

Galasso, Emanuela, and Adam Wagstaff, with Sophie Nadeau and Meera Shekar. 2017. "The Economic Costs of Stunting and How to Reduce Them." Policy Research Note 5, World Bank, Washington, DC.

Garcia, Marito, Alan R. Pence, and Judith L. Evans. 2008. *Africa's Future, Africa's Challenge: Early Childhood Care and Development in Sub-Saharan Africa.* Directions in Development Series—Human Development. Washington, DC: World Bank.

Global Education Commission. 2017. "The Learning Generation: Investing in Education for a Changing World." International Commission on Financing Global Education Opportunity, New York.

Gokcekus, Omer, Kwabena Anyane-Ntow, and T. T. Richmond. 2001. "Human Capital and Efficiency: The Role of Education and Experience in Micro-Enterprises of Ghana's Wood-Products Industry." *Journal of Economic Development* 26 (1): 103–13.

Goos, Maarten, and Alan Manning. 2007. "Lousy and Lovely Jobs: The Rising Polarization of Work in Britain." *Review of Economics and Statistics* 89 (1): 118–33.

Goos, Maarten, Alan Manning, and Anna Salomons. 2009. "Job Polarization in Europe." *American Economic Review* 99 (2): 58–63.

Groningen Growth and Development Centre. Various years. 10-Sector Database. Groningen, the Netherlands: University of Groningen, Faculty of Economics and Business, Groningen Growth and Development Centre.

Handel, Michael J. 2012. "Trends in Job Skill Demands in OECD Countries." OECD Social, Employment and Migration Working Paper, Organisation for Economic Co-operation and Development, Paris. doi:0.1787/5k8zk8pcq6td-en.

Hanushek, Eric A., and Ludger Woessmann. 2009. "Do Better Schools Lead to More Growth? Cognitive Skills, Economic Outcomes, and Causation." NBER Working Paper 14633, National Bureau of Economic Research, Cambridge, MA.

Heckman, James J., Lance Lochner, and Christopher Taber. 1998. "Explaining Rising Wage Inequality: Explorations with a Dynamic General Equilibrium Model of Labor Earnings with Heterogeneous Agents." *Review of Economic Dynamics* 1 (1): 1–58.

Heckman, James J., Jora Stixrud, and Sergio Urzua. 2006. "The Effects of Cognitive and Noncognitive Abilities on Labor Market Outcomes and Social Behavior." *Journal of Labor Economics* 24 (3, July): 411–82.

Huffman, Wallace E. 2001. "Human Capital: Education and Agriculture." In *Handbook of Agricultural Economics*, edited by B. L. Gardner and G. C. Rausser, vol. 1, ch. 7, 333–81. Amsterdam: Elsevier.

ILO (International Labour Organization). Various years. School-to-Work Transition Survey. Paris: ILO.

Kağıtçıbaşı, Cigdem. 2007. *Family, Self, and Human Development across Cultures: Theory and Applications.* New York: Psychology Press.

Kautz, Tim, James J. Heckman, Ron Diris, Bas ter Weel, and Lex Borghans. 2014. "Fostering and Measuring Skills: Improving Cognitive and Noncognitive Skills to Promote Lifetime Success." Organisation for Economic Co-operation and Development, Paris.

Kavuma, Susan, Oliver Morrissey, and Richard Upward. 2015. "Private Returns to Education for Wage-Employees and the Self-Employed in Uganda." WIDER Working Paper 21/2015, United Nations University, World Institute for Development, Helsinki.

Klinger, Bailey, Asim Ijaz Khwaja, and Carlos del Carpio. 2013. *Enterprising Psychometrics and Poverty.* SpringerBriefs in Innovations in Poverty Reduction. New York: Springer-Verlag.

Koch, Steven F., and Ssekabira Ntege. 2008. "Returns to Schooling: Skills Accumulation or Information Revelation?" Working Paper 87, University of Pretoria.

Krishnan, Pramila, and Manasa Patnam. 2014. "Neighbors and Extension Agents in Ethiopia: Who Matters More for Technology Adoption?" *American Journal of Agricultural Economics* 96 (1): 308–27.

Laajaj, Rachid, and Karen Macours. 2017. "Measuring Skills in Developing Countries." Policy Research Working Paper 8000, World Bank. Washington, DC. https://open knowledge.worldbank.org/handle/10986/26250.

Lall, Somik Vinay, J. Vernon Henderson, and Anthony J. Venables. 2017. *Africa's Cities: Opening Doors to the World.* Washington, DC: World Bank.

Leutner, Franziska, Gorkan Ahmetoglu, Reece Akhtar, and Thomas Chamorro-Premuzic. 2014. "The Relationship between the Entrepreneurial Personality and the Big Five Personality Traits." *Personality and Individual Differences* 63 (June): 58–63.

Liverpool-Tasie, Saweda, and Alex Winter-Nelson. 2012. "Social Learning and Farm Technologies in Ethiopia." *Journal of Development Studies* 48 (10): 1501–21.

Montenegro, Claudio E., and Harry A. Patrinos. 2014. "Comparable Estimates of Returns to Schooling around the World." Policy Research Working Paper 7020, World Bank, Washington, DC.

Moretti, Enrico. 2004. "Workers' Education, Spillovers, and Productivity Evidence from Plant-Level Production Functions." *American Economic Review* 94 (3): 656–90.

———. 2012. *The New Geography of Jobs*. Boston: Houghton Mifflin Harcourt.

Moretti, Enrico, and Per Thulin. 2013. "Local Multipliers and Human Capital in the United States and Sweden." *Industrial and Corporate Change* 22 (1): 339–62.

National Research Council and Institute of Medicine. 2000. *From Neurons to Neighborhoods: The Science of Early Childhood Development*, edited by Jack P. Shonkoff and Deborah A. Phillips. Committee on Integrating the Science of Early Childhood Development; Board on Children, Youth, and Families; Division of Behavioral and Social Sciences and Education. Washington, DC: National Academies Press.

Pence, Alan, and Jessica Shafer. 2006. "Indigenous Knowledge and Early Childhood Development in Africa: The Early Childhood Development Virtual University." *Journal for Education in International Development* 2 (3): 1–17.

Perotti, Valeria. 2017. "Training, Skills, and Firm Productivity in Formal African Firms." Background paper for this report, World Bank, Washington, DC.

Rankin, Neil, Justin Sandeful, and Francis Teal. 2010. "Learning and Earning in Africa: Where Are the Returns to Education High?" CSAE Working Paper 2010-02, Centre for the Study of African Economies, Oxford.

Roberts, Brent W., Nathan Kuncel, Rebecca N. Shiner, Avshalom Caspi, and Lewis R. Goldberg. 2007. "The Power of Personality: The Comparative Validity of Personality Traits, Socio-Economic Status, and Cognitive Ability for Predicting Important Life Outcomes." *Perspectives in Psychological Science* 2 (4): 313–45.

Roberts, Brent W., Dustin Wood, and Avshalom Caspi. 2008. "The Development of Personality Traits in Adulthood." In *Handbook of Personality: Theory and Research*, 3d ed., edited by Oliver P. John, Richard W. Robins, and Lawrence A. Pervin, 375–98. New York: Guilford.

Rodrik, Dani. 2016. "Premature Deindustrialization." *Journal of Economic Growth* 21 (1): 1–33.

Skinner, Jonathan, and Douglas Staiger. 2005. "Technology Adoption from Hybrid Corn to Beta Blockers." NBER Working Paper 11251, National Bureau of Economic Research, Cambridge, MA, March.

UNESCO (United Nations Educational, Scientific, and Cultural Organization). 2011. "Financing Education in Sub-Saharan Africa—Meeting the Challenges of Expansion, Equity, and Quality." UNESCO, Montreal.

———. 2016. *Education for People and Planet: Creating Sustainable Futures for All*. UNESCO Global Education Monitoring Report. Paris: UNESCO.

Uwaifo Oyelere, Ruth. 2008. "Understanding Low Average Returns to Education in Africa: The Role of Heterogeneity across Education Levels and the Importance of Political and Economic Reforms." IZA Discussion Paper 3766, Institute of Labor Economics, Bonn.

Valerio, Alexandria, Maria Laura Sanchez Puerta, Namrata Tognatta, and Sebastian Monroy-Taborda. 2016. "Are There Skills Payoffs in Low-and Middle-Income Countries? Empirical Evidence Using STEP Data." Policy Research Working Paper 7879, World Bank, Washington, DC.

van der Sluis, Justin, Mirjam van Praag, and Wim Vijverberg. 2005. "Entrepreneurship Selection and Performance: A Meta-Analysis of the Impact of Education in Developing Economies." *World Bank Economic Review* 19 (2): 225–61.

World Bank. 2007. *World Development Report 2008: Agriculture for Development.* Washington, DC: World Bank.

———. 2016a. "Kenya: Jobs for Youth." Report 101685-KE, Social Protection and Labor Global Practice, Africa Region, World Bank, Washington, DC.

———. 2016b. *World Development Report 2016: Digital Dividends.* Washington, DC: World Bank.

———. 2017. *World Development Report 2017: Governance and the Law.* Washington, DC: World Bank.

———. Various years. Doing Business database. Washington, DC: World Bank.

———. Various years. Enterprise Surveys database. Washington, DC: World Bank. http://www.enterprisesurveys.org.

———. Various years. World Development Indicators database. Washington, DC: World Bank.

Chapter **2**

Developing Universal Foundational Skills in Sub-Saharan Africa

Moussa Pouguinimpo Blimpo, David K. Evans, and Mũthoni Ngatia

Universal foundational skills are crucial both for sustained economic growth and for opportunities to benefit all members of society. As such, these investments are unambiguously wise. Even in economic downturns, they will pay for themselves over time. In many Sub-Saharan African countries, current systems to develop foundational skills are weak. Major improvements in foundational skills development will come at a cost, but the expected returns are high. However, it is essential to build on evidence of what actually creates human capital in order to ensure that investments deliver the desired results of an educated population and workforce.

These investments begin in early childhood, with crucial investments in child nutrition and stimulation. To improve the quality of primary education, evidence consistently points to improving teaching rather than improving infrastructure or inputs. Of course, infrastructure investments can pay off in places where levels are extremely low, particularly in secondary schools. Beyond primary, a massive influx of learners into secondary in recent and coming years presents both an opportunity to improve quality together with access and a massive challenge to provide learning opportunities. Quality investments are needed across the continent, but some countries will have to balance the simultaneous expansion of access with investments in quality.

Foundational skills are crucial to all three policy goals of productivity, inclusion, and adaptability. Although these objectives may also require higher-order skills, a firm foundation of cognitive and socioemotional skills is essential to achieve economic growth, to provide opportunities for the poor, and to permit individuals to adjust with the economy. At the same time, foundational skills circumvent one of the main policy trade-offs associated with investments in skills: skills for productivity vs. skills for inclusion. The same broad-based foundational skills contribute to both objectives. This chapter examines the present and potential future of Sub-Saharan Africa with regard to three key goals of systems for skill formation: access and equity, quality and relevance, and efficiency.

Looking Back: The Evolution of Access and Equity in Formal Skills Development in Sub-Saharan Africa

Access to foundational skills training has improved steadily across Sub-Saharan Africa over the last 50 years. Primary completion rates more than doubled between 1971 and 2014, and completion of lower-secondary school increased more than five times over the same period. But this consistent increase in learners completing primary and lower-secondary school—what is commonly known as basic education—masks massive variation across a heterogeneous continent (figure 2.1). While completion of primary school reached almost 75 percent in 2014, in the bottom 20 percent of countries fewer than 60 percent of children complete primary school, while in the top 20 percent of countries more than 93 percent of children complete primary school. In several countries, including Botswana, Cabo Verde, Ghana, Kenya, the Seychelles, and South Africa, virtually all students complete primary school. But in South Sudan,

Figure 2.1 Basic Education Completion Rates in Sub-Saharan Africa, 1971–2013

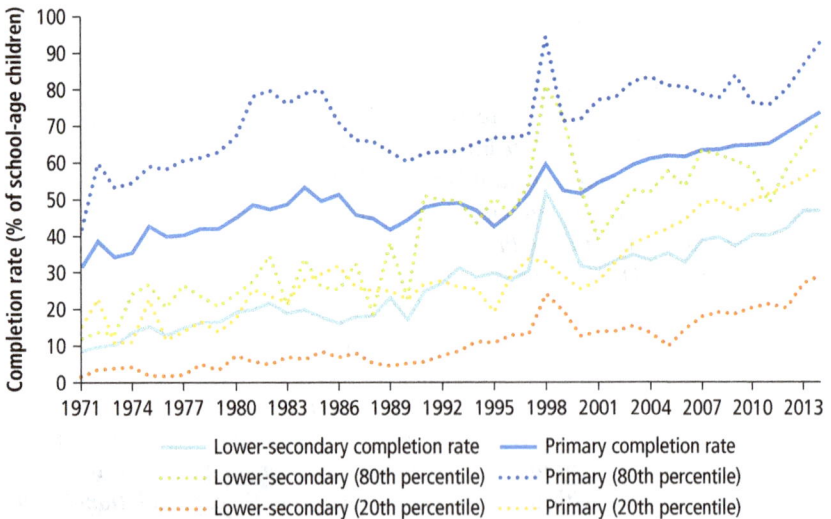

Source: Estimates based on World Development Indicators.
Note: Simple average across countries for which data are available. In an average year, observations are available for 20 (lower-secondary school) to 27 (primary school) countries.

fewer than half of students complete primary school, and several other countries have completion rates near 50 percent. Likewise, although almost half of
African children continent-wide now complete lower-secondary school,
20 percent of countries have less than 30 percent of students completing lower-
secondary school, while another 20 percent have more than 70 percent of
students completing.

That variation across the continent has grown over time. In 1965, the vast
majority of young adults (ages 20–24) in most countries had only reached primary school, ranging from 74 percent in Ghana to 99 percent in Niger. By 2010,
the landscape had become much more heterogeneous: 70 percent of young
adults had reached secondary or more in Ghana, compared with more than
90 percent of young adults with just a primary education in Niger (figure 2.2).

Yet, many economies still have far too many individuals with limited access
to formal schooling. In 13 countries across Africa, more than one-third of
young adults—ages 20–24—have no schooling at all. Again, schooling is
clearly not the only way for individuals to accumulate skills. But schooling is
the primary means for the large-scale delivery of foundational skills, and
every highly skilled nation has a high rate of school completion. Schooling is
a necessary, but insufficient, condition. The number of out-of-school children
may be even higher than current measures suggest. Household surveys miss
the most vulnerable youths, and one estimate puts the likely share of out-of-
school children at 70 percent higher than normally calculated numbers
(Carr-Hill 2012).

Figure 2.2 Access to Education in Ghana, Niger, and Uganda, 1965–2010

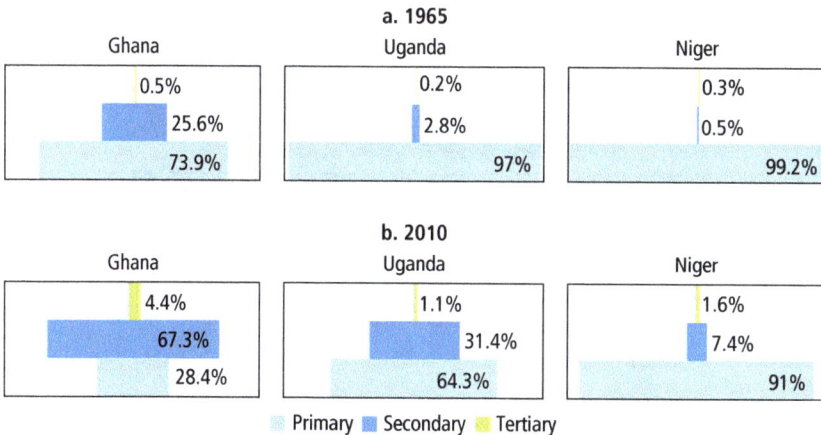

a. 1965

Ghana	Uganda	Niger
0.5%	0.2%	0.3%
25.6%	2.8%	0.5%
73.9%	97%	99.2%

b. 2010

Ghana	Uganda	Niger
4.4%	1.1%	1.6%
67.3%	31.4%	7.4%
28.4%	64.3%	91%

Primary ■ Secondary ■ Tertiary

Source: Estimates based on Barro and Lee 2015.

"In half the countries of Sub-Saharan Africa, fewer than two in every three children complete primary school."

At the other end of the spectrum, tertiary enrollment, which is the topic of chapter 4 but which relies on successful completion of basic education, remains startlingly low. Only three countries report that more than 20 percent of students are enrolled in tertiary education. Universal tertiary is not necessarily the objective, but the next generation of doctors, teachers, and engineers all emerge from tertiary education, so systems need to prepare students for that opportunity. This continued lack of access for many is focused among the poorest populations and so propagates the next generation of missed opportunities.

Access to primary education is still incomplete. Although the literature on primary education in Africa often emphasizes the true fact that much progress has been made on access, many children still lack access to primary school. While the top 10 percent of countries in the region have essentially full completion, the median primary school completion rate is only 67.5 percent (table 2.1). In other words, in half the countries of Sub-Saharan Africa, fewer than two in every three children complete primary school.

Most parents have high educational aspirations for their children; even parents with limited education themselves hope that their children will complete primary school and continue onward. Surveys from Ethiopia and The Gambia, for example, demonstrate that more than 90 percent of parents hope that their children will complete upper-secondary school (Blimpo, Evans, and Lahire 2015; Tafere 2014). Children themselves also have high aspirations: in Ethiopia, 70 percent of 12-year-olds reported a desire to complete university education, and more than 90 percent said they hope to complete secondary school. So the one-third of children failing to complete primary school is not driven by a lack of interest.

Beyond primary education, secondary education plays multiple roles in the development of young people, communities, and nations. Economically, the returns to secondary, while lower than those for either primary or tertiary, are still high at 10.6 percent on average—10.1 percent for males and 12.7 percent

Table 2.1 **Primary Completion Rates across Sub-Saharan Africa**

Percentile	Country	Primary completion rate (%)
10th	Mozambique	47.5
	Angola	49.7
25th	Côte d'Ivoire	56.9
Median	Mauritania	67.5
75th	Malawi	79.3
90th	Mauritius	97.5
	Botswana	99.7

Source: Estimates based on World Development Indicators database. Most recent year available, which is 2013 and 2014 for almost all countries.

Table 2.2 Secondary Completion Rates across Sub-Saharan Africa

Percentile	Country	Secondary completion rate (%)
10th	Malawi	21.0
	Mozambique	21.7
25th	Côte d'Ivoire	32.4
Median	Benin	41.9
75th	Zambia	55.1
	Eritrea	55.4
90th	Cabo Verde	75.7
	Kenya	83.1

Source: Estimates based on World Development Indicators database. The most recent year available is 2012, 2013, and 2014 for almost all countries.

for females (Montenegro and Patrinos 2014). Completing secondary school has a substantial impact on human capital accumulation as measured by performance on vocabulary and reasoning tests in adulthood (Özler et al. 2016). Looking at social outcomes, evidence from several countries across the continent finds that girls are less likely to get pregnant while in school (Baird et al. 2010; Gupta and Mahy 2003; Were 2007).

Secondary enrollment and completion rates, while rising, are still low. Rising primary completion rates and population growth have been creating demand for secondary education across the continent (table 2.2). The increases have been largest in poorer countries. For example, in Mali the gross enrollment ratio in lower-secondary education increased 39 percentage points. In Mozambique, it increased from 7 percent in 1999 to 34 percent in 2012. In Guinea, the gross enrollment ratio in upper-secondary education increased from 6 percent in 1999 to 28 percent in 2012 (UNESCO 2015).

Access to secondary education remains inequitable. Although secondary school participation is growing, access to a secondary education remains inequitable across the continent. Gender disparities in secondary schooling are widespread, with only one country, Eswatini, having achieved gender parity (UNESCO 2015). In the Central African Republic and Chad, both recently affected by conflict, half as many girls as boys were enrolled in secondary school in 2012. In contrast, in Lesotho, only 71 boys were enrolled for every 100 girls in 2012, a ratio unchanged since 1999, because in Lesotho—as in other Southern African countries, including Botswana and Namibia—boys are taken out of school to herd cattle. Of the 15 countries projected to have gender parity below 0.80, 11 are in Sub-Saharan Africa (UNESCO 2015). Among them, Benin, Burkina Faso, Chad, Guinea, and Mali still have low gender parity but have made strong progress. In Angola, disparity at girls' expense has deepened, from 76 girls enrolled per 100 boys to 65 between 1999 and 2011.

Looking Forward: The Future of Access and Equity in Formal Skills Development

In the coming years, the massive expansion that was observed in primary education in recent decades will shift to secondary education (figure 2.3), with the proportion of the adult population stopping after at least some secondary education rising almost 70 percent—from 29 to 49 percent—over the next 20 years (Barro and Lee 2015). The expected gains in tertiary are larger in relative terms but smaller in absolute terms (from 3 to 10 percent).

Even with this expansion, Africa threatens to remain the least educated region 25 years from now, with even further divergence from other regions at the tertiary level. What is observed is not convergence but divergence. As Africa seeks to move out of agriculture and into services, light manufacturing, and—insofar as much of the population remains in agriculture—more productive agriculture, higher levels of skills will matter more and more. And these statistics only represent access, which is a deeply limited picture of skills acquisition.

Foundational skills will grow more important with structural transformation and the overarching megatrends facing the region (box 2.1). Strong literacy and numeracy skills create a foundation for further skills acquisition and more adaptability in the future. Being ready for the next job requires strong literacy skills to read new materials and access the digital universe. More and more

Figure 2.3 Projected Educational Attainment of the Adult Population across Africa, 2010–40

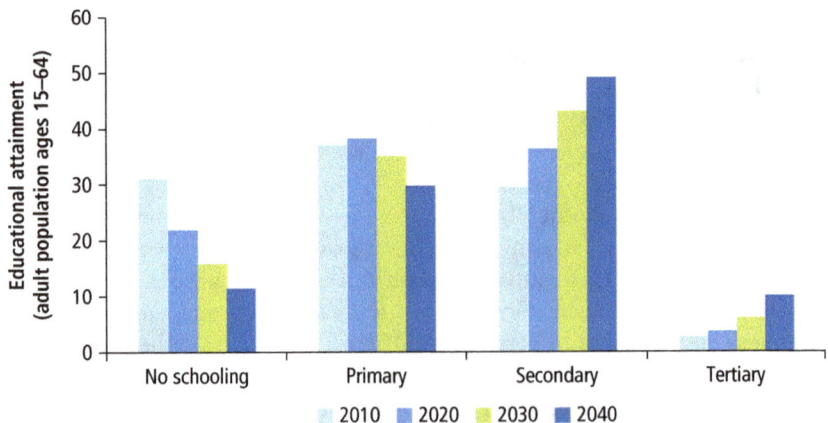

Source: Estimates based on Barro and Lee 2015.
Note: This refers to the adult population (ages 15–64) with any primary, any secondary, any tertiary education. The pattern is similar, but more muted, if only completion is included.

BOX 2.1

The Megatrends and Foundational Skills

The megatrends that are transforming Africa's economies present both opportunities and challenges for the provision of foundational skills.

Globalization means more access to global markets, which can translate into more opportunity, but only if the workforce has the foundation over which to lay needed technical skills. Manufacturing work requires technical skills, and it is difficult to provide those skills to a population that lacks literacy or numeracy, along with the ability to learn.

Urbanization means the opportunity to provide schooling at lower cost since students are located more closely together. However, it also leads to a temptation to invest all educational resources in urban areas, leaving the sizable rural population behind. Property expenses in urban areas push governments to construct larger schools, which can be more difficult to manage effectively.

Technological change holds great promise for education, particularly technological interventions that complement teachers. At the same time, it can tempt policy makers and populations with the false promise of a panacea, sometimes leading to large investments in hardware that is unsupported by existing infrastructure.

African jobs are moving from agriculture and into services, and there are hopes for growth in light manufacturing. Technical education builds on a foundation of literacy and numeracy skills.

The number of jobs in the formal sector will be limited over the coming 20 years, so individuals will have to create their own jobs. Estimates across Africa suggest that very few new wage jobs will be created between 2010 and 2020 (Fox et al. 2013). Far more are likely to move out of agriculture by 2040 (Tschirley et al. 2015), but if current trends continue, much of this shift will be into the services sector, with high concentrations of entrepreneurs. To be an effective entrepreneur requires strong foundational skills. Entrepreneurship training around Africa tends to focus on financial skills, such as accounting and budgeting, and business skills, like marketing and human resources (Valerio, Parton, and Robb 2014). These higher-order skills clearly require working literacy and numeracy skills. As a result, entrepreneurs may need a stronger, wider base of foundational skills than—for example—a long-term employee of a company with a narrowly defined task. For entrepreneurs, all tasks of the business fall to them.

For most countries in Sub-Saharan Africa, demographic trends in the coming years will lead to more pressure on education systems. A few countries—Botswana, South Africa, and Zimbabwe—have seen sufficient drops in fertility to lead to reductions or at least no shift in school-age populations over the next 15 years. But on average across the continent, the number of children who turn five in 2030 will be 25 percent higher than the number who turned five in 2015. For many countries—for example, the Democratic Republic of Congo, Mali, Niger, and Zambia—that increase will be more than one-third, creating increased pressure to expand access to education as well as to improve its quality (UNDESA 2015).

Financing for foundational skills in Sub-Saharan Africa varies dramatically across income levels. Chapter 1 shows that spending on education has grown in absolute terms, with growing economies and with spending on education reaching more than 16 percent of public spending. Spending on basic education (primary and secondary) translates to roughly US$670 per student. But spending ranges from a mere US$235 per student for low-income African countries to US$2,650 for upper-middle-income countries, more than a tenfold difference. These levels are comparable to those of countries at similar income levels outside of Sub-Saharan Africa, where per pupil spending in low- and middle-income countries is US$753 per student and spending in upper-middle-income countries is US$2,500. Is there a minimum level of spending to ensure foundational skills? Although the data do not reveal a precise floor, some countries at each level of spending are achieving better and worse educational outcomes. That said, with greatly needed investments in early childhood and in secondary education, increasing resources will continue to be needed for education. As economies are squeezed by lower commodity prices, at least in the short run, the pressure will rise to improve the quality of spending. Ultimately, the lowest-spending economies will need to increase both the amount and the efficiency of spending. Higher-spending economies will need to focus on increased efficiency.

Quality: The Need to Deliver Actual Learning

Children are going to school, but they are not learning nearly as much as they should. This becomes evident as children reach the end of basic education. For example, one of Africa's major cross-country tests—the PASEC (Programme d'Analyse des Systèmes Educatifs de la CONFEMEN), implemented in many Francophone nations—shows that more than half of students in late primary cannot carry out basic reading skills, and similar numbers fail at basic math tasks (figure 2.4); a test in Anglophone countries shows similar results (Hungi et al. 2010; PASEC 2015). Three African countries (Botswana, Ghana, and South Africa) participated in a global test for math (the Trends in International Mathematics and Science Study), and they performed in the bottom 4 of all 45 participating countries (see Bethell 2016). When adults—products of the education system—participate in exams, the results are similar: Ghana and Kenya

Figure 2.4 Proportion of Pupils Performing below a Sufficient Competency Threshold on Math and Language in Francophone Africa

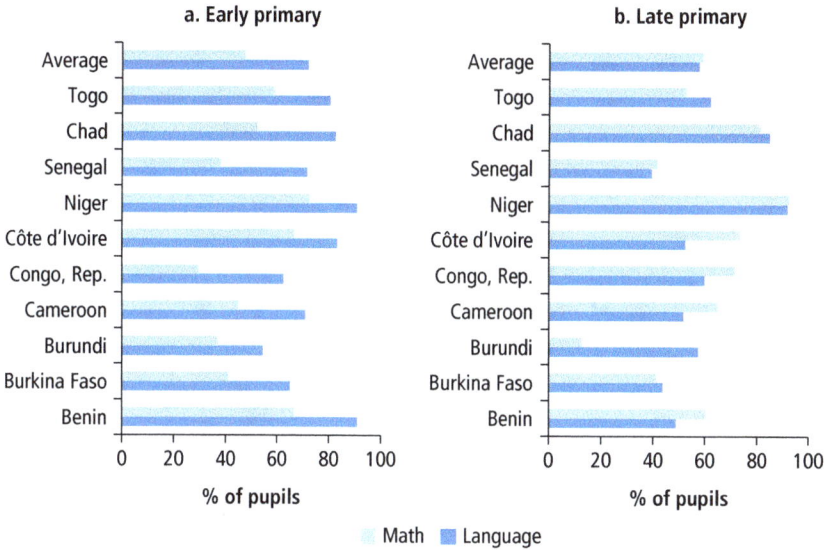

a. Early primary | b. Late primary

Math   Language

Source: Estimates based on PASEC 2015.

recently participated in an exam testing cognitive ability for urban adults, and they performed worse than Armenia, Colombia, Georgia, Ukraine, and Vietnam (Valerio et al. 2016).

That same failure to learn as much as students should be learning is manifest even in early grades. Early-grade reading assessments carried out for second graders across multiple countries show that in several countries more than 50 percent of second graders cannot read a single word of text (figure 2.5). Likewise, tests in early primary in Francophone Africa demonstrate that nearly 50 percent of students are below the threshold for sufficient competency. In East Africa, less than one-third of third-grade pupils were able to pass either a basic literacy or numeracy test (Uwezo 2013). This poor performance even in early grades reflects multiple weaknesses, including a lack of preparatory investments, low quality of teaching, and, in some cases, instruction in languages that students do not understand.

Low average levels of learning mean particularly low performance for the poorest children (figure 2.6). For example, in Tanzania, nonpoor children have a pass rate roughly double that of the ultra-poor. The differences are almost as stark in Kenya and Uganda. Most children are not receiving a quality education, and the poorest children are receiving the poorest-quality education of all.

Figure 2.5 Proportion of Second-Grade Students Who Cannot Read a Single Word of Connected Text in Select Countries

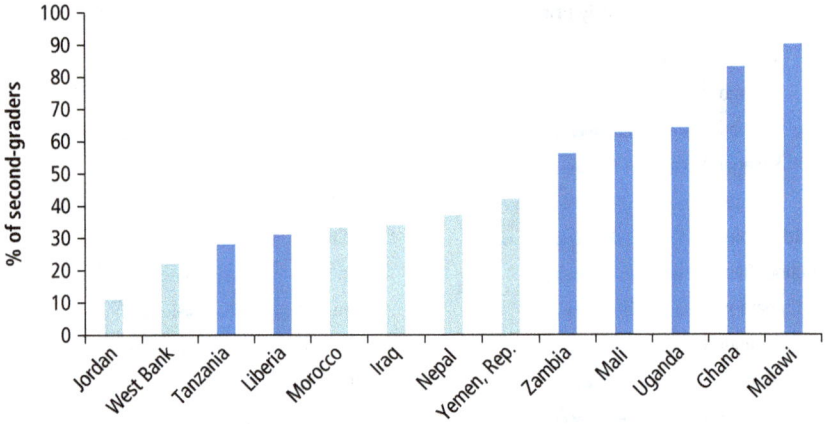

Source: Estimates based on USAID 2017b.
Note: Blue indicates Sub-Saharan African countries. Turquoise indicates other countries for which data are available, as comparators.

Figure 2.6 Average Pass Rates on Tests of Both Literacy and Numeracy in Kenya, Tanzania, and Uganda, by Household Poverty Level for All Children Ages 10 and Above

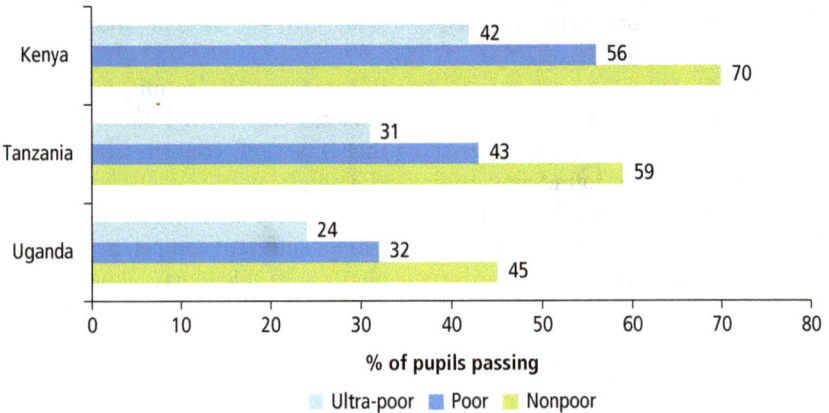

Source: Estimates based on Uwezo 2013.

The returns to education should be even higher than they are. Of all regions in the world, Sub-Saharan Africa has the highest returns to education—that is, an additional year of schooling leads to a higher increase in wages than in any other region in the world (Montenegro and Patrinos 2014). Indeed, all five countries with the highest returns in the world are from Africa: Burundi, Ethiopia, Namibia, Rwanda, and South Africa. For primary education, the average increase exceeds 14 percent. Yet the quality of education in many countries—including in those five—is low relative to the rest of the world, with many students not exhibiting the desired skills at the end of primary school. Primary education could be much more productive than it is.

Why Children Are Not Learning

Low levels of learning stem from a lack of early investments, which means that children cannot reap the benefits of schooling once they arrive, and the low quality of schooling itself. Children across the continent lack access to investments in early years, and then, when they arrive at school, the quality of education is often low, reflecting a mix of poorly trained teachers with little motivation, few supplementary inputs, and limited enabling leadership or management.

Why Children Are Not Ready to Learn When They Reach School

While an enabling developmental environment is needed at all ages for human capital formation, it is particularly crucial at early ages. The aptitude of the child to learn is path dependent, and deficiencies at young ages may determine the future possibilities for the child. Early child development (ECD) can be defined broadly as the overall well-being of a child from the womb until entering the formal education system at ages five, six, or seven, depending on the context. Early child investments include a wide range of interventions, such as prenatal care for mothers, good nutrition for young children, and cognitive stimulation in the early years. These interventions can be delivered through different technologies: parents and caregivers play an obviously crucial role, but home visits by experts and care provided in centers can also be important, depending on the age of the child and the context. Each of these investments plays a key role.

Early child investments in Africa are lacking, and it shows. This is true in terms of both physical and cognitive investments. In terms of physical investments, two in every five children are stunted across Africa (UNICEF 2013); in 15 countries, more than one-third of children are stunted (figure 2.7).[1] This is more than double the rate of the region with the second highest prevalence of stunting. Across studies and countries, stunting is associated with lower levels

Figure 2.7 Stunting Rates among Children under Five across Countries

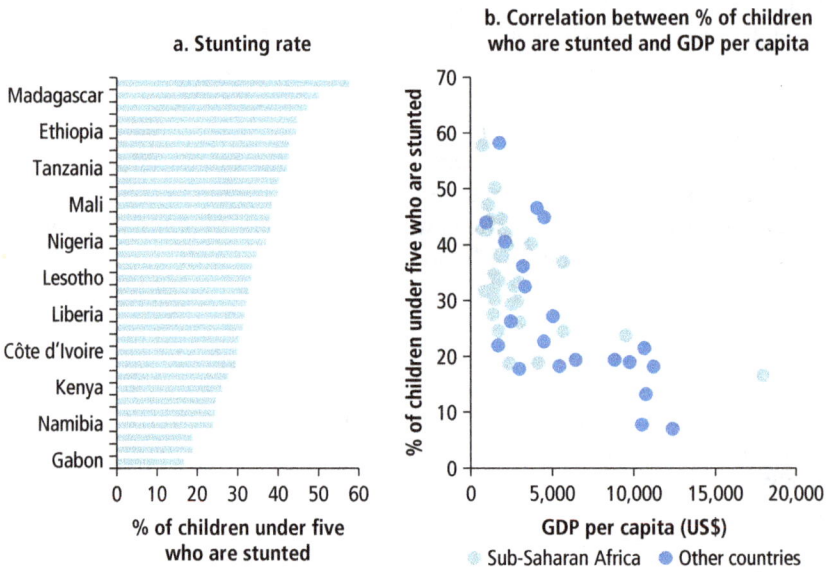

Source: Estimates based on USAID 2017a. All data are from the most recent available year of the Demographic and Health Surveys.
Note: Only some countries are labeled on panel a.

of schooling, lower cognitive ability, and subsequently lower pay (Galasso et al. 2016). Even in contexts where nutrition is less of an issue, children often do not receive as much cognitive stimulation as they need to thrive. Access to ECD is low. As of 2013, fewer than one in five children had access to preprimary education, with several countries, including Burkina Faso and the Republic of Congo with rates under 5 percent.

Data on early child development demonstrate that large socioeconomic gaps open up by school age. In Kenya, children ages seven and younger in the first year of primary school in the North Eastern region are eight times more likely to be unable to read letters than their peers in Nairobi (16 versus 2 percent; Uwezo 2015). Comparing the richest and the poorest children in countries shows that, by age five, rich children are more than twice as likely as poor children to demonstrate certain cognitive abilities (Filmer and Fox 2014). Thus, when corrective investments begin in primary school, the battle is already uphill. Children who have participated in ECD programs demonstrate higher numeracy skills at ages five, eight, and beyond (for data from Ethiopia as well as India, Peru, and Vietnam, see Favara 2016).

Figure 2.8 Prevalence of Stunting in Children under Five across Countries and Wealth Groups

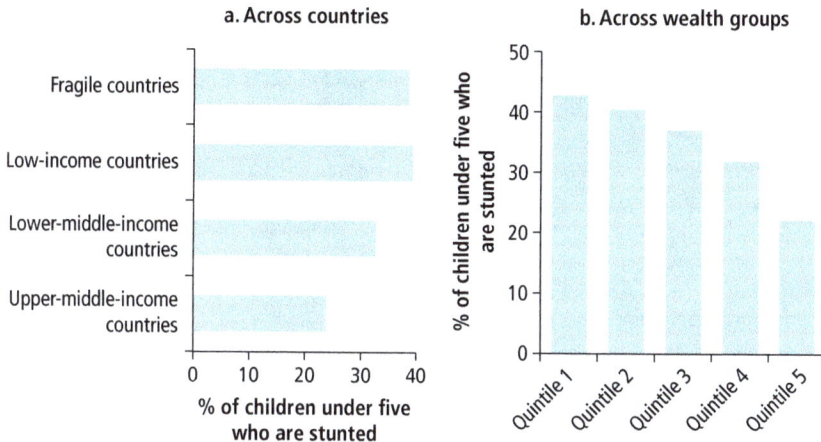

Source: Estimates based on USAID 2017a. Data are from the latest wave of Demographic and Health Surveys in the past 10 years (from 2007 to 2017) for Sub-Saharan African countries and economies except Angola, Botswana, Cabo Verde, the Central African Republic, Djibouti, Equatorial Guinea, Eritrea, Guinea-Bissau, Mauritania, Mauritius, Réunion, Seychelles, Somalia, South Africa, and Sudan.

While the overall level of children's developmental outcomes is poor on average, there is significant inequality across and within countries. The prevalence of stunting is significantly higher in low-income and fragile states on the continent.[2] In Sub-Saharan Africa, nearly 40 percent of children are stunted in low-income countries. In upper-middle-income countries, that figure falls to just under 25 percent, a better outcome, to be sure, but still dramatically high (figure 2.8, panel a).

Likewise, while the prevalence of stunting for children under five across more than 30 Sub-Saharan African countries is 36 percent, that figure drops to 22 percent for the richest 20 percent of households. This is—again—a strikingly high figure considering that these are the best-off families and that the national average for a country of similar income—like Haiti—stands around the same rate. As shown in figure 2.8, panel b, the prevalence of stunting decreases with the household wealth quintile: 22 percent of children from households in the top quintile are stunted in contrast to 43 percent of children from households in the bottom quintile. Stunting is also highly correlated with area of residence: 40 percent of children in rural areas are stunted, dropping to 27 percent in urban areas. If the mother has completed any level of education, her children's stunting rate drops 9 percentage points. Dramatic improvement is needed across the continent, especially for the poorest (box 2.2).

Stunting in Africa: What It Costs and How to Reduce It

Africa has the highest rates of stunting in the world (see map B2.2.1). This takes a steep toll on Africa's youths, weakening their ability to acquire needed skills. Stunting reduces not only physical development but also cognitive ability and socioemotional skills in both childhood and adulthood. This translates into a roughly 9 percent reduction in per capita income (Galasso et al. 2016).

Nevertheless, various countries in the world, including countries in Africa, have made significant progress in reducing stunting. Over 15 years, Kenya reduced its stunting rate from 40 to 26 percent (a one-third reduction). Ethiopia and Tanzania also made significant gains in the same time period (see figure B2.2.1).

Two countries—one in Africa and one in Latin America—have documented processes for achieving significant reductions in stunting. In Peru, a major media campaign emphasized the value of key health and nutrition services, and a conditional cash transfer program was linked more closely to nutrition services. At the same time, regular data collection and dissemination helped to garner ongoing political support. Over the course of nine years, stunting dropped from 33 to 14 percent (Marini and Arias 2016; Marini, Rokx, and Gallagher 2017).

Map B2.2.1 **Global Stunting Rates**

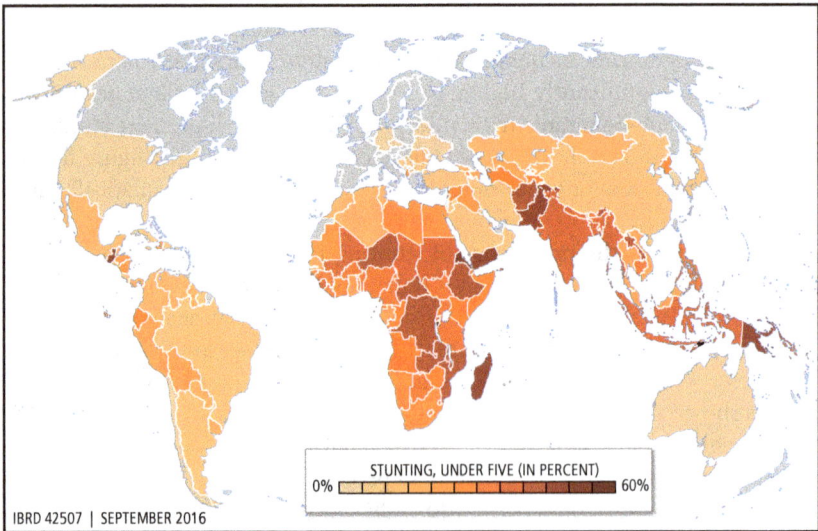

STUNTING, UNDER FIVE (IN PERCENT)
0% — 60%

IBRD 42507 | SEPTEMBER 2016

Source: Galasso et al. 2016.

(continued next page)

Box 2.2 (continued)

Figure B2.2.1 **Reductions in Stunting in Select Countries**

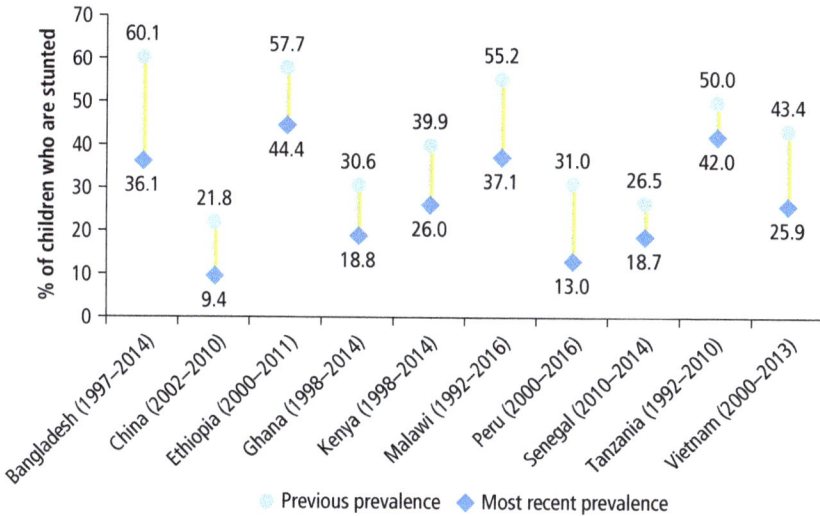

Source: Estimates based on Shekar et al. 2017; for Peru, Marini, Rokx, and Gallagher 2017.

In Senegal, stunting dropped significantly to one of the lowest rates in Sub-Saharan Africa despite uneven economic growth. How? The government created a special initiative within the prime minister's office to fight malnutrition. This initiative coordinated efforts across sectors and reduced costs by drawing on local resources. The initiative included promotion of exclusive breastfeeding, supplementation with vitamin A, and the use of nutrition and health services (Sibanda and Mehta 2017).

Why Students Are Not Learning in School

Lack of Teacher Knowledge

Teacher knowledge is startlingly low. Recent tests of teachers applied in seven countries found that few teachers know even 80 percent of the content they are required to teach (figure 2.9; Bold et al. 2016). A separate assessment in The Gambia showed similar levels of teacher knowledge (Blimpo, Evans, and Lahire 2015). Even in a middle-income country like South Africa, nearly 80 percent of grade 6 mathematics teachers do not have a complete understanding of sixth grade mathematics (Venkat and Spaull 2015). Teacher professional development—both preservice and in-service—has been critiqued as being too

Figure 2.9 Teacher Knowledge across Sub-Saharan Africa

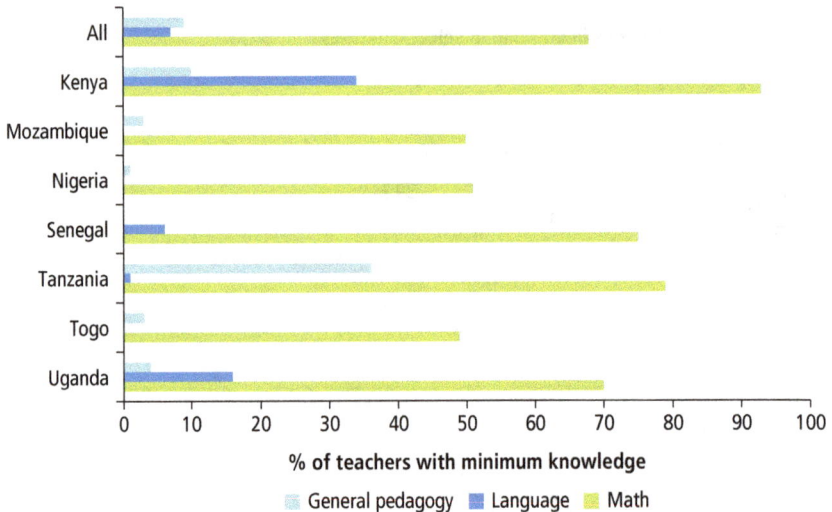

% of teachers with minimum knowledge

General pedagogy   Language   Math

Source: Estimates based on Bold et al. 2016.

theoretical, too inconsistent, and too limited to help teachers to close the knowledge gap (Lauwerier and Akkari 2015).

Teacher Absenteeism and Lack of Motivation

Much of the time, teachers do not teach. At the same time, teachers are absent from school or the classroom a great deal of the time. On average, across seven countries, teachers were absent from the classroom—they were not in the classroom when a visitor appeared unannounced to check during class time—more than 40 percent of the time, on average, and they were not even on the school premises almost a quarter of the time (figure 2.10; Bold et al. 2016). Learners cannot learn if teachers are not teaching or if teachers are teaching but do not know the content. These absences do not all reflect truancy. For example, a study in India—a country that also struggles with high teacher absenteeism—finds that teachers are absent from school almost 20 percent of the time, but less than one-seventh of that is truancy: the rest is either official duty or authorized leave (Azim Premji Foundation 2017). Whether an absence from the classroom is excused or not makes little difference to the students lacking a teacher, but it does affect potential interventions.

Teacher beliefs about students' ability to learn can play into this lack of motivation. Recent surveys in six African countries asked teachers about students' ability to use and to learn mathematics (figure 2.11; Bethell 2016). Almost all

Figure 2.10 Teacher Attendance across Africa

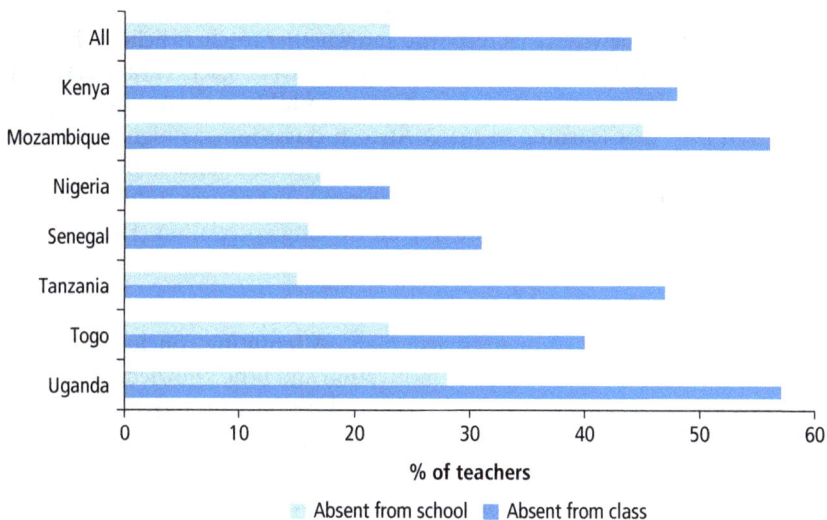

% of teachers

Absent from school ■ Absent from class

Source: Estimates based on Bold et al. 2016.

Figure 2.11 Teacher Beliefs about Students' Math Ability

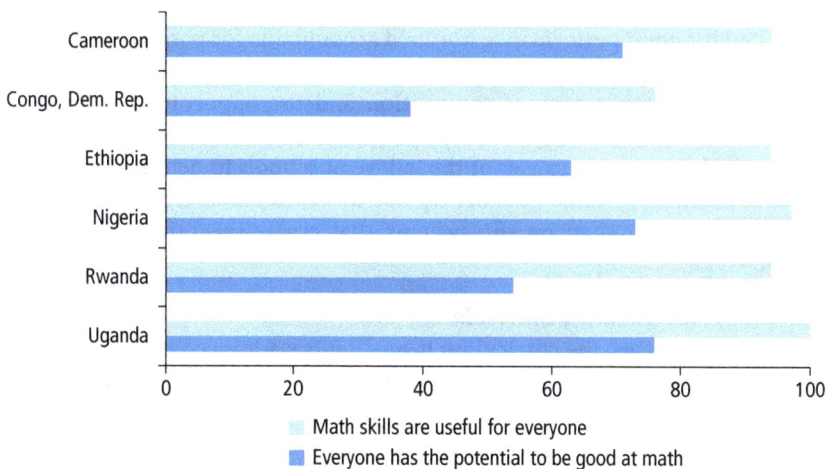

■ Math skills are useful for everyone
■ Everyone has the potential to be good at math

Source: Estimates based on Bethell 2016.

teachers said that they believe that "mathematical skills are useful for everyone," with the exception of teachers in the Democratic Republic of Congo. But there is a steep drop-off between that response and whether teachers believe that any student can be good at mathematics. Fully one-third of teachers said that they do not believe that any student can succeed at math.[3] It is perhaps not surprising, given this, that learning in many African classrooms is highly unequal. Likewise, teachers in Tanzania identified family background as being key to children's performance, such that their expectations of poorer children are significantly lower, potentially reinforcing an existing correlation (Humble and Dixon 2017).

The Environment

Teachers are a product of their environment. A tempting conclusion is that these are all bad teachers, with poor motivation and little knowledge. There is certainly value in ensuring that the best candidates have incentives to become teachers. But teachers are a product of their environment (Evans and Yuan 2018). Teachers teach in challenging settings, sometimes far from their home and with few materials to complement their efforts. Often, few students have textbooks, and teachers resort to using one of a few textbooks as a teacher's guide. For example, recent studies find that fewer than two-thirds of students have access to textbooks in Madagascar, and there is one textbook for more than 14 students in Uganda (Republic of Madagascar 2012; World Bank 2013). Teacher salaries are often delayed and may be slow to catch up with salaries of comparably trained professionals. In most systems, teachers are neither rewarded for good performance nor held accountable for poor performance. Reward does not refer exclusively to performance-based pay; it also includes professional rewards such as recognition and the opportunity to mentor others. In short, while the poor preparation and limited motivation of teachers are likely proximate causes of the failure of schools to deliver the desired levels of learning, it would be short-sighted to lay the blame entirely at the feet of teachers rather than on the systems that create incentives for exactly this behavior.

Ambitious and Outdated Curricula

At the primary level, the curriculum is much more advanced than the pace of learning in many countries, resulting in large numbers of students who fall far behind (Pritchett and Beatty 2015). At the secondary level, many programs have not been adapted to changes in the economy and focus on preemployment training (Verspoor 2008). These curricula are supply driven, neglect the informal sector, and leave students ill prepared for further learning and skills acquisition. Further still, many students do not acquire the skills specified in the national curriculum.

How to Get It Right

Make Early Investments and Build Foundational Skills

ECD programs—when done right—have a substantial direct effect on children and a significant indirect effect on women's labor force participation and household income. In high-income countries, children exposed to high-quality early child support programs have significantly better outcomes throughout their lives (García et al. 2016; Heckman et al. 2010). The same is true for middle-income countries (Gertler et al. 2014; Grantham-McGregor et al. 1991). In Mozambique, center-based preschools are found to produce significantly better child development outcomes. Caregivers are more likely to have worked in the previous month, and older siblings are more likely to attend school (Martinez, Naudeau, and Pereira 2012). Evidence from elsewhere in the world, such as Brazil and Colombia, likewise shows a mix of benefits for children and their households (Attanasio et al. 2014; Rubio-Codina, Attanasio, and Grantham-McGregor 2016).

Parents are the foundation of any successful program of early child investments. Parenting and overall family environments often determine the success of ECD programs. While evidence from Africa is still nascent on this topic, global evidence confirms it. Parental investments—from speaking and singing to their children to investing financial resources in their care—are crucial for children to succeed (Heckman and Mosso 2014). In Colombia, a multifaceted early-years investment that improved child development proved to be driven by improved parental investments, both in materials and of time (Attanasio et al. 2015). Parental investments matter for the development of children's socioemotional skills. But, on average, the poorest parents have the least time and the fewest other resources to offer their children. Therefore, enabling poorer parents and the most vulnerable families is one way to achieve greater impact.

Parenting programs include those that foster parental involvement, cognitive stimulation, and basic nutritional practices spanning from breastfeeding to nutritional supplements. Some of these programs may be highly cost-effective; even just the provision of information, which is usually cheap, has at times been effective (Cárdenas, Evans, and Holland 2015). One of the most well-known early child programs from the low- and middle-income world provided stunted children under the age of two with nutritional supplements and cognitive stimulation through weekly play. The nutrition intervention alone had no effect 15 years later, but cognitive stimulation had a persistent, positive effect on socioemotional outcomes (Walker et al. 2007). The experiences of immigrant children who arrived in the United States at different ages—and thus were exposed to the U.S. environment to varying degrees—showed that parents mattered much more than the country (Schoellman 2016). In Malawi, efforts to improve the quality of ECD programs were most effective when they incorporated parenting support (Özler et al. 2016). Parenting is the common denominator for several programs that worked both inside and outside Africa. ECD programs should therefore consider parental empowerment and the quality of parental involvement in children's lives as paramount.

A cornerstone of all ECD programs is quality: not only implementing the right programs, but also implementing them right. Around the world, ECD programs exhibit marked gaps between plans and implementation. A comprehensive review of evidence in Brazil shows that frameworks and practices often diverged (Campos, Füllgraf, and Wiggers 2006). Similarly, three early childhood programs in Cambodia all had little impact because of major implementation challenges (Bouguen et al. 2013). Many large-scale studies in Africa report major implementation challenges. Programs that prove ineffective often show a significant gap between design and implementation, stemming from an overly ambitious program design or a failure to factor in real-life challenges like staffing. For example, the quality of teachers and classroom practices is important in early education, as demonstrated recently in Ecuador (Araujo et al. 2015). This is one area that could benefit from much attention at the program design level. While programs must be designed at high quality, implementation realities vary dramatically from setting to setting and must factor into the design stage. A modest but fully implementable early-years program is better than an ambitious program that fails in implementation.

African countries should not jump-start completely new programs and practices without carefully documenting and understanding the prevailing practices. Identifying and building on existing practices is an effective way to achieve immediate impact at scale. The existing literature has often focused on evaluating well-designed packages. More comprehensive qualitative work is needed on how communities across the continent care for and raise their children and then work to eliminate bad practices and promote good ones. Even efforts to use information campaigns to eliminate practices spanning from unhealthy nutritional practices to child abuse may go a long way toward improving children's lives.

Since the success of a program is hard to establish ex ante, it is important for countries to adopt an evidence-based approach to scaling up their programs that integrates systematic and periodic evaluation. In a given context, operational realities and existing stocks of parental and community capacity are such that the right first priority in ECD may be parent training, center-based care, or something in between, such as community organizing of parents. In The Gambia, the government sought to identify the most effective way to integrate ECD into the formal school system using a series of experiments to test and then adjusting its approach (box 2.3). In Mozambique, an evaluation of a community-based preschool program that yielded positive results led to a

BOX 2.3

How to Decide Which Early Child Investments Will Work Best in Context? Test Them

In the early 2010s, the Ministry of Basic and Secondary Education of The Gambia developed a new comprehensive early childhood development (ECD) curriculum as part of its plan to scale up access. Aside from the private provision of preschool services in urban areas, the country had two other ECD services: (a) an informal community-based arrangement whereby volunteers from the communities helped families to address children's needs and (b) a more formal option called ECD annex, which added a classroom to existing primary schools to serve children ages three to six.

In order to test the new curriculum and to determine which of the two was better suited to being scaled up, the government partnered with the World Bank to run two parallel experiments. In communities with an ECD annex, some communities were randomly assigned to receive intensive teacher training and a new curriculum, whereas others received only the new curriculum. In another set of communities (without annexes), some communities were randomly assigned to a new community-based ECD structure and some were not. The government would decide on the way forward based on factors, including the effectiveness of the curriculum in improving children's outcomes, take-up rates, staffing challenges, and ease of quality assurance and monitoring.

In terms of children's learning outcomes, the study found no evidence of significant effect in the short term, with only moderate effect in the ECD annexes. On the remaining dimensions, a major trade-off emerged: the community-based ECD was associated with much higher take-up than the annexes, as households were often located quite a distance from the school. However, across all dimensions of quality, the annexes showed better results. As a result of the study, the government decided to expand the annexes, while exploring means by which to address the accessibility challenge over time. This decision was driven by the value that the government attached to quality and learning (Blimpo et al. 2017).

scale-up of the program and subsequent evaluation at scale (Martinez and Bain 2013; World Bank 2012). Piloting, evaluating, scaling up with care, and continuing to evaluate offer the greatest chance for success that combines local knowledge and experience with global evidence.

Deliver Foundational Skills at School

Get Children and Youths to School

Cutting costs is the clearest way to increase access to primary education. While the vast majority of African nations offer primary education without formal tuition fees, Africa has the highest number of countries that require fees, with Guinea, Somalia, South Africa, Zambia, and Zimbabwe all reporting fees (World Policy Center 2016). The elimination of tuition fees marked major jumps in enrollment in Kenya, Malawi, and Uganda, with smaller jumps in Cameroon, Tanzania, and Zambia (World Bank 2017). But beyond formal tuition fees, schooling comes with many costs, including the costs of transportation, uniforms, and other materials in addition to the opportunity costs that rise as children grow older.

In a wide array of countries around the world, cash transfers to extremely poor households—sometimes, but not always, conditioned on school enrollment and attendance—have significantly raised educational enrollment or completion rates. Across more than 20 impact evaluations of cash transfer programs around Africa (from Burkina Faso to Zimbabwe), all but one show significantly improved outcomes in education (Evans and Popova 2017). These positive impacts are observed for both unconditional and conditional programs, although evidence from Burkina Faso suggests that the children most vulnerable to dropout—girls overall and boys who are doing less well in school—may benefit from conditional transfers (Akresh, de Walque, and Kazianga 2013). School construction can reduce transport costs in areas with extremely low schooling density, with particularly positive impacts for girls, as recent evidence from Afghanistan and Burkina Faso attests (for Afghanistan, see Burde and Linden 2013; for Burkina Faso, see Kazianga et al. 2013 and Sawada et al. 2016).

Several African countries have successfully increased enrollment in recent years (figure 2.12) and may present lessons for others in the region. All of the countries with low initial enrollment and subsequent high gains were in post-conflict recovery, so some of the gains may be simple reversion to peacetime normalcy. All six of the gainers offered free education, five of six (all but Burundi) had economic growth above the regional average, and four of six increased the proportion of the budget for education (all but Burundi and Sierra Leone). Three—Ethiopia, Lesotho, and Malawi—used cash transfer programs as part of the strategy to increase enrollment.

Reducing fees also increases access at secondary, but it may not help students who have already fallen behind. In Ghana, providing secondary school scholarships—one way of alleviating the pressure of school fees—increased secondary school completion more than 50 percent. It also reduced fertility and increased earnings (Duflo, Dupas, and Kremer 2017). At the same time, in South Africa the elimination of school fees at the secondary level had no measurable impact on student participation. Why not? Prior school performance is a major driver of dropout, and students who have fallen far behind over many years are unlikely to remain in school even in the absence of economic constraints (Branson and Lam 2017). This is consistent with Kenyan youths in the final years of primary, where performance is a major determinant of dropout (Zuilkowski et al. 2016). Other constraints, such as distance to school, can play

Figure 2.12 **Which Countries Have Made the Largest Gains in Enrollment in the Last 20 Years?**

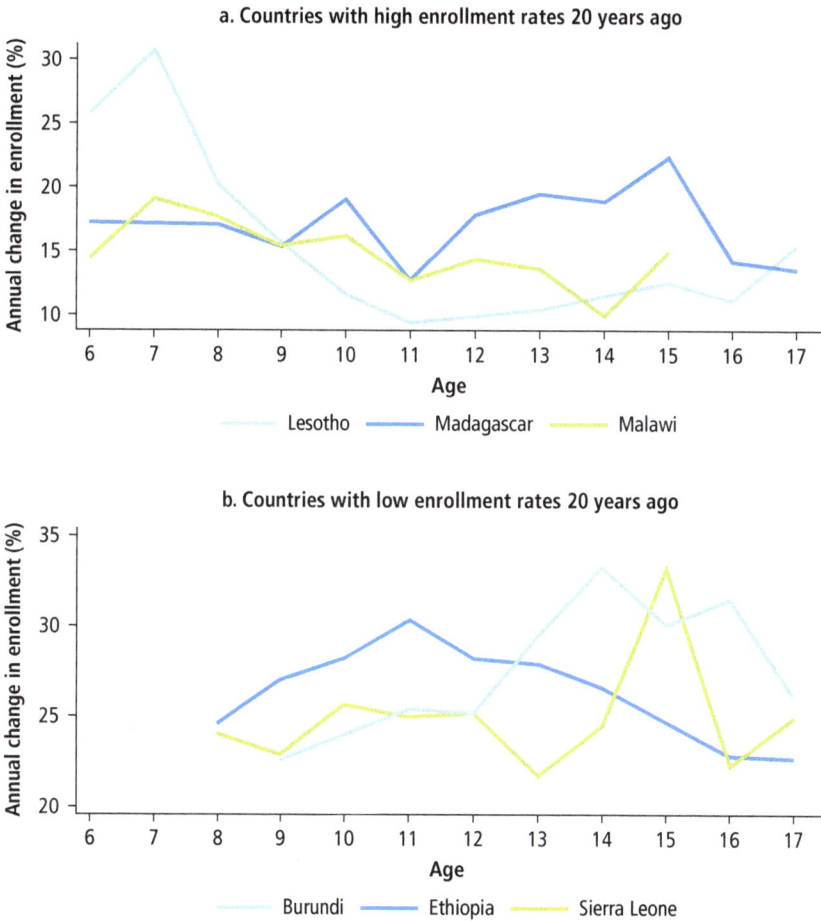

a. Countries with high enrollment rates 20 years ago

Lesotho   Madagascar   Malawi

b. Countries with low enrollment rates 20 years ago

Burundi   Ethiopia   Sierra Leone

Source: Estimates based on Filmer 2010.
Note: High and low baseline enrollment rates are determined by countries' being above or below the median of all countries in the sample.

a role (box 2.4). Besides reducing costs, one of the best ways to keep youths in secondary school is to help them to succeed in primary school.

Provide Quality Education

Once children are in school, they have to be retained with high-quality, relevant education. Households in several countries—Burkina Faso, Guinea, Niger, and others—report that low school quality is one of the main reasons for dropping out of school from age 12 onward (Inoue et al. 2015). The vast majority of

BOX 2.4

Using Bicycles to Achieve Gender Parity in Access to Secondary School

Gender disparities in secondary enrollment remain widespread. An innovative program in Bihar, India, improved access without constructing additional schools (Muralidharan and Prakash 2013). The program provided all girls who enrolled in ninth grade with funds to buy a bicycle to make it easier for them to attend school.

Being exposed to the program increased the probability of a girl between 14 and 15 years of age's being enrolled in or having completed ninth grade by 30 percent. Further, the program closed the preexisting gender gap in age-appropriate secondary school enrollment between boys and girls by 40 percent. Girls exposed to the program were 9.5 percent more likely to sit for the secondary school certificate exam, and pass rates remained constant. These results suggest that exposure to the program not only increased enrollment on paper, but also increased the number of girls who stayed in secondary school to the point of being able to take the secondary school certificate exam.

Several factors led to the success. The program was implemented effectively, with extremely low leakage even in a context of high corruption in other public programs. Based on discussions with policy makers and field officials in Bihar, the evaluators identified the following factors as leading to low leakage in the cycling program:

1. *Universal eligibility.* Since every girl enrolled in ninth grade was eligible, officials had little discretion in determining beneficiaries.

2. *Ease of implementation and monitoring.* The transfer was transparent and one-time, which made it easier to monitor than several ongoing smaller transfers. The program was highly visible to beneficiaries and communities and relatively easy to implement.

3. *Transparency.* Public ceremonies for awarding the cash to purchase bicycles in schools provided an easy platform for beneficiaries to notice irregularities and report grievances.

4. *Political commitment.* The program, which was highly visible to beneficiaries and communities and relatively easy to implement, enjoyed the commitment of the political leadership of the state and offered clear political rewards.

This kind of innovative solution holds promise in some parts of African nations with limited infrastructure.

---

the one-third of children who fail to complete primary school do start, but they drop out after a few years of education. Some of this may be because they or their families do not see the value of an education. Indeed, in an intervention in primary schools in Madagascar, providing parents and learners with accurate data on the returns to education increased both attendance and

BOX 2.5

Bringing Parents and Communities Along

Caregivers and communities are central for effective skills development. Almost no children enroll in school without the support of their caregivers. But sometimes caregiver intuition may be based on incomplete information. For example, parents may demand early education in English or French rather than a mother tongue, despite evidence that mother tongue instruction improves literacy, as parents in Kenya recently showed (Piper, Schroeder, and Trudell 2016). At the same time, caregivers may underestimate the returns to schooling. In Madagascar, one-third of caregivers were unable to predict the likely earnings if their child completed school, and among other caregivers, there was wide dispersion, with many underestimating the returns. Providing caregivers with better information on returns improved both school attendance and school performance (Nguyen 2008). Related programs—providing information on the returns to schooling—have had positive impacts in the Dominican Republic and Mexico (Avitabile and De Hoyos Navarro 2015; Jensen 2010).

learning (Nguyen 2008). Beyond the region, similar interventions have shown positive impacts in Mexico (on performance) and the Dominican Republic (on completion) (for Mexico, see Avitabile and De Hoyos Navarro 2015; for the Dominican Republic, see Jensen 2010; box 2.5). Other interventions that show the returns to education more indirectly—for example, by providing job-recruiting services or by legislating quotas for female political leadership in India—have also increased school enrollment and attainment (for the evidence on job-recruiting services, see Jensen 2012; for the evidence on female leadership, see Beaman et al. 2012). Even so, providing a higher-quality learning experience with relevant knowledge will likely increase primary completion. Although various factors enter in, the quality of education and primary completion tend to move together.

There is no single solution to improving quality, but pedagogy matters more than buildings. Recent years have seen a massive expansion of evidence from interventions to try and improve learning in low- and middle-income countries, with much of the evidence coming from Africa (Evans and Popova 2016). From an array of efforts to synthesize this evidence, one message is clear: the best improvements in learning come through improved pedagogy. In other words, while better materials and information and communications technology have a role and can be leveraged to improve teacher pedagogy, the best evidence on improving learning has been from including the quality of teaching. This is true both for the evidence specific to Africa as well as for the global evidence (for an analysis of evidence specific to Africa, see Conn 2014; for global reviews reaching the same conclusion, see Kremer, Brannen, and Glennerster 2013 and Snilstveit et al. 2016; for a synthesis of the reviews, see Evans and Popova 2016).

Improving the quality of teaching means providing teachers with quality, ongoing professional development (box 2.6). The kind of professional development that improves student learning outcomes is professional development with continuity, which means providing consistent support to teachers, not one-time, one-day trainings with the hope that teachers will subsequently implement a new method. It is professional development with concreteness, which means including support in the classroom to coach teachers in the implementation of new techniques. It is professional development with specificity, which means helping teachers to learn a particular teaching method rather than broad pedagogical theory (Popova, Evans, and Arancibia 2016).

A pedagogical approach with consistent evidence in Ghana, Kenya, and elsewhere is helping teachers to teach to the level of the child. In many countries, an ambitious, inflexible curriculum means that many learners get left behind

---

BOX 2.6

Getting the Right Teachers into the School System

In a discussion of how to improve the quality of education in Kenya, a Kenyan senior education official asked, "Can anyone be a teacher?" (Evans 2017). He and many others believe that a crucial part of improving the teaching force involves improving the quality of candidates who enter the field, as well as making it easier to remove teachers who perform poorly and do not improve with training and support. Earlier analysis of the requirements for entry into teacher training programs suggests that standards are very low (table B2.6.1). On the contrary, high-performing education systems such as in Finland and Singapore have highly selective teacher education programs in which only a few applicants are accepted.

Countries around the world have experimented with different ways to attract better candidates into the teaching profession, including creating special incentives for top students to go into teaching in Chile or raising the standards of entry into teacher training colleges in Peru (Bruns and Luque 2015). Improving the standards of entry into the profession itself can potentially improve outcomes. Although credentials and other indicators of teacher preservice performance have a mixed record of predicting teacher performance in the classroom, recent evidence from Argentina suggests that observing candidates during a brief demonstration lesson predicts their performance in the classroom (Ganimian 2015). Countries need to evaluate the most effective methods to improve the quality of teaching in their context. Because it is very difficult to predict teaching performance, one effective method would be to have teaching apprentices who can then be hired if they are effective teachers (Muralidharan 2016).

(continued next page)

Box 2.6 (continued)

Table B2.6.1 **Entry Requirements into Primary School Teacher Training**

Country	Requirement
Eritrea	Eritrean school leaving certificate (grade 12), with grade point average of 0.6 or higher on a four-point scale
Gambia, The	West African senior school certificate examination (grade 12), with one credit and three passing grades, including a passing grade in English
Lesotho	Cambridge overseas school certificate (grade 1), with four credits and one passing grade, including at least a passing grade in English
Liberia	The selection system is under development and seems likely to involve an entrance examination testing competence in English and mathematics
Malawi	Malawi school certificate of education (grade 12), with a credit in English and a passing grade in mathematics and two sciences
Uganda	O-level (junior secondary, grade 11) examination, with six passes, including English, mathematics, and one science subject
Zambia	Grade 12 certificate, with at least three credits and two passes, including at least a passing mark in English and mathematics
Zanzibar	Varies by institution

Source: Mulkeen 2010.

(Pritchett and Beatty 2015). Interventions that help teachers to target their teaching to the needs of students in the classroom have been highly effective. In Ghana, providing community assistants to help the weakest students has led to sizable gains in literacy and numeracy, especially when this assistance is given after school—in other words, it complements rather than substitutes for schooling (Duflo and Kiessel 2012). Also in Ghana, providing teachers with training to instruct students in small groups, targeted to their learning levels, had a significant impact on literacy (Duflo and Kiessel 2012). In rural Kenya, separating primary students into groups based on their initial ability led to gains for both those who were performing better at baseline and those who were performing worse at baseline (Duflo, Dupas, and Kremer 2011). In India, rather than separating students by ability for the full day, students were grouped by ability—regardless of their age or grade—for just one hour each day, still resulting in big gains in language ability (Banerjee et al. 2016). These programs are not just pilots: in both Ghana and India, the programs are being scaled up in government schools.

Is technology a promise or a pitfall? Technology holds the promise of allowing students to have an individualized learning experience. A recent evaluation in India used mathematics learning software that was adaptive. In other words, the software changed the nature of the questions it asked depending on learner performance.

For learners who were doing worse, it focused on easier questions to help them to strengthen their core skills. For learners who were doing better, it stretched them. The learning gains were impressive, with more than 0.5 standard deviation in improved mathematical skill (Muralidharan, Singh, and Ganimian 2016). Some other, simpler computer-assisted learning programs have shown positive results, just by allowing students to move at their own pace (Banerjee et al. 2007). But technology interventions come with significant risks. Many countries have rushed ahead to invest in complex technological systems only to find that the physical infrastructure in place is insufficient to support full operation or maintenance. Efforts to replace teachers with technology have been less successful by and large than efforts to complement teachers (Snilstveit et al. 2016). Technology is expensive to implement, so it is crucial to ensure that it is worth the cost; a recent intervention to replace printed textbooks with e-books on laptops in Honduras found that the returns only favored e-books if they could replace at least five textbooks (Bando et al. 2016). Technology will only fulfill its promise if it is analyzed with an eye toward cost-effectiveness and a careful, conservative view of what country systems can implement.

Being in school delivers more than just learning to read, write, and do arithmetic. Good schooling contributes to socioemotional skills. A growing literature demonstrates that some of the most important skills that children and youths accrue in their formative years are socioemotional skills—skills like persistence, self-regulation, and conscientiousness. Learners who attend school have higher rates of these skills (Heckman and Rubinstein 2001; Heckman, Stixrud, and Urzua 2006). Yet not all schools and teachers are equally good at nurturing those skills (Jackson 2016). Both measurement and evidence on how best to strengthen these skills are in their infancy, but in the coming years, African schools will want to pay more attention to how their students are developing these skills, even as most effort at the foundational level goes toward strengthening fundamental literacy, numeracy, and problem solving (box 2.7). Evidence from Peru suggests that a low-cost socioemotional intervention can even have spillovers to cognitive skills (Vakis 2017). These skills likely move together to some degree.

Private schools have been part of the landscape of African education for many years (box 2.8). One in every six students in Sub-Saharan Africa attends a private primary school. But recent developments have brought private provision of education to the headlines, including the emergence of chains of for-profit schools and moves by some governments to provide public resources to private schools through public-private partnerships (PPPs) (box 2.9). Liberia, for example, announced a large-scale initiative early in 2016 to move to a charter school model. The move was scaled back, with 90 schools in the 2016–17 school year (Hares and Sandefur 2016). Most evaluations of student outcomes for public versus private schools are complicated by the fact that students who

How to Deliver Socioemotional Skills in Low-Income Environments

Socioemotional skills demonstrate some of the highest returns of any skills. These skills are initially formed in households and subsequently strengthened in formal settings. Efforts to measure these skills, especially in a setting where the results have implications for resource allocation, for example, to schools, are still underway, but they are progressing. Some argue that it is important to deliver socioemotional skills before tackling literacy or numeracy. This is a false dichotomy. Most individuals in high-income countries learn socioemotional skills together with other skills. Efforts to develop these skills are currently underway in Chile, North Macedonia, and Peru (Arias et al. 2017; Claro, Paunesku, and Dweck 2016; Vakis 2017). In the future, as governments reform teacher pre- and in-service training, they need to help teachers to model and teach socioemotional skills as they teach literacy and numeracy. At the same time, they can be humble and recognize that there is still a lot to learn in this area.

Socioemotional skills have great value in their own right, but they also improve cognitive skills. In an intervention in Peru designed to give students a "growth mindset" (that is, to help them to see how much they could learn), students were invited to read an article entitled, "Did You Know You Can Grow Your Intelligence?", participated in a 90-minute discussion, and wrote a letter about the article to a friend. Student test scores rose by 0.2 standard deviation. The intervention reached more than 50,000 students at a cost of 20 cents per student (Vakis 2017).

Are Private Schools the Answer?

What is the role of private schools in basic education provision in Sub-Saharan Africa?

Every child has the right to a free, quality education (Gaeta and Vasilara 1998). But public education systems in many countries face challenges in providing quality education, especially to the poorest children. Many children remain out of school, and many who have been in school for many years do not have basic literacy or numeracy skills. At the same time, many households turn to private schools for education, with one in seven primary school children and nearly one in five secondary school children enrolled in private school in African countries (Baum, Cooper, and Lusk-Stover 2018). These numbers are on the rise.

There are multiple dimensions to consider with regard to the private provision of basic education. The first is the regulatory role of the state and its capacity to ensure a

(continued next page)

Box 2.8 (continued)

minimum level of quality. The second is the role of the state in providing financial resources to private schools via public-private partnerships (PPPs). The third includes the general equilibrium effects associated with private schools. In this discussion, private schools include all nonstate schools, including both for-profit and nonprofit schools.

The regulatory role of the state. The state should regulate the quality of all schools, both private and public, to ensure the quality of education provision as well as the safety of students. This regulatory function is more important in education than in some other industries, because it can be difficult for students and their families to judge the quality of the education they are receiving. (This stands in contrast to a more standard market good, like a cell phone or a piece of fruit, where quality is easily discernible.)

Student test scores are one indicator of education quality, and states can use regular testing to gauge the quality of education so that schools performing below a certain bar can—in the case of private schools—be sanctioned or closed. (In the case of public schools, the reaction may be additional support.) However, test scores cannot be the only indicator of quality, as other characteristics (such as physical safety) are also essential. Regular inspections can help. But the multiple outcomes that many expect from the education system (not only cognitive skills, but also socioemotional skills, safety, development of civic values, and sense of belonging to society) make defining, measuring, and regulating quality in education challenging. Regulatory efforts can successfully be coupled with appropriate dissemination of information regarding quality so that students and their families can make appropriate education decisions.

Providing financial resources to private schools via PPPs. Most state education funding should involve investing in high-quality public schools. (Indeed, 95 percent of World Bank funding for education goes to the public sector.) One reason for this is that private actors may have different incentives than the state (for example, profit motives or religious objectives), making it difficult to write comprehensive contracts to ensure that the incentives of private schools are aligned with the state's objectives. Contracts have to include provisions for both access and quality.

In geographic areas where the state is not able to provide education in the short run, there is a clear case for providing public resources to private providers. This may be because the government does not yet have the capacity to construct new infrastructure in remote areas. In areas where there are existing public schools, the decision is more nuanced, depending on the relative benefits of constructing new infrastructure and the expected flow of students over time. In both cases, comprehensive contracts are essential. On average, nonprofit providers may have incentives more aligned with those of the state than for-profit providers and so may be preferred, but there will be exceptions to this trend.

Scale and general equilibrium effects. A final dimension to consider when deciding whether to support private provision of basic education—how much and through what type of support—relates to scale and general equilibrium effects. When covering

---

(continued next page)

Box 2.8 (continued)

10 percent of the student population, private provision of basic education is likely to have different effects both statically and dynamically than when covering 70 percent. These dynamics are part of the strategic decision that governments must make. Overall, private provision should be viewed as a tool to improve the overall education system—both public and private.

Learning and innovation. The private sector can be a valuable source of knowledge and innovation. But as with any program—public or private—it is important to evaluate and learn from those findings. A priori, public or private systems do not inherently produce higher-quality education, and the evidence comparing student learning in public and private systems does not show consistent patterns after adjusting for differences in the initial characteristics of students. In Liberia, outsourcing public provision to private providers in a pilot of 93 schools resulted in significantly higher learning levels, on average, along with lower teacher absenteeism. But that outsourcing came at a significantly higher cost per student. Furthermore, some private providers in the group delivered large gains in learning, while others showed little or no gains (Romero, Sandefur, and Sandholtz 2017). There is still much to learn about private provision of schooling in Africa, but this initial evidence—from just one country—suggests that much will depend on the individual characteristics of the private providers, reinforcing the importance of effective monitoring.

Ultimately, education is a human right and should be provided to all children and youths. But certain members of the population will continue to purchase private education, and in some environments, public provision is scarce and private schools fill a much-needed gap. PPPs may be a way to close that gap.

BOX 2.9

Public-Private Partnerships in Secondary Schools

A promising policy option for engaging the private sector in education delivery is through public-private partnerships (PPPs). PPPs in education are long-term contractual relationships between the government and private providers for all or part of the delivery of education infrastructure and services. PPPs in education could potentially leverage public financing aimed at improving equity of access through the efficiency of private provision of education.

Specifically, a promising PPP policy arrangement consists of private schools' receiving government contracts to deliver services to low-income households. This arrangement allows the government to take advantage of existing educational infrastructure in a cost-effective way. Barrera-Osorio et al. (2016) study a PPP in Uganda where the

(continued next page)

Box 2.9 (continued)

government offered a per student subsidy to participating private schools and find that this PPP helped to absorb large numbers of eligible students in secondary schools. Specifically, after one year of participation in a PPP program, total enrollment increased by just over 100 students per private school. Additionally, the expansion in enrollment was distributed evenly between male and female students. Student performance in participating schools improved. The downside of such arrangements is that the public education system does not retain the investments in private schools so that, for example, materials and trained teachers remain with the private schools after the end of the partnership. On net, given infrastructure constraints, PPPs may be the best path forward.

---

attend private schools may have a different profile than those who attend public schools. High-quality evaluations are underway of for-profit preprimary education in Kenya and charter schools in Liberia (Hares and Sandefur 2016; World Bank 2015). Regardless of whether or not they choose to invest in private schools, African governments will have to play a crucial regulatory role in ensuring that schools provide a safe, effective learning environment for their youths.

While the case for investment in secondary education seems clear, the challenge of doing so is stark. Too few secondary schools, poorly trained teachers, and increasingly outdated curricula mean that many young people are receiving a poor-quality secondary education. Moreover, high primary completion rates and population growth are increasing the demand for secondary education. Dramatically expanding secondary education will be difficult and costly. Many countries in Sub-Saharan Africa will simultaneously have to build more schools, improve the quality of education provided, and improve the institutions governing schools.

Considerable funding will be needed to expand secondary education. The three principal sources of financing include (a) greater efficiency—reducing waste and thus getting more from what is spent; (b) additional spending from countries (governments and PPPs) and external development partners; and (c) economic growth (Verspoor 2008).

Gains can be realized by using resources more efficiently guided by evidence. Most secondary education systems in Sub-Saharan Africa are still marked by a colonial legacy of having been elite systems with few students and high costs per student compared with other regions as well as with high unit costs in primary education (Lewin 2008; Mingat, Ledoux, and Rakotomalala 2010). Whereas unit costs for secondary education are 12 percent of gross domestic product (GDP) per capita in low-income countries outside Sub-Saharan Africa, they are

40 percent in the region (Mingat, Ledoux, and Rakotomalala 2010). Sub-Saharan Africa spends a higher share of the government budget (on average, 18.4 percent in 2012) on education than other low- and middle-income regions (UNESCO 2015). Although many Sub-Saharan African countries have narrow tax bases, there is both scope to improve and successful examples across the continent such as in Zambia (Bwalya et al. 2014).

Governance of the education system and of schools has major implications for the quality of education. School governance is defined broadly "to include goal-setting for the education system, motivating service providers for delivering on these goals and holding them accountable if they do not, and the quality of management of schools and school systems" (Muralidharan 2017). Substantial evidence demonstrates that governance matters for students' learning outcomes, and a significant number of cost-effective interventions can improve governance. Increases in the frequency of unannounced school visits are strongly correlated with lower teacher absence in India (Muralidharan et al. 2017). Promising examples of inexpensive monitoring include using technology such as mobile phones. In Niger, students and the village chief received calls from supervisors on a weekly basis, resulting in higher reading and math test scores (Aker, Ksoll, and Lybbert 2012).

Communities also have a key role to play in the governance of schools. Most schools are managed by principals in conjunction with local school committees. While school principals are generally better educated than teachers, very few have specific training in school management (Mbiti 2016). The fact that principals and school committees jointly manage school finances suggests that improving their capacity should improve school management practices in general and the efficient use of school funds in particular to improve student learning. Evidence on this relationship is mixed. A four-year, large-scale experiment in The Gambia provided a grant and comprehensive school management training to principals, teachers, and community representatives in a set of schools (Blimpo, Evans, and Lahire 2015). Three to four years into the program, the full intervention led to a reduction in student absenteeism and in teacher absenteeism, but had no impact on student test scores. A school grant program in Senegal provided schools with resources and the freedom to spend them as they saw fit (Carneiro et al. 2015). Schools that invested in materials had limited improvements in learning outcomes, whereas schools that invested in programs that increased management and teacher productivity through training programs had some learning improvements. In Indonesia, a large field experiment tested alternative approaches to strengthen school committees in public schools (Pradhan et al. 2014). In one treatment, some schools were randomly assigned to implement elections of school committee members. Another treatment facilitated joint planning meetings between the school committee and the village council (called "linkage").

Pradhan et al. (2014) find that institutional reforms—in particular linkage and elections combined with linkage—were most cost-effective at improving learning, suggesting that school committees may require additional support from their communities to realize learning improvements.

The Way Forward

Investing in foundational skills is crucial for achieving sustained economic growth and creating opportunities to benefit all members of society. The stock of foundational skills is the basis on which all subsequent training rests and is the indispensable condition for the future development of the continent. There are efficiency-equity trade-offs in determining a strategy for investment in foundational skills, and many Sub-Saharan African countries are faced with limited public resources to realize the necessary improvements in foundational skills. However, a more efficient use of existing resources—together with leveraging of the private sector—can help governments to expand access and improve the quality of foundational skills. To accomplish this, governments have to play a regulatory role. They should hold schools accountable for results. Governments should monitor all providers (public and private) and take clear steps when quality falls short. Regulations for public and private actors need to be clear and inclusive to encourage diversity of supply, while ensuring the safety and achievement of students.

It is important to prioritize pedagogy over infrastructure, both to benefit the average student and to benefit the poorest students. There is a growing body of evidence of what works in improving learning in low- and middle-income countries. Improving pedagogy is more effective than improving infrastructure for increasing learning outcomes. Pedagogical strategies that allow teachers to reach students at their level—whether separating classes by ability or offering remedial lessons to lower performers—will reduce inequality by giving students who have fallen behind a chance to learn.

Cutting costs will help to get children into school, but as students reach higher grades, the quality of earlier education is also key. Universal elimination of fees for basic education should be the policy goal, but in the medium term, countries need to be judicious in their use of educational resources; in some cases, targeted scholarships or other benefits may be just as effective at getting children and youths into school. At the secondary level, eliminating fees will help those who want to attend but cannot, but for those who have fallen several years behind, it may not close the gap. This is why quality investments in primary education and before are so crucial.

Early investments are critical and need to leverage the efforts of caregivers. In an ideal world, each country would have a comprehensive early child investment program, from home visits for the youngest children to the availability of child care or preschool and nutritional supplementation. As countries work toward these goals, the first step is to provide caregivers with information about how to invest effectively in children and youths.

Improvements in governance of the education sector have great potential at each level, from increasing the number of inspections or schools to getting caregivers involved in the school community. Most countries already have school inspectors, but visits often are irregular and provide limited value to the quality of teaching. Increasing and improving inspections can improve motivation and accountability. Many countries have a strong tradition of parental involvement. Schools should be accountable to parents, and parents should work with schools to ensure that students learn. Although parental involvement may be more challenging with poorer and less educated parents, there is evidence that, when given relevant information, even poor and low-income parents make the best decisions for their children (Nguyen 2008). To expand the delivery of foundational skills, the private sector can fill some of the gap left by the public sector. Provision of foundational skills by the private sector has grown significantly. Promising examples exist, but PPPs require careful supervision by the public sector.

In leveraging private capital to deliver foundational skills, governments need to lead and coordinate. Multiple actors are providing foundational skills across the continent; governments should coordinate the multiple players to minimize duplication and ensure that a coherent education policy responds to the country's unique needs. Governments can set and monitor quality standards for teachers in both public and private institutions.

Governments have an important role to play in prioritizing the country's needs, ensuring that the delivery of foundational skills is relevant. Among many competing priorities, governments face difficult choices and limited resources. By articulating a clear policy for investment in foundational skills, based on the country's unique needs, governments can prioritize what skills need to be imparted to the population and how best to do so.

Notes

1. Stunting, or low height-for-age, corresponds to −2 standard deviation z-scores below the median of the World Health Organization child growth standards.
2. In this data set, the countries are categorized by the World Bank. The country lists are mutually exclusive. Fragile countries include Burundi, the Comoros, the Democratic Republic of Congo, Côte d'Ivoire, The Gambia, Liberia, Madagascar, Mali, Sierra Leone, and Togo. Low-income countries include Benin, Burkina Faso, Ethiopia, Guinea, Malawi, Mozambique, Niger, Rwanda, Senegal, Tanzania, Uganda, and Zimbabwe. Lower-middle-income countries include Cameroon, the

Republic of Congo, Eswatini, Ghana, Kenya, Lesotho, Nigeria, São Tomé and Príncipe, and Zambia. Upper-middle-income countries include Gabon and Namibia. Fragile states refer to countries in a fragile situation, having either (a) a harmonized average country policy and institutional assessment rating of 3.2 or less or (b) the presence of a United Nations or regional peace-keeping or peace-building mission during the past three years.

3. The median across countries is 33 percent.

References

Aker, Jenny C., Christopher Ksoll, and Travis J. Lybbert. 2012. "Can Mobile Phones Improve Learning? Evidence from a Field Experiment in Niger." *American Economic Journal: Applied Economics* 4 (4): 94–120.

Akresh, Richard, Damien de Walque, and Harounan Kazianga. 2013. "Cash Transfers and Child Schooling: Evidence from a Randomized Evaluation of the Role of Conditionality." Policy Research Working Paper, World Bank, Washington, DC. http://documents.worldbank.org/curated/en/587731468005971189/pdf/wps6340.pdf.

Araujo, María Caridad, Florencia López-Boo, Rafael Novella, Sara Schodt, and Romina Tomé. 2015. "La calidad de los centros infantiles del buen vivir en Ecuador." Inter-American Development Bank, Washington, DC.

Arias, Omar, Pedro Carneiro, Angela Duckworth, Lauren Eskreis-Winkler, Christian Krekel, Ana Maria Munoz Boudet, and Indhira Santos. 2017. "Can Grit Be Taught? Learning from a Field Experiment with Middle School Students in FYR Macedonia." AEA RCT Registry, American Economic Association, Nashville, TN. https://www.socialscienceregistry.org/trials/2094/history/15128.

Attanasio, Orazio, Sarah Cattan, Emla Fitzsimons, Costas Meghir, and Marta Rubio-Codina. 2015. "Estimating the Production Function for Human Capital: Results from a Randomized Control Trial in Colombia." NBER Working Paper 20965, National Bureau of Economic Research, Cambridge, MA.

Attanasio, Orazio, Ricardo Paes de Barros, Pedro Carneiro, David Evans, Lycia Lima, Rosane Mendonca, Pedro Olinto, and Norbert Schady. 2014. "Free Access to Child Care, Labor Supply, and Child Development." 3IE Grantee Final Report, International Initiative for Impact Evaluation, New Delhi. http://www.3ieimpact.org/evidence-hub/publications/impact-evaluations/impact-free-availability-public-childcare-labour.

Avitabile, Ciro, and Rafael E. De Hoyos Navarro. 2015. "The Heterogeneous Effect of Information on Student Performance: Evidence from a Randomized Control Trial in Mexico." Policy Research Working Paper, World Bank, Washington, DC.

Azim Premji Foundation. 2017. "Teacher Absenteeism Study: Field Studies in Education." Azim Premji University, Bangalore. http://azimpremjiuniversity.edu.in/SitePages/pdf/Field-Studies-in-Education-Teacher-Absenteeism-Study.pdf.

Baird, Sarah, Ephraim Chirwa, Craig McIntosh, and Berk Özler. 2010. "The Short-Term Impacts of a Schooling Conditional Cash Transfer Program on the Sexual Behavior of Young Women." *Health Economics* 19 (S1): 55–68.

Bando, Rosangela, Francisco Gallego, Paul Gertler, and Dario Romero. 2016. "Books or Laptops? The Cost-Effectiveness of Shifting from Printed to Digital Delivery of Educational Content." NBER Working Paper 22928, National Bureau of Economic Research, Cambridge, MA. http://www.nber.org/papers/w22928.

Banerjee, Abhijit, Rukmini Banerji, James Berry, Esther Duflo, Harini Kannan, Shobhini Mukerji, Marc Shotland, and Michael Walton. 2016. "Mainstreaming an Effective Intervention: Evidence from Randomized Evaluations of 'Teaching at the Right Level' in India." Abdul Latif Jameel Poverty Action Lab, Cambridge, MA. https://www.pov ertyactionlab.org/sites/default/files/publications/TaRL_Paper_August2016.pdf.

Banerjee, Abhijit V., Shawn Cole, Esther Duflo, and Leigh L. Linden. 2007. "Remedying Education: Evidence from Two Randomized Experiments in India." *Quarterly Journal of Economics* 122 (3): 1235–64. http://qje.oxfordjournals.org/content/122/3/1235 .short.

Barrera-Osorio, Felipe, Pierre de Galbert, James P. Habyarimana, and Shwetlena Sabarwal. 2016. "Impact of Public-Private Partnerships on Private School Performance: Evidence from a Randomized Controlled Trial in Uganda." Policy Research Working Paper 790, World Bank, Washington, DC. https://openknowledge.worldbank.org/bit stream/handle/10986/25804/WPS7905.pdf?sequence=1&isAllowed=y.

Barro, Robert J., and Jong-Wha Lee. 2015. *Education Matters: Global Schooling Gains from the 19th to the 21st Century.* New York: Oxford University Press.

Baum, Donald R., Rachel Cooper, and Oni Lusk-Stover. 2018. "Regulating Market Entry of Low-Cost Private Schools in Sub-Saharan Africa: Towards a Theory of Private Education Regulation." *International Journal of Educational Development* 60 (May): 100–12.

Beaman, Lori, Esther Duflo, Rohini Pande, and Petia Topalova. 2012. "Female Leadership Raises Aspirations and Educational Attainment for Girls: A Policy Experiment in India." *Science* 335 (6068): 582–86. https://www.ncbi.nlm.nih.gov/pmc/articles /PMC3394179/.

Bethell, George. 2016. "Mathematics Education in Sub-Saharan Africa." Report No. ACS19117, World Bank, Washington, DC. https://openknowledge.worldbank.org /handle/10986/25289.

Blimpo, Moussa P., Pedro Carneiro, Pamela Jerviz Ortiz, and Todd Pugatch. 2017. "Scaling up Children's School Readiness in The Gambia: Lessons from an Experimental Study." Working Paper, World Bank, Washington, DC.

Blimpo, Moussa P., David K. Evans, and Nathalie Lahire. 2015. "Parental Human Capital and Effective School Management: Evidence from The Gambia." Policy Research Working Paper 7238, World Bank, Washington, DC.

Bold, Tessa, Deon Filmer, Gayle Martin, Ezequiel Molina, Brian Stacy, Christophe Rockmore, Jakob Svensson, and Wally Wane. 2016. "What Do Teachers Know and Do?: Evidence from Primary Schools in Africa." Policy Research Working Paper no. 7956, World Bank, Washington, DC. https://openknowledge.worldbank.org /handle/10986/25964.

Bouguen, Adrien, Deon Filmer, Karen Macours, and Sophie Naudeau. 2013. "Impact Evaluation of Three Types of Early Childhood Development Interventions in Cambodia." Policy Research Working Paper 6540, World Bank, Washington, DC.

Branson, Nicola, and David Lam. 2017. "The Impact of the No-Fee School Policy on Enrolment and School Performance: Evidence from NIDS Waves 1–3." Southern Africa Labour and Development Research Unit, Cape Town. http://opensaldru.uct.ac .za/bitstream/handle/11090/856/2017_197_Saldruwp.pdf?sequence=1.

Bruns, Barbara, and Javier Luque. 2015. *Great Teachers: How to Raise Student Learning in Latin America and the Caribbean.* Washington, DC: World Bank. https://open knowledge.worldbank.org/handle/10986/20488.

Burde, Dana, and Leigh L. Linden. 2013. "Bringing Education to Afghan Girls: A Randomized Controlled Trial of Village-Based Schools." *American Economic Journal: Applied Economics* 5 (3): 27–40. http://pubs.aeaweb.org/doi/pdfplus/10.1257/app .5.3.27.

Bwalya, Samuel, Shantayanan Devarajan, Vinayak Nagaraj, and Gaël Raballand. 2014. "Increasing Public Revenue and Expenditure Efficiency in Zambia." In *Zambia: Building Prosperity from Resource Wealth,* edited by Christopher Adam, Paul Collier, and Michael Gondwe, 59. Oxford: Oxford Scholarship Online. https://books.google .com/books?hl=en&lr=&id=ZRCSBAAAQBAJ&oi=fnd&pg=PA59&dq=zambia+tax &ots=EUjqSJBEE-&sig=JhvMZgWe-Ajo8J5T8xZWkxAoBGg#v=onepage&q=zambia %20tax&f=false.

Campos, Maria Malta, Jodete Füllgraf, and Verena Wiggers. 2006. "Brazilian Early Childhood Education Quality: Some Research Results." *Cadernos de Pesquisa* 36 (127): 87–128. http://www.scielo.br/pdf/cp/v36n127/en_a0536127.pdf.

Cárdenas, Sergio, David K. Evans, and Peter Holland. 2015. "Early Childhood Benefits at Low Cost—Evidence from a Randomized Trial in Mexico." Society for Research on Educational Effectiveness, Evanston, IL.

Carneiro, Pedro, Oswald Koussihouèdé, Nathalie Lahire, Costas Meghir, and Corina Mommaerts. 2015. "Decentralizing Education Resources: School Grants in Senegal." NBER Working Paper 21063, National Bureau of Economic Research, Cambridge, MA. http://www.nber.org/papers/w21063.

Carr-Hill, Roy. 2012. "Finding and Then Counting Out-of-School Children." *Compare: A Journal of Comparative and International Education* 42 (2): 187–212. http://www .tandfonline.com/doi/abs/10.1080/03057925.2012.652806.

Claro, Susana, David Paunesku, and Carol S. Dweck. 2016. "Growth Mindset Tempers the Effects of Poverty on Academic Achievement." *Proceedings of the National Academy of Sciences* 113 (31): 8664–68. http://www.pnas.org/content /113/31/8664.full.

Conn, Katharine M. 2014. "Identifying Effective Education Interventions in Sub-Saharan Africa: A Meta-Analysis of Rigorous Impact Evaluations." Economics and Education, Columbia University, New York.

Duflo, Annie, and Jessica Kiessel. 2012. "Teacher Community Assistant Initiative (TCAI)." Policy Brief, International Growth Centre, London. http://www.theigc.org /wp-content/uploads/2015/07/Duflo-Kiessel-2012-Policy-Brief.pdf.

Duflo, Esther, Pascaline Dupas, and Michael Kremer. 2011. "Peer Effects, Teacher Incentives, and the Impact of Tracking: Evidence from a Randomized Evaluation in Kenya." *American Economic Review* 101 (5): 1739–74. https://www.aeaweb.org /articles?id=10.1257/aer.101.5.1739.

————. 2017. "The Impact of Free Secondary Education: Experimental Evidence from Ghana." Massachusetts Institute of Technology, Cambridge, MA; Stanford University, Stanford, CA; Harvard University, Cambridge, MA. https://web.stanford.edu/~pdupas/DDK_GhanaScholarships.pdf.

Evans, David K. 2017. "World Development Report 2018: Kenya Consultation Notes." World Bank, Washington, DC.

Evans, David K., and Anna Popova. 2016. "What Really Works to Improve Learning in Developing Countries? An Analysis of Divergent Findings in Systematic Reviews." *World Bank Research Observer* 31 (2): 242–70. https://openknowledge.worldbank.org/bitstream/handle/10986/21642/WPS7203.pdf?sequence=1.

————. 2017. "Cash Transfers and Temptation Goods." *Economic Development and Cultural Change* 65 (2): 189–221.

Evans, David K., and Fei Yuan. 2018. "Working Conditions of Teachers in Low- and Middle-Income Countries." Working Paper, World Bank, Washington, DC.

Favara, Marta. 2016. "Do Dreams Come True? Aspirations and Educational Attainments of Ethiopian Boys and Girls." Young Lives Working Paper 146, Young Lives, Oxford. http://www.younglives.org.uk/sites/www.younglives.org.uk/files/YL-WP145-Favara.pdf.

Filmer, Deon. 2010. "Education Attainment and Enrollment around the World: An International Database." World Bank, Washington, DC. http://econ.worldbank.org/WBSITE/EXTERNAL/EXTDEC/EXTRESEARCH/0,,contentMDK:20699532~pagePK:64214825~piPK:64214943~theSitePK:469382,00.html.

Filmer, Deon, and Louise Fox. 2014. *Youth Employment in Sub-Saharan Africa.* Washington, DC: World Bank.

Fox, Louise, Cleary Haines, Jorge Huerta Muñoz, and Alun Thomas. 2013. "Africa's Got Work to Do: Employment Prospects in the New Century." IMF Working Paper WP/13/201, International Monetary Fund, Washington, DC. https://www.imf.org/external/pubs/ft/wp/2013/wp13201.pdf.

Gaeta, Anthony, and Marina Vasilara. 1998. *Development and Human Rights: The Role of the World Bank.* Washington, DC: World Bank. http://siteresources.worldbank.org/BRAZILINPOREXTN/Resources/3817166-1185895645304/4044168-1186409169154/08DHR.pdf.

Galasso, Emanuela, Adam Wagstaff, Sophie Naudeau, and Meera Shekar. 2016. "The Economic Costs of Stunting and How to Reduce Them." Policy Research Note, World Bank, Washington, DC. http://pubdocs.worldbank.org/en/536661487971403516/PRN05-March2017-Economic-Costs-of-Stunting.pdf?utm_content=bufferde6d1&utm_medium=social&utm_source=twitter.com&utm_campaign=buffer.

Ganimian, Alejandro Jorge. 2015. *The Predictive Validity of Information from Clinical Practice Lessons: Experimental Evidence from Argentina.* Doctoral dissertation, Harvard Graduate School of Education, Cambridge, MA.

García, Jorge Luis, James J. Heckman, Duncan Ermini Leaf, and María José Prados. 2016. "The Life-Cycle Benefits of an Influential Early Childhood Program." HCEO Working Paper 2016-035, Human Capital and Economic Opportunity Global Working Group, University of Chicago, December. https://heckmanequation.org/assets/2017/01/Garcia_Heckman_Leaf_etal_2016_life-cycle-benefits-ecp_r1-p.pdf.

Gertler, Paul, James Heckman, Rodrigo Pinto, Arianna Zanolini, Christel Vermeersch, Susan Walker, Susan M. Chang, and Sally Grantham-McGregor. 2014. "Labor Market Returns to an Early Childhood Stimulation Intervention in Jamaica." *Science* 344 (6187): 998–1001. http://science.sciencemag.org/content/344/6187/998.short.

Grantham-McGregor, Sally M., Christine A. Powell, Susan P. Walker, and John H. Himes. 1991. "Nutritional Supplementation, Psychosocial Stimulation, and Mental Development of Stunted Children: The Jamaican Study." *The Lancet* 338 (8758): 1–5.

Gupta, Neeru, and Mary Mahy. 2003. "Adolescent Childbearing in Sub-Saharan Africa: Can Increased Schooling Alone Raise Ages at First Birth?" *Demographic Research* 8 (4): 93–106. http://www.demographic-research.org/volumes/vol8/4/8-4.pdf.

Hares, Susannah, and Justin Sandefur. 2016. "'Trying Small': Liberia's Bold Education Experiment." Center for Global Development (blog). https://www.cgdev.org/blog /trying-small-liberias-bold-education-experiment.

Heckman, James J., Seong Hyeok Moon, Rodrigo Pinto, Peter A. Savelyev, and Adam Yavitz. 2010. "The Rate of Return to the Highscope Perry Preschool Program." *Journal of Public Economics* 94 (1): 114–28. http://www.sciencedirect.com/science/article/pii /S0047272709001418.

Heckman, James J., and Stefano Mosso. 2014. "The Economics of Human Development and Social Mobility." *Annual Review of Economics* 6 (1): 689–733.

Heckman, James J., and Yona Rubinstein. 2001. "The Importance of Noncognitive Skills: Lessons from the GED Testing Program." *American Economic Review* 91 (2): 145–49. http://jenni.uchicago.edu/papers/Heckman_Rubinstein_AER_2001_91_2.pdf.

Heckman, James J., Jora Stixrud, and Sergio Urzua. 2006. "The Effects of Cognitive and Noncognitive Abilities on Labor Market Outcomes and Social Behavior." *Journal of Labor Economics* 24 (3, July): 411–82.

Humble, Steve, and Pauline Dixon. 2017. "The Effects of Schooling, Family, and Poverty on Children's Attainment, Potential, and Confidence—Evidence from Kinondoni, Dar Es Salaam, Tanzania." *International Journal of Educational Research* 83: 94–106. http:// www.sciencedirect.com/science/article/pii/S0883035517300228.

Hungi, Njora, Demus Makuwa, Kenneth Ross, Mioko Saito, Stephanie Dolata, Frank van Cappelle, Laura Paviot, and Jocelyne Vellient. 2010. "SACMEQ III Project Results: Pupil Achievement Levels in Reading and Mathematics." Southern and Eastern Africa Consortium for Monitoring Educational Quality, Gaborone. https://nicspaull.files.wordpress.com/2011/04/wd01_sacmeq_iii_results_pupil _achievement.pdf.

Inoue, Keiko, Emanuela Di Gropello, Yesim Sayin Taylor, and James Gresham. 2015. *Out-of-School Youth in Sub-Saharan Africa: A Policy Perspective.* Washington, DC: World Bank.

Jackson, C. Kirabo. 2016. "What Do Test Scores Miss? The Importance of Teacher Effects on Non-Test Score Outcomes." NBER Working Paper w22226, National Bureau of Economic Research, Cambridge, MA. http://www.nber.org/papers/w22226.

Jensen, Robert. 2010. "The (Perceived) Returns to Education and the Demand for Schooling." *Quarterly Journal of Economics* 125 (2): 515–48. doi: 10.1162/qjec .2010.125.2.515.

———. 2012. "Do Labor Market Opportunities Affect Young Women's Work and Family Decisions? Experimental Evidence from India." *Quarterly Journal of Economics* 127 (2): 753–92. http://qje.oxfordjournals.org/content/127/2/753.full.

Kazianga, Harounan, Dan Levy, Leigh L. Linden, and Matt Sloan. 2013. "The Effects of 'Girl-Friendly' Schools: Evidence from the Bright School Construction Program in Burkina Faso." *American Economic Journal: Applied Economics* 5 (3): 41–62. http://www.leighlinden.com/BRIGHT_Schools.pdf.

Kremer, Michael, Conner Brannen, and Rachel Glennerster. 2013. "The Challenge of Education and Learning in the Developing World." *Science* 340 (6130): 297–300. http://science.sciencemag.org/content/340/6130/297.

Lauwerier, Thibaut, and Abdeljalil Akkari. 2015. "Teachers and the Quality of Basic Education in Sub-Saharan Africa." Education Research and Foresight: Working Paper 11, UNESCO, Geneva. http://archive-ouverte.unige.ch/unige:73216/ATTACHMENT01.

Lewin, Keith M. 2008. *Strategies for Sustainable Financing of Secondary Education in Sub-Saharan Africa.* Washington, DC: World Bank.

Marini, Alessandra, and Omar Arias. 2016. "Peru's Success in Reducing Stunting." In *An Investment Framework for Nutrition,* edited by Meera Shekar, Jakub Kakietek, Julia Dayton Eberwein, and Dylan Walters. Washington, DC: World Bank. http://documents.worldbank.org/curated/en/758331475269503930/pdf/108645-v2-PUBLIC-Investment-Framework-for-Nutrition.pdf.

Marini, Alessandra, Claudia Rokx, and Paul Gallagher. 2017. "Standing Tall: Peru's Success in Overcoming Its Stunting Crisis." Working Paper, World Bank, Washington, DC.

Martinez, Maria Emilia, and Steve Frank Bain. 2013. "The Costs of Remedial and Developmental Education in Postsecondary Education." *Research in Higher Education Journal* 22 (February): 1–40.

Martinez, Sebastian, Sophie Naudeau, and Vitor Pereira. 2012. "The Promise of Preschool in Africa: A Randomized Impact Evaluation of Early Childhood Development in Rural Mozambique." Inter-American Development Bank, Washington, DC; World Bank, Washington, DC; Pontifical Catholic University of Rio de Janeiro. http://www.issuelab.org/resources/20195/20195.pdf.

Mbiti, Isaac M. 2016. "The Need for Accountability in Education in Developing Countries." *Journal of Economic Perspectives* 30 (3): 109–32.

Mingat, Alain, Blandine Ledoux, and Ramahatra Rakotomalala. 2010. *Developing Post-Primary Education in Sub-Saharan Africa: Assessing the Financial Sustainability of Alternative Pathways.* Washington, DC: World Bank.

Montenegro, Claudio E., and Harry Anthony Patrinos. 2014. "Comparable Estimates of Returns to Schooling around the World." Policy Research Working Paper 7020, World Bank, Washington, DC. http://documents.worldbank.org/curated/en/830831468147839247/Comparable-estimates-of-returns-to-schooling-around-the-world.

Mulkeen, Aidan. 2010. *Teachers in Anglophone Africa: Issues in Teacher Supply, Training, and Management.* Washington, DC: World Bank. http://siteresources.worldbank.org/EDUCATION/Resources/278200-1099079877269/Teachers_Anglophone_Africa.pdf.

Muralidharan, Karthik. 2016. "A New Approach to Public Sector Hiring in India for Improved Service Delivery." Paper prepared for the "India Policy Forum," National Council of Applied Economic Research, New Delhi, July 14–15, 2015. http://www.ncaer.org/uploads/photo-gallery/files/1436783346IPF%202015%20Karthik%20Conference%20Version%20Draft.pdf.

———. 2017. "Field Experiments in Education in Developing Countries." In *Handbook of Economic Field Experiments,* edited by Esther Duflo and Abhijit Banerjee. Amsterdam: North-Holland.

Muralidharan, Karthik, Jishnu Das, Alaka Holla, and Aakash Mohpal. 2017. "The Fiscal Cost of Weak Governance: Evidence from Teacher Absence in India." *Journal of Public Economics* 145 (January): 116–35.

Muralidharan, Karthik, and Nishith Prakash. 2013. "Cycling to School: Increasing Secondary School Enrollment for Girls in India." NBER Working Paper 19305, National Bureau of Economic Research, Cambridge, MA.

Muralidharan, Karthik, Abhijeet Singh, and Alejandro Ganimian. 2016. "Disrupting Education? Experimental Evidence on Technology-Aided Instruction in India." University of California, San Diego. http://econweb.ucsd.edu/~kamurali/papers/Working%20Papers/Disrupting%20Education%20(Current%20WP).pdf.

Nguyen, Trang. 2008. "Information, Role Models, and Perceived Returns to Education: Experimental Evidence from Madagascar." Economics Department, Massachusetts Institute of Technology, Cambridge, MA.http://xxpt.ynjgy.com/resource/data/20091115/U/MIT20091115040/OcwWeb/Economics/14-771Fall-2008/Readings/PaperJM%20TRANG%20NGUYEN%2022jan08.pdf.

Özler, Berk, Lia C. H. Fernald, Patricia Karol Kariger, Christin McConnell, Michelle J. Neuman, and Eduardo Fraga. 2016. "Combining Preschool Teacher Training with Parenting Education: A Cluster-Randomized Controlled Trial." World Bank, Washington, DC. http://documents.worldbank.org/curated/en/580351473691118169/Combining-preschool-teacher-training-with-parenting-education-a-cluster-randomized-controlled-trial.

PASEC (Programme d'Analyse des Systèmes Educatifs de la CONFEMEN). 2015. *PASEC 2014—Education System Performance in Francophone Sub-Saharan Africa: Competencies and Learning Factors in Primary Education.* Dakar: PASEC. http://www.pasec.confemen.org/wp-content/uploads/2015/12/Rapport_Pasec2014_GB_webv2.pdf.

Piper, Benjamin, Leila Schroeder, and Barbara Trudell. 2016. "Oral Reading Fluency and Comprehension in Kenya: Reading Acquisition in a Multilingual Environment." *Journal of Research in Reading* 39 (2): 133–52. http://onlinelibrary.wiley.com/doi/10.1111/1467-9817.12052/full.

Popova, Anna, David K. Evans, and Violeta Arancibia. 2016. "Training Teachers on the Job: What Works and How to Measure It." Policy Research Working Paper 7834, World Bank, Washington, DC. https://openknowledge.worldbank.org/handle/10986/25150.

Pradhan, Menno, Daniel Suryadarma, Amanda Beatty, Maisy Wong, Armida Alishjabana, Arya Gaduh, and Rima Prama Artha. 2014. "Improving Educational Quality through Enhancing Community Participation: Results from a Randomized Field Experiment in Indonesia." *American Economic Journal: Applied Economics* 6 (2): 105–26. https://www.aeaweb.org/articles?id=10.1257/app.6.2.105.

Pritchett, Lant, and Amanda Beatty. 2015. "Slow Down, You're Going Too Fast: Matching Curricula to Student Skill Levels." *International Journal of Educational Development* 40 (January): 276–88. http://www.sciencedirect.com/science/article/pii/S073805 9314001217.

Republic of Madagascar. 2012. "Plan intérimaire pour l'éducation [Interim Education Sector Plan] 2013–2015." Antananarivo: Ministère de l'Éducation.

Romero, Mauricio, Justin Sandefur, and Wayne Aaron Sandholtz. 2017. "Outsourcing Service Delivery in a Fragile State: Experimental Evidence from Liberia." Working Paper, University of California at San Diego, San Diego, CA.

Rubio-Codina, Marta, Orazio Attanasio, and Sally Grantham-McGregor. 2016. "Mediating Pathways in the Socio-Economic Gradient of Child Development: Evidence from Children 6–42 Months in Bogota." *International Journal of Behavioral Development* 40 (6): 483–91.

Sawada, Yasuyuki, Takeshi Aida, Andrew Griffen, Harounan Kazianga, Eiji Kozuka, Haruko Nogushi, and Yasuyuki Todo. 2016. "On the Role of Community Management in Correcting Market Failures of Rural Developing Areas: Evidence from a Randomized Field Experiment of COGES Project in Burkina Faso." Selected paper prepared for presentation at the 2016 "Agricultural and Applied Economics Association Annual Meeting," Boston, MA, July 31–August 2. http://ageconsearch. umn.edu/bitstream/236323/2/SelectedPaper_9662.pdf.

Schoellman, Todd. 2016. "Early Childhood Human Capital and Development." *American Economic Journal: Macroeconomics* 8 (3): 145–74. https://www.aeaweb.org /articles?id=10.1257/mac.20150117.

Shekar, Meera, Jakub Kakietek, Julia Dayton Eberwein, and Dylan Walters. 2017. *An Investment Framework for Nutrition: Reaching the Global Targets for Stunting, Anemia, Breastfeeding, and Wasting.* Vol. 2: *Main Report.* Washington, DC: World Bank. http:// documents.worldbank.org/curated/en/758331475269503930/main-report.

Sibanda, Menno Mulder, and Michelle Mehta. 2017. "Senegal's Nutrition Policy Development Process: A Work in Progress." In *An Investment Framework for Nutrition: Reaching the Global Targets for Stunting, Anemia, Breastfeeding, and Wasting,* edited by Meera Shekar, Jakub Kakietek, Julia Dayton Eberwein, and Dylan Walters. Directions in Development—Human Development. Washington, DC: World Bank. http://documents.worldbank.org/curated/en/758331475269503930/pdf/108645-v2 -PUBLIC-Investment-Framework-for-Nutrition.pdf.

Snilstveit, Birte, Jennifer Stevenson, Radhika Menon, Daniel Phillips, Emma Gallagher, Maisie Geleen, Hannah Jobse, Tanja Schmidt, and Emmanuel Jimenez. 2016. *The Impact of Education Programmes on Learning and School Participation in Low- and Middle-Income Countries: A Systematic Review Summary Report.* New Delhi: International Initiative for Impact Evaluation (3ie). http://www.3ieimpact.org/media /filer_public/2016/09/20/srs7-education-report.pdf.

Tafere, Yisak. 2014. "Education Aspirations and Barriers to Achievement for Young People in Ethiopia." Young Lives Working Paper 120, Young Lives, Oxford. http:// www.younglives-ethiopia.org/files/working-papers/education-aspirations-and-barri ers-to-achievement-for-young-people-in-ethiopia.

Tschirley, David L., Jason Snyder, Michael Dolislager, Thomas Reardon, Steven Haggblade, Joseph Goeb, Lulama Traub, Francis Ejobi, and Ferdi Meyer. 2015. "Africa's Unfolding Diet Transformation: Implications for Agrifood System Employment."

Journal of Agribusiness in Developing and Emerging Economies 5 (2): 102–36. http://fsg.afre.msu.edu/JADEE_2015_Tschirley_ESAAfricaDietChange.pdf.

UNDESA (United Nations Department of Economic and Social Affairs). 2015. "Population 2030: Demographic Challenges and Opportunities for Sustainable Development Planning." St/Esa/Ser.A/389, UNDESA, Population Division, New York. http://www.un.org/en/development/desa/population/publications/pdf/trends/Population2030.pdf.

UNESCO (United Nations Educational, Scientific, and Cultural Organization). 2015. "EFA Global Monitoring Report 2015. Regional Overview: Sub-Saharan Africa." UNESCO, Paris.

UNICEF (United Nations Children's Fund). 2013. "Improving Child Nutrition: The Achievable Imperative of Global Progress." UNICEF, New York. https://www.unicef.org/gambia/Improving_Child_Nutrition_-_the_achievable_imperative_for_global_progress.pdf.

USAID (U.S. Agency for International Development). 2017a. "The Demographic and Health Survey Program." USAID, Washington, DC. http://dhsprogram.com/data/.

———. 2017b. "Early Grade Reading Barometer." USAID, Washington, DC. http://www.earlygradereadingbarometer.org/.

Uwezo. 2013. "Are Our Children Learning? Literacy and Numeracy across East Africa." Twaweza East Africa, Nairobi. http://www.uwezo.net/wp-content/uploads/2012/08/2013-Annual-Report-Final-Web-version.pdf.

———. 2015. *Are Our Children Learning? The State of Education in Kenya in 2015 and Beyond.* Nairobi: Twaweza East Africa. http://www.uwezo.net/wp-content/uploads/2016/05/05-16-Kenya-small-size.pdf.

Vakis, Renos. 2017. "Peru: If You Think You Can Get Smarter, You Will." Projects and Operations, World Bank, Washington, DC, April 25. http://www.worldbank.org/en/results/2017/04/25/peru-if-you-think-you-can-get-smarter-you-will.

Valerio, Alexandria, Brent Parton, and Alicia Robb. 2014. *Entrepreneurship Education and Training Programs around the World: Dimensions for Success.* Washington, DC: World Bank. https://openknowledge.worldbank.org/handle/10986/18031.

Valerio, Alexandria, Maria Laura Sanchez Puerta, Namrata Tognatta, and Sebastian Monroy-Taborda. 2016. "Are There Skills Payoffs in Low- and Middle-Income Countries? Empirical Evidence Using STEP Data." Policy Research Working Paper 7879, World Bank, Washington, DC.

Venkat, Hamsa, and Nic Spaull. 2015. "What Do We Know about Primary Teachers' Mathematical Content Knowledge in South Africa? An Analysis of SACMEQ 2007." *International Journal of Educational Development* 41 (March): 121–30. https://nicspaull.files.wordpress.com/2011/04/venkat-spaull-2015-ijed-what-do-we-know-about-primary-teachers-maths-ck-in-sa.pdf.

Verspoor, Adriaan. 2008. *At the Crossroads: Choices for Secondary Education in Sub-Saharan Africa.* Washington, DC: World Bank.

Walker, Susan P., Theodore D. Wachs, Julie Meeks Gardner, Betsy Lozoff, Gail A. Wasserman, Ernesto Pollitt, Julie A. Carter, and International Child Development Steering Group. 2007. "Child Development: Risk Factors for Adverse Outcomes in Developing Countries." *Lancet* 369 (9556): 145–57.

Were, Maureen. 2007. "Determinants of Teenage Pregnancies: The Case of Busia District in Kenya." *Economics and Human Biology* 5 (2): 322–39. http://www.sciencedirect .com/science/article/pii/S1570677X07000287.

World Bank. 2012. "Mozambique Education Sector Support Project." Project Paper Report 65968-MZ, World Bank, Washington, DC.

———. 2013. "Service Delivery Indicators." World Bank, Washington, DC.

———. 2015. "Where Does ELP Work?" Education Brief, World Bank, Washington, DC. http://www.worldbank.org/en/topic/education/brief/early-learning-partnership-coun tries#Kenya.

———. 2017. *World Development Report 2017: Governance and the Law.* Washington, DC: World Bank. https://openknowledge.worldbank.org/handle/10986/6001.

———. Various years. World Development Indicators database. Washington, DC: World Bank.

World Policy Center. 2016. "Is Education Tuition-Free?" World Policy Center, New York. http://www.worldpolicycenter.org/policies/is-education-tuition-free/is-beginning -secondary-education-tuition-free.

Zuilkowski, Stephanie Simmons, Matthew C. H. Jukes, and Margaret M. Dubeck. 2016. "'I Failed, No Matter How Hard I Tried': A Mixed-Methods Study of the Role of Achievement in Primary School Dropout in Rural Kenya." *International Journal of Educational Development* 50 (September): 100–07. http://www.sciencedirect.com/sci ence/article/pii/S0738059316301638.

Building Skills for the School-to-Work Transition in Sub-Saharan Africa

Indhira Santos, Daniel Alonso Soto, and Shobhana Sosale

Despite the potential for technical and vocational education and training (TVET) to improve the school-to-work transition and promote aggregate productivity and inclusion, TVET systems in most of Sub-Saharan Africa remain fragmented and disconnected from labor market demands. As a result, TVET is too often seen to be failing students, employers, and taxpayers. Investments in TVET also carry a likely trade-off between investing in skills for the economic needs of today and investing in those for the needs of tomorrow; TVET systems tend to track students too early into very narrow fields of specialization, with a penalty in the labor market vis-à-vis general education that grows over time.

Hence, as TVET expands, the focus should be on (a) strengthening the evidence base for all decision making, (b) prioritizing selected growth sectors while support-ing TVET in the informal sector, and (c) strengthening the links between TVET and market demands by focusing on foundational and core business skills; partnering with the private sector, including for the provision of apprenticeships; avoiding premature tracking; and aligning financing and institutional arrangements more closely with performance or reforms to improve incentives. Higher-quality TVET following these principles could meet its promise of facilitat-ing the school-to-work transition and improving youths' life chances.

Skills Acquisition for the School-to-Work Transition through Technical and Vocational Education and Training

Preemployment TVET[1] comprises skills development programs that primarily aim to serve as a springboard into the world of work. Although not necessarily the case, most formal TVET programs are aimed at youths who are finishing primary or lower-secondary education and approaching the end of their academic education;

in addition, polytechnics and technical universities provide technical education at the tertiary level. TVET differs from general education primarily in that it focuses on technical, occupation-specific skills seen as more immediately relevant for work rather than on academic and foundational skills often aimed at preparing students for further studies as opposed to for immediate insertion into the labor market.

The duration of school-based technical and vocational education is between three and six years, depending on the country and the model. In an attempt to expose young people to preemployment skills, countries like Burkina Faso, Liberia, and Mozambique have incorporated basic vocational skills into the general lower- or junior-secondary school curriculum, while other countries wait until upper-secondary school to track students into TVET.

A significant part of TVET in Sub-Saharan Africa takes place outside of the formal education system, delivered by public, private, or nongovernmental organizations, often informally (Adams, Johansson, and Razmara 2013; Billetoft 2016; Filmer and Fox 2014). Some TVET training is workplace based, through apprenticeships or in-service training once in employment (table 3.1). On-the-job training, self-training, and traditional apprenticeships in the informal sector can account for up to 95 percent of all TVET, according to a survey carried out in Angola, Benin, Cameroon, Ethiopia, Senegal, and South Africa (Walther and Filipiak 2007). This chapter focuses on TVET that takes place within the formal education system (both in the classroom and in the workplace), while chapter 5 covers TVET that takes place outside the education system, mostly in the informal sector.

In Sub-Saharan Africa, interest in TVET is rising. In 2014, 12.2 percent of students (11.5 percent of women) in upper-secondary school were enrolled in a vocational program.[2] TVET is increasingly seen as essential to addressing the youth employment challenge facing the region (Filmer and Fox 2014). Indeed, the school-to-work transition is hard for many African youths (figure 3.1). Optimism about the role that TVET can play in supporting productivity and inclusion stems from the role that is often attributed to TVET in the economic transformation of East Asia and from the low unemployment

Table 3.1 **A Typology of TVET Provision**

Type of TVET	Other characteristics
Classroom based	Within formal education or outside of formal education
Classroom based and workplace based	Mixed, possibly in the form of a dual system
Workplace based	Preemployment: apprenticeships (either formal or informal) or internships
	In-service training during employment

Source: Adapted from the 2015 Education for All Global Monitoring Report (UNESCO 2015).
Note: TVET = technical and vocational education and training.

Figure 3.1 Youths' School-to-Work Transition in Select Sub-Saharan African Countries, circa 2014

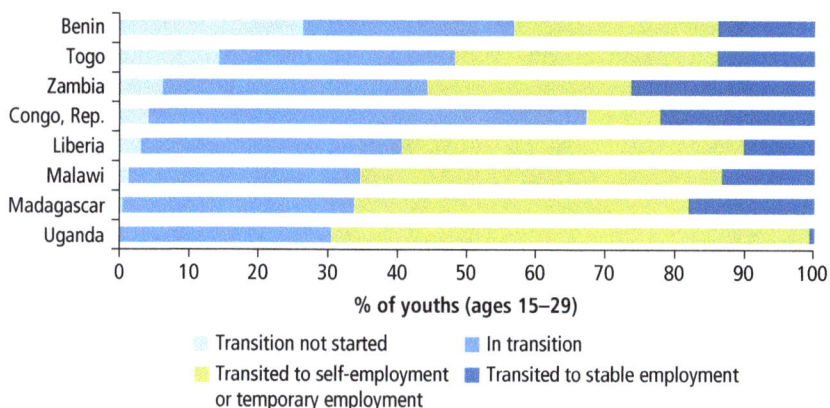

% of youths (ages 15–29)

Transition not started | In transition
Transited to self-employment or temporary employment | Transited to stable employment

Source: Based on School-to-Work Transition Surveys.
Note: Among youths who are no longer studying, "transition not started" means that they are inactive and not in education or training, with no intention of looking for work; "in transition" means that they are currently unemployed or employed in a temporary and unsatisfactory job, in unsatisfactory self-employment, or inactive and not in education or training, with an aim to look for schooling later; "transited" means that they are currently employed in a stable job, in a satisfactory but temporary job, or in satisfactory self-employment. See ILO (2014) for further details on definitions.

rates in countries with strong TVET systems like Germany.[3] Moreover, in Sub-Saharan Africa, TVET is seen as a promising route for the majority of young Africans, who lack the foundational skills, the means, or the interest to take a more academic track.

The TVET system is relatively small today, but demographic trends (chapter 1) and rising completion rates in primary and lower-secondary education (chapter 2) mean that it is likely to expand significantly in the next decades in most countries in Africa. Even with no change in the share of youths who select general versus technical education, the number of youths with TVET at the secondary level could be expected to more than quadruple in the next two decades in countries like Mali, Mozambique, Tanzania, and Uganda (figure 3.2).

High expectations about what TVET can accomplish make it critical to manage the expansion of the system smartly, balancing existing trade-offs and making necessary reforms. Chapter 1 of this report puts forward two strategic trade-offs that policy makers in Sub-Saharan Africa need to manage in skills development. These trade-offs are also present in TVET. The first trade-off is between investing in skills that maximize overall productivity growth—mostly related to catalytic sectors that can pull workers out of low-productivity activities—and investing in skills that prioritize inclusion and livelihoods.

Figure 3.2 Number of Youths (Ages 15–24) with at Least Secondary TVET in Select Sub-Saharan African Countries, 2015–40

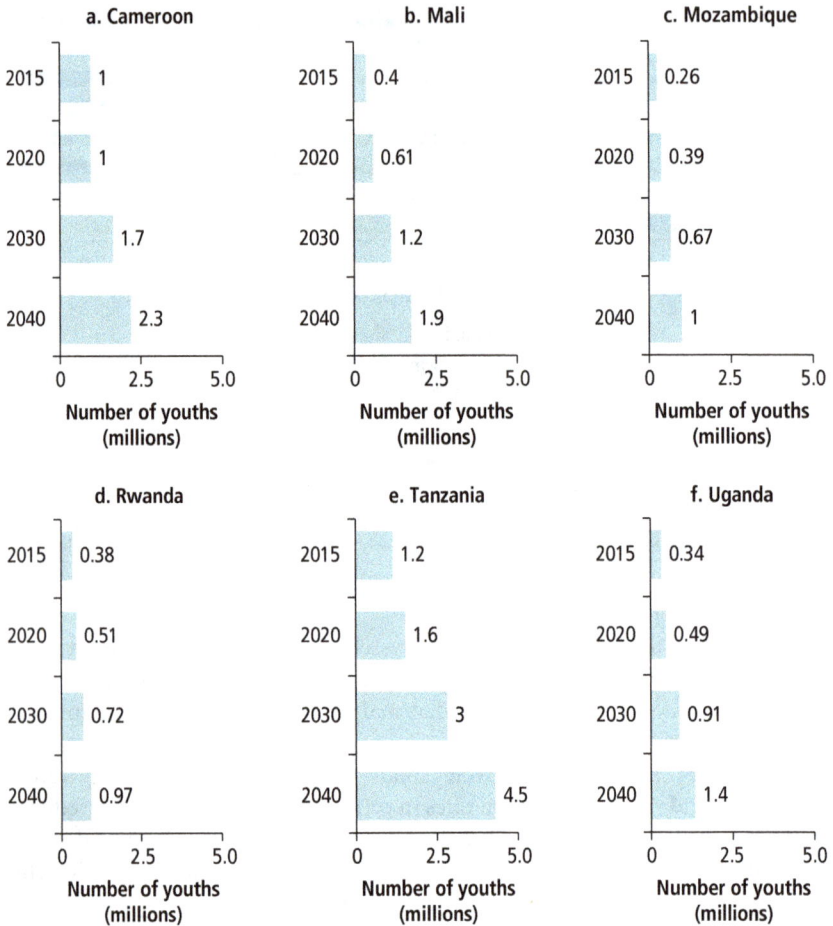

a. Cameroon

Year	Number of youths (millions)
2015	1
2020	1
2030	1.7
2040	2.3

b. Mali

Year	Number of youths (millions)
2015	0.4
2020	0.61
2030	1.2
2040	1.9

c. Mozambique

Year	Number of youths (millions)
2015	0.26
2020	0.39
2030	0.67
2040	1

d. Rwanda

Year	Number of youths (millions)
2015	0.38
2020	0.51
2030	0.72
2040	0.97

e. Tanzania

Year	Number of youths (millions)
2015	1.2
2020	1.6
2030	3
2040	4.5

f. Uganda

Year	Number of youths (millions)
2015	0.34
2020	0.49
2030	0.91
2040	1.4

Sources: Based on UIS.Stat data; Barro and Lee 2015.
Note: TVET = technical and vocational education and training.

Technical and vocational skills can contribute to aggregate productivity, as the experience in East Asia suggests.[4] Recent employer surveys conducted as part of the International Labour Organization (ILO) School-to-Work Transition Surveys in Benin, Liberia, Malawi, and Zambia show that more than 60 percent of firms think that technical skills are very or extremely important for their performance—the highest among seven possible skills (chapter 1). Yet, these skills are in short supply in Sub-Saharan Africa, including in sectors such as mining, construction, or agribusiness. Nigeria, for example, had to import welders, fitters, and scaffolders from the Philippines and the United Kingdom for construction of the Bonga oilfield (McKinsey Global Institute 2012). Similarly, due to a shortage of skilled technicians and engineers, Gabon regularly imports workers, particularly in skills-intensive sectors like mining, oil, and information and communication technology (ICT) (World Bank 2016b). To contribute more to aggregate productivity, TVET needs to be better aligned with the demands of these catalytic sectors.

However, because resources are limited, a key question for governments is how much to invest in skills for the catalytic sectors (largely for skilled workers, at least in terms of direct employment) and how much to invest in technical and complementary skills for a large number of youths and adults working in low-productivity activities (often in the informal sector and with little chance of moving up to higher-productivity activities). For this latter group, skills building is about improving livelihoods and productivity at the margin. TVET is a potential avenue to achieving this goal.

Trade-offs are even starker when placing TVET in the context of governments' attempts to balance their investments in skills for today's economic needs with investments in skills for tomorrow's needs. As discussed in this chapter—and consistent with international evidence (Hampf and Woessmann 2016; Hanushek et al. 2017)—TVET seems to be more effective than general education at helping workers to get their first job and transition from school to work, but lifetime earnings are higher among those attending general education. The lower earnings of TVET graduates over the life cycle partly reflect the fact that the students who enter TVET are often those who cannot afford a general education track (which often delays entry into the labor market), who already have weaker foundational skills, or who feel unprepared for more academic training. However, part of the explanation is also likely to be that TVET tends to build narrow technical skills that are good for entering a particular occupation but that prepare workers less well for transitioning across occupations or jobs or for moving up the earnings ladder (Hanushek et al. 2017). If skills demands in Sub-Saharan Africa evolve as they are in the rest of the world, with increased emphasis on transferable skills and adaptability associated with strong foundational cognitive and socioemotional skills (chapter 1), and TVET systems do not modernize, the gap between TVET and general education training could well widen. As a result, the advantages of vocational training in easing entry into the labor market have to be set against the disadvantages later in the job market.

While managing these trade-offs requires making some difficult choices, countries in the region have an opportunity to "leapfrog" in some aspects of TVET. The first opportunity for leapfrogging arises because countries in Sub-Saharan Africa can avoid some of the mistakes that countries in other regions have made when expanding their own TVET systems. Some countries have an opportunity to build a system on strong foundations rather than taking the very difficult path of reforming later once the system is large and legacy makes reform increasingly difficult. In general, countries in the region have both opportunities and challenges associated with strengthening TVET in a time of rapid changes associated with economic transformation, urbanization, and demographic and technological change (box 3.1).

Megatrends and Skills Building through TVET

Strong technical and vocational skills that rest on solid foundational skills can help countries in Sub-Saharan Africa to realize the potential of key megatrends—technological progress, urbanization, globalization, and economic transformation in general. First, technical skills are important for firms' ability to adopt new technologies, adapt them to local contexts, and use them productively, including in the informal sector (World Bank 2016a). Second, a two-prong TVET system—with a strategic arm that is well aligned with the needs of high-productivity, catalytic sectors and another that supports the large informal sector where most people work—can improve Africa's competitiveness in strategic sectors, while aiding urbanization and economic transformation.

These megatrends have implications for TVET in three main areas:

What skills to emphasize. In addition to the need for technical skills in traditional sectors like agriculture, low-skill manufacturing, and construction, high-productivity niches in agribusiness, mining, oil, and gas increase the demand for internationally qualified technicians and engineers. That said, narrow technical skills that may serve an individual well in a particular occupation risk leaving workers—especially young workers with long working lives ahead of them—unprepared for structural changes that may require occupational, job, and geographic mobility. Megatrends therefore make it more relevant than ever for TVET students to have strong foundational skills and wider specializations. Moreover, the megatrends and concerns about premature deindustrialization mean that TVET systems will need to pivot at least partly to catering to the service sector.

When to build these skills. If more rapid changes mean more lifelong learning, it is important for TVET to build in strong foundational skills that allow individuals to learn new skills, provide individuals with a diversity of learning options, and allow TVET to open up, rather than close, economic opportunities in the medium and long term. To do so requires building flexibility within TVET and across education tracks to allow students to combine work and study, to spend periods out of the education system and come back, and to move between technical and academic tracks if requirements are met.

(continued next page)

Box 3.1 (continued)

How to build these skills. A more dominant service sector in the economy has implications for the way practical experience is provided within TVET. Practical experience in the services sector is arguably closer to on-the-job training (often requiring an apprenticeship or internship with an employer) than practical experience in the manufacturing sector, where machines and simulations can mimic a larger part of the work experience. But the megatrends also open up opportunities for delivering services and managing TVET for results. Two key examples are urbanization and technological change. Rapid urbanization can lead to economies of scale and lower costs of provision as well as to higher urban demand that can create incentives for a larger and more diverse provision of TVET. Similarly, technological developments can open up opportunities in an array of areas, including the use of online courses to complement in-person classroom and practical training and to access cutting-edge training material worldwide, the use of technology for simulations as part of courses that can provide close-to-real-life experiences, and the effective and timely collection and dissemination of information across the system.

Revitalizing TVET, however, requires dedicated efforts from both the private and the public sectors. On the one hand, markets alone cannot generate an efficient distribution of skills due to labor market imperfections (externalities, information failures), capital market imperfections (credit constraints), coordination failures (innovation, vacancy externalities), and decision-making failures (inaccurate information about returns to investments in training or the quality of providers, inconsistent time preferences, cognitive and socioemotional limitations). So, there is a role for public action. On the other hand, as with markets, government and institutional failures—often not directly linked to labor markets—also exist and hinder accountability and the ability to strengthen links with the private sector.[5] These failures also require renewed public attention.

This chapter examines TVET in Sub-Saharan African countries with a view to considering how to strengthen current TVET systems in order to provide more *equitable, relevant, and efficient* TVET. First, the chapter provides an overview of the state of TVET in the region, including issues of enrollment, returns, and links to the rest of the education and training system. Next, it highlights the key policy challenges of providing preemployment TVET. The analysis exploits recent data from the Systems Approach for Better Education Results Workforce Development (SABER-WfD), an innovative cross-country benchmarking exercise that enables the analysis of strengths and weaknesses of TVET systems, considering the three key objectives of equity, relevance, and efficiency. The chapter ends with a discussion of overall strategic priorities for improving TVET and examples of how to achieve the necessary reforms and improvements.

The Landscape of TVET in Sub-Saharan Africa

The formal TVET system in most African countries remains small in terms of both enrollment and public expenditure. In 2014, on average around 12.2 percent of students in upper-secondary education enrolled in vocational programs, not much changed from 13.4 percent in 2010. In lower-secondary education, the share of students enrolled in vocational programs increased from an average of 2.7 percent in 2010 to 3.1 percent in 2014. Among women, the share choosing the vocational track is relatively smaller: an average of 11.5 percent in upper-secondary and 2.4 percent in lower-secondary education.[6] These levels are below what would be expected given countries' level of income and historical experience (figure 3.3).

Average figures mask significant differences across countries. Countries like Angola and Cameroon have a strong tradition of technical and vocational education, while others, like Kenya or Mauritania, have very small TVET systems (figure 3.4). In fact, tertiary TVET is where the region clearly lags other regions: the average gross enrollment ratio in tertiary technical or vocational education is only 4 percent in Sub-Saharan Africa, compared with 20 percent in Latin America and around 30 percent in higher-income countries. In terms of spending per student, the region is also below international comparators, but not so much compared with countries at a similar level of income.

Figure 3.3 Correlation between TVET Enrollment at the Secondary Level and GDP per Capita over Time and across Countries

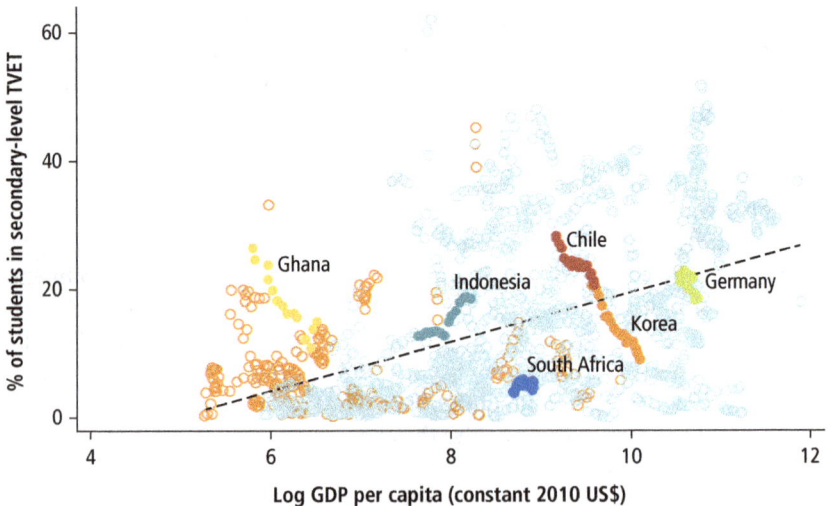

Sources: Based on UIS.Stat data; World Development Indicators.
Note: TVET = technical and vocational education and training.

Figure 3.4 Enrollment in Secondary-Level TVET, by Region and in Sub-Saharan African Countries

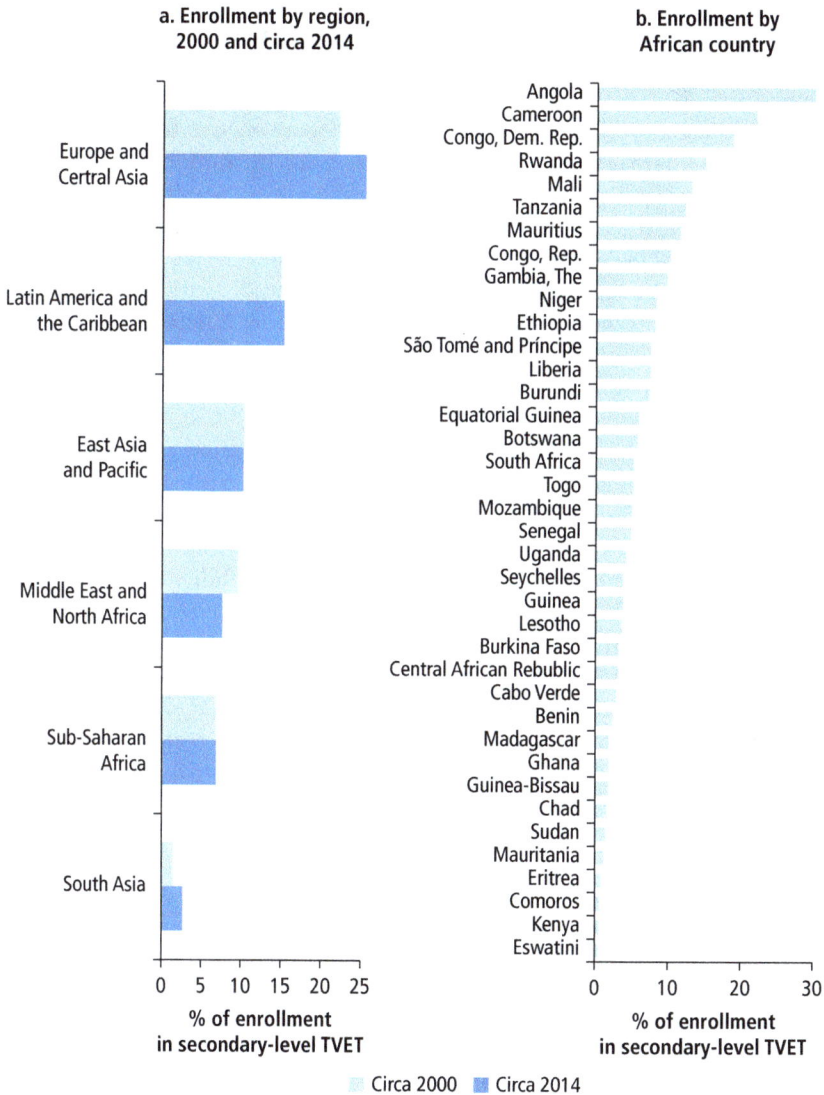

a. Enrollment by region, 2000 and circa 2014

b. Enrollment by African country

Circa 2000   Circa 2014

Source: Based on UIS.Stat data.
Note: TVET = technical and vocational education and training. On panel b, Angola = 45.2.

As in other regions, women and men enter very different TVET fields, with women often in occupations with lower average earnings. In Nigeria, there is almost a 2:1 male-female enrollment ratio in monotechnics and polytechnics at the tertiary level (World Bank 2015a). The gender gap is particularly large in architecture, ICT, accommodation or food services, and mechanics, which are male-dominated fields. Similarly, in Burkina Faso, women outnumber men in commerce, whereas men outnumber women 5:1 in the industrial sectors (mechanical, electronics, construction) (World Bank 2017b). In Uganda, three programs—construction, motor vehicle maintenance, and carpentry—account for two-thirds of male enrollment, whereas cooking or catering, beautician services, business-related studies, and tailoring account for two-thirds of female enrollment (Johanson and Okema 2011). These gender differences matter for future earnings. A study in Uganda finds that women who cross over into male-dominated sectors make as much as men and three times more than women who stay in female-dominated sectors (Campos et al. 2015). At the source of these gender differences are problems of information about opportunities in male-dominated industries and psychosocial factors regarding gender norms that kick in very early in life (see chapter 2) (Campos et al. 2015; World Bank 2011). Consequently, a major challenge for TVET—and society more generally—is to overcome the barriers that keep many individuals, especially women, from accessing higher-productivity jobs.[7]

In general, TVET in the region pays too little attention to practical training. Some countries, especially in West Africa, have a tradition of apprenticeships. In Ghana, for example, more than one-third of youths ages 25–34 report having held an apprenticeship (or internship). On average, however, across several countries in the region, only one-fifth of students enter an apprenticeship or internship (figure 3.5). Most do so informally, often with no link to formal TVET or any in-classroom training (see chapter 5; Adams, Johansson, and Razmara 2013; Franz 2017). In countries like Malawi or Rwanda, fewer than 15 percent of TVET students have ever held an apprenticeship or internship; in Burkina Faso, in 2011/12, only 4 percent of TVET students at the secondary level have participated in an apprenticeship (Tiyab 2014). In Cameroon, for example, skills testing for major occupations is mainly theoretical, and certificates, which are only recognized by the public sector, are perceived to have little impact on employment and earnings (Sosale and Majgaard 2016). In fact, many TVET institutions find it hard to place students in internships or apprenticeships, so such internships are often not required (World Bank 2017b). Employers and other stakeholders often see this lack of practical training as one of the main weaknesses of TVET systems in the region, as reflected in in-depth country and regional studies.[8]

For countries where comparable data are available, attending TVET does have positive average returns in the labor market early in the school-to-work

Figure 3.5 Share of Adults Ages 25–34 Who Report Ever Having Been in an Internship or Apprenticeship in Select Sub-Saharan African Countries

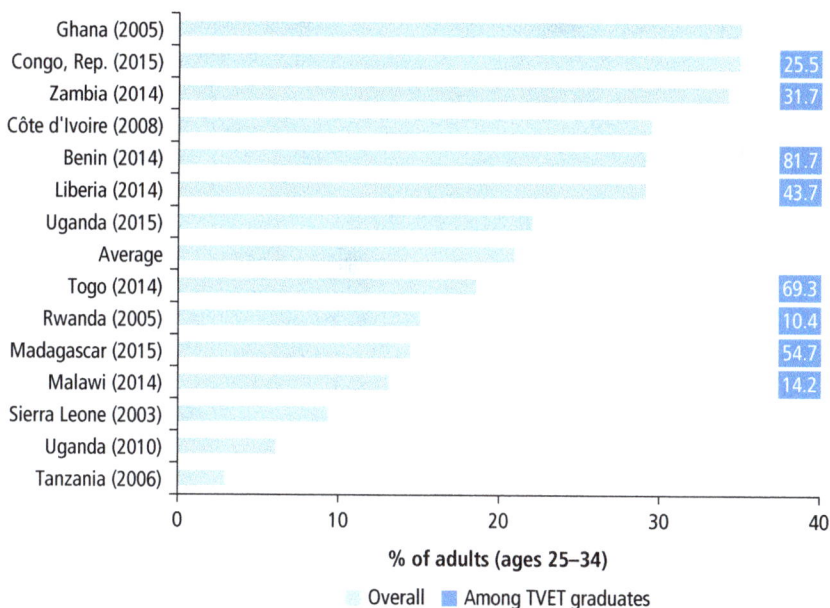

Sources: Based on School-to-Work Transition Surveys; Filmer and Fox 2014.
Note: TVET = technical and vocational education and training. No data for TVET graduates are available for Côte d'Ivoire 2008, Uganda 2010 and 2015, and Tanzania 2006.

transition, although returns often are lower than those for general secondary or tertiary education. Although it is difficult to measure with precision,[9] average returns to TVET are positive early in the school-to-work transition (figure 3.6, panel a). In the Republic of Congo and Zambia, for example, an additional year of TVET is associated with almost a 25 percent increase in wages among wage workers. But there is variation: in Benin and Madagascar, average returns are less than 10 percent per additional year of TVET. However, even when returns to TVET are positive, they are usually lower than returns to general education, particularly at the tertiary level (figure 3.6, panel b). This is the case not only for the whole population but also for younger workers.

Averages, as usual, mask significant heterogeneity. Taking a technical instead of an academic track in secondary can make sense for persons with lower earning potential and few chances of continuing to a university education. Analysis for Ghana and Kenya indicates that whether TVET or general education is the best path for an individual very much depends on the characteristics of that individual and, especially, his or her chances of continuing to university (where returns are the highest). In both countries, secondary TVET has a higher return

Figure 3.6 Returns to General Education and to TVET in Wage Employment Early in the School-to-Work Transition for Workers in Select Sub-Saharan African Countries

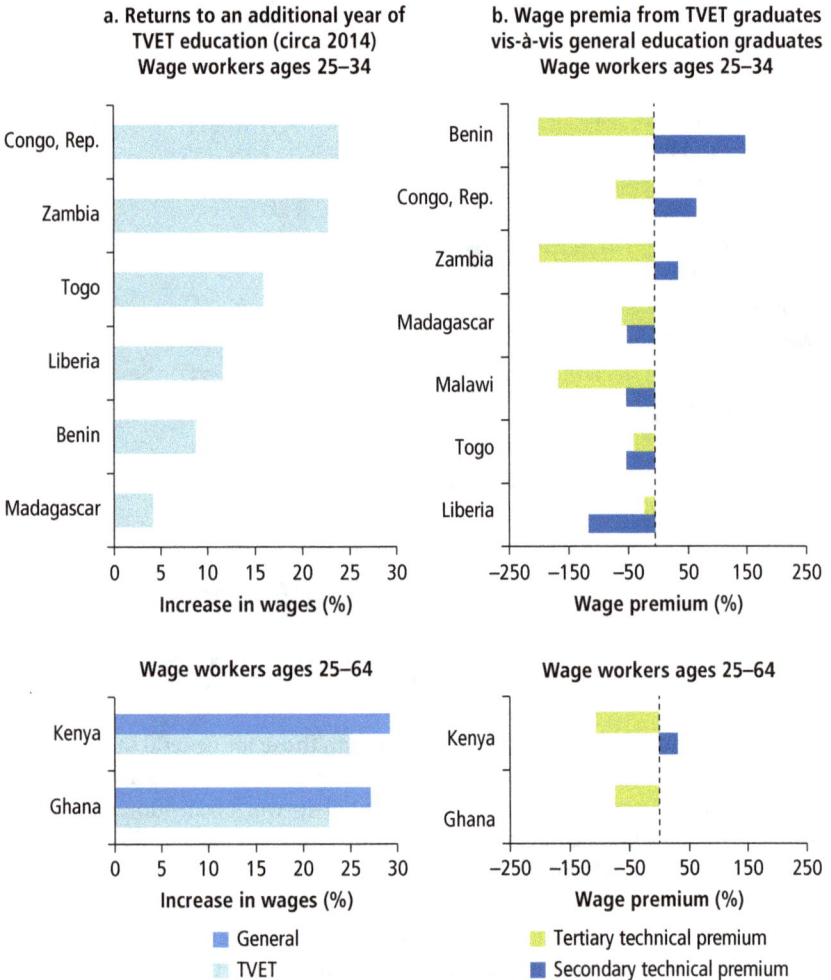

a. Returns to an additional year of TVET education (circa 2014) Wage workers ages 25–34

b. Wage premia from TVET graduates vis-à-vis general education graduates Wage workers ages 25–34

Wage workers ages 25–64

Wage workers ages 25–64

General
TVET
Tertiary technical premium
Secondary technical premium

Sources: Based on School-to-Work Transition Surveys; Skills Towards Employability and Productivity (STEP) Household Surveys.
Note: TVET = technical and vocational education and training. Estimates are for wage workers from linear regressions controlling for gender, age, and potential work experience. All coefficients are significant at the 1 percent level. Panel a shows the returns to an additional year of TVET or general education. Panel b shows the wage premium of secondary or tertiary TVET vis-à-vis general education (secondary or university). A positive premium means that TVET pays off more than general education. For Ghana and Kenya, the estimated returns for an additional year of TVET (from both wage employment but also self-employment and family work, not in the figure) are 12 and 9 percent, respectively (compared with 13 and 10 percent, respectively, for general education).

Figure 3.7 Potential Hourly Earnings in Ghana and Kenya, by Track and Estimated Percentile of Earnings

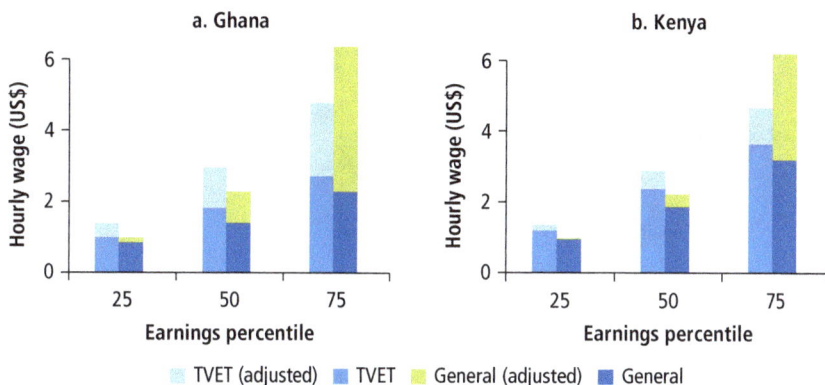

Source: Based on Skills Towards Employability and Productivity (STEP) Household Surveys.
Note: TVET = technical and vocational education and training. Estimates are from a quintile regression of earnings controlling for gender and potential work experience. The values shown are for a typical man with no work. The adjusted values account for the potential earnings after completing either tertiary technical or university studies, adjusted by the probability of accessing such studies given the worker's socioeconomic status. The probability is estimated as the proportion of university (tertiary TVET) graduates among all workers with more than a general secondary education (secondary TVET), by socioeconomic status.

than general secondary for individuals with lower earning potential (figure 3.7). For this group—who may not have the academic readiness or resources for pursuing an academic track and especially for continuing to the university level—TVET can be a better option, given the limitations they face at the time of tracking. This pattern is expected, given the high average returns associated with a university degree and how uncommon reaching this level—especially at a high-quality university—remains in most countries in Sub-Saharan Africa (chapter 4).

Lower average returns to TVET vis-à-vis general education—and possibly some of the concerns regarding quality and stigma linked to TVET—are likely to reflect a relatively more disadvantaged background and lower level of academic readiness among TVET students. Those who attend TVET, compared with those who enter a general education track, tend to come from families with lower socioeconomic status (although they are not among the poorest in the overall population), as measured by educational level of the parents (figure 3.8). TVET students are also likely to have weaker foundational skills, suggesting a lower level of academic readiness and lack of sufficient attention to these skills in TVET.[10] In Ghana, for example, TVET graduates score almost 4 standard deviations below general secondary graduates on a literacy test. In terms of probability of enrollment, scoring 1 standard deviation more on the literacy test lowers the probability of enrollment in TVET (compared with general

Figure 3.8 Odds Ratios of the Probability of Attending Secondary-Level TVET versus General Secondary in Ghana and Kenya

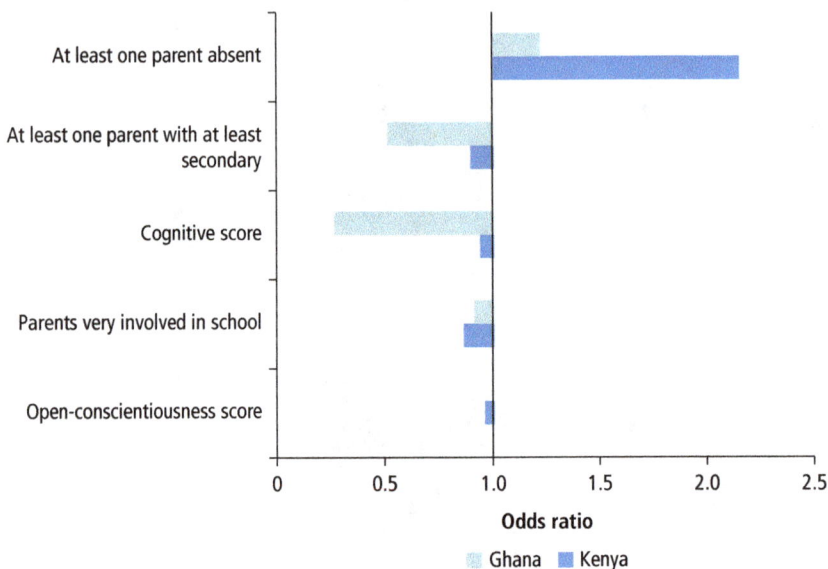

Source: Based on Skills Towards Employability and Productivity (STEP) Household Surveys.
Note: TVET = technical and vocational education and training. Estimates from a multilogit regression controlling for gender, if student started first grade at seven years of age or more, age cohort, language, and number of siblings at age 15. The cognitive score and the socioemotional score (open-conscientiousness) are measured in standard deviations. The figure represents odds ratios, in this case the ratio of the probability of attending secondary-level TVET over general secondary. If the ratio equals 1, there is no difference in the probability among the two tracks; positive values reflect factors that are associated with a higher probability of enrollment in TVET and vice versa.

education) by 75 percent in Ghana and more than 10 percent in Kenya. This result is, of course, partly by design, as access to the different tracks is often based on the students' performance in lower secondary.

The selection into TVET by youths with weaker foundational skills and from lower-income households is consistent with what has been found in other contexts and sheds light on why TVET can be an important gateway into the world of work. Controlling for several other factors, students from vocational and technical schools perform significantly worse than students from general education on the Program for International Student Assessment (PISA), an international test focused on foundational skills (Altinok 2011). Consistent with the previous discussion, students from poorer socioeconomic backgrounds in vocational schools perform better on PISA than similar students in general education schools, while the reverse is true for students from better-off households. Similarly, in South Africa, Pugatch (2014) finds a decrease of 1 percentage point in vocational enrollment in response to grade failure, compared with a decline of

40 percentage points for academic enrollment. TVET is seen as a second-rate choice for individuals with academic aptitude, but it can be a more promising avenue for others. In other words, given weak foundational skills and other disadvantages and the fact that they are unlikely to be able to attend the high-quality general education institutions that richer, better-prepared students are able to attend, TVET can be an attractive path for the less well-off. This is especially the case in countries where access to universities remains mostly limited to elites. Of course, this segregation is not ideal, and the first best option is to make sure that all students receive the appropriate foundation in basic education.

Beyond the issues of adverse selection, concerns about quality in TVET remain. Anecdotal evidence suggests that there is a generalized view among employers and the general public that a significant part of TVET is low quality (Johanson and Okema 2011; World Bank 2015a, 2017b; Zimmermann et al. 2013). This indeed seems to be the case given the large variation in average returns to TVET across and especially within fields of study (figure 3.9).

Figure 3.9 Relative Returns to TVET in Kenya and Ghana, by Field of Study

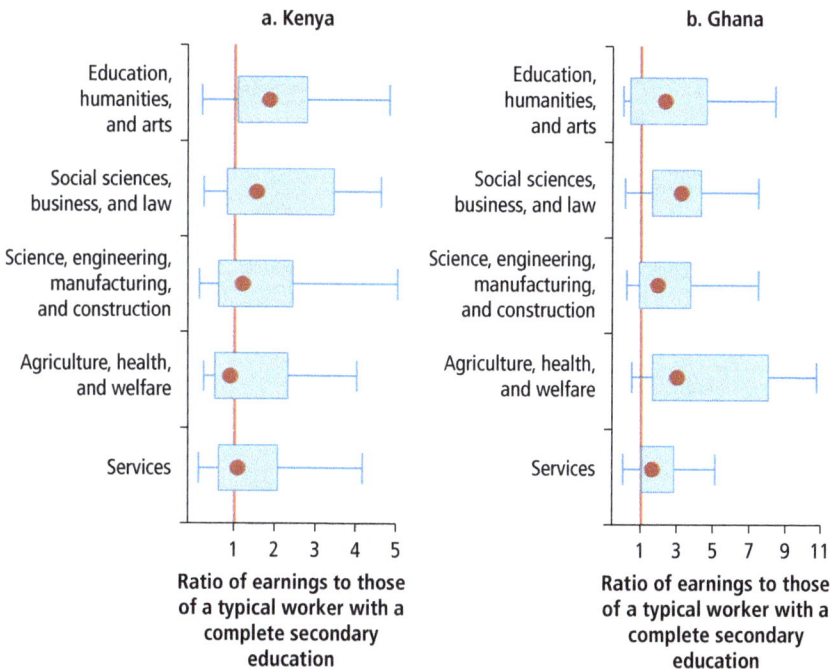

Source: Based on Skills Towards Employability and Productivity (STEP) Household Surveys.
Note: TVET = technical and vocational education and training. The red vertical line at 1 denotes parity of earnings. The red dot represents the median of the distribution. The lower end of the box represents the 25th percentile, and the upper end represents the 75th percentile. The lines outside the box represent the ratio for the highest and lowest values of earnings excluding outliers.

This large variation indicates that some TVET degrees, in some institutions, for some people, are significantly worse than others given local labor market conditions. In The Gambia, for example, a tracer study among public TVET graduates found that unemployment rates varied significantly across fields of study: from zero in fields like nursery and scientific studies to 30 percent in restaurant and bar service and more than 40 percent in software applications (Couralet, Djallo, and Akinocho 2013). For this reason, (a) quality assurance to raise standards and (b) information to help students and families to make better choices and help policy makers and the market to impose some accountability on providers are critical.

There are concerns about the medium- and long-term work prospects of TVET graduates. Young workers who went through TVET are more likely to think that their education or qualifications match well their current job than graduates from general education.[11] However, while TVET may help students to get a first job faster and allow them to have higher earnings in the early years of the school-to-work transition, graduates from TVET are, over time, more likely to be in jobs that earn less than their counterparts in general education (figure 3.10). The gaps are particularly stark at the tertiary level, but they are also present at the secondary level. This pattern is observed in countries around the world (Hampf and Woessmann 2016; Hanushek et al. 2017; Lamo, Messina, and Wasmer 2011). This life-cycle view highlights another key challenge for TVET, especially going forward: how to ensure adaptability and a solid foundation

Figure 3.10 **Earnings over the Life Cycle as a Percentage of Earnings of an Average Earner with at Most a Completed Primary Education in Kenya and Ghana**

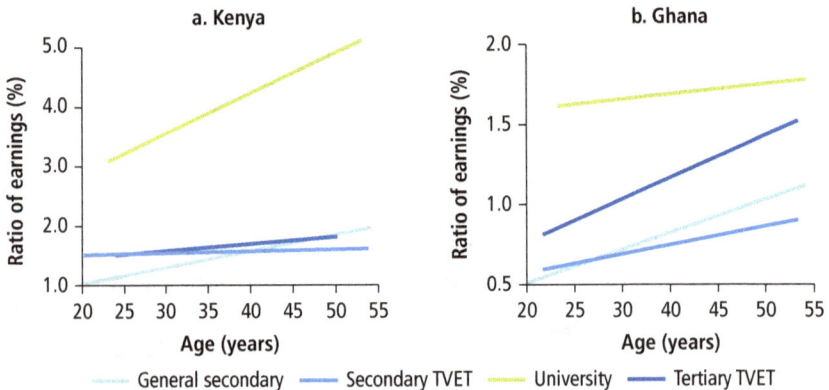

Source: Based on Skills Towards Employability and Productivity (STEP) Household Surveys.
Note: TVET = technical and vocational education and training. Results from a linear regression of earnings over age (population ages 18–55), by type of education.

among TVET graduates to allow workers to respond to changing labor market conditions and to move up the productivity ladder. Policy makers, thus, face a trade-off between investing in skills for today's needs and investing in skills for tomorrow's needs.

In some countries TVET may start too early, at the expense of building much-needed foundational skills. In a majority of African countries, TVET tracking commences at the lower-secondary education level (table 3.2). The TVET curriculum in secondary typically combines general and technical education, but more emphasis is placed on technical education. Tracking students into narrow vocational fields in lower secondary may be too early for most Sub-Saharan African countries where large numbers of students do not have strong foundational skills at the end of primary or even secondary (chapter 2). As a result, early tracking into TVET is likely to come at the expense of acquiring and reinforcing critical foundational skills and can reduce earnings potential and employment options later in life (Kutner and Gortazar 2014). Early tracking into TVET is often compounded by the difficulty of transferring to general education afterward.

Weak foundational skills, in turn, limit the capacity of workers to acquire and upgrade the very same technical skills that TVET seeks to build. In a recent paper on Kenya, Laajaj and Macours (2017) find that, even in technical areas, such as growing maize, a bundle of cognitive, socioemotional, and technical skills matters. Together, these skills explain about 12–17 percent of the variation in yields. Moreover, they find that socioemotional and cognitive skills are working partly through technical skills—that is, skills beget skills. Others have also documented these strong complementarities among different sets of skills (Psacharopoulos 1994). What is critical, therefore, is to ensure that all students arrive at the point of tracking with strong foundational skills, so that lack of

Table 3.2 Characterization of TVET Systems in Sub-Saharan Africa, by the Timing of Tracking and Paths to Tertiary Education

Possibility of further tertiary education	When tracking into TVET takes place		
	Before upper secondary	Upper secondary	Postsecondary
Only technical	Benin; Lesotho; Madagascar; Mozambique; Tanzania; Zimbabwe	Ethiopia	Eswatini
Both technical and general (although not necessarily de facto)	Burkina Faso; Burundi; Cameroon; Côte d'Ivoire; Congo, Rep.; Gabon; Guinea; Kenya; Liberia; Mali; Madagascar; Mauritania; Mauritius; Namibia; Niger; Sierra Leone; Togo; Uganda	Botswana; Chad; Congo, Dem Rep.; Gambia, The; Ghana; Malawi; Nigeria; Senegal; South Africa; Zambia	

Sources: Based on World TVET data; consultations with experts.
Note: For some countries, some technical routes can lead to universities, while others cannot. When this is the case, as in Ghana for example, the country is classified as allowing for the possibility of attending general tertiary after technical secondary education.

readiness is not the reason they enter TVET and so that, when they do enter TVET, they have a strong base for building technical skills and for adapting to changes in the labor market.

What needs to be done to improve the quality of TVET? Given overall constraints on public spending on education in most countries in the region (chapter 1), expecting a larger public spending effort on TVET may not be realistic any time soon. Moreover, expanding a low-quality system is not beneficial for anyone. Since TVET provision is estimated to be two-and-one-half to three times more expensive than general education in the region, setting priorities is particularly important (ADB 2008; Mingat, Ledoux, and Rakotomalala 2010; Tsang 1997). Many TVET centers are working with outdated technology, have underprepared teachers, and offer few opportunities for practical training (Billetoft 2016). These areas are likely to need more resources. But there are also many inefficiencies in the system, including spending on fields of study that do not pass the market test, complex national qualification frameworks (NQFs) that are difficult to implement and have potentially limited benefits, and public provision of TVET in cases where the private sector is likely to have a comparative advantage. The next section discusses possible policy priorities and options aimed at improving the performance of formal TVET with regard to equity, efficiency, and relevance.

Policy Challenges in Preemployment TVET

Equipping youths with job-relevant skills through TVET is challenging. Despite the success of TVET systems in countries like Germany or the Republic of Korea or of vocational training programs like Jobs Corps in the United States or Jovenes in Latin America (Schochet, Burghardt, and McConnell 2008), vocational training programs have often produced disappointing results. Most evaluations are of short, small programs that operate parallel to the formal TVET system, often aimed at disadvantaged youths. Even in these cases, TVET often proves difficult to get right. When designed carefully, targeted well, and with strong links to labor demand, programs can have payoffs that increase over time.[12] In Colombia, for example, between three and eight years after benefiting from training, participants were more likely to enter and remain in formal employment and had formal sector earnings that were at least 11 percent higher than nonparticipants (Kugler et al. 2015). Implementation is bound to be more difficult in systemwide interventions. In Turkey, a recent evaluation of large-scale vocational programs showed no average impacts on employment three years after the training and only transitory impacts on the quality of employment (Hirshleifer et al. 2014). In addition, a wide global literature discusses the challenges of TVET (Zimmermann et al. 2013).

Underlying this challenge in Sub-Saharan Africa are weaknesses throughout the TVET system in the countries' strategic framework, system oversight, and service delivery. These weaknesses are evidenced in the literature and in the SABER-WfD benchmarking exercise (box 3.2).[13] SABER allows for systematic documentation and assessment of the policy and institutional factors that influence the performance of workforce development systems (of which TVET is the most significant component). The countries in Sub-Saharan Africa for which SABER is available—Burundi, Cameroon, Chad, Tanzania, and Uganda—show marked weaknesses in oversight and service delivery, although they do relatively better with regard to the strategic direction of workforce development policies. While governments in the region are putting greater emphasis on workforce development, as indicated by their relatively good performance regarding strategic direction and recently completed TVET strategies,[14] the capacity of systems to go from conceptualization to policy implementation remains weak (figure 3.11).

BOX 3.2

Benchmarking TVET Systems: The Systems Approach for Better Education Results

Part of the World Bank's initiative Systems Approach for Better Education Results, SABER-WfD focuses on how well the system is equipping individuals to meet the demand for skills in the labor market and provides systematic documentation and assessment of the policy and institutional factors that influence the performance of education and training systems.

The tool is based on an analytical framework that identifies three functional dimensions of WfD policies and institutions: (1) *strategic framework*, which pertains to policies that set the direction for WfD and defines its authorizing environment; (2) *system oversight*, which relates to the "rules of the game" (including funding regimes) that guide the functioning of the system; and (3) *service delivery*, which concerns the provision of training services to equip individuals with market- and job-relevant skills.

Taken together, these three dimensions allow for a systematic analysis of the functioning of a WfD system. The focus is on the institutional structures and practices of public policy making and what they reveal about capacity in the system to conceptualize, design, coordinate, and implement policies in order to achieve results on the ground. Each dimension is composed of three "policy goals" that correspond to important functional aspects of WfD systems (detailed later in table 3.3). Data are gathered using a structured SABER-WfD data collection instrument. For each topic, the instrument poses a set of multiple-choice questions that are answered based on documentary evidence and interviews with knowledgeable informants. The answers allow each topic

---

(continued next page)

Box 3.2 (continued)

to be scored on a four-point scale against standardized rubrics based on available knowledge of global good practices. Higher values represent more mature systems. Topic scores are then averaged to produce policy goal scores, which themselves are aggregated to produce dimension scores. The results are then validated by relevant national counterparts, including the informants themselves.

In terms of how fast countries can improve the institutional framework and functioning of their TVET systems, particularly insightful are the cases of Chile, Korea, Malaysia, and Singapore, for which historical data are available. These countries—which were not that far away a few decades ago from where Sub-Saharan African countries stand today—have made significant improvements across all three dimensions: strategic framework, system oversight, and service delivery. Their experience, in addition to experience within the region, can inform reform efforts in Sub-Saharan Africa.

Source: Based on World Bank 2013.

Figure 3.11 **Relative Performance of African Countries on TVET**

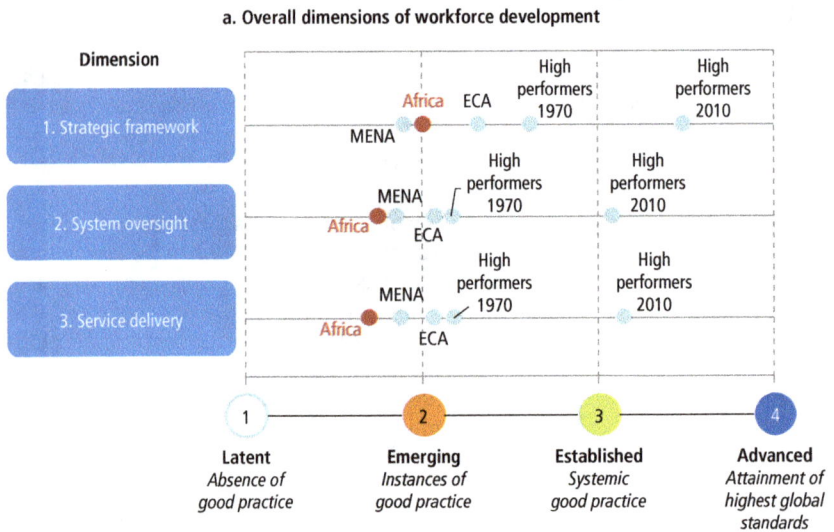

a. Overall dimensions of workforce development

(continued next page)

Figure 3.11 (continued)

b. Workforce development performance across specific policy goals, by region

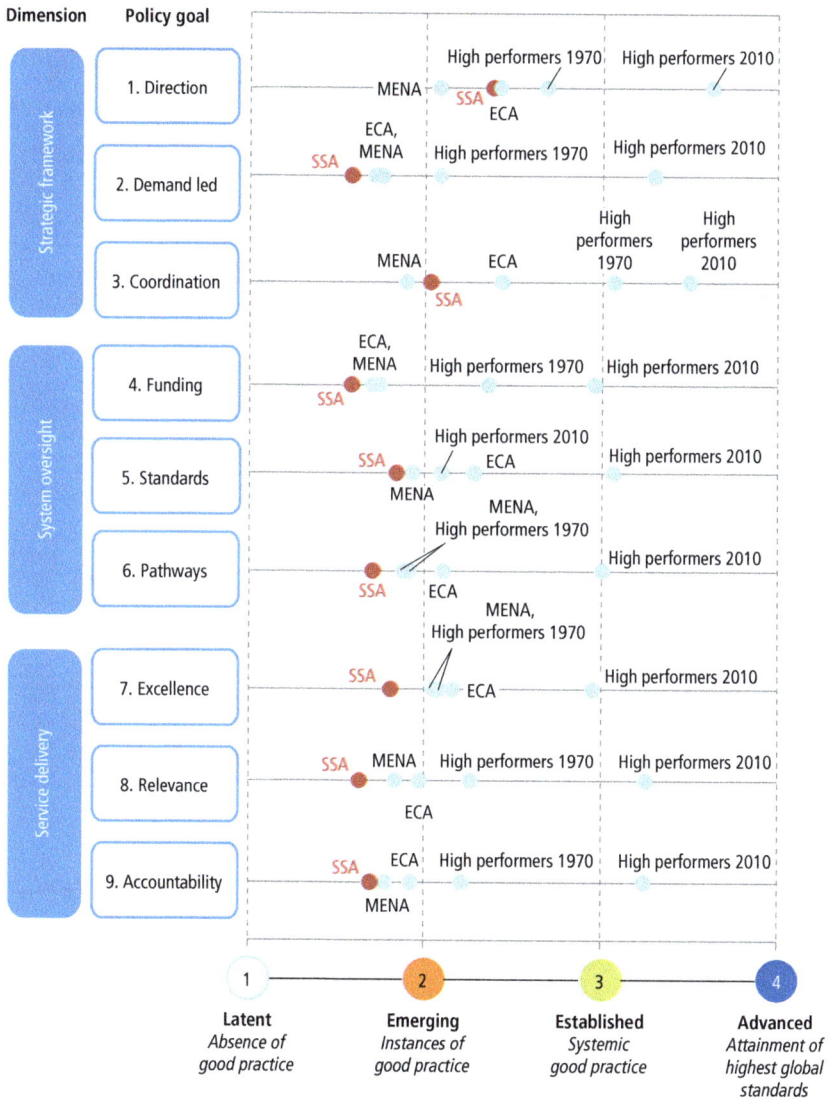

(continued next page)

Figure 3.11 (continued)

c. Country-specific performance in workforce development

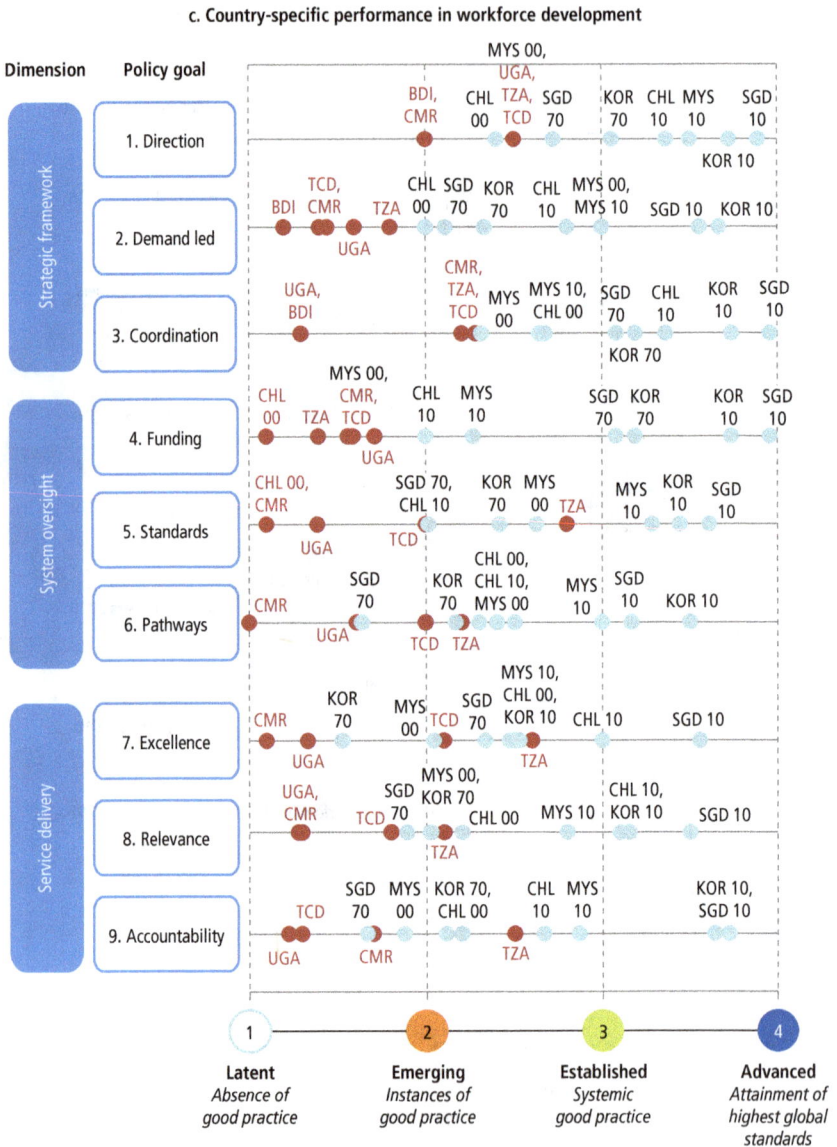

Source: Based on Systems Approach for Better Education Results Workforce Development (SABER-WfD) data.
Note: ECA = Europe and Central Asia, including Armenia, Bulgaria, Georgia, Moldova, North Macedonia, Romania, and Turkey; MENA = Middle East and North Africa, including Egypt, Arab Rep., Iraq, Jordan, Morocco, Palestine, Tunisia, West Bank and Palestine, and Yemen, Rep.; SSA = Sub-Saharan Africa, including Burundi, Cameroon, Chad, Tanzania, and Uganda. High performers 1970 = Ireland (1980), Korea, Rep. (1970), and Singapore (1970); High performers 2010 = Chile (2011), Ireland (2000), Korea, Rep. (2010), Malaysia (2010), and Singapore (2010).

The implementation of TVET strategies is made difficult by a lack of coordination and clarity of functions across different actors in the system. Some countries, including Malawi, Mauritius, and Tanzania, have established coordinating bodies and autonomous agencies for oversight. However, legislation and agreements to promote coordination among stakeholders and the multiple ministries and institutions involved in TVET often are not fully operational, have overlapping mandates, and rely on ad hoc mechanisms for coordination (Sosale and Majgaard 2016; World Bank 2012, 2015b, 2015c, 2015d, 2015e). In Cameroon, for example, there is no collective engagement among the ministries and institutions providing education or training or between the public and the private sectors; also lacking is an efficient system of standards and accreditation or a central autonomous agency for oversight and accreditation (Sosale and Majgaard 2016).

The biggest challenges, however, are related to three areas: equity, efficiency, and relevance. First, equity. Given the self-selection into general education—especially university—by individuals who are better-off and more academically ready, TVET is often the only option available for the rest. Even among those entering TVET, gender disparities, for example, abound, especially with regard to the field of study chosen. Second, efficiency. As figure 3.11 shows, weak financing and accountability arrangements are particularly fragile elements of TVET systems in the region. Financing systems that are divorced from performance and do not encourage accountability or innovation exacerbate both the equity and the relevance challenges. Third, relevance. Lack of relevance seems to be the most salient weakness, especially in countries like Cameroon and Uganda, but more broadly in the continent, as evidenced by regional and country studies. This lack of relevance stems, at least in part, from poor links between TVET and market demand. These weaknesses mean that the system's contribution to aggregate productivity, inclusion, and workers' adaptability falls short. This section discusses key areas of reform in terms of equity, efficiency, and relevance of TVET.

Responding to Equity Concerns: Generating Earning Opportunities for the Less Well-Off

In much of Sub-Saharan Africa, youths from disadvantaged backgrounds are unlikely to enroll in secondary education, whether technical or not. That said, compared with general education and among students who complete primary education, TVET disproportionally enrolls students from less well-off backgrounds or youths who are not ready for general education. A good TVET system can, therefore, help this key segment of society by easing their transition into work and equipping them with job-relevant skills.

Yet ensuring access to and adequacy of TVET to the needs of this population can be challenging. Disadvantaged students not only have liquidity and credit constraints, but also often lack access to relevant educational and labor market information.[15] In Kenya, for example, people believe that the average increase in earnings associated with training is 65 percent higher than what is estimated from survey data. People are also mistaken about the highest-earning trades (Hicks et al. 2011). Limited role models and networks may partly explain these misconceptions.[16] Often, individuals are far from TVET centers that cater to their needs, or courses are not offered at convenient times to accommodate work or family responsibilities, affecting the poorest, who need to work, or women, who bear the brunt of household and child care (Cho et al. 2015; Glennerster et al. 2011).

For these reasons, improving access among the most vulnerable will require a policy package that addresses a multiplicity of constraints. Improving affordability is one component. In Kenya, fees at the cheapest government TVET schools represent an estimated 15 percent of annual household expenditures per capita. Also in Kenya, giving out-of-school youth vouchers for vocational training increases enrollment substantially, and beneficiaries acquire an additional 0.55 year of education, on average (Hicks et al. 2015). Scholarships and financing for vulnerable youths that allow recipients to pick among recognized providers, whether private or public, can be more effective at closing equity gaps than the direct financing of institutions. Alternatively, governments could pay institutions a premium for enrolling and graduating disadvantaged students. Such premiums could be part of performance-based financing.

Most important is to improve the provision of foundational skills so that TVET can build on these skills to develop strong technical and work-readiness skills. The first best approach is to work on foundational skills in earlier levels and to delay tracking into TVET until these skills have been acquired. Since this process may take time and most formal TVET requires completed primary or lower-secondary education, targeted bridging programs that help to build these foundations and get better-prepared children and youth into TVET may also be necessary. In the United States, for example, community colleges offer catching-up programs focused on foundational skills, since it is estimated that two-thirds of incoming students lack the necessary foundational skills to complete the TVET program successfully (OECD 2014b). This policy package should include career and academic guidance to address information asymmetries early on as well as reforms to admissions and applications processes in general secondary to improve transparency and reduce biases against the poor.

Finally, but no less important, complementary measures that improve access by making TVET provision more flexible, are also necessary. In many TVET programs around the world, for example, women are disproportionately likely to drop out, related—at least partly—to household and family responsibilities (Honorati 2015). Especially for the poor, who face strong pressures to start working, it is important to make TVET "stackable" and modular, with learning blocks and due recognition of learning that lead to completed courses and qualifications but do not need to be done one right after the other. Flexibility will become increasingly important in the context of regional and global megatrends and the need for lifelong learning. This approach is being followed, for example, in Chicago College to Careers, a program that forges partnerships between community colleges and industry leaders to align curricula better with the demand in growing sectors, while at the same time being mindful of the constraints that youths who enroll in community college face. In particular, programs are both modular and stackable, as described above.[17] Similarly, digital technologies that facilitate online learning and open up new avenues for practical training by using laboratory and workshop simulations can help to manage the costs of TVET while making it more accessible. Brazil, for example, has a long history of distance learning in vocational education and training (Herd and Richardson 2011).

Increasing flexibility in TVET also requires better articulating formal, nonformal, and informal TVET streams and integrating vocational and general education to increase mobility as well as medium- and long-term opportunities for TVET students. If more rapid changes in the world of work mean more lifelong learning, it is increasingly important for TVET to have clear and flexible pathways for transfers across courses, progression to higher levels of training, and access to programs in other fields. In most cases, formal, nonformal, and informal TVET streams are disconnected from each other. Of concern is the lack of certification of learning in informal classroom or on-the-job training (chapter 5). There is also a disconnect between technical and academic streams, especially in the transition into and within tertiary education. In most countries in the region, it is very difficult to go from one to the other.[18] In order to increase the appeal of TVET, many middle- and high-income countries have introduced "bridging" arrangements that allow TVET graduates to continue their studies at academic tertiary institutions. In Sub-Saharan Africa, the Democratic Republic of Congo has two-, three- and four-year programs at the upper-secondary level offering "bridging" arrangements for TVET graduates to continue on to university.

Improving Efficiency in Preemployment TVET

Two areas that need to be strengthened are financing and accountability. Current policies and institutional arrangements fail to ensure stable funding for effective programs; neither do they foster productive partnerships with the private sector (Sosale and Majgaard 2016; World Bank 2012, 2015b, 2015c, 2015d, 2015e). It is widely agreed that some areas of TVET—such as teacher training, facilities, equipment, curricula development, and upgrading—are underfinanced, while at the same time there are great inefficiencies throughout the system.

Improving these dimensions requires diversified ways of financing and delivering TVET. Many countries in the region finance TVET through foreign assistance, income-generating activities, general public budget, training levies, tuition fees, and public-private partnerships (PPPs), among others; but financing through the general budget or training levies is the norm in most cases.[19]

Reform efforts could start with the functioning of training funds, especially given their impact on labor costs.[20] Training levies play an important role in financing publicly provided TVET in countries like Botswana, Malawi, Mozambique, Namibia, Tanzania, and Zimbabwe. Tanzania is a case in point. More than 80 percent of the Vocational Education and Training Fund is financed through a skills development levy. Employers with four or more employees pay the levy as a monthly fee of 6 percent of total payroll. One-third of the money collected goes to the Vocational Education and Training Authority (VETA), while the other two-thirds go to the general budget.[21] Employers have heavily criticized the levy (Billetoft 2016). First, in addition to increasing labor costs, the levy was introduced without sufficient consultations. Second, it is used mostly to finance non-TVET expenditures or to fund VETA's own management and training provision. Only a very small part (5 percent) benefits non-VETA centers. Third, the private sector has little to no say on how resources are used. Similar concerns are voiced around the region where these levies exist. One fundamental issue is that the formal private sector that can contribute to these funds is small, which means that the system is difficult to finance sustainably. More promising is to limit public provision only to those areas where the private sector is not willing to enter and to use resources available to finance access for those in need rather than to finance the large costs of public administration and provision. Countries could redirect a majority, if not all, of the resources levied from firms to a fund managed by the private sector itself. Brazil and Malaysia take this approach, allowing training to be better tailored to market needs.

Most critically, public funding of TVET institutions in the region needs to be linked more tightly to performance or at least to reform efforts. Most financing in the region is done on a historical basis or based on inputs or enrollment, which provides few incentives for providers to offer quality services or to innovate. There are some examples of paying for performance in higher education, such as in Mali and in centers of excellence around the region. Chapter 4 discusses these and other possible models to move gradually toward financing reform efforts and results that could apply to both universities and TVET. The main challenge is to define quantifiable and transparent indicators and to collect the data required to measure them. There is also a risk of "creaming"—that is, service providers may have an incentive to exclude individuals who are difficult to train or employ. To counter this risk, contracts can provide premiums for priority groups, as in the centers of excellence or the Employment Fund in Nepal (ADB 2014). An alternative or a complement to linking the disbursement of funds to performance could be the use of a voucher system that allows individuals to choose and directly pay training providers (whether public or private).[22] These reforms would need to be accompanied by improvements in financial management and oversight, as evidenced by the results from SABER and the lack of transparent information on financing.

Together with inadequate financing systems, weak accountability mechanisms mean that it is hard to align the incentives of regulators, service providers, students, and employers with results. Unclear governance arrangements in TVET hamper autonomy among public TVET providers and accountability for results. Even though many countries have created semiautonomous national TVET governing bodies, there is a tendency to control their operations without adequate involvement of other key stakeholders such as private businesses and nonstate TVET providers. Also, the separation of regulation and provision of TVET remains weak in many countries (Billetoft 2016). Reforms aimed at linking public financing more closely to performance or to reforms would need to be complemented by greater autonomy at the institutional level to manage curricula and human resource policies as well as select students, strengthen incentives, and empower providers to respond to local labor market needs. This approach can be especially useful in larger countries and when accompanied by stronger management capacity at the institutional level (UNESCO 2013). In addition, the public sector would need to play a role in the dissemination of performance indicators so that students and policy makers can act and bring discipline to the TVET market.

Fostering Economic Relevance and Links to Market Demands

The lack of relevance of TVET in the region and a tendency for TVET to be supply driven are concerns. The large heterogeneity of returns to TVET, especially within fields of study, and the fact that returns can be negative for many students (particularly vis-à-vis a general education track) are telling in this respect. Anecdotal evidence of quality and relevance concerns abounds (Anarfi and Appiah 2012). Even by the standards set within the system, quality seems lacking: in Burkina Faso, fewer than 40 percent of TVET students who take the final exam pass (World Bank 2017b); in Uganda, pass rates average 50–65 percent for TVET examinations (Johanson and Okema 2011). Examination performance rates are not disseminated or published by training institutions, and neither institutions nor teachers are held accountable for results.

Quality concerns stem from the misalignment of TVET with labor market needs. Many students—even before entering TVET—lack the foundational skills necessary to continue learning. Moreover, the system does not serve well the needs of the informal sector nor those of the catalytic sectors critical for the economic transformation. With skills demands changing, staying relevant requires an agility and flexibility that publicly provided TVET often lacks.

For this reason, partnering with the private sector will be critical for the future of TVET in the region.

The labor market requires workers with strong technical skills, but also with the cognitive and socioemotional skills that help them to be ready for the world of work (chapter 1). All of these skills matter, and a strong foundation is necessary to learn other skills, including technical ones. This foundation is important for on-the-job learning, but also because many graduates—even in TVET—will end up working in occupations different from the ones for which they were trained. In a tracer study in The Gambia, for example, more than one-fifth of graduates reported working in different areas than the ones for which they were trained (Couralet, Djallo, and Akinocho 2013). In visits to master craftspersons in Zambia, many of the key gaps identified were in foundational skills, specifically not being able to make measurements or read maintenance manuals in English. In addition, master craftspersons mentioned several socioemotional skills and behaviors, including bad hygiene, not showing up on time, or creating conflict at work. Similar evidence on the importance of socioemotional skills in technical tasks has been found in Kenya (Laajaj and Macours 2017) and Ghana (Ali, Bowen, and Deininger 2017).

Yet there is concern that TVET in the region is paying insufficient attention to foundational skills. Firms are more likely to train workers in technical skills than in basic literacy or socioemotional skills since the former are more likely to be firm specific (Almeida, Behrman, and Robaino 2012). Hence, the public sector has a role to play in stepping in, either ex ante or through bridge courses, to ensure that students build adequate foundational skills. Weak foundational skills are particularly problematic in TVET systems since, on average, TVET students appear to have weaker foundational skills than general education students.

Weaknesses in foundational skills mean that it is very important to avoid tracking students into TVET too early. There is a risk that students will get specialized in a narrow technical field before they gain the transferrable skills required for entering the labor market on solid footing. The risk is particularly salient in Sub-Saharan Africa, given the adverse sorting of students into TVET and the overall weaknesses in the basic education system. Singapore tracks some students into vocational education at age 13, but it does so after they have acquired a strong foundation (as evidenced by the country's performance on international tests) and keeps up the high standards of reading and math in vocational schools. In Poland, a 1999 reform that delayed tracking into TVET by one year to the start of upper secondary has been shown to improve cognitive skills development as measured by PISA (Jakubowski et al. 2011). A similar reform in Norway in 1994 also delayed tracking into TVET by a year and made transitions between general and vocational education easier, leading to lower dropout rates in TVET and higher enrollment in universities for those who completed general education (cited in Kutner and Gortazar 2014).

How do countries incorporate foundational skills into TVET? Globally, countries have followed different routes, ranging from including them as separate subjects to integrating them into the teaching of theoretical or practical subjects (UNESCO 2015). The Hung Yen University of Technology and Education in Vietnam has taken the former approach. Courses include lectures on time management and the ability to prioritize and give students time to study on their own and read extensively on a topic. Malaysian polytechnics have taken the latter approach. The Industrial Training on Soft Skills module incorporates technical training with the real-world context in which students are expected to apply the transversal skills. In addition, through a variety of class activities and real-work situations, students are exposed to the theoretical underpinnings of transversal skills prior to receiving practical training. Sub-Saharan African countries have an opportunity to leapfrog in this area before TVET systems expand significantly, by aiming for a more complete curriculum that can help to expand opportunities for TVET graduates. Some smaller programs in the region are moving in this direction, including Harambee in South Africa, a bridging program that provides a thorough training on a wide set of foundational and technical skills in order to place unemployed youths in jobs.

There is also a disconnect in the types of jobs for which the system is training workers. Formal, especially publicly provided, TVET tends to neglect the informal economy, even though the informal sector absorbs the majority of workers, even outside of agriculture. It is also disproportionately aimed at preparing workers for wage employment, often in the manufacturing sector.[23] However, recently, some public TVET has incorporated entrepreneurship and core business skills training directly relevant for self-employment and management of small enterprises.

Inflexible course times that make it difficult to combine training and work, lack of practical training, and high costs make TVET inaccessible or irrelevant for workers who already are in the informal sector or who are unlikely to get a job in the very small formal sector (Adams, Johansson, and Razmara 2013). Better incorporating the views and skills needs of the informal sector in public TVET can be a way forward, for example, by linking public TVET to existing organizations in both the informal and formal private sector. Several elements of informal TVET—links to employers, learning by doing, and flexibility—can inform reforms in formal TVET.

Thus, given the current and future needs of labor markets in Sub-Saharan Africa, entrepreneurship and management skills are arguably just as useful for future workers as job-specific technical skills. Programs such as Educate! in Rwanda and Uganda are a promising approach to introducing entrepreneurship, work readiness skills, and experiential applied teaching methodologies in secondary schools (box 3.3). TVET institutions in Kenya are often associated with business centers that provide consultancies to small-scale entrepreneurs.

BOX 3.3

Educate!: Bringing Entrepreneurship into Classrooms

Educate! is a nongovernmental organization that provides students with skills training in leadership, entrepreneurship, and workforce readiness, along with mentorship to start real businesses while in school. The program leverages community members to teach entrepreneurship alongside trained teachers in schools, relying on entrepreneurs and employees from local businesses. Educate! began in Uganda in 2009, reaching 24 schools in four districts. In 2012, after close collaboration with Educate!, the Ministry of Education in Uganda incorporated this effective approach intro national policy by rolling out a skills-based curriculum for secondary schools on the subject of entrepreneurship. Now the program reaches 12 percent of Ugandan secondary schools. In 2015, the program expanded to Rwanda; by 2024, it expects to affect 1 million students directly across Africa each year.

Educate! dedicates 12–13 percent of its budget to monitoring and evaluation and built its own tool to measure leadership, creativity, self-efficacy, and savings behavior. Data are collected in real time, allowing Educate! to monitor performance and make any necessary changes across all schools. This rapid program monitoring helps to maintain quality control. Educate! also has developed teacher associations to provide teachers with practical in-service training to develop core interactive teaching skills and ultimately to be better positioned to adopt national education reforms effectively.

Midline results from randomized control trials indicate that secondary students participating in Educate! have incomes that are doubled after they graduate from secondary school, are 64 percent more likely to start a business, and are 123 percent more likely to initiate a community project.

Sources: Based on http://www.experienceeducate.org/; Robinson, Winthrop, and McGivny 2016.

Graduates of youth polytechnics are encouraged to form business groups bringing together various disciplines, such as different construction trades to build houses. Once organized groups are formed and registered, they approach credit providers to finance their businesses.

The performance of TVET in providing skills for catalytic sectors before employment raises additional issues and suggests the need to take a narrower, more targeted approach. It takes time for reforms of the whole TVET system to take effect and alleviate the skills constraints faced by growing firms or growing sectors.[24] Several countries that have been successful in integrating skills development with the broader economic agenda—especially in East Asia—have begun by creating new institutions with explicit industry linkages or even ad hoc training centers or programs linked to specific employer needs. Then, they have institutionalized these programs or institutions as an integral part of the formal system of education and training (Ansu and Tan 2012). The idea is that, by the time the two are integrated, deep collaboration with the private sector has

BOX 3.4

Engaging the Private Sector in Building Skills for Catalytic Sectors: Lessons from Singapore

In Singapore, since the 1960s, the priority has been to align skills development with the country's industrial development strategy, which has been focused on attracting foreign direct investment to the country. However, initial efforts that were based on parallel training-cum-production workshops run by the public sector in parallel with the school system failed. So did efforts based on worker retraining schemes. The government then switched strategies, convinced that the training needed could not be provided within the regular technical education institutions. The programs offered were seen as remedial options for students who did poorly in their studies and were not producing workers quickly enough to attract foreign firms.

The new strategy—and the one that proved successful—was to affiliate with leading international industry partners with proven training systems, to learn the training business from them, and to train to their needs. The first arrangement was with the Tata Group (India's largest engineering firm at the time). The government provided the land and buildings for the training center, contributed 70 percent of the operating costs, and paid the stipends of the trainees (all of whom signed a bond to serve the training authority or any company as directed by the government for a period of five years). The training center trained twice as many people as Tata required. Tata hired the best graduates, while the rest were retained as an asset to attract other engineering firms to Singapore. In effect, the strategy was to build a pipeline of skills to grow a whole industry rather than to meet the needs of a single company.

With time, the government won commitment from leading foreign companies to participate in joint training programs. The arrangement avoided the proliferation of new institutions—each tied to a particular company—and introduced the idea of pooling training resources to serve companies in an industry cluster. The new approach contained key ingredients for Singapore to acquire the advanced skills for growing its new technology-intensive industries: secondment of experts to Singapore, the training of local lecturers and technical staff at the participating firms' overseas locations, assistance with curriculum and program development, donation or loan of equipment, commitment to upgrade equipment and software, and commitment of participating companies to remain in the scheme for at least three years. Only in the 1990s were these centers integrated into the formal education and training system.

Source: Adapted from Ansu and Tan 2012.

become ingrained in the system. The experience of Malaysia and Singapore exemplifies this approach (box 3.4).

These challenges are hard to solve in contexts of limited resources, limited capacity, and many competing demands, making it critical to rethink the role of the public sector and engage the private sector more actively in TVET.

Publicly provided TVET tends to be rigid and long, with curricula, learning materials, instruments, and training methods that are out of date and not in tune with the needs and opportunities of the labor market (Billetoft 2016). For example, of the 22 available specialties in tertiary TVET programs in Burkina Faso, 15 are defined by lists of courses dating back to 1997 or earlier (World Bank 2017b).

The disconnect between TVET and labor market demand is also explained by the poor quality of teachers and training in TVET and the outdated technology with which many of them operate. In many countries in the region, teachers' salaries typically constitute 80–90 percent of the costs of TVET, significantly more than in upper-middle-income and high-income countries outside of Sub-Saharan Africa (Billetoft 2016). Few resources are available for other inputs, including teacher training, equipment, and facilities. As in general education, weaknesses in the teaching force are seen as key to the system's poor quality. TVET teacher education is based largely in universities, with some exceptions such as the dedicated Vocational Teachers Training College in Tanzania and the Normal Schools for Teachers of Technical Education in Cameroon. In-service continuous training is also lacking.[25] Relatively few teachers in public institutions have industrial experience, in part because of requirements for a teaching certificate (Johanson and Okema 2011). Improvements in the teaching workforce can start by focusing on strategic programs, allowing the local recruitment of people with skills (but without a teaching certificate), and providing more opportunities for industry attachments for instructors. Countries could explore options for twinning arrangements with private firms and other countries to upgrade the skills of TVET teachers. This additional support could be combined with stronger performance incentives, including publishing examination results.

The lack of appropriate equipment is striking. Examples include motor vehicle mechanics taught without vehicles and health assistant training taught without laboratories (Johanson and Okema 2011; Ngome 2003). In Burkina Faso, for example, equipment often dates back to the early 1960s, and spare parts are no longer being manufactured. Instead, parts are manufactured by students, providing them with practical experience (World Bank 2017b). Exploring partnerships with the private sector and sharing equipment across institutions (especially in subjects that require high capital investments or have small classes) can be explored.

A larger role for the private sector in TVET provision can help to improve quality. Drawing from the cases of Mali and Senegal, Johanson and Adams (2004) argue that private training institutes are indeed more flexible, better able to adapt, more innovative, and better in tune with the labor market when they have the right incentives.[26] In Turkey, for example, a rigorous evaluation of TVET programs showed positive effects on trainees' labor market outcomes only when training was provided by the private sector using performance-based contracts with provisions to avoid creaming (Hirshleifer et al. 2014). Similarly, in Kenya, private providers were more likely to assist students in job search, used more up-to-date equipment in training, and were more likely to incorporate apprenticeships where students could interact regularly with clients and work on real projects (Hicks et al. 2011).

Thus, relevant TVET requires credible assessments of skills demands, continuous engagement with employers at the local level, and incentives for employers to support skills development. This is not easy, and it is not surprising that countries in the region score the lowest in this area on the SABER assessments, reflecting a supply-driven approach to workforce development. Employers and industry have a limited role and influence in shaping and implementing TVET programs in the region, including informing skills needs, specifying standards for training facilities, designing curricula, and placing students in apprenticeships for on-the-job learning (Johanson and Okema 2011; World Bank 2017b; Zimmermann et al. 2013). When the private sector is present, it is often only as a minority on the governing boards of quality assurance institutions or as ad hoc participants in general TVET discussions.

A more deliberate approach can pay off. In Tanzania, the private sector is playing an advisory role in TVET through the Tanzania National Business Council and the Association of Tanzania Employers (World Bank 2015c). Box 3.5 describes other promising approaches in Sub-Saharan Africa. Involvement of the private sector can produce positive results. In the mid-2000s, Mozambique embarked on a comprehensive reform of its

BOX 3.5

Leveraging the Private Sector in Sub-Saharan Africa for Skills Development in TVET

In the region, several public-private partnerships in TVET are now under way. One example is the Ghana Industrial Skills Development Center (GISDC), launched in 2005 to provide training in mechanical, electrical, and process engineering. The seeds for this initiative were sown when TexStyles Ghana Limited, a local subsidiary of the international firm Vlisco Helmond B.V., found that other factories shared its problem of being unable to find and retain employees who could service their machines. As a result, factories often had to fly in troubleshooters from abroad. To overcome the problem, the governments of Ghana and the Netherlands joined forces with the Association of Ghana Industries to set up the GISDC in 2005. The GISDC is now operational, with a governance arrangement that includes industry representatives on its decision-making board and an impressive list of firms among its partners.

(continued next page)

Box 3.5 (continued)

South Africa's Middelburg Higher Technical School has established successful part-nerships with companies that invest heavily in the school, provide training after school hours, and consider learners favorably for employment. For example, Toyota Motor Company provides equipment for training motor vehicle mechanics, has developed a modular training course for interested learners, and appoints teachers to provide train-ing outside school hours. Learners pay an additional fee for the training, and teachers are paid out of these funds. The learners do the first modules in the series and, once they complete their schooling, can apply for employment at Toyota, where they can complete the remaining modules as employees. Employment is not guaranteed by Toyota, but learners who achieve 80 percent or more receive a certificate stating that they completed the modules and entitling them to apply for a position at any Toyota dealer across the country. Middelburg Higher Technical School is one of 14 schools in South Africa where Toyota is involved in this way.

In Uganda, a recently launched Skills Development Facility will promote employer-led short-term training in order to address prevailing skills imbalances in both the for-mal and informal sectors, starting with agriculture, construction, and manufacturing sectors before spreading to other sectors. The scheme is to be implemented through a grant facility mechanism to be cofinanced by the private sector through a matching grant. Firms that take on students for internships, especially in vocational studies, receive a 100 percent grant.

In Nigeria, the government has started processing the certification and accredita-tion of private providers meeting certain criteria (including a governance structure that includes industry representation) to qualify as vocational enterprise institutions (target-ing persons with 9 years of schooling) or innovation enterprise institutions (targeting persons with 12 years of schooling). These institutions provide practical training in tar-get areas, among them ICT, telecommunications, computer hardware engineering, refrigeration and air conditioning, and hospitality and tourism.

Many of the initiatives are still new and require some time to be proven successful or not. But they do incorporate some of the lessons from successful new models of training: (1) coherence with the country's economic development strategy; (2) training institutions that, at least to start, are outside of the traditional education and training system and thus better able to react quickly, flexibly, and innovatively to industry needs; and (3) governance arrangements in training institutions that encourage close involvement by industry in defin-ing training curricula, in providing equipment and trainers, in providing finance, and in exposing students and faculty to industry-driven projects such as work placements.

Sources: Adapted from Ansu and Tan 2012; Centre for Development and Enterprise 2012; World Bank 2015a.

TVET system, aiming to make the system more demand driven and flexible. Key elements of the reform included industry-approved standards and quali-fications, multiple exit points, and strong consultation mechanisms. Compared with a baseline taken in 2007, a tracer study in 2015 found that 57 percent of TVET graduates had found a job or created their own job within six months in an area related to their training (in 2007, the average time for getting a job was 204 days, and only 26 percent of graduates got a job related to their area of training). In addition, 80 percent of employers reported being satisfied with the system and with graduates, compared with 25 percent in 2007 (Government of Mozambique 2016).

The potential of well-structured private and public sector partnerships in TVET is large. These PPPs could include collaboration in curriculum design, program co-management, blended theory-practicum apprenticeships, and cofinancing of training and skills development programs. Foreign investors seeking to invest in Sub-Saharan African countries, for example, have sometimes set up their own preemployment TVET support. For example, Cisco and Microsoft offer training in Kenya, Nigeria, and South Africa. Sometimes the partnerships can be with firms abroad.[27] A promising approach is being followed by recent initiatives that train youths on ICT-related technical skills, especially coding.[28]

The experience in Sub-Saharan Africa and elsewhere suggests that successful PPPs in TVET require governments that are well positioned to capitalize on the partnership in the medium and long term (Billetoft 2016). The typical model is one whereby a multinational company leases a training center, upgrades it to serve its own needs and specifications, and brings in its own management and teaching staff. Upon expiry of the contract, the center is returned to its owner and the external management and teaching staff are withdrawn. This way of practicing PPP has limited durable effect on the quality and relevance of public provision of TVET.

Beyond providing training and designing curricula, the private sector is a critical partner in increasing the exposure of TVET students to on-the-job training, whether in the formal or the informal sector.[29] This practical training is critical in TVET. In Ghana, the majority of new recruits in medium-size to large industries start their employment as apprentices, who are usually taken in for one to two years of retraining (Darvas and Palmer 2014). Annex 3A highlights formal apprenticeship systems in the region. Formal apprenticeship training, provided by companies in the formal sector, based on apprenticeship contracts and regulated through apprenticeship or TVET acts, is not uncommon in Africa, but formal apprenticeships are much less common than informal apprenticeships (chapter 5). Given the importance of practical training in TVET, apprenticeships have an important role to play as TVET systems are reformed, and there are important lessons from around the world on key principles that underpin successful ones (box 3.6).

Apprenticeships can be beneficial for both employers and apprentices. In Kenya, a program jointly carried out by the government and the Kenya Private Sector Alliance provided vulnerable youths with three months of classroom-based technical training coupled with three months of on-the-job training in private firms. The program increased employment more than a year later by 15 percent among men; it also increased wage earnings, especially among

BOX 3.6

What Defines High-Quality Apprenticeships?

A wide range of programs that can be broadly categorized as apprenticeship schemes exist around the world, ranging from informal apprenticeships, which are common in Sub-Saharan Africa (see chapter 5) and South Asia, to the well-structured formal schemes of the so-called apprenticeship countries (Austria, Germany, and Switzerland). More structured programs aim to include (a) a contract or agreement between the employer and the apprentice, (b) a structured training plan, (c) a combination of on-the-job and off-the-job training, and (d) an assessment and industry-recognized certification of acquired competencies or qualifications.

Well-designed apprenticeship systems can promote skills acquisition, facilitate the transition from school to work, and improve employment opportunities. Yet their effectiveness depends on three pillars: ensuring access to high-quality programs (coverage), making apprenticeships valuable to youths, and making them attractive to employers.

Recently, the Inter-American Development Bank (Fazio, Fernández-Coto, and Ripani 2016) identified 10 core elements of apprenticeship programs:

1. Alignment with the country's development strategy
2. Adequate levels of employer engagement
3. Appropriate governance arrangements at the legal and institutional levels
4. Sustainable funding mechanisms and incentive provisions
5. Adequate curriculum design
6. Adequate curriculum delivery
7. Robust assessment methodologies
8. Existence of industry-recognized certification, which can lead to career progression
9. Complementary support services for program beneficiaries, including but not limited to labor intermediation
10. Strong quality-assurance mechanisms for training programs in general.

Austria and Germany have good practices in implementing most of the core elements, particularly on elements 1 through 8, but many other countries, even low- and middle-income countries like India, also provide good examples that might help countries in Sub-Saharan Africa to improve their apprenticeship systems.

Regarding the first element, countries with sustainable, effective apprenticeships have developed and expanded apprenticeship strategies that are embedded in wider economic and social policy development strategies. India's 2015 National Policy for Skill Development and Entrepreneurship provides a good example of how governments can work with employers to extend apprenticeships to the service sector.

Progressively, countries with different levels of tradition and employer participation in apprenticeships have emphasized employer engagement (second element) as key for the development, sustainability, and expansion of apprenticeship programs. India, for

(continued next page)

Box 3.6 (continued)

example, is also doing a good job of engaging employers, especially small and medium enterprises, using group training organizations (first successfully pioneered in Australia) that employ apprentices and trainees and place them with host employers.

Finding the appropriate mechanisms for managing and coordinating the activities of key actors (third element) is crucial in the implementation of apprenticeships. Good practices in apprenticeships include providing a clear role for the main actors and a legal framework that establishes rights and responsibilities, including the way in which apprentices are paid, categorized, and treated during the training process.

Good practices in apprenticeship programs also include a funding strategy that allows for cost sharing among government, employers, and apprentices (fourth element). The cofinancing structure plays an important role in creating a balanced set of incentives for the participation of apprentices and employers. Incentives for employers can include cost sharing; a signing bonus for registering to hire and train apprentices, as in Canada; and a reduction of labor costs of apprentices, as in Malta. Incentives for apprentices can include remuneration (usually as a proportion of the adult minimum wage) or the provision of grants by milestone achieved and completion, as in Canada, where apprentices are eligible for a grant from the federal government on completion of the first and second years of the apprenticeship and another one on completion of the program.

Both employers and training providers typically have central roles in determining the content and standards of the curriculum (fifth element). The process typically is guided by training specialists who transfer employers' needs into a training plan for the apprentice. Curriculum design should be intertwined closely from the outset with a unified system of assessment, accreditation, and certification (sixth element), as in Australia, for example. An essential part of curriculum delivery is ensuring that both on-the-job and off-the-job trainers receive the necessary training themselves in order to deliver the curriculum successfully and to transfer both theoretical and practical knowledge and skills.

The seventh core element refers to defining and conducting the tests that best suit the different types of skills and competencies in which apprentices are being trained, in order to determine the level of qualifications that leads to a certification. There are many ways to achieve this, such as "employer endorsement," where employers themselves set the required standards, as in England, or "external verification," where a local examination board is assembled and must include an employer expert, a trade unionist, and a teacher who is usually not the employer of the apprentice, as in Germany.

Recognizing the skills acquired by apprentices with a certificate (eighth element) signals their acquired level of mastery in different occupations. It is also important for employers looking for workers with particular qualifications. In some countries, the certificate also allows apprentices to pursue other studies when there is a link to an NQF. In France, for example, apprenticeships give access to all levels of certification by means of successive contracts or via bridges with higher education courses.

(continued next page)

Box 3.6 (continued)

The ninth core element is ensuring that potential and current apprentices can get the information and counseling they need to make important career decisions before, during, and after the apprenticeship. For example, in England and the United States, programs prepare individuals to enter and succeed in registered apprenticeships, and in Australia, "apprenticeships centres" provide free information and advice.

Finally, ensuring that programs achieve the highest standards of quality is an essential component of the apprenticeship strategy. The quality control mechanisms should include periodic measurement of the quality of teaching, facilities, and learning, among others. In the United Kingdom, for instance, studies assess the wage and employment returns of individuals who hold particular qualifications. This assessment enables comparisons to be made between apprenticeships, formal education, or other learning routes.

Sources: Based on Fazio, Fernández-Coto, and Ripani 2016; OECD 2014a.

---

women and older men (Honorati 2015). This program has now been scaled up and extended nationally and to the informal sector.

Embedded into specific cultural, economic, and education traditions and norms, formal apprenticeship training differs considerably among countries in terms of organizational patterns, financing mechanisms, recognition, formalization, and nature of employer involvement. The relatively low prevalence of formal apprenticeship training is related to the small size of the formal sector in most of the region. Higher-income economies are more likely to have regulated apprenticeship systems, as in Botswana, Mauritius, and South Africa. Some countries have established modern dual systems, although they remain small in scale. In Benin, since 2006, a dual apprenticeship system with alternating phases of theoretical and practical training has been in place, albeit devoted mostly to traditional crafts such as masonry, electrical trades, and plumbing. While one day is spent at school, five days are devoted to learning on the job (Zimmermann et al. 2013).

In order to expand, apprenticeships in TVET need to cover the informal sector. The number of students involved in formal apprenticeship training is relatively small. In Kenya, the apprenticeship system only absorbs 500–600 students every year, compared with a total enrollment capacity of around 90,000. In Malawi, the number of applicants is about eight times the number of youths accepted into apprenticeship training. For practical training to expand as part of formal TVET, institutions will need to seek opportunities in the informal sector.

Employers also need to get more involved in the design and quality assurance of apprenticeships. Yet in most of Sub-Saharan Africa, the involvement of employers remains weak, reducing the systems' attractiveness and credibility among employers. A possible exception is South Africa, where employers, together with trade unions and education and training authorities, are in charge of apprenticeships and learnerships. International experience suggests that financial incentives, such as subsidies and tax breaks, are not enough to get employers on board for work-based learning. Attention should be focused instead on nonfinancial measures that improve the cost-benefit balance of apprenticeships for employers. These measures include adjusting key parameters of apprenticeship schemes, better preparing at-risk youths for apprenticeships, and providing support (for example, remedial courses, mentoring) during apprenticeships (Kis 2016).

With a larger role for the private sector in training provision, the role of the public sector becomes more focused on quality assurance. An effective system of standards and accreditation allows for recognition of what has been learned. It involves setting up competency standards, credible skills testing and certification, and accreditation standards that are enforceable (World Bank 2013). This function of quality assurance is critical and far from easy. In Uganda, for example, many private providers operate without government recognition, partly because they have few incentives to obtain government registration and the process of recognition is difficult. As a result, it is estimated that only one-fourth of private training providers are officially registered (Johanson and Okema 2011).

However, it is important to move progressively and to avoid overinvesting in complex NQFs and certification systems. Despite the importance of quality assurance, countries in the region risk investing too much in such national qualification frameworks. At least 140 countries have implemented NQFs (Keevy and Chakroun 2015). These frameworks do not ensure educational quality in and of themselves (Blackmur 2015). Young and Allias (2013) use case studies (including Botswana, Mauritius, and South Africa) to analyze the impacts of NQFs. Although it may be too early to evaluate the impact of many NQFs, there is some qualitative evidence that qualification frameworks can help to improve understanding of and communication regarding education systems and can increase the involvement of the private sector (at least in early stages), but not if complexity, bureaucracy, or cost discourage employer engagement. There is also a risk of overspecification and redundant qualifications. NQFs are found to be a possible tool for recognizing skills and learning (including informal learning), but not if there is no incentive to use them or trust to underpin recognition. Some of the issues stem from the fact that these frameworks can become overly complex, especially in contexts of high informality and many unregulated training providers; they are not necessarily as cost-effective as in more formalized, more advanced settings. Complex NQFs as in South Africa and Tanzania, for example, tend to overstretch the capacity of the TVET administration system (Billetoft 2016).

NQFs are not a prerequisite for a strong TVET system, and it is important to move gradually. Germany, well known for its strong technical and vocational education system, only set up an NQF in 2013 (World Bank 2015f). A more gradual approach requires striking a balance between establishing relevant standards and recognizing learning, on the one hand, and complexity and costs, on the other. Simpler frameworks start in selected industries (where certification is most relevant) and accredit institutions first and, only afterwards, specific programs. More advanced frameworks facilitate stakeholder interactions, support wider quality assurance, recognize learning gained outside formal education and training, and make national qualification systems more transparent to the international community (Coles et al. 2014).

Accreditation will be of limited value, moreover, if TVET systems are kept at arm's length from the private sector and if institutional and governance setups are such that they weaken rather than strengthen incentives for delivering quality TVET. An important way of managing costs and ensuring relevance of standards is to partner with business associations in this process, whether in the formal sector or—most critically—in the informal sector. If service providers have no incentive to be accredited, especially in the informal sector, there is little to be gained from accreditation. There are also unlikely to be sizable benefits from accreditation of programs and institutions or national qualification frameworks if employers have no faith in the quality of the skills acquired or in the institutions that do the quality assurance. Among the self-employed, accreditation and standards will do little if they are a noisy signal of quality and do not generate value added or ensure higher-quality products and services.

Reforming TVET: Generating Evidence, Prioritizing, and Strengthening Links with Market Demand for Skills

Despite the potential for TVET to foster economic transformation, improve youths' school-to-work transition, and equip graduates with practical skills, TVET policies in most of Africa are not based on evidence, and systems remain fragmented and disconnected from labor market demands. Demands on and expectations about TVET as a solution to the youth employment challenge in the region are undoubtedly unrealistically high. This is both because skills are just one of many possible constraints to productive employment and because getting TVET right is hard. However, even against more modest objectives, there is a recognition that if TVET is going to play a more important role, not only more resources but also significant reforms are required. Weaknesses regarding relevance, equity, and efficiency mean that today's TVET systems are

1. *Not evidence based*, affecting the quality of decisions, whether the decisions of students, firms, training providers, or policy makers

2. *Fragmented*, since the role of the public sector in TVET remains scattered among regulation, provision, financing, and spreading of resources (both financial and institutional capacity) and fails to focus on key functions necessary for the development of a relevant market for training

3. *Disconnected* from market demands, lacking links to the private sector and institutions and accountability mechanisms that create incentives for relevance and quality.

Strengthening the Evidence Base

First and foremost, governments in Africa need to make a deliberate and widespread effort to improve the information generated and disseminated around the TVET system. In The Gambia, for example, almost one-third of TVET graduates report that they had no guidance before starting TVET, and 40 percent of the TVET institutions do not have a career guidance or counseling department (Couralet, Djallo, and Akinocho 2013). Information about labor market returns across occupations, programs, and institutions can help students to make better decisions and better align their choices with the demands of the labor market; it can also be important for linking financing to results. In Kenya, Hicks et al. (2011, 2015) show that more accurate information on the earnings of different occupations leads to a switch toward TVET fields of study with higher earnings, especially among women. Improving the generation of and access to information is critical given the great variation in outcomes in TVET.

Tracer studies and labor market information systems can be useful tools here. As in the case of universities, ad hoc tracer studies of TVET have been conducted, but no systematic efforts have been undertaken. This has been the case in The Gambia, for example (Couralet, Djallo, and Akinocho 2013). Chapter 4 discusses potential cost-effective approaches to tracer studies and labor market information systems in the region, including the option of using digital technologies, especially mobile phones, creatively.

The system also lacks information about the status and practices of TVET service providers. There is very little systematic information that policy makers and providers themselves can use to benchmark themselves (facilities, equipment, funding, training delivery practices, management practices). Possible tools include an institutional assessment recently applied in Kenya or systemwide assessments such as SABER (table 3.3). These tools can guide reform efforts, measure progress, and potentially be useful for identifying good performers and even for reform-based financing.

In all of these cases, transmitting clear signals about employers' skills requirements is important to address skills gaps or mismatches. For this, better information on skills needs is required. The traditional approach of conducting sectorwide employer surveys, often followed in higher-income countries,

Table 3.3 Policy and Institutional Goals Regarding Workforce Development and Assessment of Training Providers

Functional dimensions	SABER workforce development		Assessment of training providers	
	Policy goal		**Institutional goal**	
Strategic framework	G1	Setting a Strategic Direction	IG-1	To set a strategic direction
	G2	Fostering a Demand-Driven Approach	IG-2	To develop a demand-driven approach to training
	G3	Strengthening Critical Coordination	IG-3	To establish a sustained relationship with authorities
System oversight	G4	Ensuring Efficiency and Equity in Funding	IG-4	To ensure institutional financial viability and efficiency
	G5	Assuring Relevant and Reliable Standards	IG-5	To fulfill national quality standards
	G6	Diversifying Pathways for Skills Acquisition	IG-6	To enable students to pursue education and training opportunities
Service delivery	G7	Enabling Diversity and Excellence in Training Provision	IG-7	To create a teaching/studying experience conducive to learning
	G8	Fostering Relevance in Public Training Programs	IG-8	To prepare students for the world of work
	G9	Enhancing Evidence-based Accountability for Results	IG-9	To gather and publicize data for informed decision making

Source: World Bank 2017a.
Note: SABER = Systems Approach for Better Education Results.

is unlikely to fit the needs of most sectors in Africa, given high informality and self-employment. This approach needs to be complemented with surveys focused on the informal sector as well as with more regular, less costly mechanisms for obtaining market feedback, including regular informal, but structured, consultations with the private sector, partnerships with private sector job search and matching services, and production and dissemination of information on labor market returns and graduate placements.

Finally, this agenda also calls for more systematic experimentation and learning. Getting TVET "right" is difficult, and countries could be well served by identifying critical areas where they want to improve and by setting up appropriate mechanisms to evaluate, learn, and make adjustments.

Prioritizing

Governments in the region are trying to do too much in the TVET sector; as a result, resources and capacity are being spread too thinly. Prioritization requires a focus on increasing high-quality private sector engagement and rethinking the role of the public sector. Governments in Sub-Saharan Africa should focus on addressing market and equity failures throughout the system and aim to ensure (a) *readiness*, by focusing on foundational skills; (b) *opportunities*, by ensuring equity and financing for those in need and with merit and by addressing information gaps; and (c) *incentives*, by enabling the private sector to be in the driver's seat of TVET, while providing relevant quality assurance. The returns to investment in TVET for the public sector lie in these three areas.

Prioritization, especially in countries in the early stages of economic transformation, also calls for a two-pronged approach, with one pillar better aligned to growth sectors and the other focused on TVET aimed at the informal sector. The latter subject is discussed in chapter 5. In terms of the first pillar, priority should be given to those sectors that are linked upstream or downstream to strategic sectors. A more strategic approach to TVET would also benefit from exploiting economies of scale associated with regional centers of excellence. As it is quite expensive to keep the curricula and the corresponding learning material updated, it is advisable to limit the number of trade specializations covered and to phase out courses no longer in demand. For most specialized skills, moving to a regionwide provision of these skills to take advantage of economies of scale can also boost efficiency. Centers of excellence are discussed in chapter 4.

Strengthening the Links between TVET and Skills Market Demands

TVET systems in the region need to shift from preparing students for a job to preparing students for a career. More and better information about training providers and about the labor market and more intense private sector engagement in TVET can help to ensure the relevance of TVET beyond the early school-to-work transition. Just as important is the need to strengthen foundational skills. The best way of doing so is to strengthen these skills in basic education and to avoid premature tracking into TVET. Many workers' skill deficiencies reflect weak foundational skills, as indicated by the Generation program, a very promising initiative of McKinsey and Company that follows a task-based approach to training (box 3.7). This more holistic identification of skills gaps should guide curricula, standards, assessments, recruitment, and training of instructors.

Expanding higher-quality TVET requires a more active participation of the private sector. Active participation means strengthening the role of the private sector both as a provider and as a partner in public provision through active participation in the shaping of programs and curricula and the delivery of services. It also means ensuring fair competition, especially in the public sector, when it is also a provider. At the same time, it is important to dedicate significant efforts to strengthening the on-the-job learning component of TVET by creating incentives for firms to provide apprenticeships and by bringing in the informal sector as a critical source of practical experience and future employment.

In terms of the public sector, it is necessary to improve labor market and TVET information structures for the system as a whole, as well as at the institutional and program levels. In addition, it is necessary to adopt performance-linked financing and accountability mechanisms.

BOX 3.7

Moving toward a Task-Based Approach to Training: The Generation Program

Generation is a training program for youths led by McKinsey and Company and relying on seven components:

1. Jobs and direct engagement with employers from the start
2. Student recruitment based on intrinsic motivation and effort
3. Short and intensive "boot camp" covering relevant technical, behavioral, and mind-set skills
4. Support along the way, including daily monitoring, weekly feedback, and mentoring
5. A community that follows graduates into the workplace
6. Return on investment for employers and students
7. Data tracked throughout to make sure that students are constantly learning and improving.

Training is anchored on intensive practice of the most important activities of the target profession, not only of the relevant technical skills but also of behavioral and mind-set skills. Take the example of nurses. Assessors have found that making sure that nurses show up on time or that they are able to detail in a log book what they have done for each patient is critical for improving productivity in hospitals and avoiding mistakes. All of these tasks (skills) need to be taught in the context of shift-change activity in order to ensure that learners develop full pattern recognition.

The program has been launched as a pilot in five countries (India, Kenya, Mexico, Spain, and the United States), and the initial focus has been on four sectors (health care, technology, retail and sales, and skilled trades and advanced manufacturing). In Kenya, for example, Generation seeks to place 50,000 youths in jobs by 2019 and currently offers five programs (financial services sales, consumer goods sales, retail and restaurant customer service, business process outsourcing, and apparel manufacturing). The typical Generation participant is between the ages of 18 and 29, has basic literacy and numeracy, and is either unemployed or underemployed. The program focuses on preparing participants for middle-skill jobs that feature either high scarcity or high turnover.

Initial evaluations suggest that the program has had a positive impact on both students and employers. Graduates earn above-average starting salaries relative to their peer group, and 97 percent are employed. From the employers' perspective, the retention rate is 83 percent (compared with the industry average of 65 percent), and 80 percent state that Generation graduates perform better than average.

Source: Based on https://www.generationinitiative.org/about/.

Roadmap for TVET Reform

This policy agenda can be summarized in a roadmap for TVET reform, resting on five building blocks aiming at improving access, efficiency, and relevance (box 3.8).

Finally, but no less important, TVET reforms need to be accompanied by broader efforts to improve the overall environment that determines payoffs to

---

BOX 3.8

Five Building Blocks for TVET Reform in Sub-Saharan Africa

1. *Foundational skills are key both for equity reasons and for relevance and efficiency.* Many students in TVET lack foundational skills, partly because students from better-off families and higher academic readiness try to avoid TVET. But even within TVET, insufficient attention is paid to strengthening these foundations. As a result, TVET graduates are often less adaptable to changes in the labor market.

2. *A focus on a two-pronged growth-inclusion approach to TVET.* Especially in countries still in the early stages of economic transformation, the focus is on prioritizing catalytic sectors with a strong private sector interest in partnerships, on the one hand, and on supporting TVET for low-skill occupations and in the informal sector (mostly self-employed), on the other. In most countries in the region, a few sectors are driving aggregate economic growth and have the potential to create jobs directly or indirectly through value chains. PPPs are promising in these sectors. However, the majority of youths in the region are likely to be employed over the next couple of decades in lower-skill occupations, often in the informal sector. Here, most countries already have a vibrant informal (often workplace-based) training sector. Rather than trying to regulate it, the focus should be on addressing the financial constraints of trainees or apprentices and any market failures in the system (chapter 5).

3. *A rationalized role for the public sector.* In many countries in the region, the public sector is still heavily involved in TVET provision. In sectors where the private sector alone would underprovide TVET, the public sector can finance its provision; it does not need to provide the training itself. Instead, it can competitively hire providers from the private sector under performance-based contracts. In sectors where there is already vibrant private sector provision of TVET, the most important role of the public sector is in providing regulation and quality assurance and ensuring equitable access.

4. *Light regulation of TVET, but with financing and accountability arrangements aligned with results and reforms.* The experience across Africa so far suggests that implementing complex national qualification frameworks is difficult and not necessarily

---

(continued next page)

Box 3.8 (continued)

cost-effective. With emerging institutions, it probably pays off to start less ambitiously. This would mean shifting from inputs-based regulation (for example, curriculum content, teachers, courses offered) and financing to more results- or reforms-based regulation and financing. These changes should be accompanied by incentives for enrolling and servicing youth from disadvantaged backgrounds.

5. *Focusing clearly on learning, allowing for experimentation and evaluation, and expanding approaches found to be successful.* This focus requires improving the information and generation of evidence throughout the system for students, providers, the private sector, and policy makers. Since much is still not known about what works, for whom, and in which sectors in TVET, it is important to strengthen the capacity of national systems and individual institutions to learn. Linking financing and accountability more clearly with results would allow for greater autonomy among TVET providers and more incentives to try out different approaches to TVET provision, making it easier to identify promising approaches that respond better to local labor market needs.

TVET at the national and individual levels. First, these efforts include reforms to address critical market failures in the credit and labor markets as well as institutional failures that cripple the business environment and, thus, the returns to TVET. TVET reforms will also be more effective if accompanied by reforms across the education system to ensure that all students, and not only the better off, complete basic education with solid foundational skills. Finally, reforms need to account for a country's capacity, resources, and state of economic transformation. If these complementary reforms are left undone, the payoffs of TVET reforms will be limited at best and negative at worst.

Annex 3A Formal Apprenticeship Training in Select Sub-Saharan African Countries

Country	Legal or policy framework	Institutional responsibilities	Program characteristics	Relationship with formal TVET system	Certification	Financing arrangements	Relative importance in the formal TVET system
Countries with distinct apprenticeship systems regulated parallel to other formal TVET schemes							
Botswana	Apprenticeship and Industrial Training Regulation	Madirelo Training and Testing Centre, Directorate of Apprenticeship and Industrial Training, Ministry of Labour	4-year program, divided each year into 3 months at a training center and 9 months of in-company training; operates with 26 trades	Distinct parallel delivery system	National craft certificate	Apprentice receives remuneration from employers; government bears college costs; firms are entitled to double tax deduction, but system is not used effectively	—
Ghana	Apprenticeship Training Regulation (1978) and NVTI Act (1970)	NVTI Department of Apprenticeship	Cooperative training with 10–15% vocational institution training	—	—	—	—
Kenya	Industrial Training Act	Administered by National Industrial Training Authority under Ministry of Labour	Formal apprenticeship contract, industrial training during tuition-free time, accessible to youth upon merit, only levy-paying companies can participate	Special program within formal TVET system	Formal TVET craft certificates and diplomas (postsecondary)	Apprenticeship allowances and tuition fees for TVET institutions reimbursed through levy fund	Low (500–600 apprentices annually vs. 41,000 in formal postsecondary technical college system
Mauritius	—	MITD	Different schemes: (1) dual apprenticeship training; (2) in-house apprenticeship training (firms need to provide both theory and practice); and (3) tailor-made apprenticeship training; duration is normally 1–2 years, but can be longer	—	National trade certificate	Employers have to pay stipulated apprenticeship allowances, 50% of which are reimbursed by MITD	—

(continued next page)

Annex 3A Formal Apprenticeship Training in Select Sub-Saharan African Countries (continued)

Country	Legal or policy framework	Institutional responsibilities	Program characteristics	Relationship with formal TVET system	Certification	Financing arrangements	Relative importance in the formal TVET system
South Africa	Manpower Training Act (1981) and Skills Development Act (2008)	National Artisan Moderation Body under Department of Higher Education and Training	2- to 4-year cooperative programs combining workplace learning with school-based training; 25–30% is delivered at school; the learnerships introduced in 1998 are shorter (1 year or less), are modular, and can involve different employers	Apprenticeship system is an established system of artisan training; apprenticeships and learnerships are 2 of 4 official routes to trade testing	Trade testing, regulated by Quality Council for Trades and Occupations	Employers can apply for apprenticeship grants, which are sourced from the training levy; employers are also eligible for a tax rebate	After a steep drop in 2000, apprenticeships are regaining importance. In 2012, more than 24,000 were registered in the system; numbers are higher for learnerships
Zimbabwe	Manpower Planning and Development Act (1994, 1996)	Ministry of Higher and Tertiary Education	Formal, postsecondary programs (4 years, including 1 year in college)	Alternative postsecondary TVET track	Trade test journeyman class	Training costs of companies subsidized under levy-sourced Manpower Development Fund	—
Countries with apprenticeship training as mainstream formal TVET delivery							
Ethiopia	National TVET Policy of 2008	National TVET Authority	Extended industrial attachment: all formal TVET students are required to undergo 70% of their training in-company, no formal apprenticeship contracts	Default delivery mode of formal TVET	Formal TVET certificates	No special arrangement	Mainstream delivery mode in formal TVET system; however, not always implemented

(continued next page)

Annex 3A Formal Apprenticeship Training in Select Sub-Saharan African Countries (continued)

Country	Legal or policy framework	Institutional responsibilities	Program characteristics	Relationship with formal TVET system	Certification	Financing arrangements	Relative importance in the formal TVET system
Malawi	National TEVET Policy, TEVET Act	TEVET Authority	4-year programs with 50% college-based and 50% enterprise-based training	Default delivery mode of formal TVET	TVET certificate	College-based training subsidized by TEVET Authority from levy fund	Mainstream delivery mode in formal TVET system; however, due to lack of company placements, a parallel formal TVET system, mainly school based, has developed that enrolls double the number of apprentices; in 2015, 1,283 apprentices were officially admitted (of which 394 female)
Countries with plans to introduce or reintroduce apprenticeship training							
Namibia	Policy Framework and Guidelines for Apprenticeship, Traineeships, and Internships (2016)	Namibia Training Authority	2 systems are foreseen in the policy: apprenticeship training of 3–4 years in designated apprenticeship trades, which are classical technical trades; traineeships (also called learnerships), which are shorter and mainly cover service sector occupations. The latter are based on NQF qualifications	Alternative TVET delivery mode	For apprenticeships, (postprimary) trade certificates after trade test; for traineeships, NQF qualifications at different levels	Apprentices and learners are supposed to receive allowances from employers of not less than N$400–N$700 week, depending on year; employers are suggested to be entitled to apprenticeship or traineeship grants from the government of between N$30,000 and N$40,000, depending on the year of training	Not yet implemented, but presumably substantial due to previous apprenticeship culture and relatively large formal sector
Rwanda	Labour Law, Workplace Learning Policy (2015)	Workforce Development Authority	Dual training programs in construction industry (donor supported)	Planned as parallel delivery track within formal system	National TVET certificates based on RTQF	Development and quality assurance costs are donor supported	Very small numbers

Source: Franz 2017.

Note: TVET = technical and vocational education and training; NVTI = National Vocational Training Institute; MITD = Mauritius Institute of Training and Development; TEVET Authority = Entrepreneurial and Vocational Education and Training Authority; NQF = national qualifications framework; RTQF = Rwanda TVET qualifications framework; — = no information available.

Notes

1. The United Nations Educational, Scientific, and Cultural Organization (UNESCO) defines TVET as "those aspects of the educational process involving, in addition to general education, the study of technologies and related sciences and the acquisition of practical skills, attitudes, understanding, and knowledge relating to occupation in various sectors of economic life" (UNESCO 2011).
2. Based on UIS.Stat data.
3. For East Asia, see Ansu and Tan (2012); for a discussion of Germany's dual system and youth unemployment, see Zimmermann et al. (2013).
4. See, for example, Almeida, Behrman, and Robalino (2012); Ansu and Tan (2012); Ashton et al. (2002); Kuruvilla, Erickson, and Hwang (2002).
5. For a more detailed discussion of market and government failures in TVET, see Almeida, Behrman, and Robalino (2012).
6. Based on UIS.Stat data. The diversity of TVET systems and the paucity of data in many countries in the region mean that systematic and comparable data on TVET quality are scarce.
7. However, this work on social norms needs to go beyond the TVET system, since the choice of fields of study mirrors many of the stereotypes and realities in the labor market.
8. For in-depth analysis for Burkina Faso, see World Bank 2017b; for Nigeria, see World Bank (2015a); for Uganda, see Johanson and Okema (2011); for a regionwide discussion of these issues, see Zimmermann et al. (2013).
9. Among other characteristics, youths who enter TVET are different from youths who pursue a general education, including in their socioeconomic background and academic readiness. Since in the estimates of returns many of these characteristics are unobservable, the estimates obtained are a measure not only of the returns to education but also of unobserved but associated characteristics of graduates.
10. This literacy measure is far from perfect since it does not predate the actual choice of track or studies. The lower literacy levels among TVET students could, therefore, be the result of both lower academic readiness at the moment of choosing the track and lesser attention to foundational skills in technical versus general education.
11. Calculations based on the School-to-Work Transition Surveys. In Malawi and Zambia, for example, 10 percent of youths who have at least secondary education, who work, and who have a technical and vocational education background report having important knowledge and skills gaps relevant for their job, compared with at least 20 percent among graduates of general education.
12. For Argentina, see Alzúa, Cruces, and Lopez (2016); for Colombia, see Attanasio, Kugler, and Meghir (2011) and Kugler et al. (2015); for the Dominican Republic, see Card et al. (2011), Ibarrarán et al. (2014), and Ibarrarán et al. (2015); for Kenya, see Hicks et al. (2015) and Honorati (2015); for Malawi, see Cho et al. (2015); for Peru, see Diaz and Rosas-Schady (2016).
13. In the context of this tool, workforce development refers to issues pertaining to training provision, by both public and private providers, through channels such as preemployment, on-the-job, and lifelong education and training as well as active

labor market programs, enabling individuals to acquire job-relevant skills (World Bank 2013). For more information on SABER, see http://www.worldbank.org/education/saber.

14. In Benin, for example, the Education Sector Development Plan 2006–2015 sets TVET as the second key priority, after primary education. Similarly, in Chad, the National Plan for Education for All 2002–2015 prioritizes TVET. The Gambia, Mauritius, Mozambique, Namibia, Tanzania, Uganda, and Zambia, among others, also have recent strategic documents that put TVET atop government's priorities in education (World TVET data).

15. Lucas and Mbiti (2012) find that, in Kenya, even among high-ability students with a small set of secondary schools from which to choose, many selection errors reduce the likelihood of students being admitted to top schools. These errors are significantly more likely among girls, students with lower exam scores, and students from public and lower-quality primary schools. A similar phenomenon has been found in Ghana (Ajayi 2013).

16. Jensen (2010) finds that, in the Dominican Republic, students have strong misperceptions about returns to education that affect their livelihood and choices in secondary school. Students are constrained in their role models and information sets and form their expectations on earnings and returns to education and to different occupations based on what they observe in their neighborhoods. Since in many countries in Africa there is also strong residential separation between rich and poor, this type of asymmetry in and access to role models could play an adverse role in educational choices among the more disadvantaged.

17. For more information on College to Careers, see http://www.ccc.edu/menu/Pages/college-to-careers.aspx.

18. Having these pathways is important because vocational training and academic education can be complementary investments. In Colombia, for example, a rigorous impact evaluation found that, in the medium and long term, participants in vocational training were more likely to complete secondary school and to attend and persist in tertiary education even eight years after starting training (Kugler et al. 2015).

19. See the financing sections in the World TVET data.

20. For a more in-depth discussion of financing of TVET in Africa and in low- and middle-income countries, see Almeida, Behrman, and Robalino (2012); Billetoft (2016); Johanson (2009); Walther and Uther (2014).

21. Based on World TVET data.

22. In the Technical and Vocational Vouchers Program, launched in 2008 in Western Kenya, 50 percent of youth applicants were randomly selected to receive a voucher, with the remaining applicants serving as a control group. Of those receiving vouchers, half were given restricted vouchers applicable only in public institutions. Three-quarters of voucher holders attended training compared with 4 percent of the control group, showing that high costs of accessing TVET are a barrier to accessing skills development. In addition, enrollment was 10 percentage points higher among those with vouchers that could be used to attend public or private institutions than among those with vouchers that were restricted to public providers (Hicks et al. 2011).

23. For Burkina Faso, see World Bank 2017b; for Nigeria, see World Bank (2015a); for Uganda, see Johanson and Okema (2011); for a regionwide discussion, see Zimmermann et al. (2013). In Burkina Faso, at the tertiary level, training programs are concentrated in the industrial sectors, which account for more than 75 percent of students, yet industry represents only 3 percent of total employment.
24. For a discussion of the skills needed in the natural resource industries, see de la Brière et al. (2017).
25. For an in-depth analysis of TVET teacher education in Africa and lessons from approaches followed elsewhere in the world, see European Commission (2015).
26. An estimated 35 percent of training across Africa is provided by the private sector (Mingat, Ledoux, and Rakotomalala 2010).
27. See, for example, in Kenya, "We'll Train One Million Youths for Jobs Abroad, Says Kandie," *Daily Nation,* February 17 (http://www.nation.co.ke/news/Ministry -plans-to-train-one-million-youth-for-labour-export/-/1056/3081068 /-/13ho41d/-/index.html).
28. See, for example, http://akirachix.com/ and www.decodingbootcamps.org.
29. The discussion on apprenticeships in Africa is based on Franz (2017).

References

Adams, Arvil, Sara Johansson, and Setareh Razmara, eds. 2013. *Improving Skills Development in the Informal Sector.* Directions in Development Series. Washington, DC: World Bank.

ADB (Asian Development Bank). 2008. *Education and Skills: Strategies for Accelerated Development in Asia and the Pacific.* Manila: ADB.

———. 2014. *Innovative Strategies in Technical and Vocational Education and Training for Accelerated Human Resource Development in South Asia.* Manila: ADB.

Ajayi, Kenhinde. 2013. "School Choice and Educational Mobility: Lessons from Secondary School Applications in Ghana." Boston University, Boston, MA. http:// people.bu.edu/kajayi/Ajayi_EducationalMobility.pdf.

Ali, Daniel Ayalew, Derick Bowen, and Klaus Deininger. 2017. "Personality Traits, Technology Adoption, and Technical Efficiency: Evidence from Smallholder Rice Farms in Ghana." Policy Research Working Paper 7959, World Bank, Washington, DC.

Almeida, Rita, Jere Behrman, and David Robalino, eds. 2012. *The Right Skills for the Job? Rethinking Training Policies for Workers.* Washington, DC: World Bank.

Altinok, Nadir. 2011. "General versus Vocational Education: Some New Evidence from PISA 2009." Background paper for the Education for All Global Monitoring Report 2012, UNESCO, Paris. http://unesdoc.unesco.org/images/0021/002178/21 7873e.pdf.

Alzúa, María Laura, Guillermo Cruces, and Carolina Lopez. 2016. "Long Run Effects of Youth Training Programs: Experimental Evidence from Argentina." IZA Discussion Paper 9784, Institute of Labor Economics, Bonn.

Anarfi, John, and Ernest Appiah. 2012. "Skills Defined by Curricula: Sub-Saharan Africa." Center for Education Innovations, Results for Development Institute, Washington, DC.

Ansu, Yaw, and Jee-Peng Tan. 2012. "Skills Development for Economic Growth in Sub-Saharan Africa: A Pragmatic Perspective." In *Good Growth and Governance in Africa: Rethinking Development Strategies*, edited by Akbar Noman, Kwesi Botchwey, Howard Stein, and Joseph E. Stiglitz, 462–64. Initiative for Policy Dialogue Series. Oxford, UK: Oxford University Press.

Ashton, David, Francis Green, Johnny Sung, and Donna James. 2002. "The Evolution of Education and Training Strategies in Singapore, Taiwan and South Korea: A Development Model of Skill Formation." *Journal of Education and Work* 15 (1): 5–30.

Attanasio, Orazio, Adriana Kugler, and Costas Meghir. 2011. "Subsidizing Vocational Training for Disadvantaged Youth in Colombia: Evidence from a Randomized Trial." *American Economic Journal: Applied Economics* 3 (3): 188–220.

Barro, Robert J., and Jong-Wha Lee. 2015. *Education Matters: Global Schooling Gains from the 19th to the 21st Century.* New York: Oxford University Press.

Billetoft, Jorgen. 2016. "Technical and Vocational Education and Training in Sub-Saharan Africa." Background paper for this report, World Bank, Washington, DC.

Blackmur, Douglas. 2015. "Arguing with Stephanie Allais. Are National Qualifications Frameworks Instruments of Neoliberalism and Social Constructivism?" *Quality in Higher Education* 21 (2): 213–28.

Campos, Francisco, Markus Goldstein, Laura McGorman, Ana Maria Munoz, and Obert Pimhidzai. 2015. "Breaking the Metal Ceiling: Female Entrepreneurs Who Succeed in Male-Dominated Sectors." Policy Research Working Paper 7503, World Bank, Washington, DC.

Card, David, Pablo Ibarrarán, Ferninando Regalia, David Rosas-Shady, and Yuri Soares. 2011. "The Labor Market Impacts of Youth Training in the Dominican Republic." *Journal of Labor Economics* 29 (2): 267–300.

Centre for Development and Enterprise. 2012. "Vocational Education in South Africa: Strategies for Improvement." Building on What Works in Education 3, Centre for Development and Enterprise, Johannesburg.

Cho, Yoonyoung, Davie Kalomba, A. Mushfiq Mobarak, and Victor Orozco. 2015. "Gender Differences in the Effects of Vocational Training: Constraints on Women and Drop-out Behavior." Working Paper WPS6545, World Bank, Washington, DC.

Coles, Mike, James Keevy, Andrea Bateman, and Jack Keating. 2014. "Flying Blind: Policy Rationales for National Qualifications Frameworks and How They Tend to Evolve." *International Journal of Continuing Education and Lifelong Learning* 7 (1): 17–46.

Couralet, Pierre-Emmanuel, Ezéchiel Djallo, and Hervé Akinocho. 2013. "Gambian Graduates Tracer Study: Final Report." ERNWACA (Educational Research Network for West and Central Africa), Bamako, Mali, December. http://www.rocare.org/docs/final-report-TVET-tracer-study.pdf.

Darvas, Peter, and Robert Palmer. 2014. "Demand and Supply of Skills in Ghana. How can Training Programs Improve Employment and Productivity?" World Bank, Washington, DC.

de la Brière, Bénédicte, Deon Filmer, Dena Ringold, Dominic Rohner, Karelle Samuda, and Anastasiya Denisova. 2017. *From Mines and Wells to Well-Built Minds: Turning Sub-Saharan Africa's Natural Resource Wealth into Human Capital.* Directions in Development Series. Washington, DC: World Bank.

Díaz, Juan José, and David Rosas-Shady. 2016. "Impact Evaluation of the Job Youth Training Program Pro Joven." Working Paper 94116, Inter-American Development Bank, Washington, DC.

European Commission. 2015. "TVET Teacher Education in Africa: Synthesis Report." European Commission, Brussels. http://ec.europa.eu/dgs/education_culture/reposi tory/education/library/reports/tvet-africa-report_en.pdf.

Fazio, María Victoria, Raquel Fernández-Coto, and Laura Ripani. 2016. "Apprenticeships for the XXI Century: A Model for Latin America and the Caribbean?" Inter-American Development Bank, Washington, DC.

Filmer, Deon, and Louise Fox. 2014. *Youth Employment in Sub-Saharan Africa.* Africa Development Series. Washington, DC: World Bank.

Franz, Jutta. 2017. "Apprenticeship Training in Africa." Background paper for this report, Washington, DC.

Glennerster, Rachel, Michael Kremer, Isaac Mbiti, and Kudzai Takavarasha. 2011. "Access and Quality in the Kenyan Education System: A Review of the Progress, Challenges, and Potential Solutions." Report prepared for the Office of the Prime Minister of Kenya. https://www.povertyactionlab.org/sites/default/files/publications /Access%20and%20Quality%20in%20the%20Kenyan%20Education%20System%20 2011.06.22.pdf.

Government of Mozambique. 2016. "TVET Reform in Mozambique: The Involvement of the Private Sector as a Factor of Success." Presentation given at the World Bank, Washington, DC, June.

Hampf, Franziska, and Ludger Woessmann. 2016. "Vocational vs. General Education and Employment over the Life-Cycle: New Evidence from PIAAC." IZA Discussion Paper 10298, Institute of Labor Economics, Bonn.

Hanushek, Eric A., Guido Schwerdt, Ludger Woessmann, and Lei Zhang. 2017. "General Education, Vocational Education, and Labor-Market Outcomes over the Life-Cycle." *Journal of Human Resources* 52 (1): 49–88.

Herd, George, and Alison Richardson. 2011. "World Report on TVET: The Promise and Potential of ICT in TVET." UNESCO, Paris. http://oasis.col.org/bitstream/han dle/11599/824/UNESCO%20World%20Report%20-%20ICT%20in%20TVET%20-%20 Herd%20%2B%20Mead%20Richardson.pdf?sequence=1&isAllowed=y.

Hicks, Joan Hamory, Michael Kremer, Issac Mbiti, and Edward Miguel. 2011. "Vocational Education Voucher Delivery and Labor Market Returns: A Randomized Evaluation among Kenyan Youth." A report for the Spanish Impact Evaluation Fund, World Bank, Washington, DC.

———. 2015. *Vocational Education in Kenya: A Randomized Evaluation.* 3ie Grantee Final Report. New Delhi: International Initiative for Impact Evaluation (3ie).

Hirshleifer, Sarojini, David McKenzie, Rita Almeida, and Cristobal Ridao-Cano. 2014. "The Impact of Vocational Training for the Unemployed: Experimental Evidence from Turkey." *Economic Journal* 126 (597): 2115–46.

Honorati, Maddalena. 2015. "The Impact of Private Sector Internship and Training on Urban Youth in Kenya." Policy Research Working Paper WPS7404, World Bank, Washington, DC.

Ibarrarán, Pablo, Jochen Kluve, Laura Ripani, and David Rosas Shady. 2015. "Experimental Evidence on the Long-Term Impacts of a Youth Training Program." IZA Discussion Paper 9136, Institute of Labor Economics, Bonn.

Ibarrarán, Pablo, Laura Ripani, Bibiana Taboada, Juan Villa, and Brigida Garcia. 2014. "Life Skills, Employability, and Training for Disadvantaged Youth: Evidence from a Randomized Evaluation Design." IZA Journal of Labor and Development 3 (1): 1–24.

ILO (International Labour Organization). 2014. "Labor Market Transitions of Young Women and Men in Sub-Saharan Africa." ILO, Geneva.

———. Various years. School-to-Work Transition Survey. Geneva: ILO. http://www.ilo.org/employment/areas/youth-employment/work-for-youth/WCMS_191853/lang--en/index.htm.

Jakubowski, Maciej, Harry Patrinos, Emilio Porta, and Jerzy Wisniewski. 2011. "The Impact of the 1999 Education Reform in Poland." Education Working Paper 49, Organisation for Economic Co-operation and Development, Paris.

Jensen, Robert. 2010. "The (Perceived) Returns to Education and the Demand for Schooling." Quarterly Journal of Economics 125 (2): 515–48.

Johanson, Richard. 2009. "A Review of National Training Funds." Social Protection Discussion Paper 0922, World Bank, Washington, DC.

Johanson, Richard, and Arvil Adams. 2004. Skills Development in Sub-Saharan Africa. Washington, DC: World Bank.

Johanson, Richard, and James Okema. 2011. "Business, Technical Vocational Education, and Training Sub-Sector Analysis." Technical Paper 5: BTVET Delivery, prepared for the Ministry of Education and Sports, Belgian Technical Cooperation/BTC and the World Bank, Kampala, Uganda.

Keevy, James, and Borhene Chakroun. 2015. Level-Setting and Recognition of Learning Outcomes: The Use of Level Descriptors in the Twenty-First Century. Paris: UNESCO.

Kis, Viktoria. 2016. "Work-Based Learning for Youth at Risk: Getting Employers on Board." Working Paper, Organisation for Economic Co-operation and Development, Paris.

Kugler, Adriana, Maurice Kugler, Juan Saavedra, and Luis Herrera. 2015. "Long-Term Direct and Spillover Effects of Job Training: Experimental Evidence from Colombia." Working Paper 21607, National Bureau of Economic Research, Cambridge, MA.

Kuruvilla, Sarosh, Christopher L. Erickson, and Alvin Hwang. 2002. "An Assessment of the Singapore Skills Development System: Does It Constitute a Viable Model for Other Developing Countries?" World Development 30 (8): 1461–76.

Kutner, Daniel, and Lucas Gortazar. 2014. "Technical and Vocational Education vs. General Secondary Education: Literature Review." World Bank, Washington, DC.

Laajaj, Rachid, and Karen Macours. 2017. "Measuring Skills in Developing Countries." Working Paper, Paris School of Economics, Paris. http://www.parisschoolofeconomics.eu/docs/macours-karen/skills-measurement-laajaj-macours-jan-2017-v10.pdf.

Lamo, Ana, Julian Messina, and Etienne Wasmer. 2011. "Are Specific Skills an Obstacle to Labor Market Adjustment?" *Labour Economics* 18 (2): 240–56.

Lucas, Adrienne, and Isaac Mbiti. 2012. "The Determinants and Consequences of School Choice Errors in Kenya." *American Economic Review, Papers and Proceedings* 102 (3): 283–88.

McKinsey Global Institute. 2012. "Africa at Work: Job Creation and Inclusive Growth." McKinsey Global Institute, New York. https://www.mckinsey.com/featured-insights /middle-east-and-africa/africa-at-work.

Mingat, Alain, Blandine Ledoux, and Ramahatra Rakotomalala. 2010. *Developing Post-Primary Education in Sub-Saharan Africa: Assessing the Financial Sustainability of Alternative Pathways.* African Human Development Series. Washington, DC: World Bank.

Ngome, Charles. 2003. "Overview of Skills Development in Kenya: Constraints and Prospects." Network for International Policies and Cooperation in Education and Training, Geneva. http://www.norrag.org/en/publications/norrag-news /online-version/critical-perspectives-on-education-and-skills-in-eastern-africa-on-basic -and-post-basic-levels/detail/overview-of-skills-development-in-kenya-constraints-and -prospects.html.

OECD (Organisation for Economic Co-operation and Development). 2014a. "G20-OECD-EC Conference on Quality Apprenticeships for Giving Youth a Better Start in the Labour Market: Background Paper Prepared by the OECD." OECD, Paris.

———. 2014b. *Skills Beyond School: Synthesis Report.* OECD Reviews of Vocational Education and Training. Paris: OECD Publishing. http://www.oecd.org/edu/skills -beyondschool/Skills-Beyond-School-SynthesisReport.pdf.

Psacharopoulos, George. 1994. "Returns to Investment in Education: A Global Update." *World Development* 22 (9): 1325–43.

Pugatch, Todd. 2014. "Safety Valve or Sinkhole? Vocational Schooling in South Africa." *IZA Journal of Labor and Development* 3 (2014): 8.

Robinson, Jenny Perlman, Rebecca Winthrop, and Eileen McGivney. 2016. *Millions Learning: Scaling up Quality Education in Developing Countries.* Washington, DC: Brookings Institution.

Schochet, Peter, John Burghardt, and Sheena McConnell. 2008. "Does Jobs Corps Work? Impact Findings from the National Job Corps Study." *American Economic Review* 98 (5): 1864–86.

Sosale, Shobhana, and Kirsten Majgaard. 2016. *Fostering Skills in Cameroon Inclusive Workforce Development, Competitiveness, and Growth.* Directions in Development Series. Washington, DC: World Bank.

Tiyab, Beifith Kouak. 2014. "Développement de l'enseignement post-primaire au Burkina Faso: Vue d'ensemble des enjeux et défis en matière d'accès et d'équité." Background paper for this study. Government of Burkina Faso (INS), UNESCO Pôle de Dakar, and World Bank, Ouagadougou.

Tsang, Mun. 1997. "The Cost of Vocational Training." *International Journal of Manpower* 18 (1/2): 63–89.

UIS (UNESCO Institute for Statistics). Various years. UIS.Stat database. Montreal: UIS.

UNESCO (United Nations Educational, Scientific, and Cultural Organization). 2011. "Introducing UNESCO's Technical Vocational Education and Training (TVET) Definition and Strategy." UNESCO, Viña del Mar, Chile.

———. 2013. "Status of TVET in the SADC Region." UNESCO, Paris. http://unesdoc .unesco.org/images/0022/002256/225632e.pdf.

———. 2015. *Transversal Skills in TVET: Policy Implications.* Asia-Pacific Education System Review Series. Bangkok: UNESCO.

———. 2015. *Education for All: 2000–2015: Achievements and Challenges.* Education for All Global Monitoring Report 2015. Paris: UNESCO.

UNEVOC International Center. Various years. World TVET Database: Promoting Learning for the World of Work. Paris: UNESCO.

Walther, Richard, and Ewa Filipiak. 2007. "Vocational Training in the Informal Sector or How to Stimulate the Economies of Developing Countries? Conclusions of a Field Survey in Seven African Countries." Research Department, Agence Française de Développement, Paris.

Walther, Richard, and Christine Uhder. 2014. "The Financing of Vocational Training in Africa: Roles and Specificities of Vocational Training Funds." Agence Française de Développement, Paris. http://www.adeanet.org/sites/default/files/afd-financing-voca tional-training-africa.pdf.

World Bank. 2011. *World Development Report 2012: Gender Equality and Development.* Washington, DC: World Bank.

———. 2012. "SABER Workforce Development Country Report: Uganda." SABER Country Report 2012. World Bank, Washington, DC.

———. 2013. "What Matters for Workforce Development: A Framework and Tool for Analysis." SABER Working Paper 6, World Bank, Washington, DC.

———. 2015a. "Nigeria: Skills for Competitiveness and Employability." World Bank, Washington, DC.

———. 2015b. "SABER-Workforce Development Country Draft Report for Burundi." World Bank, Washington, DC.

———. 2015c. "SABER-Workforce Development Country Draft Report for Chad." World Bank: Washington, DC.

———. 2015d. "SABER-Workforce Development Country Draft Report for Liberia." World Bank, Washington, DC.

———. 2015e. "SABER-Workforce Development Country Draft Report for Tanzania." World Bank, Washington, DC.

———. 2015f. "Secondary Vocational Education: International Experience." World Bank, Washington, DC.

———. 2016a. "Skills Development and Employability Project. Project Appraisal Document." Report PAD1156, World Bank, Washington, DC.

———. 2016b. *World Development Report 2016: Digital Dividends.* Washington, DC: World Bank.

———. 2017a. "Training Assessment Project—TAP—Methodology Note." World Bank, Workforce Development Project, Washington, DC, August.

———. 2017b *Post-Primary Education Development in Burkina Faso: Achievements, Challenges, and Prospects.* Vols. 1 and 2. Washington, DC: World Bank.

———. Various years. SABER-WfD Ratings and Data. Washington, DC: World Bank. http://saber.worldbank.org/index.cfm?indx=8&pd=7&sub=1.

———. Various years. Skills Towards Employability and Productivity (STEP) Survey. Washington, DC: World Bank.

———. Various years. World Development Indicators database. Washington, DC: World Bank.

Young, Michael, and Stephanie Allias, eds. 2013. *Implementing National Qualification Frameworks across Five Continents.* New York: Routledge.

Zimmermann, Klaus, Costanza Biavaschi, Werner Eichhorst, Corrado Giulietti, Michael Kendzia, Alexander Muravyev, Janneke Pieters, Nuria Rodrıguez-Planas, and Ricarda Schmidl. 2013. "Youth Unemployment and Vocational Training." *Foundations and Trends in Microeconomics* 9 (1-2): 1–157.

Chapter **4**

Building Skills for Productivity through Higher Education in Sub-Saharan Africa

Indhira Santos and Omar Arias

Targeted, smart investments in university education are crucial for African countries' productive transformation and sustained economic growth. Yet these investments potentially carry the most significant trade-off between the goals of productivity and inclusion, a trade-off that is stronger for countries with a low skills endowment, in the early stages of their productive transformation, or lacking an enabling environment for workers and countries to generate adequate returns from university education investments.

Lessons from international experience suggest that countries should manage carefully the expansion of higher education, first, by ensuring that youths acquire solid foundational skills in basic education as a prerequisite for college readiness and by promoting equitable access and, second, by building early on the institutional foundations that can make higher education investments pay off both for individuals and for the economy at-large. Of prime importance are financing mechanisms that are aligned with merit and families' ability to pay and governance structures that strengthen the links to the private sector and are conducive to more active learning practices.

Introduction

The success of many African countries in boosting enrollment and completion in primary and, increasingly, secondary education is increasing the demand for more affordable and better-quality higher education across the continent.[1] The average gross enrollment rate in tertiary education—of which higher education accounts for around 80 percent—is 10 percent in the region.[2] The variation across countries is large, however: enrollment rates range from 42 percent in Mauritius to 1–2 percent in Malawi and Niger. But these rates are set to rise: the larger number of students completing secondary education (see chapter 2), coupled with rising expectations, is increasing the pressure on governments to expand access to higher education as well as to improve its quality and relevance. But this expansion needs to be well managed if it is to create more skilled workers and avoid unfulfilled aspirations. The recent university student protests in South Africa highlight not only the increasing demand for higher education but also many of the equity, quality, and efficiency issues that affect (or will soon affect) many university systems on the continent. Similar concerns have been raised in recent years around the world through student protests in Bangladesh, Canada, Chile, and the United Kingdom, to name a few.

This demand for more and better higher education is augmented by the changing and rising demands of employers and local economies. The investments, delivery mechanisms, and financing of higher education need to be fit to the changes in the world economy and the world of work that will be brought about by the megatrends described in box 4.1.

Smart investments in university education are indeed crucial for Africa's productive transformation and sustained economic growth. Workers' skills,

---

BOX 4.1

The Megatrends and Higher Education

As in the rest of the education and training system, demographic changes, global integration, and technological changes are profoundly affecting what universities do, how they do it, and for whom. Along these dimensions, the megatrends bring both opportunities and challenges for the university systems of Sub-Saharan African countries.

First, demographic forces imply that the number of youths completing secondary education will continue to grow—fueled by demographic youth bulges and urbanization—increasing the demand for higher education. At the same time, urbanization and the rise of new middle-income economies in Africa, coupled with the structural transformation of these economies, is increasing the demand for a more skilled but also a more adaptable workforce. University education is critical for achieving these goals. Urbanization also is likely to increase the demand for university education, since most universities are located in urban areas, where returns to education are the highest.

Second, global economic integration and technological changes are changing the nature of work and skills demands, putting a premium on cognitive and socioemotional skills that complement new technologies and add most value to global production chains. Many of these skills are cemented in the university system. More rapid changes such as those already observed in high-income countries will require greater adaptability from workers, who will change jobs more often or—even within the same

---

(continued next page)

Box 4.1 (continued)

job—perform tasks that are ever evolving. The need for adaptability is a challenge for university education, which struggles to deliver practical learning experiences and often hinges on a linear university-to-work transition that is rapidly being rendered obsolete. Analysis of the International Labour Organization (ILO) School-to-Work Transition Surveys suggests that, while in most Sub-Saharan African countries, many students combine studies and work, employment often does not directly apply what is being learned, limiting potential synergies.

All in all, university education becomes increasingly critical in more urbanized, integrated, and technologically advanced countries. As documented in this report, returns to skills are systematically higher in countries that have grown faster in the recent past, which is consistent with skills being particularly relevant for adapting to dynamic changes in the economy (Hanushek et al. 2016). More modern firms—those that export and innovate, for example—also report that skills are more of a constraint to their operations (chapter 1). University education, in particular, may be most important for improving productivity and expanding the catalytic sectors of both today and tomorrow. Given their role in innovation and in high-value-added sectors, science, technology, engineering, and mathematics (STEM), in particular, are likely to become more important for countries in the region, especially those that are more advanced in their economic transformation (Moretti 2004, 2010; Valencia Caicedo and Maloney 2014).

These megatrends open up opportunities for leapfrogging. Global integration and new technologies facilitate new delivery mechanisms in higher education. These mechanisms include opportunities for studying abroad, for joining forces across countries to develop centers of excellence, and for developing online and distance learning that can provide access to higher education courses to more people, in more fields, globally (and may reduce costs). Introducing practical elements in courses becomes easier through digital technologies. At the system level, technology also can facilitate the generation, synthesis, analysis, and dissemination of relevant information for decision making and adaptive learning.

---

particularly those obtained through higher education, are considered critical for technology development and adaptation (Lucas 1988; Romer 1986, 1990) and necessary for drawing on global knowledge and applying it for local growth (Valencia Caicedo and Maloney 2014). Higher education also provides the foundation for a nation's innovation capacity (Carnoy et al. 1993; Cloete et al. 2011). In addition, there are externalities related to interdependencies between higher education investments and broader capital formation, particularly between skills agglomeration and technological innovation. It is thought, for example, that having a supply of qualified engineers and highly skilled workers has been critical to China's ability to adopt and adapt Western technologies and grow at an unprecedented rate (Yuchtman 2017). Similarly, early investments in engineering schools in the early 19th century, even before the massive expansion of secondary education took place, are credited with some of the success of the United States in igniting its innovation capacity (Valencia Caicedo and Maloney 2014). Countries or regions lacking a minimum level of college-educated workers are less likely to attract more technology-intensive and research and development (R&D)–intensive domestic or foreign investments. This lack of investment holds back the private returns to higher levels of education under an educational expansion. The ensuing slowdown in the transition to higher educational grades, in turn, hinders technology upgrading and reinforces the low-skill, low-innovation cycle.

There is also evidence of spillovers into aggregate productivity and aggregate demand as university graduates agglomerate in economic centers. In the United States, it is estimated that a 1 percentage point increase in the supply of university graduates increases the wages of high school dropouts 1.9 percent, those of high school graduates 1.6 percent, and those of tertiary graduates 0.4 percent (Moretti 2004). Also in the United States, it has been found that one additional job held by a college graduate in the tradable sector generates 2.5 jobs in local goods and services. The corresponding multiplier for unskilled jobs is 1 (Moretti 2010). Similar evidence has been found in Mexico and Turkey, with multipliers for skilled jobs estimated at 4.4 and 3.9, respectively (World Bank 2017a). In addition to a host of other development benefits and externalities such as better health, average private returns to higher education—at 20 percent—are also high (figure 4.1; see Montenegro and Patrinos 2014). Returns to higher education across the region are, on average, slightly higher for women than for men.

However, this payoff in terms of economic growth only materializes if higher education can build on strong foundational skills. Skills beget skills: simply adding years of schooling at the university level without ensuring quality institutions and a minimum level of foundational skills among entering students has no impact on growth and often comes at a much higher cost (Hanushek 2016). In fact, the achievement levels of students at an earlier age are a very good indicator of the aggregate skills of students at the end of their schooling, since each level of schooling builds on earlier knowledge. Beyond economic growth, skills building in universities can contribute to achieving more and better earning opportunities and to amassing an adaptable and agile workforce fit to the demands of a modernizing economy. Investments in university education need, therefore, to focus on quality and account not only for current needs, but also for the changing needs of a dynamic environment.

Moreover, despite these potentially high private and social returns, higher education investments potentially carry the most significant trade-off between countries' productivity and inclusion goals. As shown in this chapter, university education in Sub-Saharan Africa is accessible largely to students from better-off families. Simply expanding higher education under current governance and financing structures can exacerbate inequality, given current failures in early

Figure 4.1 Returns to Tertiary Education, by Region and Select Sub-Saharan African Countries

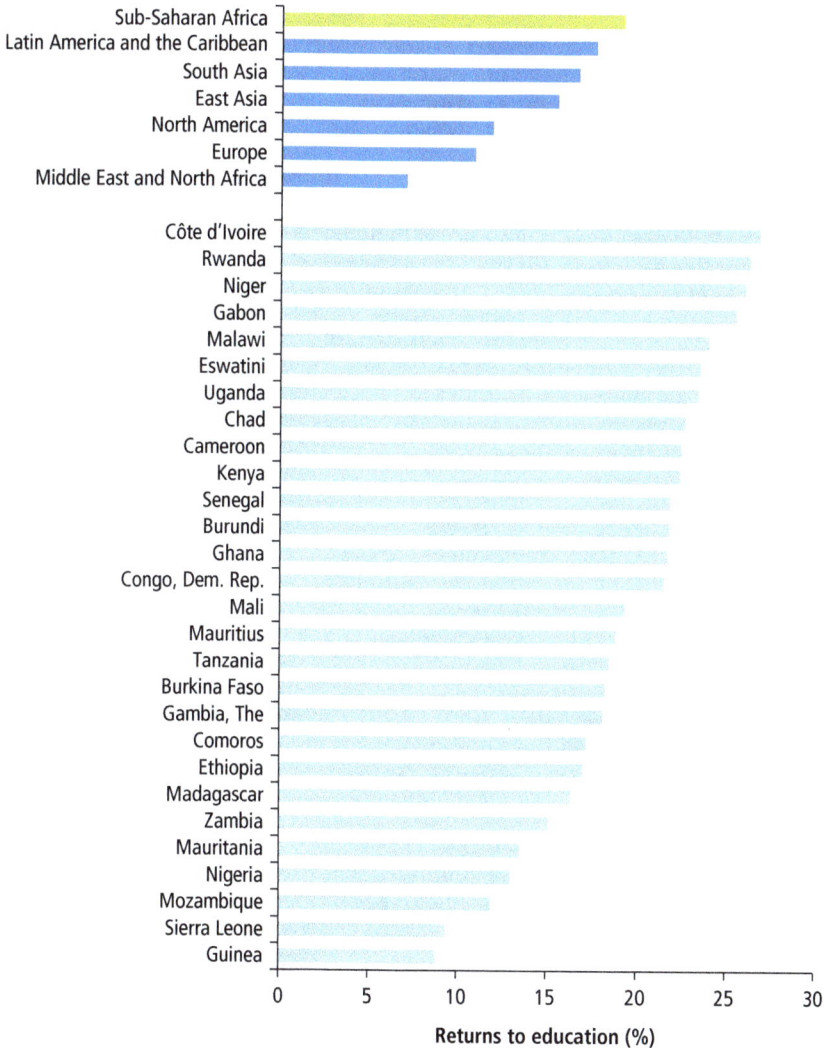

Source: Based on Montenegro and Patrinos 2014.

and basic education that mostly affect the poor. This chapter discusses how this trade-off can be lessened and better managed.

The potential trade-off between productivity and inclusion inherent in higher education investments depends on countries' ability to produce high-quality graduates from across the socioeconomic ladder and economies' capacity to absorb new college graduates. As discussed below, returns are likely lower in countries or regions with a policy environment that is not conducive to private investment and sustained job creation. Such a policy environment holds back the demand for college graduates and thus the ability to maintain attractive private returns to higher education. The trade-off between a country's productivity and inclusion goals is stronger in countries with a low skills endowment, in the early stages of their productive transformation, or lacking an enabling environment for workers and countries to generate adequate returns from investments in university education. These factors will mediate how much and how countries can optimally invest in higher education.

Against this backdrop, this chapter seeks to answer three questions: (1) How much should Sub-Saharan African countries invest in university education? (2) Are current investments well aligned with current needs of the economy and the labor market as well as with expected changes in the world of work? (3) What are key strategic and policy priorities for putting university education to work in Africa? To answer these questions, the chapter first examines the expansion of coverage of higher education in the region. Then it analyzes the expansion of access through the lens of the goals of an education system: equity, efficiency, and quality (relevance). Finally, it discusses the policy reforms that are critical for investments in higher education to pay off.

University Education in Sub-Saharan Africa

The university system across most of Sub-Saharan Africa remains small, albeit growing, although it is not growing fast enough to catch up to the rest of the world. Figure 4.2 compares the evolution of enrollment in Sub-Saharan Africa over the last four and a half decades with that of other regions. Despite the important gains in the last decade, on average, Sub-Saharan African countries have continued to lose ground to low-income and lower-middle-income economies in access to higher education. Today, the gross enrollment rate in tertiary education is 10 percent, on average, just slightly higher among men (10.4 percent) than among women (8.8 percent). There is wide variation across countries in the region, however. While in some countries like Botswana and Mauritius enrollment is above 30 percent, in others like Malawi and Niger it is only 2 percent. In more than a third of countries in the region, enrollment is at or below 5 percent. The coverage of higher education in Sub-Saharan Africa is also low by historical global experience. When comparing the evolution of tertiary education enrollment across the development path, countries in Sub-Saharan Africa have lower enrollment rates in tertiary education than other countries have had at similar levels of income (figure 4.3).

Figure 4.2 Gross Enrollment Rates in Tertiary Education, by Region, 1970–2015

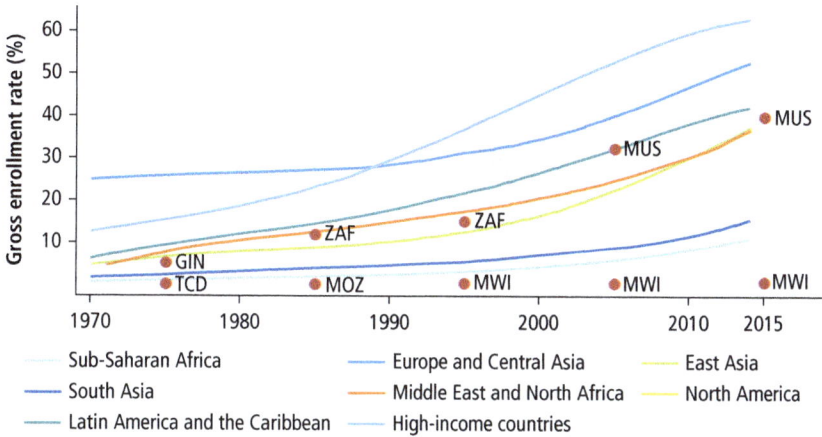

Source: Based on UIS.Stat data.
Note: Average enrollment is estimated using an unbalanced panel of countries. Tertiary enrollment is gross enrollment in advanced postsecondary schooling, including International Standard Classification of Education (ISCED) levels 5, 6, 7, and 8, which are labeled as short-cycle tertiary education, bachelor's or equivalent level, master's or equivalent level, and doctoral or equivalent level, respectively. GIN = Guinea; MOZ = Mozambique; MUS = Mauritius; MWI = Malawi; TCD = Chad; ZAF = South Africa.

Figure 4.3 Gross Enrollment Rates in Tertiary Education and GDP per Capita, by Region

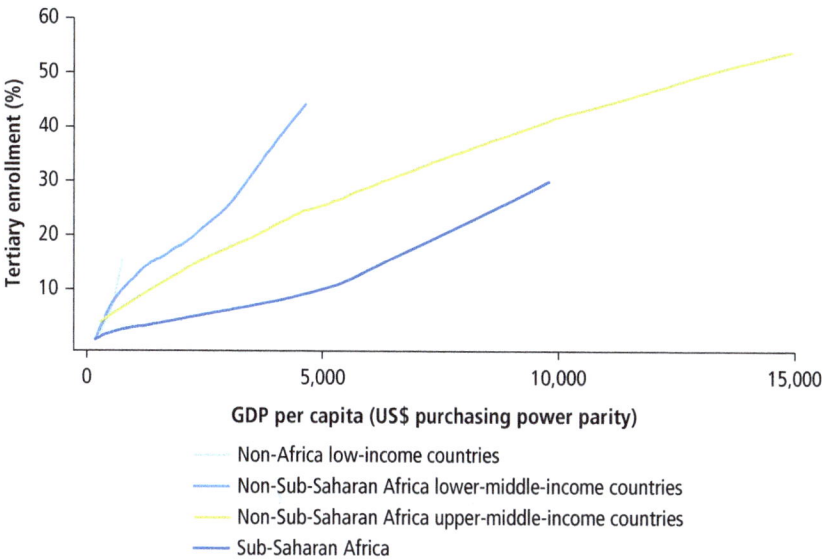

Sources: For gross tertiary enrollment, UIS.Stat data. For GDP per capita, World Development Indicators.

Despite low overall enrollment rates, the size of the university system has been increasing at a pace commensurate with countries' historical educational and economic trajectories as well as their business environments. As discussed in chapters 1 and 2, most Sub-Saharan African countries historically have lagged in their progression on basic education and average educational attainment. As expected, countries' enrollment in tertiary education goes hand in hand with the share of the population with basic education, a policy environment that facilitates job creation and rewards skills, and countries' state of economic transformation (figure 4.4).

But there are notable exceptions. On the one hand, in Ghana and Senegal, enrollment rates in tertiary education are lower than would be expected for their stage of economic transformation and policy environment. On the other hand, in Angola, Cabo Verde, and Sudan, university enrollment is relatively high, given the lack of a policy environment necessary to reap many of the social and private returns from investments in university education or the nascent stage of their economic transformation. Yet the evidence so far suggests that, for higher education to generate economic growth, it must be accompanied by policy reforms that are conducive to private investment and a robust basic education system that advances students' foundational skills (Hanushek 2016).

Figure 4.4 Gross Enrollment in Tertiary Education in Sub-Saharan Africa and the World, by GDP per Capita, Share of Population That Has Completed at Least Secondary Education, and Enabling Business Environment

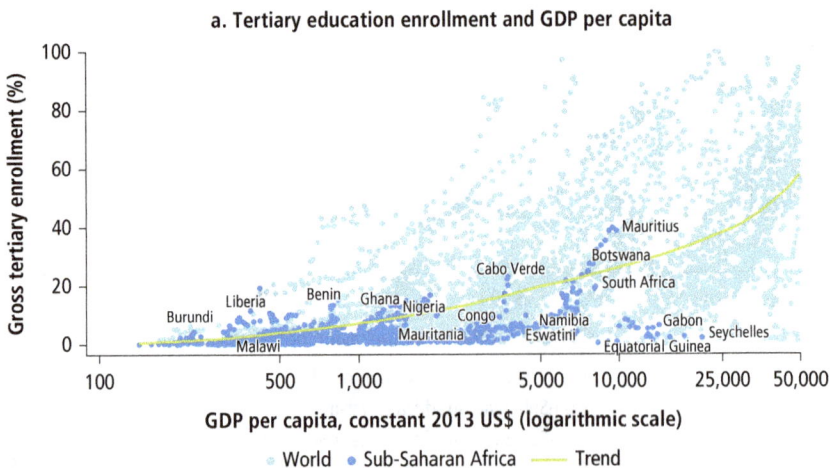

a. Tertiary education enrollment and GDP per capita

(continued next page)

Figure 4.4 (continued)

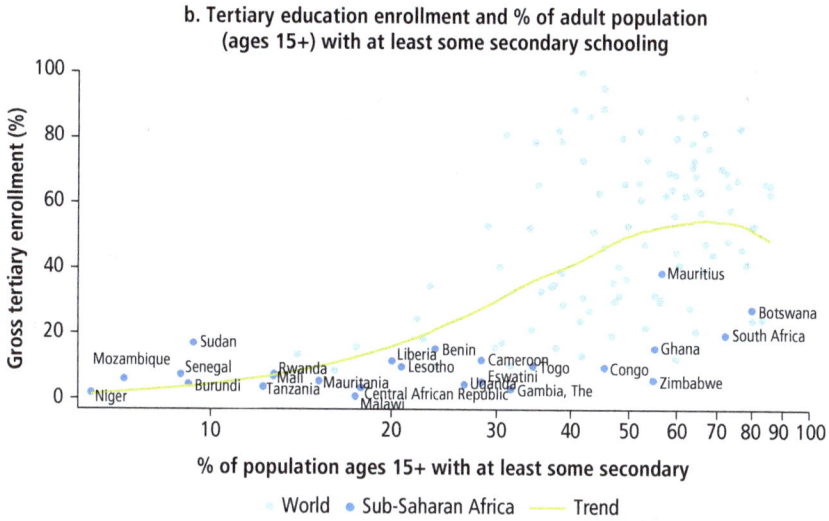

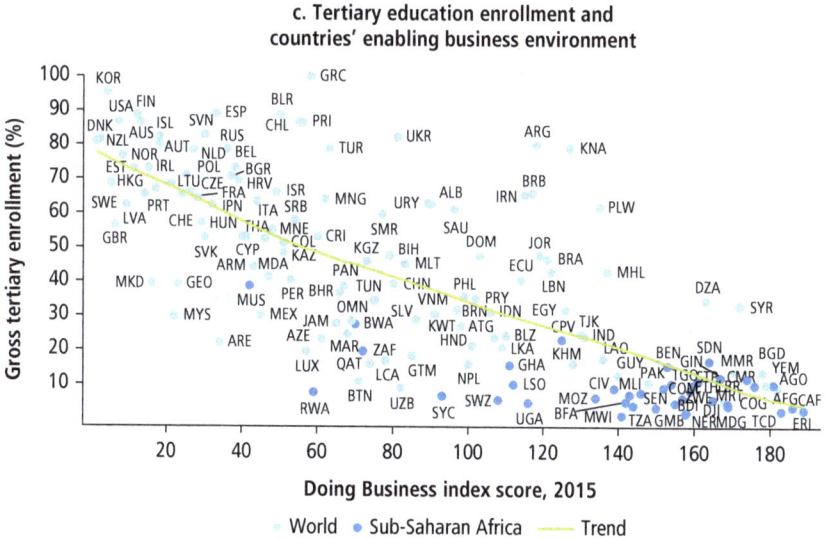

b. Tertiary education enrollment and % of adult population (ages 15+) with at least some secondary schooling

Gross tertiary enrollment (%) / % of population ages 15+ with at least some secondary

World • Sub-Saharan Africa — Trend

Labeled countries: Mozambique, Sudan, Niger, Senegal, Burundi, Rwanda, Mali, Tanzania, Mauritania, Malawi, Central African Republic, Liberia, Benin, Lesotho, Uganda, Eswatini, Cameroon, Togo, Gambia, The, Congo, Ghana, Zimbabwe, Mauritius, Botswana, South Africa

c. Tertiary education enrollment and countries' enabling business environment

Gross tertiary enrollment (%) / Doing Business index score, 2015

World • Sub-Saharan Africa — Trend

Source: For panel a, World Development Indicators and UIS.Stat data. For panel b, Barro and Lee 2015 and UIS data. For panel c, Doing Business 2015 data and UIS.Stat data.

There is significant pressure on the tertiary education systems in Sub-Saharan Africa to expand in order to absorb the increasing number of secondary school graduates, yet weaknesses in equity, efficiency, quality, and relevance remain. Over the next 20 years, the share of the adult population with at least some tertiary education (mostly university education) will increase from 3 percent today to 10 percent (see chapter 2). Yet the university system in most countries in the region is in a bad equilibrium, consisting of large inequalities in access and success in higher education, high inefficiencies, and low quality and relevance overall, especially in key areas that matter for an economy's structural transformation such as the STEM fields. These systematic weaknesses generate a disconnect between the aspirations of youths and their families and the reality. The factors behind these weaknesses regarding equity, efficiency, quality, and relevance are discussed next.

Improving Equity in Access to Higher Education

Socioeconomic Inequities

As in many other countries, investments in universities in Sub-Saharan African countries have so far disproportionally benefited the better-off. As discussed by Darvas, Favara, and Arnold (2017), there are considerable gaps in access across socioeconomic groups. In Malawi, only 1 percent of students enrolled in universities come from households in the bottom 20 percent of the income distribution; only 3 percent come from the second poorest quintile. In contrast, 80 percent of university students come from the richest quintile (World Bank 2013a). Overall, in the region, gross enrollment rates in tertiary education stand at 16 percent among the richest quintile of the population, but at only 2 percent among the poorest (figure 4.5). Even controlling for other factors, such as academic performance in primary and secondary school, cognitive ability, socioemotional skills, and parental involvement in school, socioeconomic background—proxied by parental educational attainment—matters a lot for higher education access. In urban Kenya, for example, having one or both parents with at least secondary education makes a person 3.5 times more likely to attend university (figure 4.6).

Gender and Spatial Inequities

In addition to socioeconomic background, there are vast gender and geographic differences in access within countries.[3] While, on average for the continent, men are more likely than women to access tertiary education, differences are relatively small. However, the average masks very large gender differences in individual countries. In Benin, Cameroon, Chad, Ghana, Guinea, Mali, and Togo, men are at least 5 percentage points more likely than women to be

Figure 4.5 Gross Tertiary Enrollment Rate in Sub-Saharan Africa, by Income Quintile

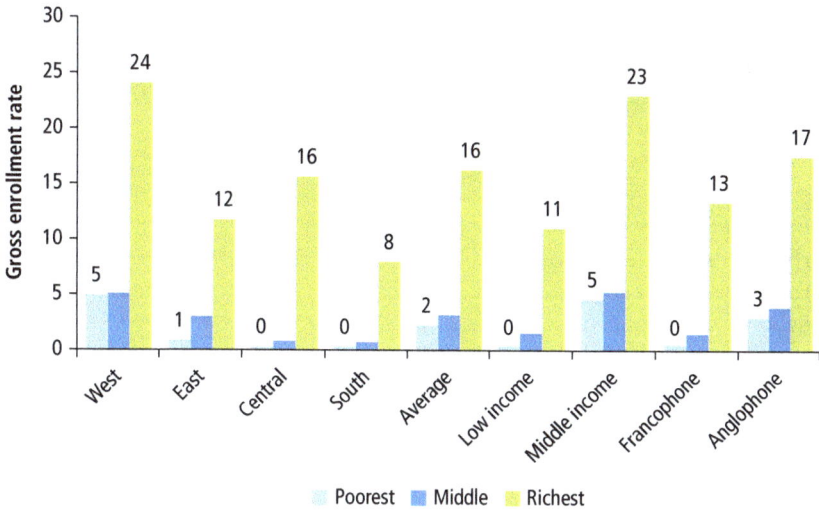

Source: Darvas et al. 2017.

Figure 4.6 Odds Ratio for the Probability of Attending University in Urban Kenya

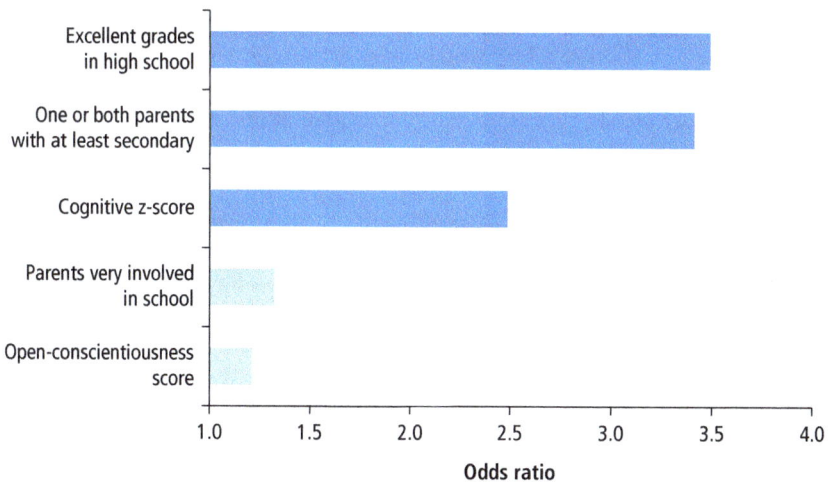

Source: Based on Skills Towards Employability and Productivity (STEP) Household Surveys.
Note: Based on multivariate regressions. The bars depict the odds of attending university. Coefficients that are significant at least at the 10% level are depicted in dark blue. Controls for whether the individual started school late for his or her age (started first grade at the age of 7 or older), number of siblings, age, gender, and mother tongue are included.

enrolled in tertiary education. In Botswana, Cabo Verde, Mauritius, Senegal, the Seychelles, and South Africa, women are disproportionately more likely to attend tertiary.[4] Differences in college readiness, gender differential opportunity costs in different contexts, work prospects after graduation, and other gender-specific barriers (such as social norms) are likely to explain these gaps (Banerjee et al. 2013).

Geography also matters. In Nigeria, for example, 18 percent of adults in the Southwest region—which includes Lagos— have at least some tertiary education compared with only 5 percent in the Northwest (World Bank 2015a). An urban-rural divide is also salient in most countries in the region, given that urban areas have a higher concentration of universities, higher enrollment and quality of basic education, and larger numbers of better-off households with a better chance of being able to afford the cost of a university education.

International experience suggests that university education often starts being biased toward the elite and becomes more equitable as it expands, provided the right policies are in place. For example, between 2000 and 2013, participation in higher education grew for all income groups in Latin America and the Caribbean, but growth was significantly faster for persons in low- and middle-income groups. Inequality in participation declined by an average of 25 percent. In Chile, for example, participation by the poorest half of the population more than doubled during this time, in part due to a progressive student loan scheme (World Bank, forthcoming). However, equitable expansion is not guaranteed. In Asia, access to higher education has expanded greatly and gender parity has nearly been achieved, but access for persons in the lowest wealth quintiles remains disproportionately low, with little growth (UIS 2014). One of the challenges for university systems in Sub-Saharan Africa—as well as in many other countries globally—is to ensure more equitable access to and retention in quality universities.

Policy Focus

What should be the focus of policy action aimed at improving equity? Basically, countries have to address the reasons for the bias in higher education toward the elites. The reasons are threefold. First, attending university can be costly, especially for the poor, even if tuition is covered. In addition to the heavy burden of the direct costs of college (tuition, transport, housing, materials), the poor also face a higher opportunity cost in the form of forgone earnings from work that could have been done at home or in the labor market. Students from low-income families also often come from rural areas with no university close by, raising the monetary and nonmonetary costs of studying.

Second, and related, families may underinvest in schooling—both university education and earlier levels—because the full benefits of the investment are too remote. Families must invest in their children's schooling for a span of many years before reaping the benefits, especially when returns to education markedly increase with the level of education and when diploma or "sheepskin" effects mean that returns accrue to individuals completing a degree (for example, secondary or university graduates), as has been widely documented around the world and in many Sub-Saharan African countries (Montenegro and Patrinos 2014). The inability to borrow against future higher earnings (due to adverse selection, moral hazard, and lack of acceptable collateral) can lead to underinvestment in education, beginning in the early years. All of these constraints and market failures disproportionally affect the poor. Kaufmann (2012) shows that in Mexico poorer students require higher expected returns in order to be induced to enroll in higher education, suggesting that they face higher direct and indirect costs associated with college enrollment. Given that progress in and completion of basic education depend partly on the "option value" of attending higher education (where returns are the highest), and faced with uncertain prospects to reach these education levels, children from low-income families are more likely to drop out of school, even before liquidity constraints become binding. Low probabilities of obtaining a university education, thus, affect earlier investments in education, creating a negative feedback loop.

Third, having attended lower-quality basic education, students from disadvantaged backgrounds have lower chances to enroll in universities (especially high-quality ones) and to complete a degree even if they enter. In Ghana and Kenya, for example, adults with at least primary education from poorer families—proxied by having less-educated parents—score 45 and 30 percent below their more privileged counterparts, respectively. This finding echoes large gaps in performance in basic education between rich and poor children (chapter 2). Indeed, other studies also indicate that access to and equity in higher education are fundamentally determined by access to and equity in good-quality secondary education (Lulwana, Ouma, and Pillay 2016).

Investing in foundational skills early on is, thus, the best way to manage the productivity-inclusion trade-offs of investments in higher education. Because disadvantaged youth are more likely to be unprepared for the academic and nonacademic demands of university studies due to inequities in access to quality basic education, it is very difficult (and ultimately costly) to address inequities in higher education comprehensively without addressing inequities at lower levels of education. When additional barriers to access exist—associated with socioeconomic status, gender, or location, for example—complementary measures are also likely to be required.

Ensuring Value for Money and Improved Efficiency

Public Spending

Sub-Saharan African countries spend a significant share of their education budget on university education, with average per capita spending three times

Table 4.1 Average Public Spending on Higher Education in Sub-Saharan Africa and the World, by Income Level, 2010–15

Region	Public spending on higher education (% of GDP)	Public spending on higher education (% of total public expenditure on education)	Spending per student (constant US$)
Sub-Saharan Africa	0.96	20	2,445
Low-income	0.96	21	1,713
Middle-income	0.85	16	2,872
Upper-middle-income	1.10	14	6,089
Outside of Sub-Saharan Africa			
Low- and lower-middle-income	0.70	16	817
Upper-middle-income	0.95	20	1,873

Source: Based on UIS.Stat data.
Note: The table reports spending on postsecondary academic-level education. The average is taken over the three most recent years of data between 2010 and 2015.

higher than elsewhere in the low- and middle-income world. On average, the region spends 1 percent of gross domestic product (GDP) or 20 percent of total public education expenditure on higher education (table 4.1). This level of spending is above the average for low- and lower-middle-income countries in the rest of the world and on par with what upper-middle-income countries spend.

In the region, the average spending per student on higher education also is above international norms. The region spends, on average, US$2,445 per student, three times more than what low- and lower-middle-income countries elsewhere spend (and 1.3 times more than upper-middle-income countries elsewhere). While on average, per capita spending on higher education increases with countries' income, the global experience is quite diverse (figure 4.7). Nevertheless, some countries spend relatively little (Liberia, Zambia). In these countries, there is a risk of problems characteristic of underfunding (and lack of accountability), including overcrowded classrooms and lecturers who are absent and moonlighting at second jobs.[5] In contrast, Southern African countries such as Botswana, Eswatini, and Lesotho, but also Ghana, Malawi, and Rwanda, are among the countries (with available data) with the highest per capita expenditures on higher education, although several of them have seen declining costs per capita as they have gotten richer.

Education Costs

On average, governments in the region spend four times more per higher education student than they spend per basic education student. This ratio is 1:1 in low- and lower-middle-income countries and less than 1:1 in upper-middle-income countries. Out-of-pocket expenses (for example, tuition, housing, materials), especially for private universities, can also be significant for families

Figure 4.7 Correlation between Spending per Student on Tertiary Education and GDP per Capita

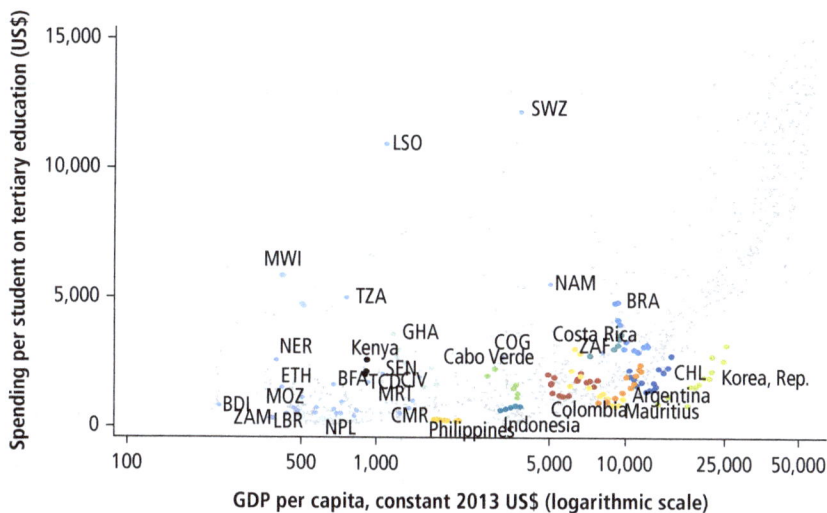

Sources: Based on UIS.Stat data; World Development Indicators.
Note: BDI = Burundi, BFA = Burkina Faso; BRA = Brazil, CHL = Chile, CMR = Cameroon; COG = Republic of Congo, ETH = Ethiopia, GHA = Ghana; LBR = Liberia, LSO = Lesotho, MWI = Malawi; MOZ = Mozambique, MRT = Mauritania; NAM = Namibia; NER = Niger, NPL = Nepal, PHL = the Philippines, SEN = Senegal, TZA = Tanzania, and ZAM = Zambia.

and individuals (Darvas 2016). In countries such as Burundi, Côte d'Ivoire, and Rwanda, more than half of tertiary enrollment is in private institutions.

These high unit costs stem largely from substantial blanket subsidies and other inefficiencies. The lack of economies of scale given the small size of the system only explains a minor part of the costs, since, overall, spending per capita is largely unrelated to enrollment. High costs arise, first, from the use of significant public resources to pay for subsidies for most students, including students from richer families who could afford to pay for themselves or to take out loans (World Bank 2010). In addition, throughout Sub-Saharan Africa, about 18 percent of tertiary budgets are spent on scholarships to study outside of Africa, and these scholarships typically go to students from privileged backgrounds. Although such scholarships can have significant benefits, they also have costs (box 4.2). Botswana, Lesotho, and Mauritius spend significant portions of their tertiary budget on scholarships to send students abroad, limiting the public externality benefits of such high levels of spending.

Dropout and noncompletion rates tend to be high in Africa, raising costs both for the system and for individuals. In South Africa, for example, around 30 percent of university students drop out within five years (van Broekhuizen, van der Berg, and Hofmeyr 2016). In Madagascar, about 40 percent of students

BOX 4.2

When Students Go Abroad for University Studies

An estimated one in nine Africans with a tertiary education is living in a high-income country in Europe, North America, and elsewhere. This represents a 50 percent increase in the past 10 years, more than in any other region in the world (OECD 2013). In countries such as Mauritius and Zimbabwe, more than 40 percent of migrants are highly educated. In many countries, the proportion of tertiary students studying abroad is very significant (figure B4.2.1). Particularly in small countries, such as Cabo Verde, the Comoros, and Eswatini, the percentage of tertiary students abroad is multiple times the number of students enrolled in tertiary education locally.

The consequences for source countries are ambiguous. On the one hand, there is possible brain drain, whereby the departure of (future) doctors, teachers, engineers, scientists, and other highly skilled workers reduces the human capital and fiscal revenues of sending countries (Bhagwati and Hamada 1974). On the other hand, a highly educated diaspora can be a potent force for developing the local economy through remittances, trade, foreign direct investment, and knowledge transfer, with the experience of China and India in setting up technology firms as a result of the diaspora working in Silicon Valley a prominent example (Saxeenian 2002).

There is a growing literature with empirical evidence regarding the impacts of migration. For example, Gibson and McKenzie (2012) study five countries, including Ghana, and find that there are large benefits from migration, including postgraduate education and remittances from high-skill migrants from poorer countries, but that involvement in trade and foreign direct investment is a rare occurrence. They also find that there is considerable knowledge flow from both current and return migrants about job and study opportunities abroad, but little net knowledge sharing from current migrants to home-country governments or businesses. Finally, the fiscal costs vary considerably across countries and depend on the extent to which governments rely on progressive income taxation. In addition, the literature has found that countries combining relatively low levels of human capital and low rates of skilled emigration are more likely to experience a beneficial brain drain (net positive effect; see Beine, Docquier, and Rapoport 2008) and that small states are the main losers (Beine, Docquier, and Schiff 2008). As a result, the situation of many small countries in Sub-Saharan Africa is worrisome.

Not every Sub-Saharan African country is at risk of brain drain. Rwanda, for example, holds onto the best and brightest and at the same time attracts international talent. Rwanda tops the World Economic Forum's list of Sub-Saharan African countries able to retain their top talent, followed by Côte d'Ivoire, Kenya, and South Africa. Moreover, there is evidence that the younger generation of Sub-Saharan Africans studying at foreign universities wants to come home. Being close to their families is a big factor. However, they also weigh the risks and the rewards. African governments and initiatives run by various nongovernmental organizations are promoting the

(continued next page)

Box 4.2 (continued)

Figure B4.2.1 **Number of Tertiary Students Studying Abroad as a Share of Total Tertiary Enrollment in Sub-Saharan Africa and Other Regions, 1999 and 2013**

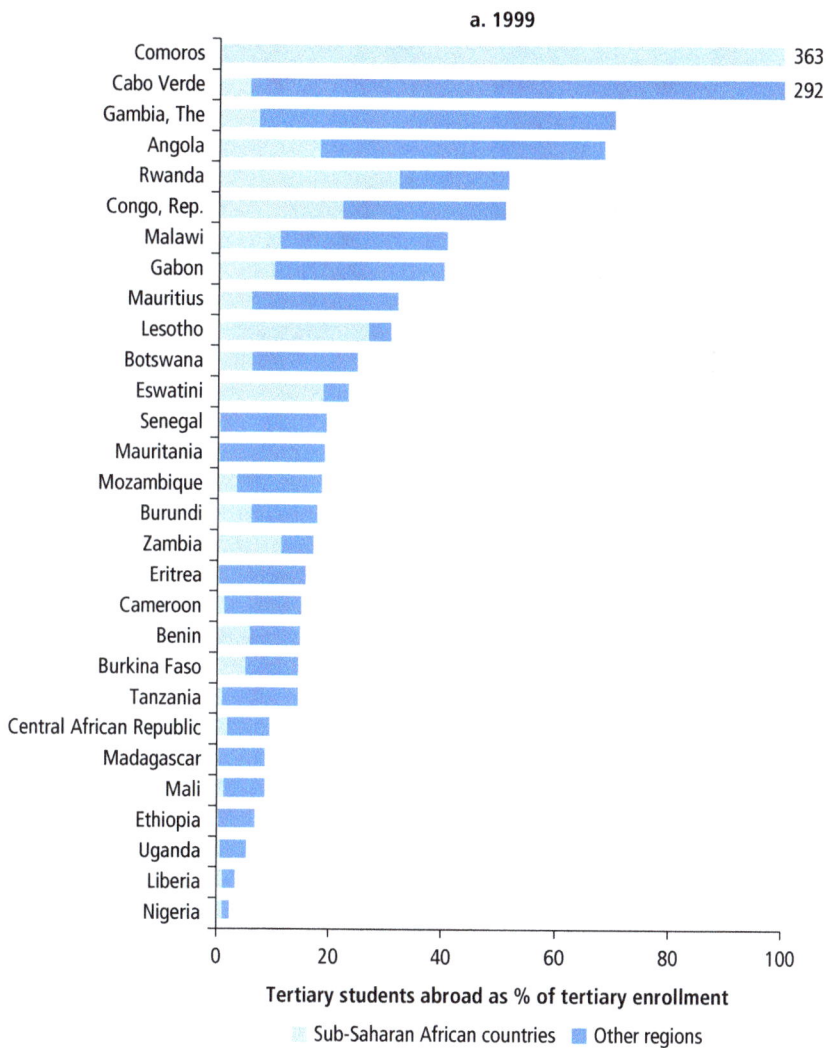

a. 1999

Country	
Comoros	363
Cabo Verde	292

Tertiary students abroad as % of tertiary enrollment

Sub-Saharan African countries ■ Other regions

Source: Based on UIS.Stat data.

(continued next page)

Box 4.2 (continued)

Figure B4.2.1 (continued)

b. 2013

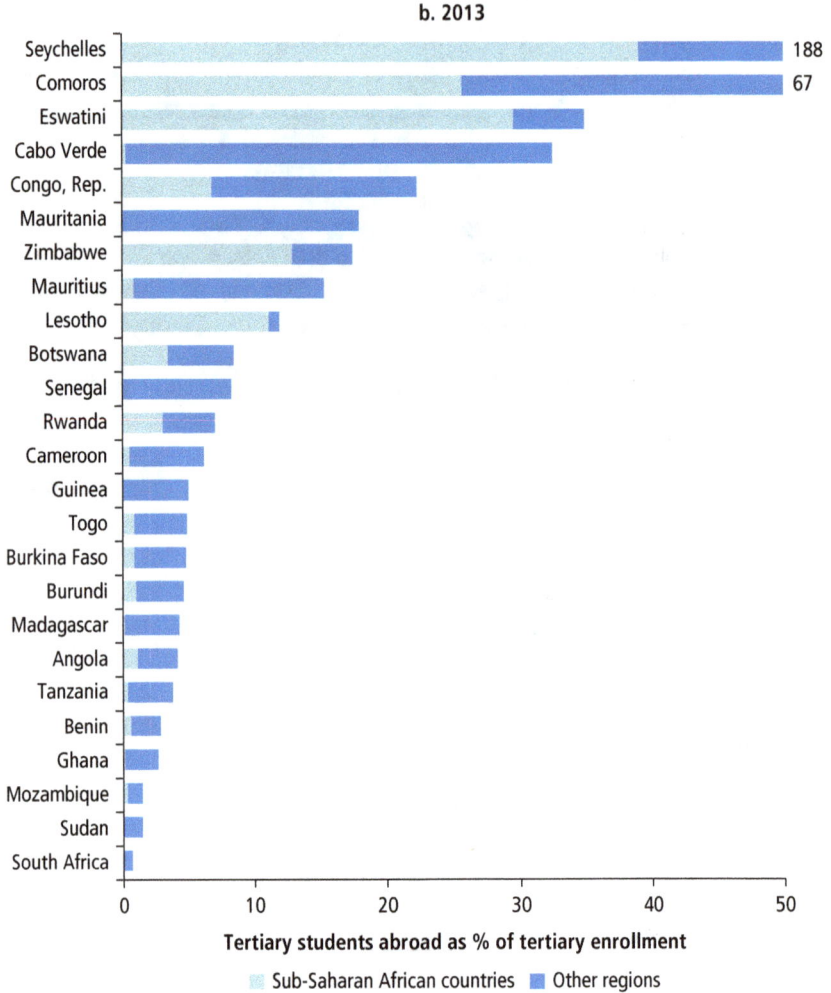

Seychelles						188
Comoros						67

Tertiary students abroad as % of tertiary enrollment

Sub-Saharan African countries ▪ Other regions

Source: Based on UIS.Stat data.

(continued next page)

Box 4.2 (continued)

"rewards" and calling on Africans to return home. These organizations include the New Partnership of Africa's Development and the Homecoming Revolution. The latter focuses on South Africa and states that 359,000 South Africans have returned home in the last five years. Moreover, for every skilled person who returns home to South Africa, an estimated nine new jobs are created in the formal and informal sectors. Therefore, the potential exists to harness the diaspora and encourage skilled workers to return to the continent. Now the enabling environment for them to want to return and for their return to pay off in terms of further job creation also needs to be there.

---

fail in the first year, and only about 27 percent of incoming students end up graduating (Sack and Ravalitera 2011). Students who are from disadvantaged backgrounds and less college ready are more likely to drop out and more likely to delay completion (Chimanikire 2009; van Broekhuizen, van der Berg, and Hofmeyr 2016). The quality of institutions, particularly the quality of faculty and teaching, has also been linked to higher dropout rates (Lulwana, Ouma, and Pillay 2016). Not all of these university costs are a waste, of course. In a group of seven Sub-Saharan African countries, youths with some university education still earn more than secondary education graduates, although 70 percent less than those who have completed a university degree.[6]

Higher unit costs also likely stem from other inefficiencies in the use of resources in the system. High recurrent costs, primarily in the form of salaries, and poor management of human resources without corresponding quality and outputs in the form of skilled graduates and research, are major sources of inefficiency (Darvas 2016). In Madagascar, Malawi, and Zambia, universities have a disproportionately large number of administrative staff relative to students and workloads (Mambo et al. 2016; Sack and Ravalitera 2011; World Bank 2015c). In Zambia, while the ratio of students to academic staff in public and private universities is similar (at around 18 or 20 to 1), the story is very different for nonacademic staff: the ratio is around 15:1 in the private sector and 73:1 in public universities—that is, almost five times higher (World Bank 2015c). Budgeting processes, which often rely on historical allocations rather than per-student or performance-based formulas, are another source of inefficiency (World Bank 2013a).

Policy Focus

Considering existing budgetary constraints and competing demands for human capital investments and beyond, it becomes imperative to find efficiencies in public spending in university education before continuing the rapid expansion of the system, especially in countries where per capita spending is already very high.

Achieving Higher Quality and Relevance

Returns to Tertiary Education

For persons who have access, a university education does pay off in the region, on average. Higher education is associated with higher and better employment and more positive labor market trajectories over time than is just completing secondary education or completing nonuniversity tertiary education (chapter 3). In fact, the private returns to higher education are higher in Africa than in any other region in the world, reflecting the relative scarcity of tertiary graduates and much smaller systems. On average, across countries in the region, the returns to tertiary education stand at 20 percent.[7] Within Sub-Saharan Africa, returns to tertiary are significantly higher than returns to primary or secondary education (14 and 11 percent, respectively) (Montenegro and Patrinos 2014). Côte d'Ivoire, Gabon, Niger, and Rwanda have the highest returns to tertiary education (above 25 percent), while Guinea and Sierra Leone have the lowest (below 10 percent; see figure 4.8).

In approximately half of the countries, returns are higher for men than for women, while in the other half, it is the other way around.[8] In most cases, the gap in returns is less than 5 percentage points. However, in Chad, The Gambia, and Niger, returns are more than 10 percentage points higher for men than for women; in the Democratic Republic of Congo, returns favor women.

Overall, higher levels of education, particularly higher education, are associated with lower working poverty rates (UNESCO 2016). This association is important in Sub-Saharan Africa, where more than 70 percent—nearly 64.4 million—of working youths live in poverty (ILO 2016).

Figure 4.8 Returns to Tertiary Education in Africa and Latin America, by GDP per Capita and Enrollment

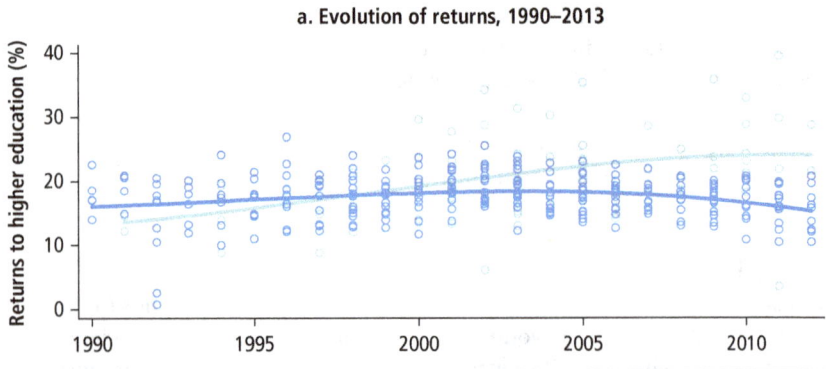

a. Evolution of returns, 1990–2013

(continued next page)

Figure 4.8 (continued)

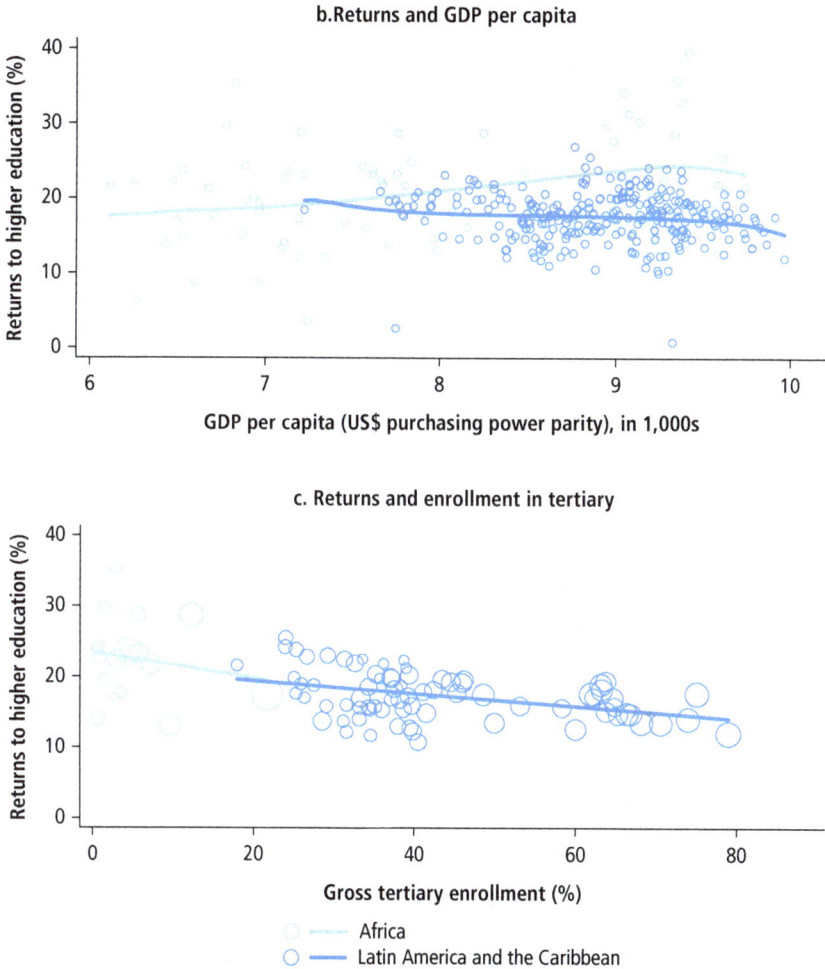

b.Returns and GDP per capita

c. Returns and enrollment in tertiary

Sources: Urzua 2016. For returns to higher education, Montenegro and Patrinos 2014. For gross tertiary enrollment, World Development Indicators. For GDP per capita, International Monetary Fund.
Notes: On panel c, GDP per capita defines the size of marker. Countries reporting information on all three variables: for Latin America and Caribbean, Argentina, Bolivia, Chile, Colombia, Ecuador, Paraguay, Peru, Uruguay, and Venezuela, RB; for Africa, Burkina Faso, Cameroon, Chad, Ethiopia, Ghana, Kenya, Malawi, Mozambique, Niger, Nigeria, Rwanda, and Tanzania.

Figure 4.9 Share of Adults Using Reading, Writing, Numeracy, and Computer Skills in Urban Kenya, by Intensity and Educational Attainment

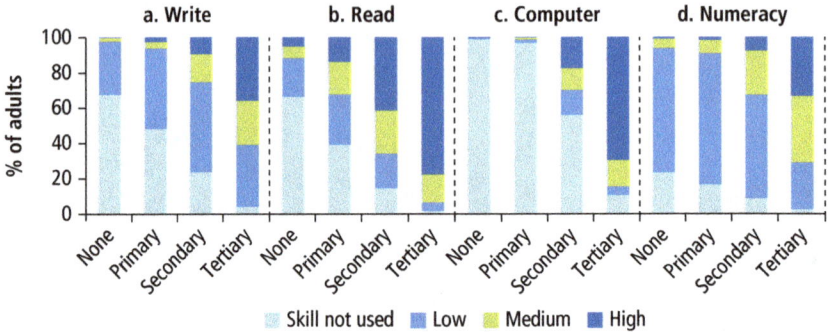

Source: Sanchez Puerta and Perinet 2015, based on 2013 Skills Towards Employability and Productivity (STEP) Household Survey.
Note: Excludes those currently enrolled in the education system.

These high average returns to completing a university degree are consistent with countries' level of income and low enrollment at the tertiary level. As figure 4.8 shows, returns to tertiary education have been rising over time, despite rising enrollment.[9] However, as countries in the region grow and tertiary systems expand, returns are expected to fall.

Not surprisingly, higher education is, on average, associated with more advanced skills. In Kenya, for example, graduates of tertiary education are the only urban adults who make intensive use of reading, writing, numeracy, and information and communication technology (ICT) skills (figure 4.9). These skills are precisely some of the skills that are becoming increasingly critical in mid- and high-skill occupations and in modernizing sectors and economies; they can be crucial to countries' economic transformation in the region. In Ghana, more than two-thirds of urban workers with at least some tertiary are in high-skill occupations, compared with only 20 percent of those with at most completed secondary education (figure 4.10). This use of skills at work reflects—at least partly—higher cognitive abilities.[10]

Misalignment between Skills Taught and Skills Needed

Despite high average returns, there is evidence of misalignment among university graduates' skills, the labor market, and the needs of transforming economies. As discussed in chapter 1, many employers in the region—particularly larger exporting and innovating firms—consider inadequate skills to be one of the most binding constraints to their business. Employers are

Figure 4.10 **Share of Workers in Urban Ghana, by Skill Level of Occupation and Educational Attainment**

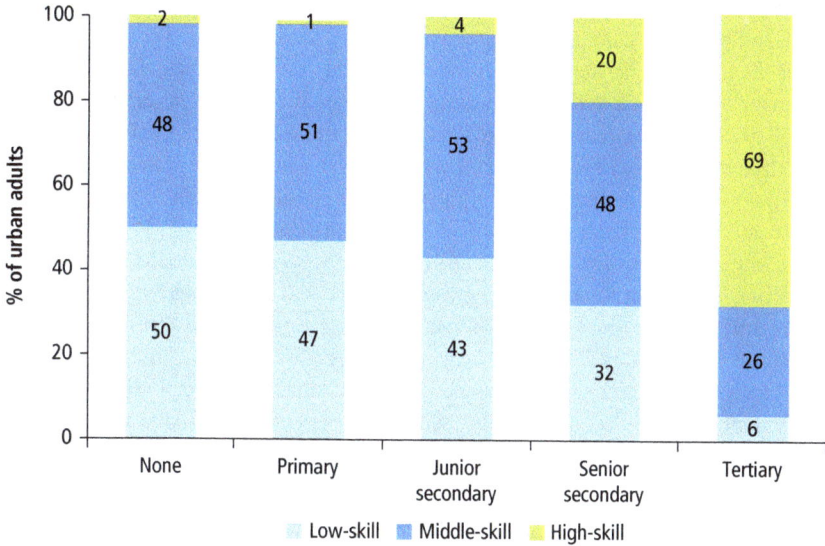

Source: Darvas, Farvara, and Arnold 2017, based on 2013 Skills Towards Employability and Productivity (STEP) Household Survey.
Note: Low-skill occupations include agricultural, forestry, and fishery workers, craft and related trades workers, plant and machine operators and assemblers, and elementary occupations. Middle-skill occupations include technicians and associate professionals, clerical support workers, and service and sales workers. High-skill occupations include managers and professionals.

increasingly feeling the pinch of skills gaps as economies in the region grow and other constraints to business operations are addressed. These pressures are likely to increase as employers demand an ever wider and more complex set of skills. Quality higher education is critical, especially in catalyzing sectors that can drive economic transformation. Yet a university degree, for many, is far from being a job guarantee, especially a job that meets graduates' expectations. In many countries in the region—and elsewhere in the world—unemployment rates tend to be higher for young university graduates than for other youths (Filmer and Fox 2014).[11] On average, it takes university graduates in the region a year to get a job after graduation.[12] That is, too often employers cannot find the skills they look for in university graduates, and graduates cannot find employment (Blom et al. 2016).

Misalignment stems, first, from a widespread lack of quality in university education, despite the presence of several high-quality universities in the region. The Times Higher Education world universities ranking, for example, places two of South Africa's universities in the top 200 of the worldwide rankings: the

University of Cape Town, ranked 148, and Wits University, ranked 182 (Times Higher Education 2016). But world-quality universities are highly concentrated. Among the top 10 universities within Sub-Saharan Africa in the same ranking, 8 are in South Africa, 1 is in Ghana, and 1 is in Nigeria. In most cases, students leave the university system still lacking basic skills. In Kenya, fewer than 1 percent of tertiary-educated adults who completed a reading skills test achieved level 4 or 5 of proficiency (for example, synthetizing or integrating information from multiple texts); more than a quarter were at level 1 or below, meaning that they could not identify a single piece of information requested from a simple text or enter personal information into a document (figure 4.11). Similarly poor results were found in Ghana on the same test (Darvas, Favara, and Arnold 2017). More than one-fifth of private firms in Liberia report that young workers, including those with higher education, have very poor ICT and writing skills.[13]

These poor results reflect the lack of university readiness of many students, who arrive at the tertiary level lacking foundational skills. As a result of these early deficiencies (chapter 2), many students in Sub-Saharan Africa—poor and nonpoor—reach the university level without the foundational skills needed to navigate higher education and acquire the advanced academic skills intended. Failures in the development of foundational skills either at home or in basic education hinder a young person's readiness to be prepared for the strong demands of a college education. In countries requiring university entrance exams, many secondary school graduates fail to meet minimum standards on exams, as was the case in 2016 in Liberia, when nearly all students failed the university entrance exam, according to the West African Examinations Council.

Figure 4.11 Reading Proficiency in Urban Kenya, by Educational Achievement

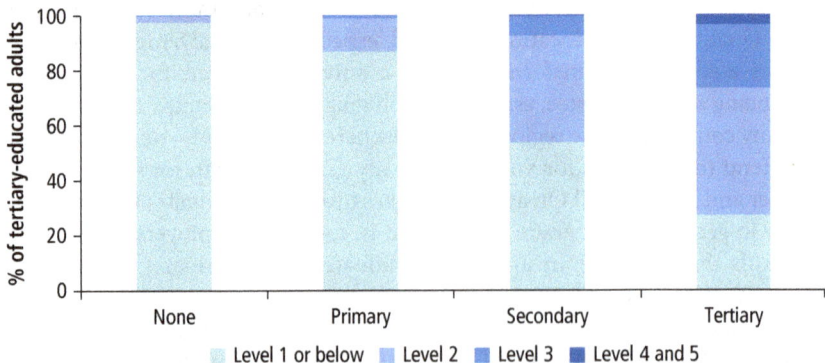

Source: Sanchez Puerta and Perinet 2015, based on 2013 Skills Towards Employability and Productivity (STEP) Household Survey.

Figure 4.12 Performance on the High School Leaving Exam and University Outcomes in South Africa

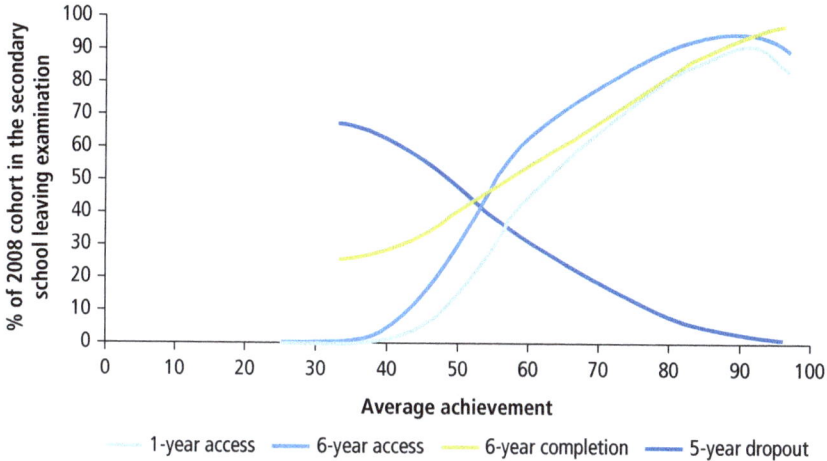

Source: van Broekhuizen, van der Berg, and Hofmeyr 2016.

As discussed, foundational skills matter for accessing higher education, even after controlling for socioeconomic status and other individual and household characteristics. But because standards are often lax, readiness remains a constraint among matriculated students. In South Africa, for example, university readiness—proxied by performance on the high school leaving exam that is used for admission into universities—is a strong predictor of performance once in higher education: the higher the university readiness, the sooner students enter universities, the higher the likelihood that they complete the degree within six years, and the lower the likelihood that they drop out in the first five years (figure 4.12). As higher education systems expand, they tend to draw from a pool of increasingly less college-ready students, so ensuring readiness of university students will become an increasingly relevant policy issue in Sub-Saharan Africa: the deficits in generic skills affect the capacity of high school graduates to develop these generic skills and to acquire new technical skills in their pursuit of a higher education degree.

In addition and related to quality, misalignments stem from a lack of relevance and disconnect from employers' and local labor demands. Part of this misalignment with the needs of the private sector is reflected in the fact that, on average, around 50 percent of university graduates in the region work for the public sector (Hino and Ranis 2014).[14] In addition to lacking academic skills, university students leave the education system lacking practical experience and not ready for the world of work. In Nigeria, recent surveys have shown that, although 96 percent of chief academic officers at universities believe that they are doing a good job of preparing students for employment, only 11 percent of business leaders agree that graduates have the requisite skills for success in the workforce (McKinsey Global Institute 2012). In Liberia, Malawi, and Zambia, more than one-fifth of employed youths below 29 years of age and with higher education report having important knowledge and skills gaps vis-à-vis the work they are expected to do.[15] In countries where many are unlikely to find quality wage employment, self-employment or work in a household enterprise may be the most promising path; yet universities in the region consistently fail to impart entrepreneurship and business skills. This misalignment is a major source of inefficiency, arising from weak links between higher education institutions and the labor market, inadequate or misaligned course offerings and curricula, and a lack of information among students about returns to various fields of study or institutions. In Malawi, the core university curriculum is reviewed every two years with the goal of reducing duplication and improving relevance with the labor market and development needs, but this process is only weakly linked to the private sector; as a result, enrollment and curriculum remain inadequately aligned to the needs of the labor market (Mambo et al. 2016; Salmi 2016). Not much different, in Madagascar, as in most other countries in the region, a poor-quality curriculum coupled with a lack of relevance to the labor market is seen as one of the largest sources of inefficiency in higher education (Sack and Ravalitera 2011).

Many youths are seen to be pursuing careers and degrees with limited labor market prospects, and there is a specific concern about skills shortages in the STEM fields. Too many students enter saturated or dead-end professions (humanities, communications, social sciences) and end up in jobs unrelated to their acquired qualifications (the "horizontal qualification mismatch"). Figure 4.13 shows enrollment in tertiary education in Sub-Saharan Africa and middle-income countries in other regions by field of study. Enrollment in STEM fields—in this case, science, health, ICT, engineering, and agriculture—is 29 percent, on average, in the region; around half of enrollment in social science and education alone and lower than enrollment in middle-income countries in other regions (39 percent). STEM fields represent the lowest share of enrollment in Benin (16 percent) and Mali (21 percent), and the highest in The Gambia and Niger. At 23 percent, enrollment in STEM fields is significantly lower among women than among men. Average shares of enrollment in STEM have been constant since the 2000s, although enrollment in science and health has risen a bit, while enrollment in agriculture and engineering has fallen slightly.

These STEM skills are critical to the region's capacity to develop knowledge-intensive industries through national science and innovation systems in the context of global patterns of trade and technology diffusion (Valencia Caicedo and Maloney 2014). However, either the demand for these skills does not

Figure 4.13 Evolution of Enrollment in Tertiary Education, by Field of Study, Average, 2010–15

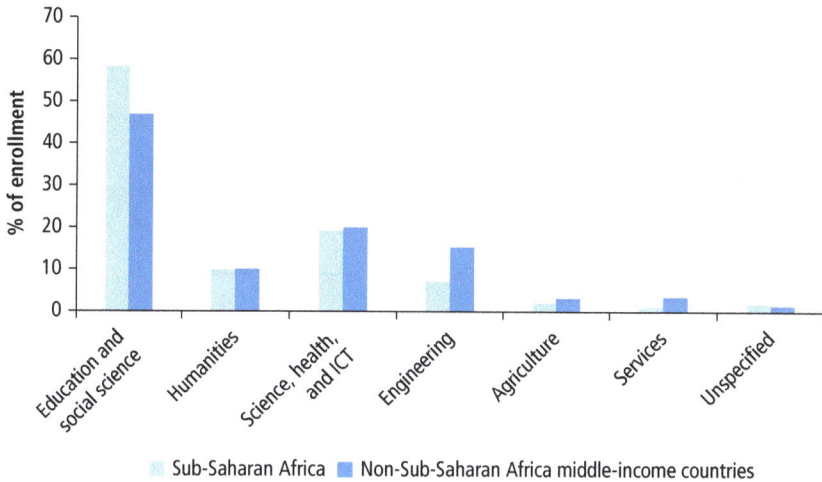

Sub-Saharan Africa   Non-Sub-Saharan Africa middle-income countries

Source: Based on UIS.Stat data.
Note: ICT = information and communication technology.

yet exist, or the quality of STEM graduates is particularly low, because returns to higher education *across* fields of study, at least in Ghana and Kenya, where relevant data are available, are not that different. Median earnings across fields of study are around four to five times higher than for a typical earner who has only completed secondary education (figure 4.14).

More than disconnects in the choice of fields of study in higher education, however, the more relevant problem is *skills* mismatches. Often, the discussion of mismatches centers on whether workers are active in occupations that traditionally fall within their field of study. Yet an individual holding a job that does not directly match his professional qualifications need not be a mismatch. As discussed before, broad shifts in skills demand are driven by the need to match workers' skills to the tasks they need to perform in a job. Workers are matched to jobs based on a multiplicity of skills, not just their educational qualifications. For several years now, the finance industry has been hiring math graduates and physicists into relatively high-paying "quant" jobs. Economists and statisticians permeate the world of sports. These apparently mismatched workers typically earn more because they increase the productivity (and profitability) of the business. The key is to focus on skills, more than diplomas, especially given the poor track record of the region in building skills in higher education (and earlier).

As a result of the low quality and relevance of the skills acquired in most universities in the region, too often a university education is not a profitable investment.

Figure 4.14 Distribution of the Ratio of Earnings from Different Fields at University to Those of a Typical Earner Who Has Completed Secondary Education (Whether Technical or General) in Urban Ghana and Kenya

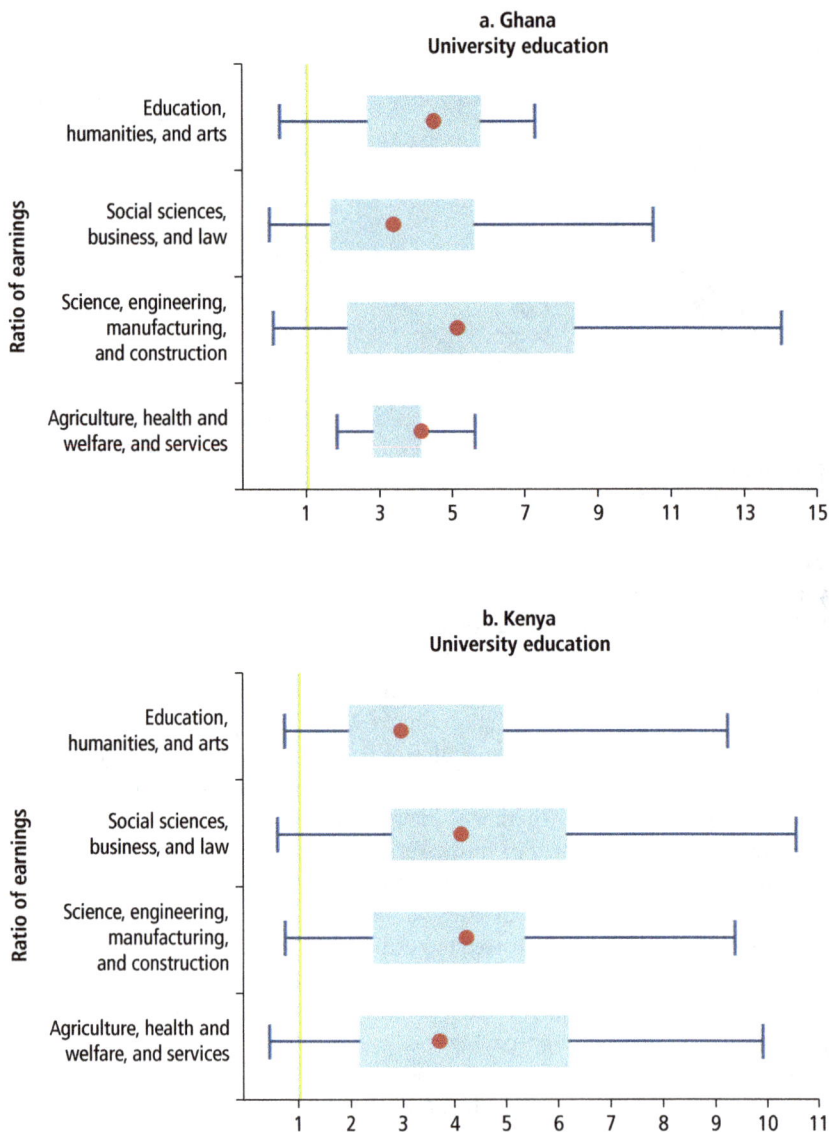

a. Ghana
University education

b. Kenya
University education

Source: Based on Skills Towards Employability and Productivity (STEP) Household Surveys.
Note: TVET = technical and vocational education and training. The green vertical line represents parity. The red dot represents the median of the distribution. The lower end of the box represents the 25th percentile, and the upper end represents the 75th percentile. The lines outside the box represent the minimum and maximum values without outliers.

The lack of quality and relevance is reflected in negative perceptions about the university system on the part of employers and a corresponding large heterogeneity in returns, especially *within* fields of study. In the 2016 World Economic Forum's Competitiveness Index, on average, countries in the region score 3.4 out of 7 in terms of quality of higher education, the same as the average for low- and lower-middle-income countries in other regions, but with scores ranging from 4.38 in The Gambia to 2.38 in Burundi. Correspondingly, within countries, there is a wide variation in the returns to higher education across programs and institutions, driven partly by systematic differences in students' university readiness. In Ghana, for example, a graduate of a STEM field—manufacturing and construction—can end up earning less than a typical earner with just secondary education; the 25th percentile graduate will earn around twice as much, while the 75th percentile graduate can earn eight times as much as the secondary education graduate (figure 4.14). This large heterogeneity in returns—coupled with a lack of information on the quality of institutions and programs or effective mechanisms for quality assurance—exacerbates inequities in the university system since disadvantaged youths are more likely to attend second-tier universities and programs. For many, the net returns from attending university are actually negative (figure 4.15). Under some scenarios, a quarter to a third of graduates lose money over their lifetime by going to university. That is, a sizable share of the university student population would be better off not attending university and simply working and putting savings in the bank.

Policy Focus: Providing Quality STEM Education

Producing quality STEM graduates is critical for long-term economic growth (Valencia Caicedo and Maloney 2014), but it can be difficult and costly to produce a good base of skills in these fields. Establishing and maintaining quality STEM programs requires expensive equipment and skilled professors and can take a significant amount of time to develop fully. For this reason, STEM is more costly than other fields. Administrative data from the largest universities in Ghana and Kenya, for example, suggest tuition can be around 25 to 30 percent more expensive for STEM fields than for humanities or social science. Not surprisingly, private universities often shy away from offering STEM programs.

A shortage of qualified faculty, high costs of laboratory equipment and technology, and a weak base of foundational skills, coupled with the pressure to expand overall access to higher education, has resulted in low-quality investments in STEM. There is a shortage of faculty with the capacity to teach STEM-related programs of sufficient quality to meet recognized standards. For example, in Kenya, fewer than 20 percent of faculty in these disciplines hold a doctoral degree (Blom et al. 2016). Given the costs, providers have incentives to focus on "softer" fields. But just as important, most students lack the strong foundational skills that are required for STEM. The success of STEM programs in higher education depends on students and faculty having

Figure 4.15 Present Value of Lifetime Incomes in Ghana and Kenya, Net of Opportunity and Direct Costs

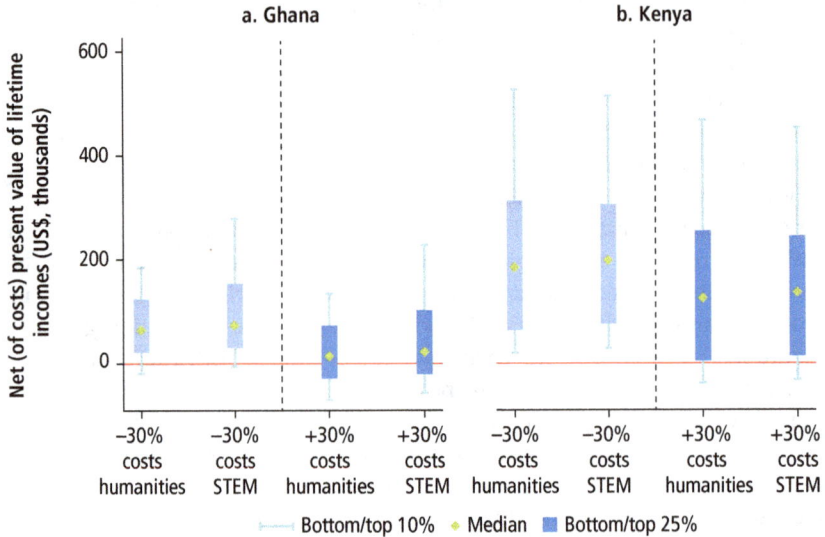

Source: Based on Skills Towards Employability and Productivity (STEP) Household Surveys and universities' administrative data.
Note: The values shown are the sum of discounted net returns (incomes minus costs) over the lifetime. Costs account for the opportunity costs of not working and the direct tuition costs of attending university. Two scenarios are presented for costs with plus or minus 30 percent, since not all costs are included in the calculations and costs vary across universities. A discount rate of 5 percent is used. Humanities = education, humanities and the arts, social sciences, business, and law; STEM = science, engineering, manufacturing, construction, and health.

this foundation. In many countries in the region, more than 50 percent of mathematics teachers do not possess even the minimum knowledge of the subject; students' math skills are equally weak (chapter 2). For example, in Sierra Leone, in 2011, 99 percent of students in the country sat for the mathematics portion of the West African senior school certificate examinations assessment, but only 3 percent passed (World Bank 2013b). Because a passing score on the mathematics portion of the exam is necessary to enter STEM programs in universities, most students were ineligible. These quality issues, together with weaknesses in complementary factors in the innovation ecosystem and the enabling environment, may explain why the returns to a higher education are not higher in STEM than in other fields (figure 4.14).

As a result, while enrollment in STEM fields is not much lower in Sub-Saharan Africa than in comparator countries, output is lower than would be expected from a quality STEM education. Sub-Saharan Africa produces less than 1 percent of the world's research despite being home to more than 12 percent of the world's population, and STEM research accounts for only 29 percent of the region's research outputs compared with 68 percent in Malaysia and Vietnam (Blom et al. 2016). Almost no international R&D projects are destined for Africa, while 4.3 percent go to Latin America and the Caribbean and nearly 30 percent go to China and India alone (UNESCO 2015). The researcher-to-population ratio is low across the continent, with only 45 researchers per 1 million inhabitants in Burkina Faso and 38 per 1 million inhabitants in Nigeria; the average is 481 in Latin America and 1,714 in East Asia (World Bank 2014b). In agriculture, an industry critical to the region's transformation, Ghana alone produces a critical mass of doctoral graduates to advance the industry (UNESCO 2015).

With limited financial and human capital resources to develop quality STEM programs across the region, investments need to be targeted and strategic. Ghana has had a goal of enrolling at least 60 percent of tertiary students in STEM fields for a considerable period of time, yet the ratio of graduates from STEM fields remains well below 25 percent (Darvas 2016). Nigeria, with a federally controlled admissions process, has adopted a 70:30 science-to-arts admissions ratio coupled with quotas for students from "educationally less developed states" to address both the STEM shortage and the inequalities in tertiary education (Asein and Lawal 2007). Yet the goal should not be so much to increase the number of graduates, but to improve quality.

As in other areas, public action requires a focus on ensuring readiness, providing opportunities, and generating appropriate incentives. In STEM, this means ensuring that a good proportion of students arrive at higher education with the necessary foundational skills. This agenda needs to start early in the life of the child, given the gaps already present in primary education, with a focus on basic mathematics, science, and higher-order cognitive skills associated with creativity, problem solving, and critical thinking. Despite the importance of quantitative skills in the 21st century, Beninese students' enrollment in math and science courses, for example, has declined since the 1980s; in some schools, the math and science track has been cancelled altogether (J-PAL 2017).

Promoting quality STEM education also requires focusing on equity, to make sure that everyone has an opportunity to develop the necessary foundational skills to access these fields. Here, gender is of particular concern. STEM fields have long been dominated by men from relatively better-off backgrounds in all parts of the globe (World Bank 2016b). Some countries, including Lesotho, Namibia, South Africa, and Zimbabwe, have achieved near gender parity among STEM graduates, while in Burkina Faso, women make up only 18 percent of STEM graduates. Women's participation in agriculture programs in the region has been rising steadily, and women make up more than 40 percent of agriculture graduates in Eswatini, Lesotho, Madagascar, Mozambique, Sierra Leone, South Africa, and Zimbabwe. The share of women graduating in engineering has also been on the rise. Benin, Burundi, Eritrea, Ethiopia, Madagascar, Mozambique, and Namibia have seen increases of more than 5 percent since 2000, although female participation in the field remains low overall (UNESCO 2015). Despite this progress, women in the region are still often constrained by family and household responsibilities as well as by negative attitudes toward women participating in higher education generally and in STEM fields in particular (Campos et al. 2015; World Bank 2011).

To address these issues, several African countries, have gender strategies that focus on improving opportunities in science and technology for women; the African Union recently established an award for female scientists to incentivize and enhance the prestige of female scientists in the region. While these initiatives can be helpful at the margin, the gender gap needs to be addressed much earlier. As discussed in chapter 2, already in primary school girls do more poorly than boys on math tests, and teachers appear to have strong gender stereotypes that consider girls as less adept than boys at hard science. Explicit teacher training on these issues, as well as other interventions aimed at fostering a growth mind-set and grit (chapters 1 and 2), can be helpful. Magnet programs in primary and secondary schools to mentor young girls and to assist female students to transition to university STEM-related studies can also be part of the policy toolkit.

Finally, promoting quality STEM also calls for governments to think about incentives and to focus on addressing key market failures present in the production of these skills. Three market failures are of particular interest:

- *Information.* Governments can play a critical role in making sure that students, teachers, and parents understand early on not only the potential returns but also the requirements associated with a career in STEM.

- *Externalities.* Given the role that STEM can play in innovation and in catalytic sectors, there can be a rationale for using public resources to finance these fields, especially among disadvantaged students. Quotas for scholarships aimed at STEM fields are one option. In addition, experimenting with higher remuneration and nonfinancial rewards for STEM professors could help to retain and attract high-quality professors; using public financing instruments to incentivize private providers to expand the provision of quality STEM and partnering with the private sector for research and innovation can be a start.

- *Coordination failures and economies of scale.* Given the large costs associated with STEM education, pooling resources across entities and even across countries is a promising avenue. Governments can play a coordinating role and seek public-private partnerships (PPPs) for this.

Among the promising regional initiatives are the African Centers of Excellence (ACEs). These aim to enhance regional capacity to meet development needs while also creating economies of scale by pooling resources across countries, with the goal of creating high-quality specialized centers like the ACE for Mathematics, Informatics, and ICT in Senegal, the ACE for Climate Change in Côte d'Ivoire, and the ACE for Drug Development and Therapeutic Trials in Ethiopia. The Association for African Universities plays a role in the ACE programs that includes coordination, quality assurance, and knowledge sharing to maximize regional effectiveness. The Partnership for Applied Sciences, Engineering, and Technology (PASET), an African-led partnership to promote applied sciences, is another important step toward improving science and technology opportunities in higher education. This regional benchmarking initiative helps African universities in applied science, engineering, and technology disciplines to choose comparable institutions and indicators through a comprehensive analytical framework and to learn from global best practices. Smaller countries have an opportunity to benefit from this regional approach in higher education.

In addition to initiatives within the continent, Sub-Saharan Africa can draw lessons from other regions on how to balance this expansion. For example, Brazil has focused on developing small yet internationally competitive and high-quality STEM programs at the tertiary level, while improving performance and equity at lower levels of education (box 4.3). Malaysia has also used a holistic STEM improvement plan spanning basic and tertiary education to address

BOX 4.3

Brazil's Targeted Tertiary STEM Expansion

Brazil has made impressive gains toward building a knowledge-based economy to serve national development needs through targeted investments in STEM fields. Brazil has focused on developing small, high-quality STEM programs at the tertiary level rather than seeking a rapid expansion of overall STEM participation and has developed a relative strength in agriculture and life sciences. Brazil has established six high-quality research centers focused on sustainable development, industrial innovation, energy, agriculture, and the improvement of national research capacity. Between 2005 and 2014, Brazil's publications in scientific journals grew 118 percent, and the country has become one of the top two patenting destinations in the world, with the lowest rate of R&D outsourcing other than China, India, or the Russian Federation. Brazil has also developed strategic forecasting capabilities in order to ensure that research efforts,

(continued next page)

Box 4.3 (continued)

industry needs, and economic development priorities are aligned. In addition, Brazil has one of the highest levels of female representation across STEM fields in the world.

Education and training policies and programs have been critical to Brazil's overall STEM development, with a focus on quality more than simply the number of graduates. Among tertiary students, 12 percent are enrolled in STEM fields. Brazil spends 1 percent of GDP on higher education, and 61 percent of all government research funding goes to universities. Admission to Brazil's universities is highly competitive, with higher education assessments to measure learning and rate institutional quality. In 2007, the Ministry of Science, Technology, and Innovation published the "Action Plan for Science, Technology, and Innovation," calling for additional funding for R&D, an increase in scholarships for STEM research, and funding for professional development of higher education faculty. In addition, the plan established 400 new vocational centers and 600 new distance learning centers, expanded the national mathematics Olympiad to 21 million participants, and granted more than 10,000 new scholarships at the secondary level. The Science without Borders international exchange program aims to build national scientific capacity by leveraging international partnerships. This program provides scholarships to Brazilian students to study in STEM fields in the world's leading universities and provides grants to international researchers to pursue projects with local researchers.

In addition to building high-quality STEM programs at the tertiary level, Brazil has sought to improve the quality of secondary education and access to higher education for disadvantaged students. While still high, inequality in access declined more than 50 percent between 2001 and 2012, possibly due to the expansion of private institutions and scholarship programs. Brazil still performs low on international standards, but it also had the largest improvement in Program for International Student Assessment (PISA) scores of any country between 2003 and 2012.

Sources: UIS.Stat data; OECD 2015; World Bank, forthcoming.

---

the cycle of underperformance in STEM fields (UNESCO 2015). Many countries, including Brazil, Chile, the Republic of Korea, and Vietnam, have turned to international exchange programs in order to help faculty develop the necessary skills to contribute to quality improvement at home.

Policy Focus: Developing Assurance and Accountability Mechanisms

With so much variation in returns to a university degree, the expansion of higher education calls for stronger quality assurance mechanisms for both public and private providers. Much of the expansion of university education so far has occurred in the absence of quality assurance and accountability mechanisms for public universities, and weak regulatory capacity to ensure quality in private universities. For instance, in Malawi, despite the establishment of the National Council for Higher Education in 2011, the system still lacks a functional accreditation system, has not adequately defined quality assurance procedures, and has not established a mechanism to assess academic staff, which makes it difficult to determine the quality of institutions (Mambo et al. 2016). That said, licensing, accreditation, external examiners, and academic audits are increasingly being used to ensure quality, often within a quality assurance agency. By 2010, for example, one-third of countries in the region had national, structured quality assurance mechanisms (Materu and Righetti 2010).

Where quality assurance mechanisms have been put in place, they have often revealed widespread noncompliance of numerous higher education institutions with minimum quality standards. In Nigeria, for example, in recent years around one-third of undergraduate programs have lacked full accreditation, putting them at risk of having to close.[16] However, countries often lack the human and institutional capacity or political capital to carry out these complex processes in a credible and timely manner (Darvas 2016). These weaknesses in quality assurance raise doubts about the capacity of some providers to ensure that students graduate with the requisite skills, and not just diplomas.

In short, managing the existing trade-offs in higher education investments, especially between aggregate productivity and inclusion, involves pursuing the system's goals of expanding coverage with equity and achieving efficiency with quality and relevance. This effort requires addressing the market and policy failures that lead to poor incentives and institutional weaknesses in higher education in the first place. Information failures, credit constraints, and externalities, combined with policy failures in governance and financing (both in higher education and earlier in the education system), lead to suboptimal outcomes in terms of the efficiency, equity, and relevance of higher education. The next section discusses policy priorities for governments in the region to address both market and policy failures in pursuit of a university education that is more relevant, more inclusive, and more sustainable.

Prioritizing Investments and Managing the Expansion of Higher Education in Sub-Saharan Africa

Since most systems in the region remain small, Africa has a unique opportunity to "leapfrog" in its expansion of higher education. Aiming to improve the impact of university education investments on both economic growth and inclusion, countries in the region are in the process of implementing significant governance, quality assurance, and financing reforms. These reform efforts are very timely, not only because the pressures of expansion are growing, but also because this is a time of tremendous opportunities: (a) opportunities to learn from the experience of other regions that have experienced periods of rapidly expanding higher education, such as East Asia and Latin America; and (b) opportunities to rethink financing and delivery models of higher education in a more enabling environment than in the past, thanks to technological progress, urbanization, and economic integration. Drawing lessons from how different countries in the region and around the world have managed the expansion of higher education, building on successes, and harnessing the potential benefits associated with the global megatrends will be critical to identifying promising pathways for reform.

A first step in this process is to prioritize university investments depending on each country's initial conditions, base of skills, and enabling environment. This chapter argues that investments in advanced skills—more than any other skills investments—carry significant productivity-inclusion trade-offs. These trade-offs are likely to be present *within* university education, but also *between* university education and other education investments. Within the university system, expanding coverage without significantly strengthening accountability and quality assurance mechanisms can come at the cost of quality. Across education levels, limited financial resources are likely to mean that spending more on university education can come at the cost of spending less on basic education or on technical and vocational education and training (TVET). The recent #FeesMustFall student protests at South African universities exemplify this trade-off.

The trade-offs between productivity and inclusion associated with higher education investments vary across country contexts. These trade-offs are stronger for countries with a low skills endowment, those that are still in the early stages of their economic transformation, or those that do not have an enabling environment for workers and firms to capitalize on investments in general education. This is because strong foundational skills, which are usually acquired in early childhood and basic education; labor demand for advanced skills, which is associated with more modern economies; and a good overall business environment are critical *complements* to investments in advanced skills at the university level. If these complements are weak or missing, investments in high-quality basic education should take priority over the expansion of higher education; the same goes for reforms aimed at improving the overall business environment. After all, the goal is to put higher education to work, not just to produce higher education graduates.

In addition to strategic trade-offs, there are also significant financial and institutional constraints to a rapidly expanding university education. Many countries in the region are spending a large share of their education budget on higher education, despite the small size of the system. Spending per student is often multiple times higher than in comparator countries. In most of Africa, today's financing arrangements for higher education are, therefore, likely to come under increased pressure and to become unsustainable due to demographics and higher completion rates in basic education. And beyond financial constraints, in many cases the institutional capacity to manage this expansion may prove to be limited.

Thus, while smart investments in university education are crucial for Africa's productive transformation and sustained economic growth in the long run, the expansion needs to be managed carefully, with a strong emphasis on reforms. An important part of this reform agenda needs to be centered outside of the university system: in basic education to ensure university readiness and in the business environment to ensure that the skills acquired translate into higher productivity and earnings (chapter 1). Within the university system, while the challenges and opportunities for higher education vary across countries, types of institutions, and programs, there are five cross-cutting guiding principles for reform:

1. *Be market driven,* through agile mechanisms and governance reforms to provide future self-employed, household enterprise, and wage workers with relevant skills by linking them with employers and markets, preferably at the local level. Leveraging the private sector as a partner in provision, in shaping curricula, and in providing active learning opportunities is critical.

2. *Rethink financing to improve equity, efficiency, and quality.* Restructure financing mechanisms (a) to shift blanket subsidies toward means-test, merit-based scholarships, while ensuring that students come to university with the required foundational skills for university readiness; and (b) to be better aligned with results, while striving to increase economies of scale.

3. *Selectively and gradually support STEM university education,* as economies transform with an emphasis on building engineering and managerial human capital and ensuring the complementary factors for these investments to pay off.

4. *Adopt more active learning practices and a "careers" approach,* including more work-based learning. This principle should guide course offerings, curricula, standards, assessments, evaluations, and recruitment of professors and should facilitate access to diverse pathways.

5. *Be results oriented and evidence based* and enable students, policy makers, university authorities, and employers to make informed decisions by providing regular access to quality data on institutional performance, labor demand, and graduates' employment and earnings prospects.

Be Market Driven

Improving the market relevance of higher education will require aligning teaching and research activities at public and private universities with market imperatives. Too often, curricula, course offerings, and number of spaces per program are determined in a top-down manner, without enough links between industry and providers. Both Botswana and Mauritius have established curriculum advisory and review boards that include faculty and departments as well as stakeholders from both the public and private sectors to ensure that curriculum and skills development are aligned effectively with labor market needs (Cloete et al. 2011). In Mauritius, this process has helped universities to become strategic resources for the government during sectoral transformations and economic planning and is seen as having improved the alignment of graduates' skills with labor market demands.

The weak link between higher education institutions and employers reflects, at least partly, a lack of information on what works and poor legal and financial incentives to connect. Governments have a role to play in sharing local and international best practices regarding collaborations between the private sector and universities on everything from curriculum development to setting up university incubators, as is done as part of PASET (box 4.4). Similarly, governments can offer incentives to set up and strengthen industry-university links by, for example, bringing in intermediaries or providing matching funds. The Science and Technology Education Post-Basic Program (STEP-B) in Nigeria is a promising example of this approach (box 4.5). PPPs in specific initiatives or programs can also be promising, as

---

BOX 4.4

Leveraging New Partners and Regional Collaboration: PASET

The Partnership for Applied Science, Engineering, and Technology is a recent African-led initiative designed to coordinate and strengthen investment in developing skilled human capital in Sub-Saharan Africa by leveraging the knowledge and experiences of Asia, Latin America, and other regions. It aims to bring together governments, the private sector, and new partners including Brazil, China, India, and the Republic of Korea to work together to build a critical mass of skilled human capital necessary to solve Africa's development challenges. The primary focus is on maximizing investments in key sectors and improving the capacity of universities and research centers to generate relevant knowledge and skills, particularly in the fields of applied science, engineering, and technology. Current priority sectors include agriculture, mining, manufacturing,

---

(continued next page)

Box 4.4 (continued)

electrical power, infrastructure and construction, ICT, and health and financial services. Specific goals include the following:

1. Support Sub-Saharan African countries in building a skilled labor force by focusing on the entire continuum of skills

2. Target skills in applied science, engineering, and technology (ASET) for specific priority sectors to complement and maximize returns from domestic and foreign investment in these sectors

3. Promote strategic partnerships between governments, business, and partner countries from other regions to invest in skills in ASET in Sub-Saharan Africa

4. Strengthen mechanisms that promote regional institutional collaboration in specific programs and areas within ASET

5. Strengthen ASET systems and institutions in Africa, including through improved policies, systems, standards, and mechanisms to assure quality and relevance, to monitor progress, and to ensure focus on results

6. Enable the systematic sharing of knowledge and experience among Sub-Saharan African countries and between the region and partner countries in building ASET capacity to promote development.

These larger goals are pursued through complementary programs, including regional scholarship and innovation funds and country ASET plans, which include benchmarking and strategic planning to identify key skills, institutions, and investments. Additional forthcoming programs include TVET centers of excellence (similar to the African Centers of Excellence), quality assurance mechanisms to ensure regional quality in ASET development efforts, and a large-scale data initiative to support improved data collection and analysis in Africa.

Source: World Bank 2017b.

---

in the partnership between Senegal's Ministry of Higher Education and Research and Intel. This partnership uses innovative financing and loan guarantees to support university students' digital learning, provide broader access to online courses, and provide students with tools to personalize and deepen learning. The partnership allows students to purchase and own their laptops through a combination of cost reduction mechanisms (such as no tariffs and special pricing) and low-interest-rate loans. The partnership also includes local banks, computer manufacturers, and telecommunications operators and has allowed more than 50 percent of students to buy and own their first laptop (Galvin and Sow 2017).

BOX 4.5

Leveraging the Private Sector for STEM: Science and Technology Education Post-Basic Program in Nigeria

The STEP-B project, between 2008 and 2013, aimed to produce more and better-qualified science and technology graduates and higher-quality and more relevant research. Moreover, the project aimed to build capacity within participating federal post-basic education institutions to manage, monitor, and evaluate merit-based science and technology funding according to international best practices. STEP-B represented a paradigm shift in the government's approach to STEM by focusing on demand-driven, merit-based, competitive funding and institutional interaction with other institutions and regulatory agencies. The project also strengthened incentives for students to obtain innovation grants to enable them to complete their studies—the Innovators of Tomorrow Program—and promoted 11 science and technology centers of excellence through collaboration between universities and research institutions in Nigeria and abroad, particularly involving the regional African University for Science and Technology.

The project showed some positive results, including stronger capacity for continuing to promote quality STEM going forward. About 30 eligible institutions benefited from 45 grants of up to US$3 million. Key collaboration and partnerships yielded positive results in many areas of science and technology R&D. For example, the University of Agriculture Abeokuta has pioneered innovation in biotechnology research in both plants and animals, focusing on yam, poultry, and palm wine production through partnerships with research centers in Italy (Center for Genetic Engineering) and the United States (International Livestock Research Institute and Cornell University). These partnerships have allowed the university to build capacity through, for example, staff and student exchanges. Similarly, collaboration and partnership of institutions with the Africa University of Science and Technology yielded significant science and technology benefits in mechatronics, materials R&D, and nanotechnology.

Sources: World Bank 2015a, based on World Bank 2013c.

Greater differentiation of institutions at the tertiary level can also improve the relevance, as well as efficiency, of university education. Even in high-income countries, a significant share of tertiary students do not attend academic universities. Not all students have an academic inclination, many lack the necessary foundational skills, and a technical education is likely to be more relevant than an academic one for many jobs. The creation and strengthening of institutions such as community colleges, polytechnic institutions, and TVET institutions can help to manage some of the pressures on the university system from youths and parents who see academic universities as the only viable route for a postsecondary education (chapter 3).

One important risk of diversification is that it can end up creating a second-class tertiary education system for the unprepared and the poor. But this need not be the case. First, the process requires making sure that all students complete secondary education with the necessary foundational skills and information on returns to different tertiary tracks, regardless of their family circumstances or where they attend school. Second, it requires establishing pathways to move across institutional types, including necessary bridging programs (see chapter 3). Finally, it requires providing public financing of talented, disadvantaged students regardless of the type of education they choose.

Successfully managing the expansion of the university system is likely to be accompanied by an increasing role of the private sector as a provider. It is a priori ambiguous whether public or private provision of higher education is preferable. Private providers have an incentive to provide higher-quality education in order to compete with public institutions, provided data on quality are readily available, but they also have incentives to reduce costs that may undermine quality (Sekhri and Rubenstein 2011). Greater private sector participation in the provision of higher education in Africa has helped countries in the region accommodate the growth in the sector in the past decade. The share of tertiary enrollment in private institutions has increased from 32 to 58 percent in Angola, from 28 to 43 percent in Botswana, from 27 to 49 percent in Côte d'Ivoire, and from 8 to 24 percent in Madagascar in the last 10 years.[17] Private provision is likely to continue expanding, as the experiences in East Asia and Latin America suggest (World Bank, forthcoming).

For this expansion in the role of the private sector to be accompanied by improvements in quality and equity, the government needs to play a constructive role in regulating the sector by protecting consumers and promoting competition. Government regulation is necessary, given market failures associated with imperfect competition and information asymmetries. Some countries have only a few universities, whether public or private, which means that they can exercise market power. Even when entry into the sector is sizable, effective competition can be lacking because products tend to be differentiated by geographic location, program type, student peer ability, academic rigor, and content (World Bank, forthcoming). In addition, information on quality of programs and institutions is often lacking or imperfect, making it difficult for students and families to make informed decisions. This calls for combining regulation of the sector with appropriate facilitation of choice across programs and institution types so that students can vote with their feet and enact market discipline.

Regulations, however, can also be used to stifle competition and protect the privileges of insiders and incumbents, which is to be avoided. Especially larger, traditional public universities may seek protection through regulations to limit entry to the higher education market by smaller, private providers or to protect staff through civil service status (Darvas 2016). There is a need to ensure that public and private institutions compete on an equal footing by, for example, allowing them to compete both for public research funding and for students with access to public subsidies (either scholarships or student loans). When policy makers subsidize public institutions but provide no financial aid for students attending private universities, they create a captive demand for the former. This situation can weaken the incentives for public universities to perform well. Ensuring that regulations and policies facilitate, rather than hinder, the entry of private sector providers through clear and efficient regulation and information is a first step.

In addition to promoting competition, regulations should aim to ensure a minimum standard of quality and relevance in both private and public universities. There is widespread concern that quality in many universities is low and that the rapid expansion of the system—in the absence of strong quality assurance mechanisms—will make the situation worse. As the system expands and more diverse students enter the system, low-quality providers and programs with considerable market power over a segment of uninformed consumers may also enter. Of concern is the entry of students whose families and themselves are financially illiterate, have poor access to information on higher education programs and returns, and are academically unprepared for a university education. This segment is likely to attract low-quality, high-priced providers, as the experience in Latin America clearly shows.[18] Something similar has happened in more mature university systems in Africa. South Africa, for example, has a high-end segment of universities and programs with selective admissions and a low-end segment of universities with lower-quality programs and looser admissions standards; the better-off, who are also more likely to have attended high-quality high schools, are concentrated in the former. The fact that not all students gain access to the same option (largely because of differences in academic readiness and socioeconomic background) partly explains the heterogeneity in returns that is found across institutions for the same field of study.

Over the past decade, many Sub-Saharan African countries have set up agencies to conduct assessments and accreditation, but capacity remains limited. As discussed in Darvas, Favara, and Arnold (2017), in practice, quality assurance mechanisms range from simple licensing of institutions by the ministry responsible for higher education to comprehensive systemwide program accreditation and national qualification frameworks (NQFs).[19] By 2012, 21 African countries had established quality assurance agencies, and a dozen other countries were at relatively advanced stages of doing so. Francophone Africa was lagging behind, with only five such agencies (Shabani 2013). These quality assurance agencies seem to be playing a role in basic quality control, with some agencies having closed or some low-quality programs having been prevented from opening, although mostly by imposing input-based requirements on faculty, curricula, and infrastructure. However, many of these agencies lack the capacity to implement their mandates effectively. Shabani (2013) argues that, at least by 2012, 60 percent of quality assurance agencies in the region lacked appropriate capacity. Even if they had the appropriate capacity, the (limited) international evidence on quality assurance processes and accreditation agencies is mixed, suggesting that design issues are of paramount importance. Despite this context, many countries in the region are still aiming to create full NQFs (World Bank 2009). Yet this effort might be premature. In Ethiopia, for example, Tadesse (2014) concludes that complex quality assurance systems have brought only partial benefits and some unintended ill effects.

Since building complex qualification frameworks can take time, countries should focus first on building simple yet solid foundations for quality and enabling a bigger role for market discipline. In some countries, self-assessments and academic audits are gradually being adopted to supplement traditional quality assurance methods (for example, through the use of external examiners) (Darvas 2016). Doing this systematically and through the use of standardized tools can help policy makers and providers to identify weaknesses in the system. These efforts need to be complemented by mechanisms that enable a bigger role for market discipline. In Nigeria, for example, the National Universities Commission publishes an annual ranking of universities in the country, which gathers significant public and media attention (National Universities Commission 2017).[20] Generating relevant information on education institutions and making it accessible would also help to create demand for higher quality on the part of users of the system, primarily students, their families, and employers. This approach, while less ambitious, could be effective given financial and capacity constraints.

Yet even a more targeted and gradual approach to quality assurance requires significant capacity building and resources. In Mozambique, for example, Zavale, Alcantra, and da Conceição (2015) find that there are many challenges when implementing a quality assurance system, even at the institutional level. In particular, these challenges are associated with linking the mechanism to actual decision making and a funding strategy; training human resources and allocating funds for the system to operate and be sustainable; enabling the system to be assimilated by the university community; and defining measurable and objective quality standards to enable an unbiased classification of performance.

For public universities, promoting innovation in curricula, programs, teaching methods, and partnerships requires, in addition, greater effective autonomy. In some countries, most often in Francophone countries, universities are run as part of the state; in others, most often in Anglophone countries, they enjoy autonomous status, with the capacity to hire staff, charge fees, acquire materials, and invest in infrastructure (Darvas 2016; World Bank 2009). Yet, de facto, decision-making autonomy in public sector institutions remains poorly developed even in the latter cases (World Bank 2009). For example, it is not uncommon for the state to appoint university administrators and to determine student and staff composition. Even the curriculum and budget sometimes have to be approved by the government. In Liberia, any increase in tuition has to be approved by the legislature (Darvas 2016). Although academic and procedural autonomy can be improved across the board, this agenda is most urgent in middle-income, large countries, given the size of the system and the diversity of local needs. Having insufficient autonomy to select the staff they need and to shape their academic programs makes it difficult for universities to deliver what the market needs, especially at the local level. When greater autonomy is granted, the government can make use of financing instruments such as innovation grants or performance-based financing to incentivize desired outcomes or reforms.

Reforms to bring greater autonomy need to be matched by appropriate financing and governance arrangements that strengthen accountability, create incentives, and provide the state with effective tools to oversee and improve equity, efficiency, and relevance in higher education. First, accountability toward nongovernment stakeholders, whether the private sector, faculty members, or students, can be improved. Delegating more power to transparent and diverse institution boards and providing students with the information to choose and the opportunity to move across institutions can help to strengthen accountability to these groups. With greater autonomy, accountability to the government needs to be developed further. Policy instruments that can complement the regulatory approach to accountability are discussed next.

Rethink Financing to Improve Quality, Efficiency, and Equity

Well-intended, but misguided, financing policies weaken performance incentives for universities, students, and regulators, exacerbate inequities in the system, and risk unsustainability. Concerns about quality and equity, despite reasonable spending levels, also raise questions about the efficiency of the higher education system. Part of these inefficiencies may stem from weak or pervasive incentives. Students in highly subsidized public universities are not held accountable for their performance; in some countries, they face no real admissions requirements, nor do they face a limit in their time-to-degree. Public financing for institutions is delinked from outcomes or reform efforts. Little funding is awarded competitively to universities for their research, a factor that may help to explain why there are so few graduates in science. Well-thought-out financing can complement other governance reforms and help to align the incentives of different actors with the system's goals of quality, efficiency, and equity.

Improving higher education financing in Africa requires tackling what has been called the "twin problems" of inadequate resources and poor use of existing resources (Devarajan, Monga, and Zongo 2011). In cases where the financing envelope for higher education remains a constraint, options include introducing or increasing user charges and creating incentives for diversification of financing sources (for example, PPPs, consulting, or short-term courses tailored to the specific needs of a sector or firm). In Ghana, for example, 30 percent of university funding has to come from internally generated funds, and institutions are permitted to charge fees to Ghanaian students who otherwise would not have gained entrance (Darvas 2016).

Given equity concerns and overall tight budget constraints, however, an urgent priority across-the-board is to focus on improving the allocation and governance of public financing in higher education. The good news is that there is significant scope for improvement and significant opportunities to learn from higher education systems around the world. From this international experience, financing reforms aimed at achieving sustainability, but also at improving the performance of higher education in terms of relevance, efficiency, and equity, should focus on three main elements: (a) strengthening the links between public financing, university performance, and reform efforts; (b) prioritizing the use of public resources for investments expected to have significant positive externalities and aiming for larger economies of scale; and (c) eliminating public subsidies for better-off youths, while increasing subsidies for highly able, low-income youths.

More closely linking public financing to performance, or at least to reform efforts, can be an important tool for aligning the incentives of private and public providers with the ultimate goals of equity, efficiency, and quality. Public financing of public higher education institutions is based mostly on inputs.[21] Formula-based financing is calculated most commonly using the actual cost of inputs such as number of staff or staff salaries or cost per student, as in Kenya and Rwanda. Other countries, such as Ghana and Nigeria, use normative unit costs derived from prescribed student-teacher ratios by discipline and the recommended cost of goods and services for a teaching unit by discipline. Yet financing in this form creates very few incentives for cost saving, innovation, or improved outcomes for students or for the labor market.

The shift toward performance- or reform-based financing can be made gradually. Experiences in the region and globally suggest possible approaches (box 4.6). One possible instrument consists of innovation (competitive) funds such as the Teaching and Learning Innovation Fund in Ghana or the Quality Innovation Fund in Mozambique. These funds are discretionary and aim to steer promising reforms and innovations in the system around issues such as increasing access to tertiary education, improving the quality of teaching and learning, or improving the management and efficiency of institutions. Funds are ideally provided in a competitive and transparent manner, following the submission of detailed proposals and a peer review process (World Bank 2009).

A more ambitious approach is to move the bulk of public financing to a performance-based system. In India, for example, a performance-based model ties university funding to measures of equity and access, graduates' employability, and strength of institutional governance (World Bank 2016a). In Sub-Saharan Africa, early experimentation with performance-based systems is starting to yield important lessons (box 4.7). Effective results-based finance programs, however, require high-quality, timely, and reliable data and information systems, making this approach unrealistic for many African countries today. A possible stepping stone to performance-based financing is to focus—at least initially—on reforms and not necessarily on outcomes, as was done in Chile.

BOX 4.6

Chile's Performance-Based Agreements: Using Financing to Steer Reforms

Chile's Higher Education Quality Improvement Program (MECESUP, by its initials in Spanish) is an example for Sub-Saharan African countries of how to move gradually toward financing for results. Implementing a full-fledged results-based financing system requires institutions to meet a basic level of development and requires the state to have a clear framework for measuring results as well as effective systems for doing so.

Chile experienced a rapid expansion in tertiary enrollment in the 1990s and early 2000s. This expansion was funded largely by private resources and created an opportunity for the strategic use of public finance to target specific reform areas. As a stepping stone to improve quality and complement public finance, Chile implemented a finance-based improvement plan through the program. MECESUP focuses on three critical areas for improvement: (a) development of a national accreditation system; (b) enhancement of links between tertiary education and national development; and (c) improvements in the quality of services at all levels (undergraduate, postgraduate, technical). To achieve these goals, the government devised performance-based agreements as a complementary tool to increase direct public funding and obtain more public goods and results.

By linking public financing to predefined targets, the Ministry of Education was able to incentivize the implementation of plans likely to improve the quality and relevance of tertiary education, while increasing the accountability for performance. Tertiary institutions were empowered to define and pursue institutional goals and targets through performance-based agreements. They were also empowered to implement targeted activities that would improve teaching and learning outcomes through a more targeted performance-based agreement. These institutions were pushed to strengthen management and administrative capacity by coordinating and integrating efforts to reform

---

(continued next page)

Box 4.6 (continued)

curricula, programs, and departments and by working to oversee the implementation of performance agreements.

Performance-based agreements have generated a new form of dialogue between the Chilean government and universities. The government and universities agree on common objectives, negotiate the ways and resources to achieve them, promptly report on initiative effects, and interpret progress to identify possible actions and ensure a joint orientation toward results. The universities are autonomous and make decisions independently.

Resources allocated by performance-based agreements represent only a fraction of total funding and are allocated competitively. Institutions must contribute their own income or obtain resources from other sources. This scheme enables institutions to have a combination of funding sources for their institutional improvement plans and enables the government to pass a "market" test for desired reforms. Another critical feature of the performance agreements in place in Chile is the ability to redesign resource allocation dynamically in order to ensure results. This adaptability facilitates dealing with the uncertainty and complexity of processes, given the difficulty of fully anticipating the most effective actions. Feedback and learning are key.

Sources: Based on Arango, Evanst, and Quadri 2016; Reich 2015; Yutronic et al. 2010.

BOX 4.7

Paying for Results in Higher Education in Africa: The Experience of Mali and the African Centers of Excellence

The Mali Higher Education Support Project and African Centers of Excellence are two of the first examples in the region where payment to higher education institutions is based on results. In the Mali Higher Education Support Project, financing of up to US$200,000 is made available to each of the four participating higher education institutions to meet the costs of developing an accredited program in consultation with the private sector, training teachers to deliver accredited programs, or increasing their financial resources. This focus aims to improve the overall governance of higher education institutions and to develop new programs that are well aligned with labor market demands, increasing the likelihood that graduates will be able to obtain good jobs upon graduation.

The ACE project, in contrast, aims to promote regional specialization among participating universities in areas that address specific regional development challenges and to strengthen the capacity of these universities to deliver quality, market-relevant

(continued next page)

Box 4.7 (continued)

postgraduate education. There is a rigorous, competitive, and transparent process for selecting each ACE. Governments pay the centers of excellence for results—for example, US$2,000 per student in internship, US$600,000 per international accreditation, US$2,000 per male student in a master's program, and US$2,500 per female student. The latter feature aims to address one of the most common criticisms of pay-for-performance arrangements: that tying funds to results can strain access and equity in higher education by limiting the resources that institutions dedicate to support disadvantaged students and by creating pervasive incentives to serve those best prepared to succeed (usually those already better-off).

Both projects illustrate some of the potential but also some of the challenges involved in implementing pay-for-performance in higher education in the region. For example, universities may try to game the pay-per-results system. Similarly, the focus on results does not reach the individual faculty member. In addition, since quality and relevance are difficult to measure, these programs can distort institutional behavior by tying the quest for educational excellence to financial incentives at the expense of academic ethics and ethos, which are traditionally expected to shape academic behavior.

However, if these drawbacks are well managed and programs are applying lessons learned to help overcome them, this radically different way of financing projects can help to change outcomes and achieve objectives. Since payments are made on the basis of results rather than on the basis of inputs, the approach fosters performance, reform, and institutional strengthening as well as improves sustainability.

Sources: Based on Blom 2016; World Bank 2014a, 2015b.

This approach focuses on linking financing to inputs deemed necessary for a high-quality and efficient system.

Public financing can also be a tool to align fields of study more closely with national needs. Given tight budgets, countries need to be selective when deciding priorities for public funding. Some of the outputs of higher education are public goods, and several fields of study are likely to have important externalities. Research is an example of the former, while STEM and pedagogy fields are examples of the latter, because inadequate or insufficient STEM skills can constrain the development of certain industries (such as high-value-added manufacturing or ICT) or innovation more generally. Providing higher levels of financing to programs focused on these areas and giving some preference on the demand side to students who enroll in these programs are some ways of doing this.

In order to improve efficiency, it is also important for financing and governance arrangements to factor in economies of scale. Launched in 2014, the African Centers of Excellence offer an opportunity to integrate regionally and to maximize scarce resources to improve the quality, relevance, and accountability of higher education throughout the region, particularly in fields deemed critical for development. Small countries stand to benefit from this regional approach. Today, centers of excellence exist in 16 countries in the region, including one focused on health in Benin, one focused on information technology in Cameroon, and two focused on agriculture in Uganda. The ACE initiative provides funding and technical support to universities through a competitive process to assist in the development of advanced specialized studies in science, technology, engineering, mathematics, health, agriculture, and applied statistics. Economies of scale in financing and in staff can be obtained by promoting regional specialization among participating centers and reducing the need to have universities in every location. Regional specialization also ensures that the breadth of skills needed to meet labor market and development needs are addressed adequately within a region.

Finally, financing of higher education in the region needs to refocus on talented, disadvantaged students. Large blanket subsidies for higher education can be regressive and end up reducing access among the disadvantaged. In Latin America, universal free tuition resulted in high dropout rates and long completion times in many countries because of a lack of incentives to graduate on time and the limited risk associated with dropping out (World Bank, forthcoming). Unrestricted blanket subsidies are most common in Francophone countries and are often coupled with guaranteed admissions that disproportionately benefit the wealthy (World Bank 2010). On average, there is less cost sharing at the tertiary level in Africa than in other regions, but some countries have tried to move progressively away from fully free higher education and toward cost-sharing arrangements. Malawi, Uganda, and Zambia have shifted some costs, including living expenses, to students, and Botswana, Ethiopia, and Lesotho have implemented deferred cost-sharing programs in which students can repay tuition incrementally after graduation (World Bank 2010). Yet in most countries in the region, public universities have free or highly subsidized tuition, which is usually not means tested. A few countries have implemented more progressive means-tested support, including Kenya, Mauritania, Mauritius, Namibia, Rwanda, South Africa, and Tanzania (World Bank 2010). As a result, given tight budget constraints, current financing arrangements crowd out potential support for the more disadvantaged, exacerbating inequities in the system. Given competing financial needs, free university for all at this stage of development inevitably means less education for many, especially many disadvantaged youths.

Tuition charges closer to cost recovery, coupled with needs-based financial assistance for high-ability youth, can help to improve both efficiency and equity and to support the expansion of higher education in a more sustainable manner. Subsidizing tuition and other costs for students whose families can afford it or who would qualify for a loan is largely a waste of public resources, given the large private benefits associated with higher education. Of course, the political economy of these reforms is complex, as university students usually have a strong impact on public opinion. It is important, therefore, to identify in the public debate the winners and losers of the status quo and to highlight the regressive nature of today's arrangements. Public subsidies should be a priority for high-ability, low-income students.[22] Liquidity constraints for such individuals subtract not only from equity but also from efficiency, since the economy misses the opportunity to realize their full productive potential. Credit markets do not work well for this group, and public financing should seek to address this market failure. Redirecting today's blanket subsidies toward targeted scholarships based on merit and conditional on performance to low-income, academically talented individuals is a win-win for growth and inclusion.[23]

In response to the sustainability and equity concerns associated with current patterns of financing, several countries have introduced soft loan schemes for higher education. Approximately 70 countries around the world offer some form of loans for higher education (Darvas 2016), including Botswana, Burkina Faso, Eswatini, Ethiopia, Ghana, Kenya, Lesotho, Malawi, Nigeria, Rwanda, South Africa, and Tanzania. In principle, loans can help to improve efficiency and equity in higher education by providing students with the funds to pursue a higher education. There is evidence that student loans can indeed increase enrollment. In South Africa, a rigorous evaluation of university loans aimed mostly at middle-class households led to an increase of 22–25 percentage points in the probability of enrollment—a 50 percent increase over the baseline enrollment rate (Gurgand, Lorenceau, and Melonio 2011).

Loan programs, however, are hard to design and implement well. Given imperfections in the credit market for higher education loans, there is a role for government.[24] For student loan schemes to be effective, countries need consistent sources of lending capital for this group, reliable taxation and information systems, means-testing capabilities, and benchmarks for establishing reasonable repayment amounts, as well as adequate administrative, legal, and data frameworks to enforce loan repayment (World Bank 2010). Student loan schemes also require significant public financing since they usually come with heavy public subsidies and take significant capacity to recoup (even if this role is outsourced).

One of the most critical issues limiting the success of student loan schemes is the difficulty of ensuring repayment. In Africa, this issue is made particularly challenging due to the additional hurdles of establishing effective debt collection capabilities and data systems, educating borrowers about loans and loan conditions, building legal capacity to handle issues of default, and establishing mechanisms to ensure that loans target those who need them, as well as addressing the uncertainty of employment opportunities for many graduates. Due to high informality, the limited reach of the tax system, and overall weaknesses in asset- and income-reporting mechanisms in most African countries, it is often difficult to implement even means-tested loans, let alone income-contingent loans.[25] In the bursary scheme in Zambia, which is a loan scheme, none of the beneficiaries has repaid in its history (World Bank 2015c).

Despite these challenges, expanding loan schemes remains an attractive option for countries in the region looking to increase cost sharing and equity in higher education. Doing so will require drawing on lessons from the international experience, especially in Latin America, where university education has expanded significantly in recent decades. There are also several examples of promising loan schemes and solutions in the region. For example, Ghana's Student Loan Trust carries sufficient interest and has established strong administrative and loan default policies, minimizing government loss and improving cost sharing. Kenya, Rwanda, and Tanzania have designated special-ized agencies to collect loan repayments. In Namibia, repayment rates increased more than 50 percent when the Ministry of Education began collecting employ-ment information from the Social Security Commission in order to track and follow up with borrowers (World Bank 2010). A few countries, including Botswana, Ethiopia, and South Africa, have created alternatives to loan repay-ment in the form of public service as teachers (Ethiopia) or for specialization in a field facing a shortage of skilled labor (Botswana). Other steps toward improv-ing the effectiveness of loan schemes in the region include improving means-testing capabilities and accuracy. Moving in this direction will require increased efforts to link tax, social assistance, secondary education, and other relevant databases that can provide a more complete picture of households' economic situation.[26] In addition, other possible measures include setting time limits on time-to-degree, implementing fees associated with repayment schedules, strengthening the capacity of legal systems to follow up on loan defaults, and providing grant options for students from the lowest-income backgrounds.

When financial aid programs are available, it is just as important to make sure that students and parents have this information at the appropriate moment, when relevant decisions are made. Information can make a difference. Dinkelman and Martinez (2011) show for Chile that providing information to eighth-grade students and their parents on merit-based scholarships and gov-ernment loans for tertiary education improved their knowledge of these programs and increased their desire to continue to tertiary education.

While the focus here has been on financing, improving equity in higher edu-cation will also require addressing additional barriers to access and successful completion of higher education that affect youths of a particular gender or com-ing from a specific location. Attanasio and Kaufmann (2009) show, in the con-text of Mexico, that youths' expectations and perceptions about returns to higher education matter for university enrollment. Yet lack of accurate information can be a constraint, especially among women and in rural areas (Banerjee et al. 2013). In addition to the impact of information, there is some evidence that access to role models changes beliefs and expectations about what is possible for women to achieve, in turn increasing the demand for education (Beaman et al. 2012; Jensen 2012). Since it is not desirable to aim to have a university everywhere in a country, student mobility should be encouraged so that distance is not a constraint for those living far from a university. Information and scholarships that include a mobility premium can be helpful. In addition, closing the spatial gaps in access to quality higher education also requires investing in access to quality basic education in those areas as well as ensuring that relevant information on universities' admissions policies and offices reaches more remote areas in a timely manner.

More equality in access and retention should not come at the cost of university-readiness or lower standards, however. And it does not have to, if the appropriate groups are targeted. The priority has to be providing access to high-ability, low-income students who can succeed at the university level. It will not help the country, nor the individual, if university acceptance is given to students who are not academically ready. Many talented, low-income students today have no access to universities, and this group needs special attention from governments in the region.[27]

Heavily subsidizing the cost of attending university among high-ability, low-income youths is important, but attention to this group needs to start even earlier. Some of these individuals may be university ready, but need support in accessing relevant information or help in the process of applying to university. Hence, in addition to scholarships, it is equally important to think about pathways and programs that can help to address remediable deficiencies in university readiness among this group and support comprehensively the transition from secondary to higher education. "Talent academies" aimed at supporting youths from disadvantaged backgrounds in the last two years of high school and mentorship programs can be helpful. Bridge programs are another option. In Namibia, the Pathways Program at the University of Namibia targets students from the marginalized Owambo ethnic group, with a focus on preparing them to study science and engineering at the tertiary level (MacGregor 2008).

This shorter-term efficiency- and equity-enhancing agenda needs to be accompanied by a longer-term agenda that can gradually, but *effectively*, improve equity in higher education. While measures like quotas and affirmative action can play a role in promoting equity in higher education for historically disadvantaged groups,[28] their effects are likely to be limited if not accompanied by measures aimed at improving equity, not only in the number of students but also in the quality of education with which students from different backgrounds leave the university system.[29] This agenda needs to start by improving early childhood investments and the quality of basic education for disadvantaged children to ensure that they have a shot at reaching and succeeding in higher education. Measures that address the underlying causes of inequity are likely to take longer to achieve, but they can lead to more sustainable gains that go beyond just increasing the number of students.

Selectively and Gradually Support STEM University Education

The contribution of higher education to innovation and productivity growth requires complementary policies and institutional factors that are largely absent in many low-income countries in Sub-Saharan Africa. Several countries in Sub-Saharan Africa have started to focus on supporting universities to conduct more R&D activities, particularly in STEM fields. International experience, however, indicates that there are important prerequisites for investments in this area to pay off. R&D spending may not translate into technological diffusion or indigenous innovation—and thus productivity growth—without complementary institutional factors. Goñi and Maloney (2014) show that the returns to R&D vary across country context, tending to follow an inverted U-shape: returns increase as countries move up the technology frontier (the expected catch-up effect), peak for countries at middle-income levels, and fall as countries get closer to the frontier. More important, the existence of positive returns depends on complementary policy and institutional factors, such as a strong business environment, adequate human capital, research infrastructure, and a dynamic private sector that can link R&D activities with production. These factors are largely absent in the region's low-income countries.

The experience of East Asian economies in supporting higher education to build innovation capacity offers useful lessons for the region. East Asia's new industrial economies, such as those of Korea and Singapore, gradually supported postsecondary education's R&D activities in close links with the adoption and application of existing technologies by enterprises, particularly in connection with export sectors. Meanwhile, China significantly increased spending on R&D in conjunction with its expansion of higher education, but there are concerns regarding the quality of R&D investments. While government subsidies have contributed to an increase in the number of patent applications, many of these patents are of low quality and may be driven by subsidies received for patent registration and not their use in creating economic value. Support for R&D in higher education is not linked as tightly with technological adoption and diffusion in low-technology industries, where the majority of firms with potential for catch-up reside. As a result, the contribution of R&D spending and the university education system to productivity growth remains unrealized. Most of the country's success resides in areas where the university system has been linked with multinational firms that facilitate the transfer and adoption of technology.

Sub-Saharan African countries can prioritize development of engineering and managerial capacities as a stepping stone to leverage higher education investments and build their innovation capacity. Valencia Caicedo and Maloney (2014) provide historical and empirical evidence on the central role of a country's engineering capacity for technological transfer, adoption, and innovation, and thus long-term growth. Through a review of the literature and their own empirical analysis, they conclude that having a higher number of engineering graduates, as a proxy for a higher level of scientifically oriented human capital and innovation capacity, predicts significant long-term differences in a country's income per capita. They argue that the United States, for instance, started relatively early to invest in the establishment of engineering colleges, even before the massive expansion of secondary education took place. The international evidence also indicates that the private sector's managerial capabilities are a particularly important factor for productivity growth through organizational and process innovations. A core capability underpinning this upgrading is management quality that allows firms to learn to compete on the basis of intangible assets, such as organizational structures, design, brand, and modern management in the areas of long-run planning and talent management, that are necessary for technology adoption and innovation. Thus, countries in the region can prioritize building a critical mass of engineering and business graduates in their gradual expansion of higher education. Again, these investments will need to be coupled with reforms to establish a policy-enabling environment, foster close links to private enterprises, and attract foreign direct investment.

Adopt More Active Learning Practices and a "Careers" Approach

Lack of practical experience is one of the main limitations that employers identify in young workers.[30] In Uganda, for example, in a 2002 survey of around 100 employers, 26 percent of firms cited lack of practical experience as the most critical need, the highest share among more than 35 options (MISR 2006).

This agenda starts with design of the curriculum. First, academic subjects need to be combined with hands-on classes that focus on the underlying skills necessary at work. Some of these skills are academic, but many are not. The task-based approach exemplified by the Generations program (described in chapter 3) is one way of doing this. Since what matters is whether workers have the skills to perform the tasks that form their job, the development of NQFs that define and accredit qualifications tied to workers' skills should focus on the skills that employers require, not just on diplomas.

Second, introducing more work-based learning, through apprenticeships or internships and work environment simulations, can also help. Many countries in the region have or are in the process of generating national apprenticeship and internship frameworks with a view to enhancing the workplace experience of youths—including university graduates—before they officially enter the world of work. Such frameworks are to be encouraged, and the international evidence suggests that—when well designed—they can indeed improve employability (chapters 3 and 5). Since some students in the region work while studying, incentivizing universities to form partnerships with the private sector early on to ensure that students who work get relevant experience can be helpful. Similarly, incentivizing flexible schedules that allow students to work and study can make studies more relevant, while reducing the opportunity cost of attending university. That said, the experience in Latin America suggests that it is critical to avoid the risk that students will be overburdened with work, which can lead to dropouts (World Bank, forthcoming). Practical experience can also be enhanced in the classroom, through simulations or university projects that aim to address actual problems of enterprises, for example.

Third, a "careers" approach to university education that recognizes the needs of the economy today, but also those of tomorrow, can improve alignment and adaptability. Given the structure of most Sub-Saharan African countries' economies, strengthening entrepreneurship education in universities, both directly and indirectly, has to be a priority. Many universities on the continent have established incubation centers that allow and encourage students to try out new ideas and take them to market. At the same time, especially in higher education, graduates are likely to experience a rapidly changing world of work, with the nature of work shifting increasingly into nonroutine tasks that put a premium on higher-order cognitive and socioemotional skills (chapter 1). As in other levels of education, the focus of university education needs to shift from memorization to problem solving, from following rules to creativity.

Finally, such a shift in skills and ways of learning will not be possible without paying equal attention to university professors. In some countries in the region, there are 50 percent more students per professor than the global average.[31] Promoting and training professors to shift gradually toward a more "student-centered" approach in classroom training is not easy since professors in university classrooms usually adopt a "teacher-centered" approach to instruction, with little scope for student interaction, discussion, or teamwork. Reviewing recruitment and remuneration policies, improving accountability, strengthening retraining, and encouraging international exchanges can help to improve the quality of today's professors.

Since these changes will take time, countries in the region should continue fostering the international partnerships that give the most promising students access to the best universities in the continent and in the world. Today's digital technologies make such access easier. For example, the Massachusetts Institute of Technology and a consortium of 15 other top universities have started to offer micro-master's programs that only require one full semester on campus in the United States (MIT 2016).

Be Results Oriented and Evidence Based

Strong information systems are the cornerstone of many of the reforms needed in higher education in Africa. More and better information is required by different actors in the higher education ecosystem—students, families, service providers, policy makers, the private sector, and employers.

The lack of relevant information (and accompanying support) can lead students to enroll in low-quality programs, while also taking on large loans. This is a risk in the region, given the vast heterogeneity in returns across programs and institutions, discussed earlier. The risk is likely to be greater for low-income students and parents, who face more severe asymmetries of information and lower capacity to act on this information, especially with regard to assessing the quality and variety of higher education programs and comparing the long-term costs and benefits of alternative career paths and financing options.[32] Providing information on university choices and processes and complementary support in filling out forms, for example, can make a difference if done in a timely and accessible manner. In the United States, for example, the Expanding College Opportunities project provided individualized information about colleges' net prices, resources, curricula, students, and outcomes. The intervention has raised students' applications to, admissions at, enrollment in, and progress at selective colleges (Hoxby and Turner 2013).

Graduate tracer studies and employer surveys also can be useful tools for monitoring the relevance and quality of programs offered by universities. Many countries are tempted to address information failures and perceived skills mismatches by trying to forecast the types of workers that firms will be needing in the future. This approach usually proves unsuccessful, since it is difficult to know the skills that firms will be requiring in the future, and in most cases firms do not even explicitly plan, say, five years ahead. A more promising approach is, therefore, to try to use the signal that the labor market provides and make sure that this information reaches all relevant stakeholders—students, workers, firms, government—in an accessible and timely manner. Tracer studies that follow the employment and earnings trajectory of graduates can be a central part of these efforts. Universities need to be motivated and equipped to run such assessments, either through government regulation on quality assurance or results-based financing. In addition, the public sector, in partnership with formal and informal business associations, can carry out regular employer surveys and other surveys to collect information on the private sector's need for skills and views on the strengths and weaknesses of recent graduates as well as workers' fields of study, institutions attended, and labor market outcomes.

Despite some ad hoc attempts to conduct tracer studies in specific universities or at the regional level, no country in the region carries out regular tracer studies of its university graduates.[33] This is not entirely surprising given that, in environments of high informality, tracer studies can be costly. However, these studies could be conducted on a sample basis every four to five years, for example. In the Western Cape in South Africa, a tracer study of the 2010 cohort of university graduates in the region was carried out in 2013 (Cape Higher Education Consortium 2013). A potential model for other countries, this tracer study was carried out by the Cape Higher Education Consortium, which brings together representatives from different private and public universities as well as government officials. In trying to obtain more regular information on graduates' labor market outcomes, the University of Cape Town, in particular, uses an innovative mechanism of gathering information on employment at graduation ceremonies. This approach could be replicated and provide some initial information on immediate placing. Mobile technology can also help in improving response rates and allowing for more regular surveying of graduates. This approach is being followed in Nigeria, where the National Universities Commission is carrying out a pilot tracer study in selected universities and selected fields of study, using both the Internet and text messages to boost response rates.[34]

In upper-middle-income countries, these instruments can be complemented by regional or national "employment observatories." These observatories have been set up in many countries, especially in Europe and Latin America. In Africa, a labor market observatory is being set up in Kenya and Nigeria, and precursors exist or have existed in Ghana, Lesotho, Namibia, Mauritius, and Senegal, for example. Since they can be quite complex, it is important to start small. Also, observatories are probably most useful in middle- or upper-middle-income countries that have the capacity to generate up-to-date information on labor markets, including in the informal sector.[35] Employment observatories can take many forms, but they aim to provide appropriate labor market and educational information so that actors can take the right decisions: students can decide what fields to study, whether to choose vocational or higher education, and where to study, while policy makers and service providers can decide which areas to strengthen, update, or promote. Observations can start with a small office in charge of collecting labor market information and conducting specialized labor-related analysis, as in Poland, and then develop into more sophisticated outfits able to provide information about earnings, labor conditions by sectors, and type of firms and jobs, as in Chile and Colombia. Later on, they can, for example, collect and provide information on educational institutions' placements in labor markets and carry out tracer studies, in combination with data collected thorough the systems of public revenue offices.

Information and evidence are equally relevant for governments and providers to learn from their own experiences and to guide and incentivize reform. As in the case of TVET systems, in higher education, universities, quality assurance institutions, and governments are conducting policy blindly, with very little evidence on which to base their decisions. Institutionalizing tools, such as the Systems Approach for Better Education Results (SABER) Tertiary Education, that gather information at the system level, but also tools that gather similar information at the institutional level, is equally critical. As discussed above, the use of tools that link financing with reforms can be a driver of change in higher education systems in the region.

Given the many challenges associated with successfully managing the expansion of higher education, governments need to be careful in using the policy instruments at their disposal. The market alone will not achieve the social optimum in higher education, due to the presence of externalities, liquidity constraints, information-related problems, and imperfect competition. Each of these failures requires a different set of public policy instruments, and all such instruments will likely be required to manage the expansion of higher education in Africa. This is one of the lessons from the expansion in Latin America (box 4.8). Possible externalities associated with STEM or research require targeted government subsidies in those areas; liquidity constraints most likely require both government subsidies for the poorest and support for student credit markets; information-related problems require information provision and consumer protection; and imperfect competition requires enabling competition through student choice, while also monitoring and regulating the sector. As discussed in World Bank (forthcoming), these policy tools complement each other. For example, subsidies that improve access

---

BOX 4.8

Expanding University Education: Lessons from the Latin American Experience

In Latin America and the Caribbean, enrollment in higher education has expanded significantly, growing from 21 to 43 percent 2000 and 2013. This large expansion has resulted from changes in both supply and demand that offer possible lessons for Sub-Saharan African countries. Just as is expected to happen in Sub-Saharan Africa, the primary source of change in demand was an increase in the number of students completing secondary school. At the same time, families experienced an increase in their ability to pay for higher education, and many governments began offering public funds to increase participation in higher education, including free or heavily subsidized tuition, loan schemes, and scholarships. The increase in supply stemmed from both the expansion of existing institutions as well as the establishment of new institutions and programs, both public and private. On average, the market share of private higher education institutions rose from 43 to 50 percent between the early 2000s and 2013.

The Latin American experience makes evident that quality, variety, and equity of higher education systems are interdependent. It also illustrates useful lessons regarding effective, more equitable, and efficient expansion in other regions, including the

---

(continued next page)

important lesson that expanding access alone does not automatically result in greater equity or a more skilled population. The following are some of the key lessons.

Countries with the largest growth in access to higher education implemented explicit policies targeting expansion; as a whole, countries in the region strategically leveraged participation from various stakeholders, including the private sector, and increased secondary school completion rates, expanding the pool of potential higher education students. Examples of enabling policies include Chile's state-guaranteed loan program to incentivize participation (with some drawbacks as well) and Ecuador's increase in the size and number of public higher education institutions. Some countries also adopted policies to facilitate the expansion of private institutions. However, simply expanding access without improving quality and relevance will not produce a more skilled society on its own.

One policy area in which Latin America may lag is regional collaboration. In Sub-Saharan Africa, with programs like PASET and ACE, regional collaboration shows promise for improving access, quality, and efficiency in higher education. In addition, higher education authorities in nine countries in Latin America and the Caribbean do not participate in long-term strategic planning processes, or the processes do not exist. This lack of long-term planning limits the ability of higher education to contribute to the long-term goals of national development and growth in the way that improved regional and strategic planning could.

Public funding is necessary for expansion, but choosing appropriate funding mechanisms is critical because they affect the number and type of students who enroll in and complete higher education programs. All countries in Latin America and the Caribbean subsidize higher education to varying extents, ranging from completely free public higher education for all students to selective admissions with loan schemes available for students in need. The experience demonstrates that, while offering free tuition and unrestricted access to students may be an effective way to increase access, as in Argentina, it also has high fiscal costs and can be an inefficient use of public resources, offering little incentive for students to complete their studies in a timely manner or at all, and resulting in significant waste. However, offering loan schemes alone may result in inequity by excluding students from low-income backgrounds. Brazil and Colombia use hybrid approaches combining selective admissions with merit-based funding for qualified students in public universities, as well as loans and other funding for students in private universities. These hybrid funding mechanisms have resulted in increased enrollment and, which is important, increased completion.

Careful attention to private sector involvement is crucial. The adoption of policies to facilitate access to private higher education institutions can help to build private sector participation and expand access. In Brazil, Chile, and Paraguay, private providers make up more than 70 percent of higher education institutions, while in Argentina, Bolivia, Panama, and Uruguay, they comprise less than 25 percent. In many countries, private institutions develop their own admissions criteria, curriculum, and program offerings. This independence can enable them to establish stronger connections with the private

(continued next page)

Box 4.8 (continued)

sector and to be more flexible in offering programs better suited for employability. However, these institutions often charge higher fees and are restricted to wealthier students, especially when public loans and scholarships are not available. In the absence of regulations, countries often have a larger number of private providers, but this autonomy can result in significant variation in the quality of providers and create perverse incentives to maximize profit with little regard for relevance and quality, particularly in the case of for-profit institutions. However, excessively strict regulations limit the ability of private institutions to respond to the market.

Accountability and quality frameworks and incentives are key. Without concrete accountability frameworks, the policies, funding mechanisms, and leveraging of the private sector will still leave room for wasted resources and ineffective institutions. While significant variation persists and there is still room for improvement, Latin America and the Caribbean has successfully implemented accountability measures for higher education systems. For example, Brazil, Colombia, Mexico, and the Caribbean Examinations Council use learning assessments to measure student progress. Colombia has established a national system for ranking higher education institutions and an employment observatory for tracking students' labor market outcomes over time (at least among formal workers). Finally, the region has been successful at using results-based financing and discretionary funds to provide incentives to institutions and systems to work toward improvement.

Source: Based on World Bank, forthcoming.

---

to higher education among high-ability, low-income students can further improve the efficiency of the system if students can freely choose what type of institution and program to attend and have relevant information with which to make informed decisions, and if providers are overseen in ways that ensure a minimum standard of quality. For policy makers, a useful criterion is the extent to which tools incentivize the desired behaviors among students, providers, regulatory authorities, and the private sector, while considering the vast heterogeneity in constraints and preferences among these actors. Serious consideration of the issue of incentives can help to avoid negative unintended effects, some of which have been discussed in this chapter.

Conclusions

The expansion of higher education in Africa needs to balance youths' aspirations, economies' needs, and financial and institutional sustainability. The ultimate goals of higher education—contributing to economic growth, inclusion, and adaptability—are likely to be very similar across countries, as are the systemwide goals of improving access, efficiency, and relevance of higher education. This chapter has argued, however, that investments in higher education carry very significant trade-offs between the goals of productivity and inclusion, and that these trade-offs are stronger for countries with a low skills endowment, in the early stages of their productive transformation, or lacking an enabling environment for workers and countries to generate adequate returns from university education investments.

These trade-offs, together with demographic, economic, and technological changes, mean that countries in Africa should manage carefully their expansion of higher education. Countries should first identify and follow through with win-win policies for equity and efficiency—for example, shifting resources from subsidies for high-income youths to subsidies for high-ability, low-income youths and investing in solid foundational skills. Then, countries should try to align the rest of the policies with the desired behavioral changes, balancing possible trade-offs and avoiding unintended consequences. In addition to reforms within the university system, reforms need to address weaknesses in foundational skills—especially among disadvantaged groups—and in the business environment. Only then will a university education pay off for most graduates, especially amid an expansion of graduates. The fact that most systems in the region remain small provides an opportunity to make reforms early, learn from the experience of others, and set up the basis for a healthy expansion of the system.

Many of the required reforms to achieve a healthy expansion of higher education are complex and politically challenging. They require reforming governance in many instances, introducing new legislation, and using political capital. Such changes can be hard to accomplish in higher education, especially where university systems tend to be fully or partially autonomous. To achieve broad and sustained results, policies and reforms need to establish credible commitment, support coordination, and promote cooperation among all actors. To this end, they must tackle the politics of policies and create incentives to align the behaviors of all stakeholders with the pursuit of national skills development goals.

Countries in Sub-Saharan Africa also should strive to build coalitions for reform. In addition to tilting public opinion through information on the performance of graduates and institutions, countries can create coalitions that foster cooperation and shift the balance of power toward good policies and reforms. Cooperation requires recognizing the multiple, often competing and evolving, interests of stakeholders. For instance, results-oriented financing reforms can be derailed when insufficient resources and lack of support undermine morale and distract the attention of principals and the academic community from achieving results. Policies that combine increased resources tied to performance-improvement plans with reforms and mechanisms to improve accountability for results may have a better chance of buy-in.

Notes

1. This chapter focuses on higher education. However, some of the data available do not separate universities from tertiary education more generally. As a result, some of the data presented cover all of tertiary education (including technical and vocational education). However, as discussed in chapter 3, tertiary technical education in Sub-Saharan Africa remains fairly small.
2. UIS.Stat data for gross enrollment in tertiary education. International Standard Classification of Education (ISCED) 5–8 refer to, regardless of age, the percentage of the total population of the five-year age group beginning with secondary school leaving.
3. For a discussion of other dimensions of inequality in access to higher education—associated with disability, for example—see Darvas et al. (2017).
4. Based on UIS.Stat data.
5. See http://ent.arp.harvard.edu/AfricaHigherEducation/index.html.
6. Based on School-to-Work Transition Surveys for seven countries: Benin, the Republic of Congo, Liberia, Madagascar, Malawi, Togo, and Zambia. Results are based on a Mincer regression, controlling for gender and experience among youths ages 15–29 years.
7. These returns are based on a simple Mincer regression and cover only wage employees (Montenegro and Patrinos 2014).
8. Based on UIS.Stat data.
9. Rising returns in Sub-Saharan Africa can be misleading because the coverage of countries varies a lot over the years. However, the data set is more balanced closer to the year 2000, and returns continue to trend upward afterward (although less steeply).
10. For Kenya, see Sanchez Puerta and Perinet (2015); for Ghana, see Darvas, Favara, and Arnold (2017). As discussed in this chapter, the more advanced skills observed among higher education graduates are likely to reflect the fact that, on average, higher-skill individuals are those who continue on to higher education in the first place.
11. These higher unemployment rates are likely to reflect the fact that university graduates are disproportionally from richer households and hence can more easily afford to remain unemployed. It also likely reflects underemployment in addition to unemployment, given higher expectations in terms of job quality among university graduates.
12. Based on the most recent School-to-Work Transition Survey for 10 countries in the region.
13. Based on School-to-Work Transition Survey.
14. In this sector, pay is often tightly linked to educational qualifications (not necessarily passing the market test) and accompanied by job stability and a package of benefits often not available in the private sector.
15. Based on the most recent School-to-Work Transition Survey.
16. For Nigeria's National Universities Commission's accreditation results for undergraduate programs, see http://nuc.edu.ng/undergraduate-accreditation-results/.
17. Based on UIS.Stat data.

18. In Latin America and the Caribbean, on average, the market share of private higher education institutions rose from 43 to 50 percent between the early 2000s and 2013 (World Bank, forthcoming).
19. NQFs are discussed in more detail in chapter 3.
20. Contrary to many international rankings, however, this ranking is not accompanied by a breakdown of the factors considered or the data justifying the ranking. This information may exist, but it is not easily available to the public.
21. For a comprehensive discussion of financing mechanisms for higher education in Africa and policy options, see World Bank (2010).
22. The concern about credit constraints and education financing for this group is present in basic education as well (chapter 2). Improving their access at that level is the first step toward improving their chances of accessing higher education. International evidence suggests that, for example, scholarships for low-income students to attend secondary education boosted higher education enrollment significantly among beneficiaries (Barrera-Osorio et al. 2011).
23. Some of these scholarships can come from the private sector. Many private and public universities around the world partner with the private sector to provide merit scholarships to university students. Partial scholarships are often given to better-off students, and full scholarships are given to students from disadvantaged backgrounds.
24. Higher education loans typically lack the collateral or guarantee required by banks, as students borrow to finance an investment embodied in themselves. These loans can also be a risk for banks, which do not have full information about the probability of repayment. The student herself may be uncertain about the probability of her graduation or the long-term returns of her higher education.
25. In income-contingent student loans, repayment obligations depend on postgraduation salaries. While these types of loans have been adopted in countries such as Australia, the United Kingdom, and the United States, the requirements in terms of information systems and enforcement are arguably too high to be worthwhile in most low- and middle-income countries.
26. The issue of means testing for student loans is similar to that faced in social programs, and lessons can be found there about how to use valid proxies for income. Social programs can also provide lessons pertaining to community targeting, because families often colocate with other families of similar socioeconomic status. For further discussions on this topic, see, for example, Tekleselassie and Johnstone (2004).
27. In South Africa, for example, university access is limited, even among learners who perform relatively well on the national high school exit exam (van Broekhuizen, van der Berg, and Hofmeyr 2016).
28. Ghana, Kenya, Nigeria, Tanzania, Uganda, and Zimbabwe, for example, have either lowered the academic threshold for women or allocated females bonus points on admissions exams (Morley et al. 2010). In Uganda, a quota system was introduced to select students from each district, persons with disabilities, and sports men and women who meet the minimum requirements of specific institutions and programs (Darvas 2016).
29. There are two key concerns with affirmative action programs: (a) targeting, the extent to which the policies give access to the truly disadvantaged (as opposed to well-off members of disadvantaged groups), and (b) mismatch, the idea that giving

disadvantaged students access to a program of study ill-suited to their preparation and credentials may have little impact or actually make them worse off. Bertrand, Hanna, and Mullainathan (2010) and Robles and Krishna (2012) study affirmative action in India favoring lower-caste students in higher education, and both find a likely trade-off between inclusion and aggregate productivity; Bertrand, Hanna, and Mullainathan (2010) find positive returns for both high- and low-caste graduates, but smaller returns for lower-caste graduates. The smaller magnitude of the returns for lower-caste students suggests that the policy leads to aggregate economic losses, but that important distributional impacts exist and need to be set against these losses. Moreover, Robles and Krishna (2012) find that academic readiness matters. Minority students who enroll in selective majors as a result of affirmative action policies appear to earn lower wages than they would have earned if they had chosen a less selective major. Minority students enrolled in selective majors fall behind their peers in the general student population.

30. Based on School-to-Work Transition Surveys.

31. Based on UIS.Stat data.

32. Several studies have documented the information gaps that families and students have with regard to tuition costs and the applications process and find that this awareness is positively related with parents' education level and income (Hoxby and Avery 2013; Hoxby and Turner 2015). There is also evidence that the complexity of the applications process for financial aid can discourage students from even applying to universities (Bettinger et al. 2012).

33. For a sample of these studies, see http://ingradnet.org/tracer-studies/africa.html.

34. For further information, see http://nuc.edu.ng/pilot-graduate-tracer-study/.

35. Johanson and Adams (2004) analyze the experience of labor market observatories in select countries in Africa. They note that many countries failed to achieve their objectives because they had too many requirements, including lack of capacity for high-quality research, lack of sustained leadership, which can take many years to build, and lack of appropriate incentives throughout for all stakeholders to participate.

References

Arango, Maria, Stuart Evanst, and Zaitun Quadri. 2016. "Education Reform in Chile: Designing a Fairer, Better Higher Education System." Graduate Policy Workshop, Woodrow Wilson School of Public and International Affairs, Princeton University, Princeton, NJ, January.

Asein, Judith, and Yusuf Lawal. 2007. "Admission into Tertiary Institutions in Nigeria." Joint Admissions and Matriculation Board of Nigeria.

Attanasio, Orazio P., and Katja M. Kaufmann. 2009. "Educational Choices, Subjective Expectations, and Credit Constraints." Working Paper 15087, National Bureau of Economic Research, Cambridge, MA, March.

Banerjee, Abhijit, Paul Glewwe, Shawn Powers, and Melanie Wasserman. 2013. "Expanding Access and Increasing Student Learning in Post-Primary Education in Developing Countries: A Review of the Evidence." Post-Primary Education Initiative Review Paper, Abdul Latif Jameel Poverty Action Lab (J-PAL), Cambridge, MA.

https://www.povertyactionlab.org/sites/default/files/publications/PPE%20Review%20 Paper%20April%202013.pdf.

Barrera-Osorio, Felipe, Marianne Bertrand, Leigh Linden, and Francisco Perez-Calle. 2011. "Improving the Design of Conditional Transfer Programs: Evidence from a Randomized Education Experiment in Colombia." *American Economic Journal: Applied Economics* 3 (April): 167–95.

Beaman, Lori, Esther Duflo, Rohini Pande, and Petia Topalova. 2012. "Female Leadership Raises Aspirations and Education Attainment for Girls: A Policy Experiment in India." *Science* 335 (6068): 582–86.

Beine, Michel, Frederic Docquier, and Hillel Rapoport. 2008. "Brain Drain and Human Capital Formation in Developing Countries: Winners and Losers." *Economic Journal* 118 (528): 631–52.

Beine, Michel, Frederic Docquier, and Maurice Schiff. 2008. "Brain Drain and Its Determinants: A Major Issue for Small States." IZA Discussion Paper 3398, Institute of Labor Economics, Bonn.

Bertrand, Marianne, Rema Hanna, and Sendhil Mullainathan. 2010. "Affirmative Action in Education: Evidence from Engineering College Admissions in India." *Journal of Public Economics* 94 (1-2): 16–29.

Bettinger, Eric, Bridget Terry Long, Philip Oreopoulos, and Lisa Sanbonmatsu. 2012. "The Role of Application Assistance and Information in College Decisions: Results from the H&R Block FAFSA Experiment." *Quarterly Journal of Economics* 127 (3): 1205–42.

Bhagwati, Jagdish, and Koichi Hamada. 1974. "The Brain Drain, International Integration of Markets for Professionals, and Unemployment: A Theoretical Analysis." *Journal of Development Economics* 1 (1-2): 19–42.

Blom, Andreas. 2016. "Africa Centers of Excellence: Success and Pitfalls of Results-Based Financing in Higher Education." Presentation at World Bank, Washington, DC, December 7.

Blom, Andreas, Reehana Raza, Crispus Kiamba, Himdat Bayusuf, and Mariam Adil. 2016. "Expanding Tertiary Education for Well-Paid Jobs, Competitiveness, and Shared Prosperity in Kenya." World Bank, Washington, DC.

Campos, Francisco Moraes Leitao, Markus P. Goldstein, Laura McGorman, Ana Maria Munoz Boudet, and Obert Pimhidzai. 2015. "Breaking the Metal Ceiling: Female Entrepreneurs Who Succeed in Male-Dominated Sectors." Policy Research Working Paper 7503, World Bank, Washington, DC.

Cape Higher Education Consortium. 2013. "Pathways from University to Work: A Graduate Destination Survey of the 2010 Cohort of Graduates from the Western Cape Universities." Cape Higher Education Consortium, Cape Town, South Africa. http://www.chec.ac.za/files/CHEC%20Graduate%20Survey%20FULL%20REPORT %20WEB.pdf.

Carnoy, Martin, Manuel Castells, Stephen Cohen, and Fernando Henrique Cardoso. 1993. *The New Global Economy in the Information Age: Reflections on Our Changing World*. University Park: Pennsylvania State University Press.

Chimanikire, Donald. 2009. "Youth and Higher Education in Africa: The Cases of Cameroon, South Africa, Eritrea, and Zimbabwe." Council for the Development of Social Science Research in Africa (CODESRIA), Dakar.

Cloete, Nico, Tracy Bailey, Pundy Pillay, Ian Bunting, and Peter Maassen. 2011. "Universities and Economic Development in Africa." Center for Higher Education Transformation (CHET), Wynberg, South Africa.

Darvas, Peter. 2016. "Tertiary Education in Sub-Saharan Africa." Background note for this report, World Bank, Washington, DC.

Darvas, Peter, Marta Favara, and Tamara Arnold. 2017. *Stepping Up Skills in Urban Ghana: Snapshot of the STEP Skills Measurement Survey*. Directions in Human Development Series. Washington, DC: World Bank.

Darvas, Peter, Shang Gao, Yijun Shen, and Bilal Bawany. 2017. *Sharing Higher Education's Promise beyond the Few in Sub-Saharan Africa*. Washington, DC: World Bank Group. http://documents.worldbank.org/curated/en/862691509089826066/Sharing-higher -education-s-promise-beyond-the-few-in-Sub-Saharan-Africa.

Devarajan, Shantayanan, Celistin Monga, and Tertius Zongo. 2011. "Making Higher Education Finance Work for Africa." *Journal of African Economies* 20 (3): 133–54.

Dinkelman, Taryn, and Claudia Martinez. 2011. "Investing in Schooling in Chile: The Role of Information about Financial Aid for Higher Education." Working Paper 216, Center for Economic Policy Studies, Princeton University, Princeton, NJ, February.

Filmer, Deon, and M. Louise Fox. 2014. *Youth Employment in Sub-Saharan Africa*. Washington, DC: World Bank.

Galvin, John, and Aissatou Sow. 2017. "Leveraging ICTs and Innovative Financing for Education and Economic Development: Lessons from Intel in Africa." Presentation at the World Bank, Washington, DC, February 9.

Gibson, John, and David McKenzie. 2012. "The Economic Consequences of 'Brain Drain' of the Best and Brightest: Microeconomic Evidence from Five Countries." *Economic Journal* 122 (560): 339–75.

Goñi, Edwin, and William Maloney. 2014. "Why Don't Poor Countries Do R&D?" Policy Research Working Paper 6811, World Bank, Washington, DC.

Gurgand, Marc, Adrien Lorenceau, and Thomas Melonio. 2011. "Student Loans: Liquidity Constraint and Higher Education in South Africa." Working Paper 117, Agence Française de Développement, Paris, September.

Hanushek, Eric. 2016. "Will More Higher Education Improve Economic Growth?" *Oxford Review of Economic Policy* 32 (4): 538–52.

Hanushek, Eric, Guido Schwerdt, Simon Widerhold, and Ludger Woessmann. 2016. "Coping with Change: International Differences in the Returns to Skills." IZA Discussion Paper 10249, Institute of Labor Economics, Bonn.

Hino, Hiroyuki, and Gustav Ranis. 2014. *Youth and Employment in Sub-Saharan Africa: Working but Poor*. New York: Routledge.

Hoxby, Caroline, and Christopher Avery. 2013. "The Missing 'One-Offs': The Hidden Supply of High-Achieving, Low-Income Students." *Brookings Papers on Economic Activity* (Spring): 1–66.

Hoxby, Caroline, and Sarah Turner. 2013. "Expanding College Opportunities for High-Achieving, Low-Income Students." SIEPR Discussion Paper 12-014, 201, Institute for Economic Policy Research (SIEPR), Stanford University, Stanford, CA.

———. 2015. "What High-Achieving Low-Income Students Know about College." *American Economic Review* 105 (5): 514–17.

ILO (International Labour Organization). 2016. "World Employment Social Outlook: Trends for Youth 2016." ILO, Geneva.

———. Various years. School-to-Work Transition Survey. Geneva: ILO. http://www.ilo .org/employment/areas/youth-employment/work-for-youth/WCMS_191853/lang--en /index.htm.

Jensen, Robert. 2012. "Do Labor Market Opportunities Affect Young Women's Work and Family Decisions? Experimental Evidence from India." *Quarterly Journal of Economics* 127 (2): 753–92.

Johanson, Richard, and Arvil Adams. 2004. *Skills Development in Sub-Saharan Africa.* Regional and Sectoral Studies Series. Washington, DC: World Bank.

J-PAL (Abdul Latif Jameel Poverty Action Lab). 2017. Description of upcoming impact evaluation, "The Impact of Supplementary Math Courses for Girls in Benin." J-PAL, Cambridge, MA. https://www.povertyactionlab.org/evaluation/impact-supplemen tary-math-courses-girls-benin.

Kaufmann, Katja. 2012. "Understanding the Income Gradient in College Attendance in Mexico: The Role of Heterogeneity in Expected Returns." Working Paper, Department of Economics, Innocenzo Gasparini Institute for Economic Research, Bocconi University, Milan.

Lucas, Robert. 1988. "On the Mechanics of Economic Development." *Journal of Monetary Economics* 22 (1): 3–42.

Lulwana, Peliwe, Gerald Ouma, and Pundy Pillay. 2016. "Challenges in Post-School Education in Sub-Saharan Africa: Selected Case Studies." Education Commission, Washington, DC.

MacGregor, K. 2008. "Case Study: Namibia—University of Namibia." In *Pathways to Higher Education: A Ford Foundation Global Initiative for Promoting Inclusiveness in Higher Education.* Washington, DC: Ford Foundation.

Mambo, Michael M., Muna Salih Meky, Nobuyuki Tanaka, and Jamil Salmi. 2016. *Improving Higher Education in Malawi for Competitiveness in the Global Economy.* World Bank Studies Series. Washington, DC: World Bank Group.

Materu, Peter, and Petra Righetti. 2010. "Quality Assurance in Sub-Saharan Africa." *Research in Comparative and International Education* 5 (1): 3–17.

McKinsey Global Institute. 2012. "Africa at Work: Job Creation and Inclusive Growth." Report, McKinsey Global Institute, New York, August.

MISR (Makerere Institute of Social Research). 2006. "Graduate Tracer and Employers' Expectations in Uganda, 2002." MISR, Kampala, February. http://www.unche.or.ug /publications/tracer-studies/tracer-study-and-expectations.html.

MIT (Massachusetts Institute of Technology). 2016. "Thirteen Universities Adopt MicroMasters and Launch 18 New Programs via edX." *MIT News,* September 20. http://news.mit.edu/2016/thirteen-universities-adopt-micromasters-and-launch-18 -new-programs-via-edx-0920.

Montenegro, Claudio, and Harry Patrinos. 2014. "Comparable Estimates of Returns to Schooling around the World." Policy Research Working Paper 7020, World Bank, Washington, DC.

Moretti, Enrico. 2004. "Estimating the Social Return to Higher Education: Evidence from Longitudinal and Repeated Cross-Sectional Data." *Journal of Econometrics* 121 (1-2): 175–212.

———. 2010. "Local Multipliers." *American Economic Review: Papers and Proceedings* 100 (May): 1–7.

Morley, Louise, Linda Dzama Forde, Godwin Egbenya, Fiona Leach, Amandina Lihamba, Kattie Lussier, and Rosemarie Mwaipopo. 2010. "Widening Participation in Higher Education in Ghana and Tanzania: Developing an Equity Scorecard." University of Cape Coast, Ghana; University of Sussex, United Kingdom. https://assets.publishing.service .gov.uk/media/57a08afbed915d622c000a0d/60335-FinalReport.pdf.

National Universities Commission. 2017. "Accreditation Results Undergraduate Programs." National Universities Commission, Abuja. http://nuc.edu.ng/under graduate-accreditation-results/.

OECD (Organisation for Economic Co-operation and Development). 2013. "World Migration in Figures." A joint contribution by United Nations Department of Economic and Social Affairs and the OECD to the United Nations High-Level Dialogue on Migration and Development, October 3–4. OECD, Paris. http://www .oecd.org/els/mig/World-Migration-in-Figures.pdf.

———. 2015. "Education Policy Outlook: Brazil." OECD, Paris. www.oecd.org/educa tion/policyoutlook.htm.

Reich, Ricardo. 2015. "Chile's New Program for Quality Improvement." International Higher Education, Boston College, Boston, MA. https://ejournals.bc.edu/ojs/index .php/ihe/article/viewFile/6949/6166.

Robles, Veronica C. Frisancho, and Kala Krishna. 2012. "Affirmative Action in Higher Education in India: Targeting, Catch Up, and Mismatch at IIT-Delhi." Working Paper 17727, National Bureau of Economic Research, Cambridge, MA, January.

Romer, Paul. 1986. "Increasing Returns and Long-Run Growth." *Journal of Political Economy* 94 (5): 1002–37.

———. 1990. "Endogenous Technical Change." *Journal of Political Economy* 98 (pt. 2): S71–S102.

Sack, Richard, and Farasoa Ravalitera. 2011. "Tertiary Education in Madagascar: A Review of the Bologna Process (LMD), Its Implementation in Madagascar, the Status of Recent World Bank Analyses and Recommendations, and Suggestions for the Immediate Future." World Bank, Washington, DC.

Salmi, Jamil. 2016. "Tertiary Education and the Sustainable Development Goals: In Search of a Viable Funding Model." Education Commission, Washington, DC.

Sanchez Puerta, Maria Laura, and Mathilde Perinet. 2015. "Kenya STEP Survey Findings." World Bank, Washington, DC.

Saxeenian, Anna Lee. 2002. "The Silicon Valley Connection: Transnational Networks and Regional Development in Taiwan, China and India." *Science Technology and Society* 71 (1): 117–49.

Sekhri, Sheetal, and Yona Rubenstein. 2011. "Public Private College Educational Gap in Developing Countries: Evidence on Value Added versus Sorting from General

Education Sector in India." Working Paper, University of Virginia; London School of Economics and Political Science, November. http://people.virginia.edu/~ss5mj/col legesnov2011.pdf.

Shabani, Juma. 2013. "Quality Regimes in Africa: Reality and Aspirations." *International Higher Education* 73 (May): 16–18.

Tadesse, Tefera. 2014. "Quality Assurance in Ethiopian Higher Education: Boon or Bandwagon in Light of Quality Improvement?" *Journal of Higher Education in Africa* 12 (2): 131–57.

Tekleselassie, Abebayehu A., and Bruce Johnstone. 2004. "Means Testing: The Dilemma of Targeting Subsidies in African Higher Education." *Journal of Higher Education in Africa* 2 (2): 135–58.

Times Higher Education. 2016. "World University Rankings 2016." Elsevier, Amsterdam. https://www.timeshighereducation.com/world-university-rankings/2016/world -ranking#!/page/0/length/25/sort_by/rank/sort_order/asc/cols/stats.

UNESCO (United Nations Educational, Scientific, and Cultural Organization). 2015. *UNESCO Science Report: Towards 2030.* Paris: UNESCO Publishing.

———. 2016. *Education for People and Planet: Creating Sustainable Futures for All; UNESCO Global Education Monitoring Report.* Paris: UNESCO.

UIS (UNESCO Institute of Statistics). 2014. "Higher Education in Asia: Expanding Out, Expanding Up; the Rise of Graduate Education and University Research." UIS, Montreal.

———. Various years. UIS.Stat database. Montreal: UIS.

Urzua, Sergio. 2016. "Lessons from Latin America for Higher Education in Sub-Saharan Africa." Background note for this report, World Bank, Washington, DC.

Valencia Caicedo, Felipe, and William F. Maloney. 2014. "Engineers, Innovative Capacity, and Development in the Americas." Policy Research Working Paper 6814, World Bank Group, Washington, DC.

van Broekhuizen, Hendrik, Servaas van der Berg, and Heleen Hofmeyr. 2016. "Higher Education Access and Outcomes for the 2008 National Matric Cohort." Working Paper 16/16, Stellenbosh University, South Africa.

World Bank. 2009. *Accelerating Catch-up: Tertiary Education for Growth in Sub-Saharan Africa.* Directions in Development Series: Human Development. Washington, DC: World Bank.

———. 2010. *Financing Higher Education in Africa.* Directions in Development Series: Human Development. Washington, DC: World Bank.

———. 2011. *World Development Report 2012: Gender Equality and Development.* Washington, DC: World Bank.

———. 2013a. "Malawi Skills Development Project. Public Appraisal Document." World Bank, Washington, DC.

———. 2013b. "Republic of Sierra Leone: Higher and Tertiary Education Sector Policy Note." World Bank, Washington, DC.

———. 2013c. "STEP-B Implementation Completion and Results Report." World Bank, Washington, DC.

———. 2014a. "Africa Higher Education Centers of Excellence Project: Project Appraisal Document." World Bank, Washington, DC. http://documents.worldbank.org/curated /en/192751467992763313/pdf/PAD3320PAD0P12010Box385466B00OUO090.pdf.

———. 2014b. "World Bank to Finance 19 Centers of Excellence to Help Transform Science, Technology, and Higher Education in Africa." Press release, World Bank, Washington, DC, April 15. http://projects.worldbank.org/P150394/?lang=en&tab =overview.

———. 2015a. "Nigeria: Skills for Competitiveness and Employability." World Bank, Washington, DC.

———. 2015b. "Republic of Mali: Higher Education Support Project; Project Appraisal Document." World Bank, Washington, DC. http://documents.worldbank.org/curated /en/677371468056064986/pdf/PAD11620PAD0P1010Box391421B00OUO090.pdf.

———. 2015c. "Zambia: Education Public Expenditure Review." World Bank, Washington, DC.

———. 2016a. "Higher Education Quality Improvement Project." World Bank, Washington, DC. http://projects.worldbank.org/P150394/?lang=en&tab=overview.

———. 2016b. "What Matters Most for Tertiary Education: A Framework Paper." World Bank, Washington, DC.

———. 2017. "Local Job Creation Multipliers in Turkey." Macroeconomics and Fiscal Management Focus Note, World Bank Group, Washington, DC. http://documents .worldbank.org/curated/en/963901509977684250/Local-job-creation-multipliers-in -Turkey.

———. 2017b. *The Partnership for Skills in Applied Sciences, Engineering, and Technology (PASET)*. Washington, DC: World Bank Group. http://documents.worldbank.org /curated/en/405111468197982834/The-partnership-for-skills-in-applied-sciences -engineering-and-technology-PASET.

———. Forthcoming. *At a Crossroads: Higher Education in Latin America and the Caribbean*. Washington, DC: World Bank.

———. Various years. Skills Towards Employability and Productivity (STEP) Survey. Washington, DC: World Bank.

———. Various years. World Development Indicators database. Washington, DC: World Bank.

Yuchtman, Noam. 2017. "Teaching to the Tests: An Economic Analysis of Traditional and Modern Education in Late Imperial and Republican China." *Explorations in Economic History* 63 (January): 70–90.

Yutronic, Jorge, Ricardo Reich, Daniel Lopez, Emilio Rodriguez, Juan Pablo Prieto, and Juan Music. 2010. "Performance-Based Agreements and Their Contribution to Higher Education Funding in Chile." *Revista Educación Superior y Sociedad* 15 (2).

Zavale, Nelson, Luisa Alcantra, and Maria da Conceição. 2015. "Main Features and Challenges of Implementing Quality Assurance within African Higher Education Institutions: The Case of Eduardo Mondlane University." *International Journal of African Higher Education* 2 (March): 101–34.

Chapter 5

Addressing Skills Gaps: Continuing and Remedial Education and Training for Adults and Out-of-School Youths in Sub-Saharan Africa

Mūthoni Ngatia and Jamele Rigolini

More than two-thirds of workers in Africa have left the formal education system without completing their primary education (UNESCO 2015), and more than 300 million workers are illiterate. This chapter explores ways to provide labor market–relevant skills to people who have already left the formal education system. In addressing the skills needs of this population, policy makers must contend with two sets of trade-offs: (a) between building skills aimed primarily at increasing aggregate productivity and those aimed at improving livelihoods, and (b) between addressing the skills needs of today and those of tomorrow. Much of the training of out-of-school workers happens informally, and policy makers should make greater efforts to improve the quality of informal training. Informal apprenticeships and programs to support self-employment and small-scale entrepreneurship are among the most common. Their impact varies widely, although comprehensive programs that combine training with other forms of support appear to demonstrate more consistent positive impact. The use of technology is a promising avenue to improve the effectiveness and lower the cost of training programs. To avoid excessive fragmentation, policy makers should also pay greater attention to the institutional arrangements in the implementation of training programs.

Introduction

Learning should be lifelong. All persons, at every stage of their lives, should be able to access the knowledge and skills they need in order to pursue their aspirations and contribute meaningfully to their community. Lifelong learning allows workers to upgrade their skills and allows firms to catch up with newer, more productive technologies. However, for the majority of African workers, lifelong learning is more: it is one of the few paths that may lead to a better life out of poverty.

More than two-thirds of workers in Africa have left the formal education system without completing their primary education (UNESCO 2015), more than 300 million workers are illiterate, and more than two-thirds (70 percent) are in low-productivity, low-quality jobs partly because they do not possess the skills sought by labor markets that are becoming increasingly sophisticated (Horne, Khatiwada, and Kuhn 2016). Lack of labor market–relevant skills also drives many people out of labor markets—in particular, formal ones—either because they cannot find employment or, in extreme cases, because they have become too discouraged to look for employment. For these workers, receiving additional training—as part of a comprehensive package of support and in the context of broader reforms—is less a question of boosting economic growth than of helping them to escape unemployment or poorly remunerated and precarious jobs that are often associated with poverty. This chapter explores ways to provide labor market–relevant skills to the significant number of people who have left the formal education system.

Training poor and low-skill youth and workers is a monumental task. In many African countries, a significant proportion of young adults have no education at all (figure 5.1). Overall, 571 million people in Africa are of working age, and at least 300 million are deemed to be illiterate. Each year, millions of poorly trained youths join the ranks of poorly skilled workers. Box 5.1 discusses how the megatrends referred to throughout the report have implications for continuing and remedial education.

This is not, however, a reason to desist from imparting workers with labor market–relevant skills. Even if out-of-school training may lead to modest economic growth, due to the large number of unskilled or low-skill adults, it can make a significant dent in poverty. Taking education as fundamental for the exercise of many human rights, large skill gaps, such as functional illiteracy, are a serious obstacle that goes beyond the mere economic dimension, affecting central aspects of life such as health and active participation in social and civic life.

In addressing training needs, policy makers must contend with various trade-offs: (a) between building skills aimed primarily at increasing aggregate productivity and those aimed at improving livelihoods, (b) between addressing

Figure 5.1 Share of Adults Ages 20–24 with No Education in Sub-Saharan African Countries and Economies

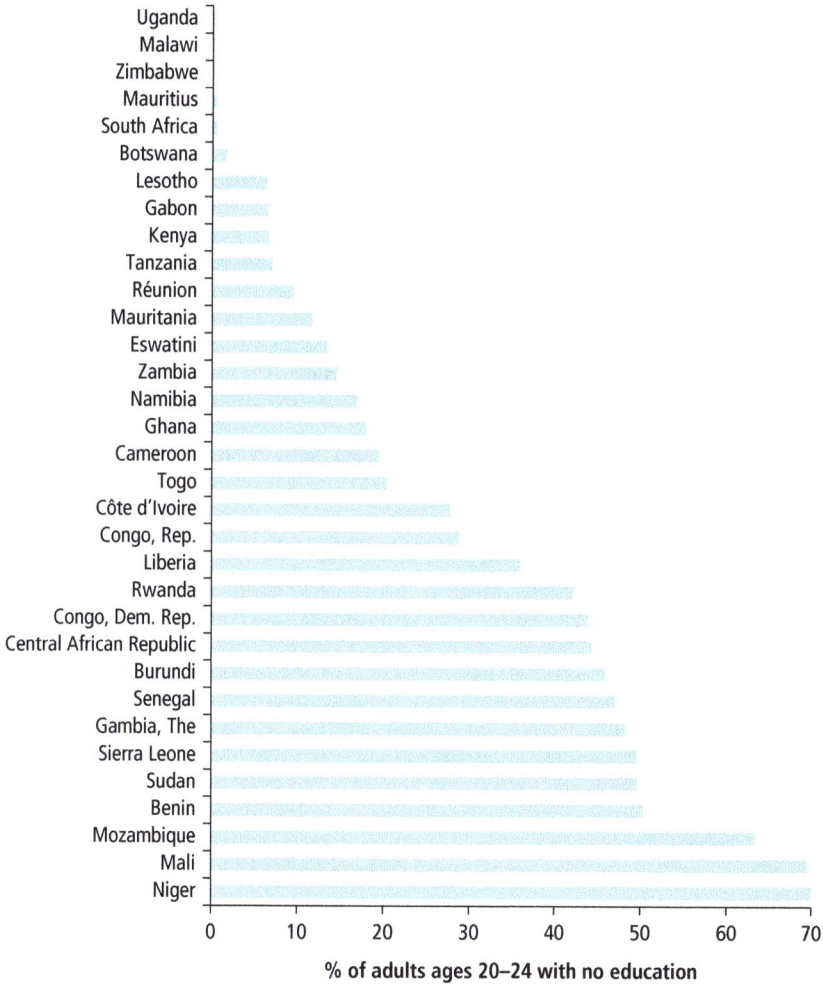

Source: World Development Indicators.

the skills needs of today and those of tomorrow, which may be more foundational, and (c) between investing in today's generation of workers and tomorrow's workers. These trade-offs are reinforced by the fact that, depending on the balance that is chosen, investments would benefit different groups of workers: for instance, high-skill formal sector workers versus low-skill informal sector workers.

BOX 5.1

Megatrends and Continuing and Remedial Education

The megatrends described in chapter 1 will only increase the relevance of—and the challenges faced by—continuing education and training.

Africa has great potential to reap a *demographic dividend* as younger cohorts in the working-age population rise and lower fertility rates free resources to be invested in skills development. However, the high stock of inadequately skilled youths and the increasing flow of entrants into these cohorts create a challenge for Africa's ability to reap the full benefits from the demographic dividend. *Urbanization*, another population trend that is concurrent with the structural transformation of the continent, is characterized by a shift of workers out of agriculture and into services. This shift has impacts on the set of skills demanded by labor markets. At the same time, the agglomeration of workers in urban centers may present opportunities for skills building, as proximity to centers of industry can make training cheaper and better.

The integration of Africa into *global value chains* will promote the adoption of new technologies, which will require retraining and improving the skills of the workforce. Production, manufacturing, and services take place in interlocked global value chains that are currently dominated by China and other East Asian economies. African economies until today have had relatively minor involvement in global value chains. However, this situation is changing. As African economies are improving their investment climate and developing their infrastructure and financial sectors, and as labor costs continue to rise in East Asia, labor-intensive manufacturing is shifting slowly to the continent; however, it is doubtful that manufacturing will be able to absorb the number of workers that it has in other regions (Rodrik 2016). With this shift come opportunities for knowledge transfer and skills upgrading of the workers who take up these jobs.

The third trend is the impact of *digital technologies* and robots and the rapidly changing world of work. As tastes and technologies continue to change rapidly, investments to upgrade skills are important for maintaining economies' competitiveness, innovation, and growth and for allowing economies to appropriate all of the returns from technological progress (Almeida, Behrman, and Robalino 2012). As technology improves, continuing education and training can encourage the adoption of new technologies and the more productive use of existing technologies. Acemoglu and Zilibotti (1999) argue that many of the technologies in use in low- and middle-income countries were developed in Organisation for Economic Cooperation and Development (OECD) countries and, as such, are designed to make optimal use of the skills of richer countries' workforces. Thus, the mismatch between technology and skills in low- and middle-income countries can lead to sizable differences in total factor productivity and output per worker, highlighting an additional role for continuing

(continued next page)

Box 5.1 (continued)

education and training. If strategically adopted, the diffusion of new technologies can simplify the teaching of new skills. Mobile phones, for instance, allow more direct, regular contact with trainees, even in relatively remote and sparsely populated areas. The diffusion of digital technologies also changes the skills needed for work. It is thus important for workers to have an opportunity to learn the skills they need to keep up with new technologies.

Policy makers also need to contend with large differences in the profiles and skills of workers in need of training. Even among low-skill workers, one-size-fits-all solutions do not work. Skills gaps and training needs differ significantly among the worker population, and solutions need to be tailored to the specific needs and profiles of workers and the local labor market. For many rural workers, adult literacy programs coupled with livelihood support may be the most appropriate approach. In urban settings with few employment opportunities, entrepreneurship and self-employment programs can be one way to generate employment for workers with an entrepreneurial mind-set. Finally, training and labor intermediation programs may prove to be effective in settings with job opportunities. Policy makers must also contend with social differences that may affect labor market aspirations and outcomes of subsets of the population, notably gender. All over Africa, women face greater barriers to labor market participation, and unless some of these barriers are addressed, women's training and employment outcomes will remain limited. Ultimately, there will be some workers for whom training may produce few impacts or for whom the cost of training may surpass the ultimate benefits.

The chapter is structured as follows. The first section reviews efforts in Africa to help formal sector workers to adapt to changing production methods and technologies. These formal sector programs are referred to in this chapter as continuing education and training, and the discussion focuses specifically on on-the-job training (OJT) in formal sector firms. The second section discusses programs that address skills gaps caused by educational systems that fail to deliver the skills sought by labor markets. These programs are referred to as remedial education and labor market training programs, which include adult literacy programs, productive inclusion programs (that is, entrepreneurship and self-employment programs), the training components of active labor market programs, and informal apprenticeships. The final section proposes a comprehensive, evidence-based approach to developing continuing and remedial education and training policies on the continent.

Continuing Education and Training

This section examines continuing education provided through OJT by (mostly formal sector) firms. In high-income countries, approximately one-quarter of the human capital that individuals accumulate over their lifetimes is achieved after the schooling process is completed (Heckman, Lochner, and Taber 1998). Workers acquire skills on the job in a variety of ways: in formal courses, informally from colleagues or others engaged in the same occupation, or through learning by doing. Formal firms are more likely to invest in OJT, and information about OJT in the informal sector remains fairly limited. This section therefore focuses mostly on formal sector firms.

Firms invest in workers' skills in order to improve their productivity and to exploit advances in technology, production, and business management. A large body of evidence, mostly from high-income countries, shows that OJT is positively associated with workers' higher wage growth and firms' productivity and innovation (Acemoglu 1998; Barron, Berger, and Black 1997; Bartel and Sicherman 1993). Studies on low- and middle-income countries also suggest that returns from OJT may be larger in low- and middle-income countries (Rosholm, Nielsen, and Dabalen 2007; Sekkat 2011). Estimates from the World Bank Enterprise Surveys reveal strong heterogeneity in countries' provision of OJT—and, overall, firms in Sub-Saharan Africa seem to provide slightly less of it than firms in other regions (figure 5.2).

On average, about 30 percent of formal sector firms in Sub-Saharan Africa provide on-the-job training, compared with 35 percent in the rest of the world. There is, however, variation across regions, and Sub-Saharan Africa's training

Figure 5.2 Share of Formal Sector Firms Offering Formal Training, by Region

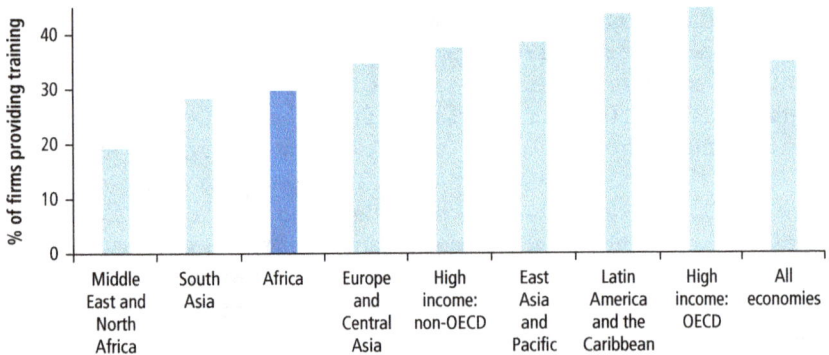

Source: Calculations from World Bank Enterprise Surveys.
Note: OECD = Organisation for Economic Co-operation and Development.

incidence is comparable to that in South Asia, higher than in the Middle East and North Africa, but lower than in East Asia and Pacific, Europe and Central Asia, or Latin America and the Caribbean.[1]

Even within Africa, strong cross-country heterogeneity in formal sector training persists. The percentage of firms offering training varies from 9 percent in Sudan to as high as 55 percent in Rwanda (figure 5.3). Some firm characteristics associated with a higher probability of providing training are the same across all regions: the incidence of OJT is higher among firms that are large or export (figure 5.4) than among firms that are small or do not export. In Sub-Saharan Africa, in particular, 23 percent of smaller firms provide training, compared with 41 percent of medium firms and 52 percent of large firms. Similarly, 29 percent of nonexporter firms provide training compared with 41 percent of exporter firms.

The incidence of training among microfirms is generally even lower than for small firms. In a handful of Sub-Saharan economies, data also exist for formal microfirms (with fewer than five employees; figure 5.5). Microfirms are even less likely to train their workers than small firms—in many cases, less than 10 percent of microfirms do so. There are, however, some notable exceptions: in Burkina Faso and Togo, almost a quarter of microfirms report training their workers.

OJT in the informal sector appears to be much less frequent, although fewer data are available about training in the informal sector. Results from the Kenya Skills Towards Employability and Productivity (STEP) Household Survey (Puerta and Perinet 2016), described in figure 5.6, show that, while almost 30 percent of formal wage workers participated in a training course over the last 12 months, only 7 percent of informal workers did. The results also reveal that self-employed and unpaid workers are less likely to participate in any kind of training. Adams, Johansson, and Razmara (2013) report that in Tanzania, people working in the nonfarm informal sector are less likely to receive any form of training than people working in the private formal sector. They also report that in Ghana, Kenya, Nigeria, Rwanda, and Tanzania, the main factors behind the shortfall in skills include unequal access to training by firms in the informal sector, underdeveloped markets for skills provision to the informal sector, lack of attention from public training providers to the needs of the informal sector, and market constraints to training for small and household enterprises in the informal sector, specifically financial and informational constraints.

The public sector also does not appear to offer substantial OJT, although the data are limited. Data from the International Labour Organization's (ILOs) School-to-Work Transition Surveys suggest that there is limited training, with some variation among countries—close to no training in Benin, one-fifth of the public workforce in Tanzania, one-quarter in Zambia, and more than one-third of the public workforce in Liberia.

Figure 5.3 Share of Firms Offering Formal Training, by GDP per Capita, 2015

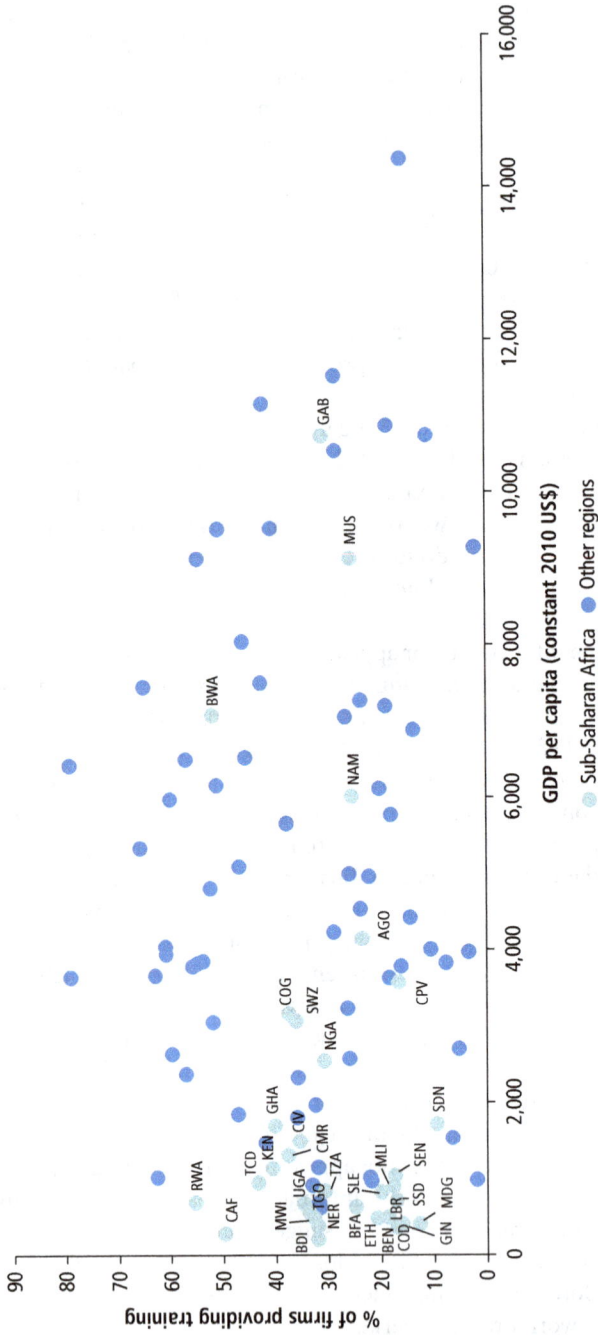

Source: Calculations from World Bank Enterprise Surveys.

Figure 5.4 Share of Firms Providing On-the-Job Training, by Size of Firm and Region

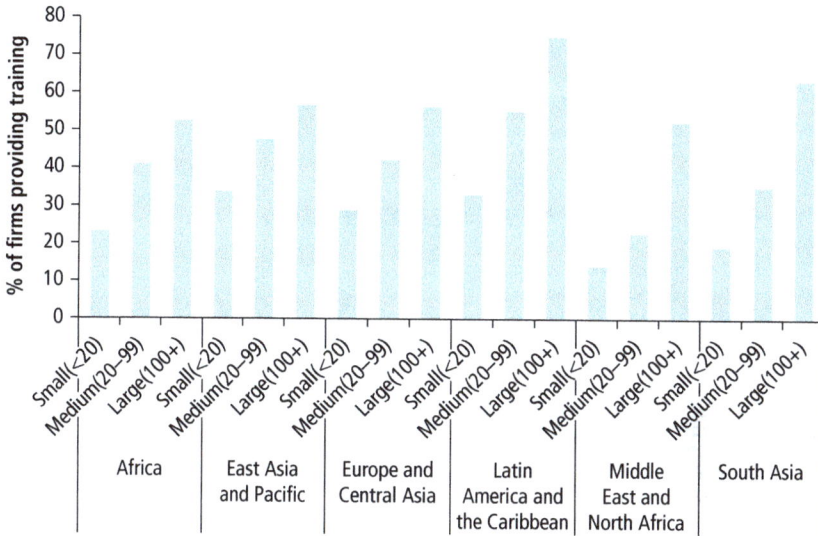

Source: Calculations from World Bank Enterprise Surveys.

The training received is likely to be heterogeneous in its quality and intensity. One additional dimension to consider is how relevant the training is for workers' productivity. Receiving training in a big firm on a sophisticated piece of machinery is not the same as receiving three hours of training in a microfirm on basic bookkeeping principles. Unfortunately, given the existing data, it is not possible to gauge either the quality or the intensity of training. These factors need to be considered when assessing the effectiveness and pertinence of training and its impact on productivity.

Larger firms, exporting firms, foreign-owned firms, and firms assessing the obstacle of "inadequately educated workers" (or "skills") as being more severe than other obstacles are more likely to provide training. Perotti (2017) identifies correlates of training using regression analysis and pooled Enterprise Survey data from all regions and for Sub-Saharan Africa separately. Results from the pooled regressions confirm the finding that larger firms and exporting firms are more likely to provide training. In addition, firms with at least 10 percent foreign ownership are also more likely to train their workers than entirely domestically owned firms. Firms in the Enterprise Surveys also are asked to rate the severity of each of 15 business environment obstacles. Firms whose assessment of the obstacle "inadequately educated workers" (or "skills") as being more severe than their average assessment for all 15 obstacles are also more likely to

Figure 5.5 Share of Firms Providing Training in Sub-Saharan Economies with Enterprise Survey Data on Microfirms, by Size of Firm

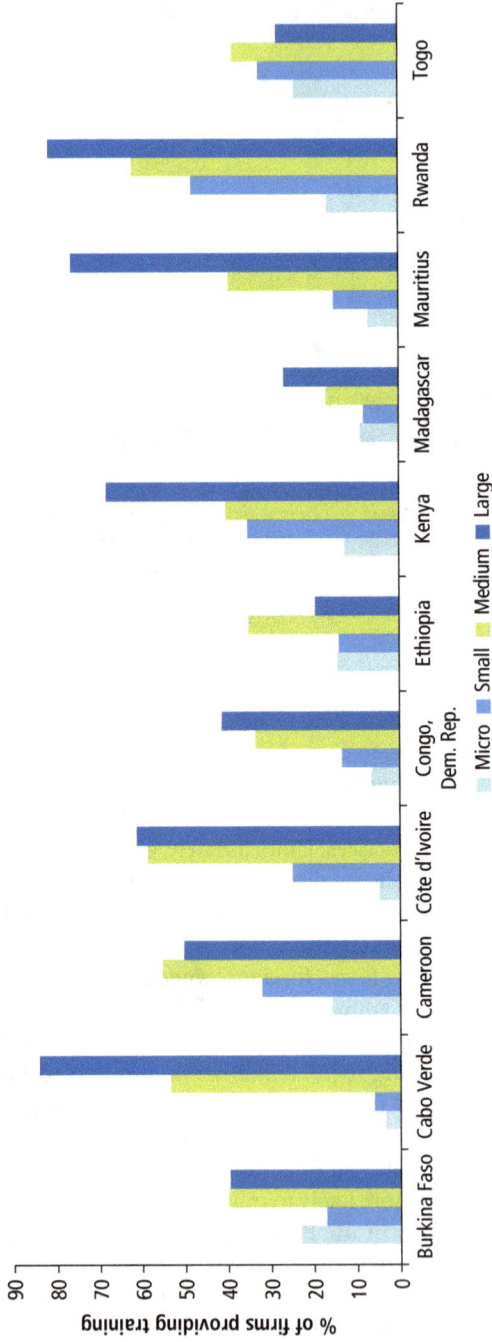

Source: Calculations from World Bank Enterprise Surveys.

Figure 5.6 Participation in Training Programs in Kenya, by Type of Worker, 2013

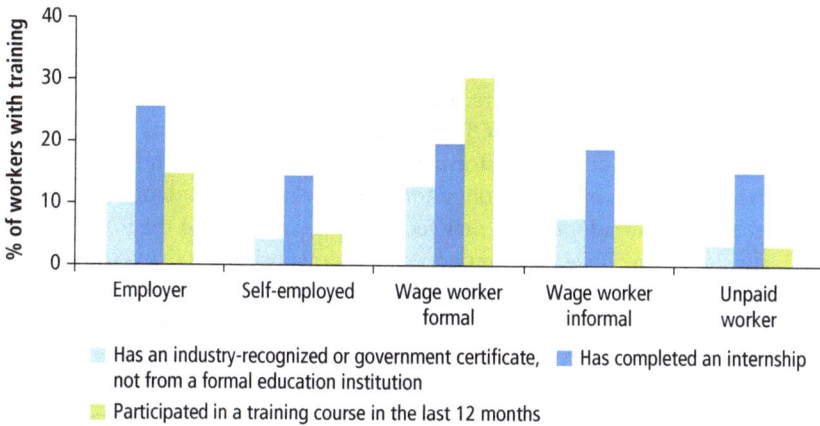

Source: Puerta and Perinet 2016, based on Skills Towards Employability and Productivity (STEP) Survey findings.

provide training. Finally, higher labor productivity (of either manufacturing or services firms) is associated with a higher probability of providing training. When the analysis is restricted to the Sub-Saharan Africa region, however, neither the exporting status nor foreign ownership appears to matter for training. In contrast, years of experience of the top manager are strongly and positively correlated with the provision of training. In addition, results seem to suggest that the "skills" obstacle only matters for training when it is perceived as the top obstacle, not when it is just more severe than the average obstacle. As in the pooled results, firms with higher labor productivity are also more likely to provide training.

Addressing the complex environment in which some African firms operate may help to improve investments in OJT. Many African countries are characterized by low population density and much higher ethnolinguistic diversity than other regions, leading to less mingling and merging of peoples and poor market integration (Collier and Gunning 1999). A high level of diversity may increase the costs of OJT and limit the ability of firms to take advantage of economies of scale. Trust in the judicial system also appears to be low overall on the continent. Fafchamps (1996) reports that fewer than 10 percent of Ghanaian firms said that they would go to court following a dispute with a supplier or a client. Fafchamps (2003) presents evidence that African manufacturing firms operate in an environment characterized by the risk of contractual nonperformance. These uncertainties may reduce firms' propensity to make long-term investments, including in OJT. For some firms, credit constraints may also limit training. Gunning et al. (2003) show that, among firms with a demand for credit, only a quarter obtain a formal sector loan, which may impede investments in OJT, especially for small and medium firms.

Public sector interventions may have a role to play in encouraging more OJT on the continent. A question remains about whether governments *should* directly subsidize formal firms' OJT. To the extent that structural factors, such as credit constraints or lack of information about returns, are binding, training subsidies may be an effective policy tool. However, to the extent that deeper factors, such as low adoption of new technologies, are behind the low levels of OJT, subsidies may have little impact or end up subsidizing firms that would have trained their workforce anyway.

The public sector can also play a role in promoting skills development in the informal sector. The informal sector faces several barriers that may prevent skills upgrading. These barriers include the high opportunity cost of time spent in training for workers in small informal sector firms; credit constraints; the failure of training to respond to the multiskill needs of the informal sector; and information asymmetries, in that informal firms may be less likely to know about the opportunities that exist and the returns to training (Adams, Johansson, and Razmara 2013). Successful interventions may need to address more than one factor. In addition, the question of financing is far from trivial (box 5.2).

BOX 5.2

National Training Funds

National training funds are financial mechanisms, usually outside normal government budgetary channels, intended to incentivize training. Johanson (2009), in a review of national training funds, reports that in Sub-Saharan Africa payroll training levies are the principal source of financing. Earmarking payroll levies in the context of volatile budgets can provide a protected source of steady funding for training, but it is important to redistribute funds equitably across firms. There is, for instance, strong unevenness in training rates between small, medium, and large enterprises (Paterson and Du Toit 2005). Since small firms generally operate in different sectors than larger firms, sectoral levies may exacerbate disparities in training offered by locking resources within rather than across sectors.

Johanson (2009) synthesizes the best practices in the design and operation of levy-financed training funds and suggests the need to take the following factors into account:

- *Financing.* Governments should consider carefully which levies work best and under what circumstances. For instance, payroll levies may not be appropriate in

---

(continued next page)

Box 5.2 (continued)

low-income countries where the industrial base is limited and capacity to generate income from levies is weak. Governments should consider how to collect funds efficiently with minimal administrative overhead and should periodically adjust the levy rate to respond to shortfalls or surpluses. These funds should be secure and not diverted to other government purposes.

- *Coverage.* Global coverage may be desirable since it permits funds to be allocated where needs are greatest, but governments have to balance these needs against the need for ownership, which sectoral levies provide. Allowing firms more say in the administration of training funds can increase their buy-in, since they pay the taxes used to finance these funds. Funds also need to consider how to cross-subsidize training for the informal sector (such as in South Africa, where 20 percent of funds go to the National Skills Fund to train the unemployed).

- *Training providers.* Funds should minimize giving preference to funding training providers that they own because such preference may lead to inefficiencies in training and crowd out other private or nongovernmental actors.

Addressing Skills Gaps of Poor and Vulnerable Workers: Remedial Education and Training

Most workers in Africa, young and old, have large skills gaps that affect their employability and productivity in both formal and informal labor markets. Many workers do not possess the foundational or technical skills needed to make use of more advanced technologies; some also lack the socioemotional skills required to operate in increasingly complex environments, where skills such as punctuality, critical thinking, and ability to work in teams are of growing importance.

These skills gaps affect both firms' productivity and workers' earnings and employability. They also contribute to the difficult transition that many young people face when leaving school and looking for job opportunities. Skills gaps affect not only the present employment prospects of youth, but also their ability to climb the income ladder by acquiring the skills required by better-remunerated jobs.

The sheer magnitude of these skills gaps calls for action to mitigate some of their negative impacts. In the following discussion, training programs aimed at bridging the skills gaps of the current workforce, arising from deficiencies in their formal education years, are denoted as remedial education and training. These programs include adult literacy programs, comprehensive programs that mix training with internships and labor market insertion, and informal apprenticeships. The section reviews the typical components of these programs, how widespread they are in Africa, the labor market impacts they should be expected to have, and implementation challenges they are facing.

Hard, but Feasible: The Complex Task of Training Out-of-School Workers

Although it may seem paradoxical, a healthy dose of skepticism is in order. The impacts of remedial education and training programs should be gauged against what they are designed to accomplish—patching skills gaps and mitigating some of the effects. Their impacts are therefore likely to remain modest. One cannot expect people to assimilate in a few weeks or at most months what the formal education sector has failed to provide over years or even decades. Moreover, schooling is only one of the many factors affecting learning outcomes. Among other factors, the household environment is also essential to foster learning, and many people in need of remedial education and training come from socioeconomic backgrounds that hinder, rather than favor, learning. Compared with children, youths and adults may also have higher opportunity costs associated with their time and be less inclined to spend many hours in training. Finally, as box 5.3 highlights, the older one becomes, the more challenging it is to learn new skills.

BOX 5.3

Adults Do Learn—Although Differently

Recent evidence from cognitive psychologists and neuroscientists demonstrates that the adult brain is capable of learning. Cognitive psychologists have shown that engaging in learning tasks can strengthen cognitive skills throughout adulthood, even into the seventh and eighth decades of life, and recent advancements in brain imaging have allowed neuroscientists to verify the theories developed by cognitive psychology within the structure of the brain.

In the absence of ongoing learning, aging is accompanied by declines in cognitive ability. However, engagement in learning activities or tasks that require significant cognitive processing attenuates and even reverses these declines. Additionally, positive developmental attributes of aging, such as emotional self-control, insight, and improved self-efficacy, provide a positive "scaffolding effect" that enhances learning (Hoare 2006).

Literacy acquisition in adulthood is a special case of learning, given the complexity of the task and the number of brain areas implicated. Reading is not a skill learned passively or automatically. Learning to read, even for children during the optimal period of brain development, requires instruction and studying. Reading is a skill that involves multiple regions (lobes) of the brain, beginning with visual recognition of letters and words and culminating in comprehension (Abadzi 2006).

The first stage of learning is the process of *decoding*. Beginner readers of any age tend to start by recognizing small "graphemic" units (letters and syllables) and translating the graphemic units phonologically into their associated sounds. Over time, the reader is then able to process larger graphemic units or words (Aker and Sawyer 2017).

(continued next page)

Box 5.3 (continued)

Decoding skills and word-level accuracy are critical to achieving *automaticity* in reading. Defined as "the ability to read quickly and fluently," automaticity is the second phase of literacy development and contributes to sentence-level comprehension. Research suggests that adults who learn to read in adulthood read more slowly than those who learn to read as children, even when they are as accurate in their decoding (Dehaene et al. 2010). However, continued instruction and practice in decoding may improve reading speed and performance, which implies that adults may need more study and practice than children to achieve the same level of automaticity.

Finally, the third phase of literacy development is *comprehension*. For this phase, metacognitive monitoring—also known as "thinking about thinking"—is critical. Metacognitive monitoring helps the reader "to detect a lack of understanding so that it can be corrected" (Cromley 2005). While adults develop strong metacognitive abilities in daily life (for example, problem solving around work tasks), these skills do not automatically translate to reading comprehension. And because metacognitive monitoring interacts with decoding and background knowledge during reading, it is often more difficult for readers to use metacognitive monitoring if they have a low level of decoding skills (Cromley 2005).

Learning to read, especially the process of decoding, also involves changes in the left posterior brain region (occipital lobe), known as the visual word form area (VWFA) (McCandliss, Cohen, and Dehaene 2003). Unlike children, adults who learn to read exhibit competition in the VWFA between face and word recognition or decoding (Dehaene et al. 2010). The limited plasticity of the VWFA in adulthood implies that adults may require additional instruction, studying, and practice to learn decoding skills. Curricula for literacy programs need to be tailored to the ways adults learn and their lifestyles.

Most adult literacy programs, unfortunately, manage to teach adults decoding skills, some automation, but more rarely comprehension, limiting the benefits that adults can draw from these programs (although impacts on numeracy, also an essential skill, are somewhat higher). Programs are often poorly tailored to adults' lifestyles, leading to high dropout rates, low motivation, and few opportunities to practice what they have learned.

Accordingly, the few impact evaluations of adult literacy programs in low- and middle-income countries tend to find modest impacts. The majority of empirical research on adult education programs in Sub-Saharan Africa has focused on the impact that different teaching methods or pedagogical (andragogical) approaches have on learning. Overall, these studies find that adult education classes have larger impacts on math skills than on reading skills and primarily on decoding as opposed to comprehension. Many of these studies have also found impacts of relatively small magnitude; even if the impacts on decoding are statistically significant, few adults achieve the threshold of 1.5 words per second (Aker and Sawyer 2017). These modest effects are also explained by low enrollment and high dropout and are characterized by rapid skills depreciation (Royer, Abadzi, and Kinda 2004).

Source: Aker and Sawyer 2017.

Figure 5.7 Impact on Earnings Outcomes across Categories of Youth Employment Programs

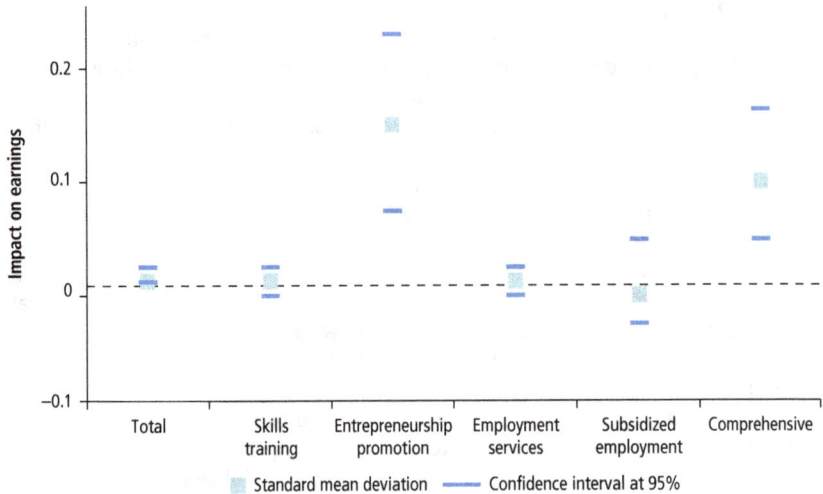

Source: Goldin and Hobson 2015, adapted from Kluve et al. 2017.

For all of these reasons, remedial education and training programs show, on average, modest impacts. Apart from adult literacy programs, training programs are usually part of a more comprehensive labor activation package that may include the injection of capital in the form of grants or loans for programs supporting small-scale entrepreneurship or job-search support for programs supporting wage employment. Because such programs are part of a package of services, it is sometimes challenging to assess their effectiveness in promoting employment and earnings. These caveats notwithstanding, some lessons are emerging from an increasingly large number of evaluations. A meta-analysis of youth employment programs from Kluve et al. (2017) summarizes the findings and shows that most employment programs deliver positive but relatively small impacts—even on youths, who, among the workforce, may be the most apt to be trained (figure 5.7).

The meta-analysis also provides a few additional lessons. First, there is a fair amount of heterogeneity across programs, largely because each category includes programs with substantially different design features, and even small changes in design can make a substantial difference in impacts. Table 5.1 shows the heterogeneity in characteristics of training programs (Valerio, Roseth, and Arias 2016). The duration of training ranges from a few days to a year; the content delivered ranges from pure technical training to socioemotional skills; costs

Table 5.1 **Variation in the Characteristics of Remedial Education and Training Programs**

Characteristic	Detail
Duration	Between three days and one year
Type of training	In classroom, on the job
Type of content	Vocational, life skills, socioemotional skills, job market, business development, business management
Type of beneficiaries	Rural youth, existing business owners, long-term unemployed, former soldiers, many more
Delivery	Public training providers, private training providers, nongovernmental organizations, local artisans
Cost	Between US$400 and US$30,000 per participant
Financing	Stipends, grants, vouchers, taxes, out-of-pocket (work, family)

Source: Adapted from Valerio, Roseth, and Arias 2016.

range from a few hundred to several thousand dollars; and there is high varia-tion in the target population, the underlying vulnerabilities that programs aim to address, and the ability of beneficiaries to improve their employment and earnings opportunities.

A second lesson is that training is most effective when associated with other program components, such as internships, capital injection, certification, or labor insertion support. Accordingly, comprehensive programs, which often include training as part of a broader package that usually also comprises intern-ships and labor insertion support, have on average a larger impact than pro-grams of narrower scope. Finally, for many youths—especially in low-income countries—capital constraints seem to be an important obstacle to better employment and higher earnings. This is reflected in the relatively high average returns of a new wave of entrepreneurship programs, many of which include, for new entrepreneurs, a grant component to start a new business. This also reflects the reality of many unskilled workers in Africa who often start their career working in a small shop as an unpaid family worker or an apprentice and who may not have the resources to become independent.

The diversity in training programs also reflects the diversity in workers' pro-files that these programs need to address. Although most poor and vulnerable workers are active in the informal sector, their profiles can differ significantly. Some workers may be literate, while others may not be able to read. A signifi-cant proportion may be working in agriculture, while others may be working in small urban shops. And there are also significant differences across gender (box 5.4). Accordingly, one-size-fits-all solutions are not likely to work—it is important to develop a system that directs beneficiaries to programs addressing their specific needs.

BOX 5.4

Adapting Training and Employment Programs to Gender-Specific Needs

An important factor behind the modest impacts of many training programs is their failure to adapt to the profile and needs of the beneficiary population. An often overlooked dimension is gender. Chakravarty, Das, and Vaillant (2017) identify several constraints that may put women at a disadvantage with respect to men:

- *Skills.* Education systems and families often fail to build adequate skills for productive employment. Women are disproportionally affected due to lower average educational attainment, possibly tied to social norms or lower expected returns to human capital investment.

- *Capital.* Asset endowments and access to finance are a stronger barrier to business creation and growth for women than for men, which limits the impacts of entrepreneurship training on women.

- *Networks and role models.* Poor signaling of skills and trust and weak institutions for contract enforcement lead employers to rely on word-of-mouth for hiring—implicitly favoring men in the labor market and diminishing the attractiveness of training for women.

- *Time, family formation, and care responsibilities.* Family formation and domestic responsibilities limit the amount of time available to women for training and work.

- *Occupational choice.* Women tend to be concentrated in low-return sectors, again diminishing the attractiveness of training.

- *Safety and mobility.* Lack of safe transport and working conditions leads to suboptimal allocations of labor and may affect women's dropout from training.

If programs fail to consider these potential constraints, they may face lower take-up rates for women, leading to higher dropout and lower impacts. At the same time, not all constraints are always binding.

Source: Adapted from Chakravarty, Das, and Vaillant 2017.

The overall picture suggests that training out-of-school youths is hard, but feasible, and that program design matters. Some of the less successful programs may not be tailored to the way the target population learns, may not teach properly the skills that the target population needs to succeed in the labor market, and may not pay proper attention to labor market demand. One of the lessons to draw from the average modest impacts shown in figure 5.7 is the need to experiment more with *how* to teach skills to improve labor market outcomes and to evaluate programs properly, as lessons can be drawn from both successes and failures. Emerging successes from programs that are making efforts to adapt curricula to beneficiaries' profiles and vulnerabilities are discussed below.

Adult Literacy and Second-Chance Programs

In spite of substantial progress, many adults in Sub-Saharan Africa remain illiterate and have poor numeracy skills. The United Nations Educational, Scientific, and Cultural Organization (UNESCO) Institute for Statistics estimates that adult literacy rates in Sub-Saharan Africa are approximately at 60 percent, implying that 4 adults out of 10 are not able to read functionally (figure 5.8).[2] There are also significant gender disparities, with close to two-thirds of adult males being literate, compared with half of adult women in the region.

A large literature has demonstrated how basic literacy and numeracy skills allow people to operate better in the labor market and, ultimately, to access better jobs. Figure 5.9 uses comparable labor force surveys across countries to estimate earnings premiums to reading literacy. It shows that, apart from Armenia, people with reading literacy earn a premium that varies between 10 and 30 percent. And premiums are at their highest levels in the two African countries in the sample—Ghana and Kenya—possibly because of the relatively lower number of people with reading literacy.

Figure 5.8 Adult Literacy Rates, by Region, circa 2015

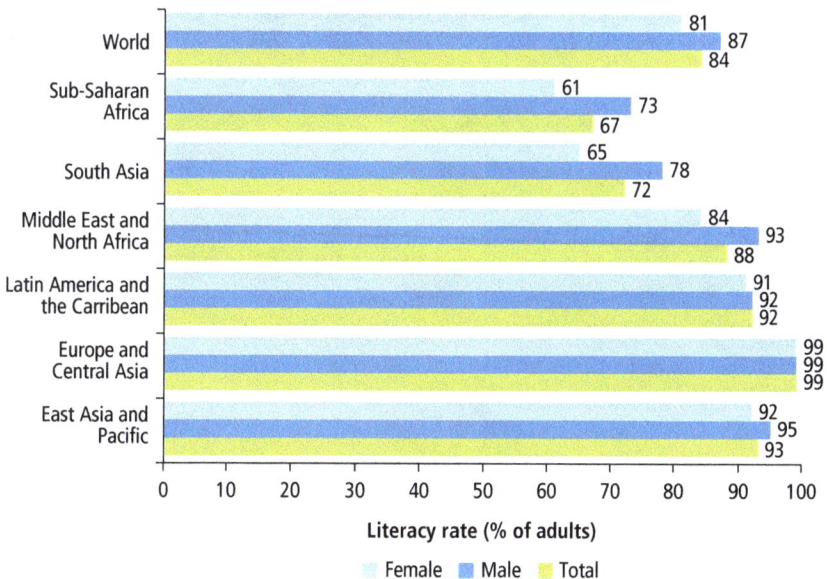

Literacy rate (% of adults)

Female ■ Male ■ Total

Source: World Development Indicators.

Figure 5.9 **Earnings Premium to Reading Literacy in Select Countries**

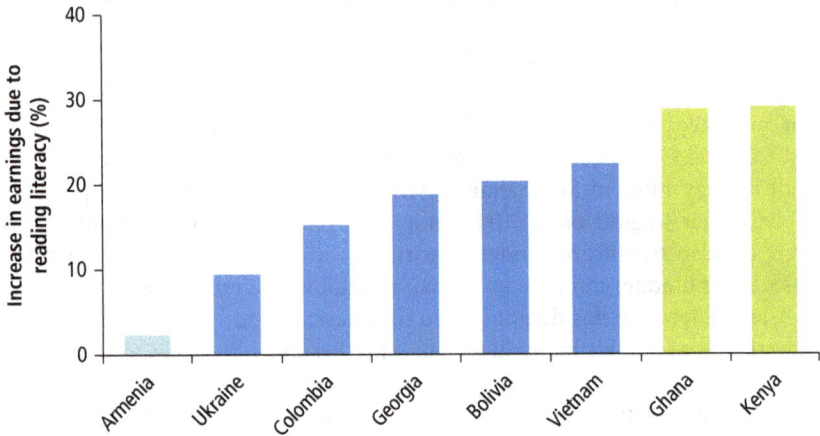

Source: Valerio et al. 2016.
Note: Workers 25–64 years old in urban areas.

There is therefore a strong rationale for adult literacy and second-chance programs, which have been widely implemented across the continent but suffer from important flaws that have led to modest impacts (box 5.5). In addition to programs led by nongovernmental organizations (NGOs), most governments implement adult literacy, basic education, and second-chance programs. A 2009 UNESCO review finds that most programs remain small in scale and coverage given the scope of illiteracy (Aitchison and Alidou 2009). Program coverage is estimated to be about 100,000 for Eritrea, 130,000 for Kenya, 200,000 for Malawi, 410,000 for Mozambique, 30,000 for Namibia, 390,000 for Nigeria, 1,300,000 for Tanzania, 230,000 for Uganda, 40,000 for Zambia, and about 20,000 for Zimbabwe. It also finds that programs have weak links with the Ministry of Education and that staff tend to be poorly paid and poorly trained (Aitchison and Alidou 2009). Many programs are also characterized by low and volatile attendance rates, high dropout rates, limited skills attainment, and rapid skills depreciation (Aker and Sawyer 2017). Similarly, some programs have facilitators who are inadequately pedagogically prepared.

Improving the impacts of adult literacy programs may also help to promote gender equity. Literacy is an essential element of empowerment, both socially and through the labor market. Sub-Saharan Africa not only displays the lowest literacy rate in the world, but also, together with South Asia, one of the highest gender gaps (figure 5.8). And despite the gender disparity, or

BOX 5.5

The Kha Ri Gude (Let Us Learn) Adult Literacy Program, South Africa

The Kha Ri Gude Adult Literacy Program is a multilingual national adult literacy program in South Africa, implemented by the Department of Basic Education. The program began in 2008 with the goal of enabling 4.7 million adults (above 15 years old) to achieve literacy and numeracy in 1 of the 11 official languages by 2012. The program includes people living with disabilities.

By 2012, the program had helped 2.8 million learners to become literate, with teaching delivered by 40,000 educators (volunteers who receive a stipend) and managed by approximately 4,000 supervisors and 400 coordinators. The program has achieved a remarkably high completion rate of 90 percent (McKay 2015).

The program was designed with key principles of adult learning in mind: instruction includes a strong focus on basic literacy skills, including decoding and automaticity; "dosage" of instruction is higher than most programs, offering 240 hours of instruction over six months (usually through three classes of approximately three hours per week), which is, for example, more than twice the average of American literacy programs; class sizes are also relatively small, with 15–18 students per educator.

The program's curriculum teaches the foundational skills of reading, including decoding skills such as phoneme-grapheme isolation, phoneme identification, and phoneme categorization, and develops automaticity through word cards and phonic domino games. The goal is for students to achieve a reading speed of 45 words per minute.

Source: Aker and Sawyer 2017.

perhaps because of it, gender is rarely a focus of the adult education agenda (Aker and Sawyer 2017; Hayes and Flannery 2000). To close the gap, programs not only need to make efforts to enroll women (which they often do—literacy programs tend to cover more women than men), but also need to address women's constraints beyond the training sessions (which they often do not). These approaches may include adapting the hours to women's schedules, offering safe transportation and child care services, and coupling literacy training with socioemotional interventions that help to empower women in the household and in the labor market.

In spite of the challenges, adult literacy programs remain an important tool in helping the most destitute to achieve more productive and socially more active lives. There should be more experimentation in designing programs that suit the way adults learn and that fit the many constraints they face in terms of motivation, time, and competing demands. Aker and Sawyer (2017) posit that adult literacy programs should consider the following aspects:

- *Ensure that teaching material is sequenced properly, from decoding to automaticity to comprehension.* While this is not so different from learning in children, adults may need to "work harder" to respecialize to a new task (that is, decoding new information).

- *Provide more practice to "make things stick"* (Knowland and Thomas 2014). Given the limits of brain plasticity and the difficulty for adults to "respecialize," exercises and practical applications are especially relevant for adults. Such approaches include having aids to assist with decoding and automaticity as well as group discussions to assist with comprehension and evaluation.

- *Ensure that the curriculum focuses on metacognitive skills, not just decoding.* Metacognitive skills are critical for comprehension, yet difficult to teach, and little research has been done on their impact on adult learning.

- *Recognize the opportunity costs to learning for busy adults.* A substantial body of research suggests that school dropout in some countries increases significantly at the age when children can start working. Strategies to address this connection have included linking social assistance programs with the demand for social services, such as conditional cash transfers and agricultural extension programs. Similar strategies may be required for adults, although more research is needed. The use of technology also shows promise: for instance, the use of mobile phones means that learners do not have to be physically present in a classroom. Further still, linking learning to goals that adult learners may have (such as learning numeracy skills to be able to operate their mobile phone) can lead to further success. In addition, women who have lower literacy may face particular constraints to achieving literacy. Box 5.6 presents a promising program in India that made it more likely that women would enroll in and complete literacy classes.

- *Ensure that teaching pedagogy is specific to adult learners* (that is, andragogy), rather than a "one-size-fits-all" approach to education.

Training Programs Supporting Livelihoods and Small-Scale Entrepreneurship

Training programs supporting livelihoods and small-scale entrepreneurship are among the most widespread remedial training programs on the African continent. They take various forms, including public works with a training component supporting entrepreneurship in West Africa, comprehensive programs with a significant training and coaching component aimed at improving the productivity of the rural poor, and programs promoting small-scale

BOX 5.6

The Saakshar Bharat Adult Literacy Program, India

The Saakshar Bharat Adult Literacy Program is a nationwide literacy program in India, designed to address low literacy among adult women in particular. The program was launched in 2009 to address the persistent gender gap in literacy rates and is administered by the Indian Department for School Education and Literacy. The program's goals include raising the national literacy rate to 80 percent and reducing the literacy gender gap to 10 percent by providing basic literacy to 70 million people, 60 million of whom are women. The program is available to persons between the ages of 15 and 35 who have aged out of the formal education system.

The program organizes and delivers classes through adult education centers that have been established in gram panchayats (local governments at the village level). Each adult education center is staffed by two coordinators, at least one of whom must be a woman. Local residents are trained to be adult educators and provide literacy classes to 8–10 learners per class. The adult education centers also offer additional resources, such as library facilities, athletics, and other courses. This is part of the program's objective of establishing an institutionalized adult education system that will be operated in conjunction with the formal education system for children.

The program seems to be moving toward achieving its goals. The 2011 census showed that India's literacy rate is 74 percent, an increase of 9 percent from the 2001 census. While the women's literacy rate remains lower than men's (65 and 82 percent, respectively), the gender gap in literacy rates has improved by more than 5 percentage points (declining from 22 percentage points in 2001 to 16 percentage points in 2011).

Source: Aker and Sawyer 2017.

entrepreneurship and improvements in the productivity of existing small-scale entrepreneurs. Their impacts vary considerably, although programs that combine training with grant support have shown more consistent positive impacts.

In rural areas, comprehensive programs aimed at improving the productivity of the rural poor have had encouraging results (box 5.7). An evaluation of the pooled impacts of six similarly designed productive inclusion programs in Ethiopia, Ghana, Honduras, India, Pakistan, and Peru finds positive impacts on consumption, income, food security, households' assets and financial position, and mental health (Banerjee et al. 2015). These pilots were comprehensive in scope and included a one-time transfer of a productive asset; a regular transfer of food or cash for a few months to about a year; technical skills training on managing the particular productive assets; high-frequency home visits; savings promotion strategies; and, except for the Ethiopian program, a health component. Although they tend to be relatively expensive (usually a few

BOX 5.7

Agricultural Extension Programs

More than half (56 percent) of Africa's labor force work in agriculture, where, especially among smallholders, productivity is dismally low. In many countries, Sub-Saharan Africa's farmers have strikingly low levels of formal education, an average of less than four years for rural adult males and less than three years for rural adult females (World Bank 2007). Improving farmers' skills can have significant impacts on productivity, for instance, through the adoption of improved seeds and better farming techniques.

Efforts to improve the skills of farmers are often delivered as part of agricultural extension services, which cover the spectrum of services to support people engaged in agricultural production. Skills upgrading among farmers includes transferring information from the global knowledge base and from local research to farmers and stimulating desirable agricultural development (van den Ban and Hawkins 1996). Extension operations have been among the largest individual-based development operations undertaken to date. Some effective community-based and farmer-to-farmer extension approaches have had large, positive cost-benefit ratios of 7.7 in Ghana, 6.8–11.6 in Malawi, and 14.2 in Uganda (Wellard et al. 2013). In spite of the potential, however, agricultural extension in Africa has not lived up to expectations. Technological adoption is still woefully low, and many farmers do not know about the existence of technological innovations, much less how to use them.

Publicly provided agricultural extension systems in many African countries are very limited. In Malawi and Zambia, these expenditures currently account for less than 15 percent of total annual public expenditures in agriculture. By contrast, input subsidy programs in these countries have accounted for more than 60 percent of public agricultural expenditures in recent years (Goyal and Nash 2017).

Several challenges have led to low levels and low quality of agricultural skills provision. Agricultural extension services are prone to information asymmetries, since farmers may not know the potential gains from upgrading the skills or where to go to get them. In addition, given that many of the small-scale farmers who need to receive agricultural skills training are often small and spatially dispersed and given poor transportation infrastructure, the costs to reach them are often high. This may lead to equilibria where the poorest farmers in greatest need of skills upgrading are underserved.

The externalities of farmer skills upgrading, together with the strong evidence of its potential benefits through well-executed agricultural extension, make a strong case for public intervention. Advancements in information and communication technology (ICT) potentially are also making it less costly and easier to reach smallholder farmers. Among others, ICT can overcome problems of access by reducing the cost of extension visits, enabling more frequent two-way communication between farmers and agents, and improving agents' accountability (Cole and Fernando 2012).

thousand U.S. dollars per beneficiary), with the exception of the Honduran program, all of the programs achieved benefits greater than their costs (ranging from 133 percent in Ghana to 410 percent in India). Although the impacts of training alone have not been evaluated in rural livelihoods programs, follow-up is a core element of their design. The Building Resources Across Communities' (BRAC) Targeted Ultra-Poor Program in rural Bangladesh, for instance, offers initial classroom training, followed by livestock specialist visits to beneficiaries every one to two months for the first year of the program and program officer visits every week for the first two years (Bandiera et al. 2013).

From a public policy perspective, scaling up these programs presents a few challenges—notably their costs and how to provide comprehensive support through a series of interlinked programs (as opposed to pilots in which the same service provider can provide all of the services). In spite of these challenges, efforts to scale up these pilots through national programs are showing encouraging results (Escobal and Ponce 2015). In scaling up these pilots, it will be important to identify the elements of the comprehensive support that are essential for the program's success. These elements will, most likely, depend on the specific context and households' main vulnerabilities, although training will always be an essential component.

Complementing these rural programs, especially in urban settings, are comprehensive small-scale entrepreneurship and firm training programs. These programs provide training alone or a mix of business skills training and cash support to a variety of target populations, including vulnerable youths, women, university graduates, and small-scale entrepreneurs.

Some firm training programs have shown promising results, even among medium firms. For instance, Bloom et al. (2013) provided free consulting on modern management practices to a randomly chosen set of medium firms in India. The training raised average productivity 11 percent, increased decentralization of decision making, and increased the use of computers. The authors suggest that information barriers were the primary factor explaining the lack of prior adoption.

Overall, however, the efficacy of business training programs targeting small and medium enterprises has been mixed—in particular, when training is provided in the absence of start-up capital. McKenzie and Woodruff (2013) review several impact evaluations of business training programs (mostly targeted to small firms). They find that training has relatively modest impacts on survivorship of existing firms and some evidence that training programs help prospective owners to launch new businesses more quickly. Moreover, firm owners tend to implement some of the practices taught in training, although the magnitude of these improvements is often modest.

Business training programs may be relatively less effective for women, although a new wave of programs is showing promising results.

Unfortunately, few evaluations of business training programs compare the impacts of training on women and men (McKenzie and Woodruff 2013), but the evidence suggests that business training may be less effective for women than for men. Giné and Mansuri (2011) find that the impacts of a business training program in Pakistan were mostly observed for men. Berge, Bjorvatn, and Tungodden (2015) also find that the effects of a training program in Tanzania were weaker for women in terms of investments in profitable sectors, improved sales, and improved profits. A new wave of programs has, however, been testing alternative forms of training, and evidence is emerging that women may respond better to personal initiative training than to traditional business training. A program in Ethiopia (the DOT Reach Up! training program) offering women training on basic technology and business skills, combined with modules fostering self-esteem and entrepreneurial spirit, led to 30 percent higher profits than in the control group (Alibhai, Buehren, and Papineni 2016). A program in Togo is finding similar results for both men and women.

These low average impacts do not mean that entrepreneurship and self-employment training programs do not work. Rather, more efforts should be invested in understanding what are, given the local context, the main constraints to entrepreneurship and in adapting training and overall program design to these constraints. As with all programs, target population, context, design, and implementation issues can affect returns substantially. For instance, Honorati and Cho (2013) look at 37 impact evaluation studies of entrepreneurship programs and find that financing support is more effective for women, while business training is more effective for existing entrepreneurs. In Togo, Campos et al. (2016) provided training to existing entrepreneurs and compared training on how to improve business practices and personal initiative training aimed at helping entrepreneurs to become more proactive and resilient to obstacles. They find that personality-based training in soft skills has greater short-term impact, resulting in higher sales and profits, to a large extent because owners who received entrepreneurial personality training tend to work longer hours and are more likely to introduce new products. In South Africa, Anderson, Chandy, and Zia (2016) look at how different types of business training benefit entrepreneurs with different profiles. They find that marketing-sales skills are significantly more beneficial for firm owners who have had less exposure to different business contexts. In contrast, finance-accounting skills are significantly more beneficial for entrepreneurs who have been running a more established business prior to training. McKenzie and Puerto (2017) also study the impact of the ILO's Gender and Enterprise Together training program for low-income female business owners and find that, after three years, women who participated in the program were earning 15 percent higher profits and experiencing improvements in their mental health and subjective well-being.

Again, providing comprehensive support that addresses individuals' multi-faceted vulnerabilities helps to improve impacts. Liberia's Economic Empowerment of Adolescent Girls and Young Women (EPAG) skills training program was designed to alleviate the barriers facing young women entering the labor market. The program provided six-month training in either job skills targeted to sectors with high demand or business development skills; six-month support for job placement or links to microcredit, depending on the training received; and other training and support, such as life skills training, small group learning, a business plan competition, mentorship, savings accounts, child care, and transportation. The project proved to be a cost-effective intervention for women entering the business skills track (where, based on increased earnings, the cost of the intervention could be recovered within three years), although less so for women entering the job skills training (where 12 years would be needed to recover the cost of the intervention; Adoho et al. 2014).

Recent programs mixing training with cash grants to address credit constraints also appear to have had good impacts (box 5.8). In Ethiopia, Blattman and Dercon (2016) compare the attractiveness of a small-scale entrepreneurship program giving participants business training plus US$300 versus providing a job in low-skill manufacturing. While manufacturing workers showed a high propensity to quit for better and less hazardous employment opportunities, participants in the entrepreneurship program raised earnings 33 percent and were able to work steady hours. In a successful program in Uganda, youths were invited to form groups and submit grant proposals for vocational training and business start-ups. The selected groups received grants of US$382 per member. Blattman, Fiala, and Martinez (2014) find that the program increased business assets 57 percent, work hours 17 percent, and earnings 38 percent.

BOX 5.8

Public Works and Training in Côte d'Ivoire

A new generation of public works includes a training component in participants' work programs. The evaluation of a public works project targeting youths in Côte d'Ivoire shows some of the challenges in integrating training components directly into safety net projects.

The project offered a subset of beneficiaries two types of training: *basic entrepreneurship training* (100 hours) aimed at building skills to help youths to set up and manage a small nonagricultural microenterprise and *training on wage job-search skills* and sensitization to wage job opportunities (80 hours), which provided information on wage job opportunities, job-search skills and techniques, a more professional

(continued next page)

Box 5.8 (continued)

environment during the public works programs, and skills certification to facilitate signaling on exit from the program.

Both components led to modest, if any, impacts, although the trainings were effective in improving participants' knowledge of basic entrepreneurship and job-search skills. They also led youths to apply these skills in practice, either by intensifying their search for a wage job (for example, using a curriculum vitae for a job search, using ads for a search, or applying independently) or by setting up a new activity (for example, undertaking a market study or preparing a business plan). However, these changes in skills and practices were not sufficient to generate earnings beyond those generated by the basic public works program (Bertrand et al. 2017). Findings are similar for a public works program in Sierra Leone that also attempted to integrate a training component, with limited success.

Experience from other regions also highlights the challenges of integrating training into social assistance. El Salvador's public works program, for instance, added a training component for urban youths. The program led to positive but modest medium-term improvements in beneficiaries' labor market outcomes that persisted after the program ended, but dissipated over time (Beneke de Sanfeliú 2014). These modest impacts are not a reason to desist. The evaluation in El Salvador suggests that greater impacts could have been achieved by adapting the training better to beneficiaries' skills and employment opportunities in the labor market and by improving intermediation efforts. To be successful, training and labor market programs have to pay greater attention to people's skills and the local context and to focus on the beneficiaries of safety net assistance who show a higher likelihood of succeeding in the labor market.

Training Programs Supporting Self- and Wage Employment

Training programs supporting self- and wage employment rarely stand alone: they usually form part of a larger comprehensive package that may include technical and soft skills training and job search support. This trend is welcome news, both because training alone tends to have much lower impacts and because pure classroom training without on-the-job learning tends to be ineffective (Almeida, Behrman, and Robalino 2012).

The distinction between self-employment and wage employment is often blurred. For instance, Kenya's Youth Empowerment Project targeted unemployed youths between 15 and 29 years of age with at least eight years of schooling. It provided a mix of life skills and technical training, with on-the-job experience provided through internships in the private sector. Although the program was designed to foster wage employment by encouraging employers to retain interns at the end of the training, some elements of entrepreneurship support were introduced for youths interested in starting a new business (Honorati 2015).

A first group of interventions supporting self- and wage employment comprises programs training vulnerable beneficiaries (often out-of-school youths) with a mix of classroom and on-the-job training, internships, and job-search support. These programs tend to be based on the design of Latin America's Jovenes programs, which, on average, have been shown to have positive, albeit relatively small, impacts on employment, often relatively more concentrated among women (González-Velosa, Ripani, and Rosas Shady 2012). The experience with Liberia's EPAG training program also shows the need to consider the labor market and the availability of job opportunities when designing interventions aimed at improving wage employment. Box 5.9 describes a promising private sector, self-sustained initiative that trains workers in the garment industry in Cape Town.

BOX 5.9

A Private Sector Self-Sustained Initiative: Cape Town's Feel Good Project

Not all training programs need public support, particularly when the private sector sees the benefits of training potential workers. Established in 2008, the Feel Good Project (tfgP) is an innovative civil society project between Learn to Earn, a nongovernmental organization, and the Foschini Group, a South African retailer.

The Feel Good Project is a training program based on a retail supply chain business model consisting of three functional departments: stores, garment repair, and warehouse distribution. Twice yearly, trainees are recruited into these three departments

THE **FEEL GOOD** PROJECT

Doing good never goes out of fashion.

(continued next page)

Box 5.9 (continued)

and provided with classroom and on-the-job training in the skills required by each department. The training happens in tfgP stores, which buy customer returns, limited samples, rejects, and overruns from the various Foschini Group brands, recondition them, and then sell them in the stores. Proceeds generated from the sales across tfgP stores are fed back into the project, and the costs of training are covered by sales from the shops, leading to a self-sustaining financial model.

Upon successful completion of the six-month training program, trainees are given the opportunity to undertake a six- to eight-week internship with an organization whose business is related to the skills trained within the tfgP stores, garment repair, and warehouse departments—usually within the Foschini Group. In 2014, around 75 trainees began the training, and 56 managed to complete it. Both trainees and the Foschini Group benefit from the partnership. Participants receive training and employment opportunities; the Foschini Group receives access to a prescreened, trained workforce.

Sources: Interviews with tfgP staff; http://www.learntoearn.org.za.

A second group of programs aims to strengthen formal vocational and training centers as well as national qualifications and certification frameworks. These programs are widespread, especially in countries with a tradition of formal apprenticeships. The effectiveness and challenges faced by these programs are discussed in chapter 3.

Finally, a third group of programs aims to strengthen existing informal training arrangements—in particular, apprenticeship training in the informal sector, which is by far the most widespread skills development channel throughout Africa, as it caters mainly to the poor and youths with low educational attainment (Adams, Johansson, and Razmara 2013; Franz 2016). For instance, Darvas and Palmer (2014) estimate that in 2005–06, more than 440,000 Ghanaian youths ages 15–24 were participating in informal apprenticeship training. Informal sector training accounted for 80 percent of all basic skills training, public sector training accounted for 7 percent, and private training institutions accounted for 13 percent. In Rwanda, 81 percent of all small and medium enterprises employ apprentices, and around 43 percent of all employees in the surveyed companies had undergone training as apprentices (Johanson and Gakuba 2011). In Senegal during the mid-2000s, an estimated 384,000 apprentices were employed in the automotive sector (Walther and Filipiak 2008).

Apprenticeships in the informal sector differ from apprenticeships in the formal sector along various dimensions, including length, contractual arrangements, quality of training, certification, and costs (table 5.2). In particular, information about training opportunities is lacking; most master craftsmen

Table 5.2 Common Patterns of Apprenticeship Training in the Formal and Informal Sectors

Characteristic	Formal sector	Informal sector
Target group	New labor market entrants, young people with or without prior technical and vocational training	Young people, with or without prior work experience
Duration	Long term	Long term, but also sometimes shorter and product specific
Location of training	Combination of workplace learning and school-based training	Workplace is main learning location, rarely complemented by school-based basic training modules
Objective	Obtain a formal qualification	Reach occupational proficiency
Certification	National certification, in some cases also company-specific certification	Declaration of completion by master craftsmen or business association, if any; usually no nationally recognized certification
Contractual arrangements	Formal apprenticeship contract, based on labor or apprenticeship legislation, safeguarding of basic labor rights	Written or oral agreement between master and apprentice or his family, no formal protection of labor rights
Financial arrangements and social security	In most cases (but not always), apprentice is entitled to apprenticeship wage or allowances (compensation payment), as well as basic social security stipulated by law or collective agreement	Differs from country to country—apprentice may pay a training fee to the master, but may also receive some support for living expenses and some wage with increasing productivity
Training contents and standards	Defined through curriculum and training plan and according to stipulated training standards	Traditionally no curriculum or training standards
Entry requirement	Formal education certificate	Traditionally no or low education entry requirement, but level of education required is increasing
Entry and access	Formal sector recruitment procedures or facilitated by training institution	Informal, network-based arrangements between master and family

Source: Adapted from Franz 2016.

operate in a heavily constrained environment with limited opportunities for updating their skills; many youths land informal apprenticeships without key foundational skills; and the quality of the training provided varies widely.

While all informal apprenticeships have a training objective, differences between and within countries are large. In some countries, such as Benin, apprentices or their families have to pay master craftsmen to be hired as apprentices, and master craftsmen decide when the apprentice is ready to graduate—often for an additional fee, which may lead to situations where trained workers remain "trapped" as apprentices even though they have been trained successfully (Davodoun 2011). In Senegal, no initial fee is required, and apprentices often leave training before it is completed (Aubery, Giles, and Sahn 2016). And although apprenticeship training in Senegal often follows early school leaving, apprentices in Malawi are relatively old (23.4 years on average) when they start their informal training, having tried other options before embarking on an informal apprenticeship (Aggarwal and Hofmann 2010). Reflecting their informal nature, strong differences persist even within countries. In Senegal, for instance, training lasts 5 years on average, but can extend up to 10 years (Aubery, Giles, and Sahn 2016). Important gender differences are also evident: the same survey reports that in Senegal a third of working-age men have been apprentices, compared with only 11 percent of women. Women and men also select different trades, and apprenticeships tend to be much shorter for women— 2.6 years for women compared with 4.3 years for men.

In spite of being often a second-best choice, given how widespread informal apprenticeships are, it is important to explore ways to make them more productive. Informal sector apprenticeships became the subject of development interventions on a larger scale during the 1980s. The National Open Apprenticeship Scheme, which started in 1987 in Nigeria (Adam 1995), the Informal Sector Training and Resources Network (ISTARN) project in Zimbabwe (ISTARN 1999), and initiatives in Benin and Togo (Walther and Filipiak 2008) are early examples of government or development partners investing in informal sector apprenticeship training. Nowadays, interventions to strengthen and develop informal sector apprenticeship training can be found in many countries. For example, in 2000 in Benin, SwissContact introduced dual training in the informal sector. Especially in Benin and Togo, the reorientation toward traditional apprenticeship training was embedded in a broader technical and vocational education and training (TVET) policy, which moved toward introducing dual training principles into informal sector apprenticeship training (Walther and Filipiak 2008).

Key elements in those and subsequent interventions usually include measures to improve the quality of training through the introduction of dual training principles (that is, classroom and OJT), the training of master craftsmen, and technology upgrading; measures to improve working conditions and inclusion in informal sector training (promotion of gender equality, occupational health and safety); measures to introduce formal recognition or certification of informally trained artisans and to improve recognition of the existing (traditional) certification system; and measures to institutionalize or improve quality assurance, with the involvement of local business associations (Franz 2016). In spite of these attempts, little has been evaluated formally, and attempts to give structure to informal apprenticeships and bring them closer to formal ones have failed to pick up scale. For instance, the National Vocational Training Institute in Ghana conducted 27,000 trade tests annually between 2001 and 2007, covering a broad range of trade areas (construction, mechanical, automotive, electrical, agriculture, textile, hospitality, printing); of these, only a small number of candidates were apprentices from the informal sector, while the majority came from public and private training institutes (Darvas and Palmer 2014). Similar findings have been reported from Malawi (Aggarwal and Hofmann 2010).

Ultimately, informal apprenticeships exist for the same reasons that an informal sector exists. Policy interventions should not attempt to make informal apprenticeships look like formal ones. Unless the deep, underlying drivers of informal activity are being resolved, attempts to formalize informal apprenticeships will likely have low take-up and modest impacts. Rather, the policy question should be how to improve the learning process of apprentices while recognizing the informal (and weakly enforceable) nature of the underlying training agreements.

What's Next? Toward a Roadmap for Effective Continuing and Remedial Education and Training Policies in Africa

The success of training programs depends very much on their ability to adapt to the profile of trainees and to respond to the needs of labor markets (box 5.10). But even under ideal implementation standards, some programs appear to work better than others. At the same time, some of the best-performing programs may not be scalable, and the modest impacts of some other programs must be gauged against the deep and widespread vulnerabilities they try to remedy. In designing continuing and remedial education and training policies, it is important to weigh carefully all of these complex—and at times opposing—elements. Adding to the complexity is the fact that, in spite of a surge in rigorous evaluations, there is still much we do not know about what works and what does not and even less about *why* programs may or may not work.

Overall, further efforts could be invested in improving the quality, cost-effectiveness, and coverage of existing programs, which are insufficient to address the enormous training needs of the out-of-school workforce. Many of the successful interventions that have been reviewed in this chapter are relatively small and expensive. Part of the challenge resides in the low public investments in remedial education and training of the out-of-school workforce. There are, unfortunately, no cross-country data on spending on remedial education and training. But data on spending on active labor market programs (which include, in part, training programs) from the World Bank's ASPIRE (Atlas of Social Protection Indicators of Resilience and Equity) database suggest that overall spending is low: from a sample of 22 Sub-Saharan countries for which data are available, median spending on active labor market programs is 0.1 percent of gross domestic product (GDP). Whether spending should be higher depends, in part, on competing and equally justified priorities, some of which relate to the megatrends. But undoubtedly, it is not possible to cover all of the needs for better and greater coverage of remedial education and training programs with the limited resources that many countries have allocated.

Next, the chapter sketches what could be relatively effective continuing and remedial education and training policies in Africa. Much more experimentation

BOX 5.10

Tailoring Programs to People: The Importance of Profiling

It is now widely recognized that obstacles to effective early child development can substantially affect long-term labor market performance. And differences in well-being, skills, personality, and preferences grow wider with age, affected by the family and community in which children and youths live, the quality of the schooling they receive, the role models with whom they are in contact, and the (lack of) opportunities they are given in life. By the time youths are ready to enter the labor market, differences in technical and socioemotional skills, motivation, aspirations, contacts, preferences, and socioeconomic status are such that the ability to find employment differs significantly across labor market entrants. Moreover, the type of employment where people will likely be more successful also will depend on the characteristics of their profile.

It is therefore important to tailor programs and their objectives to the profile of candidates that a program aims to attract. A frequently overlooked corollary of this statement is that standardized programs covering a wide range of the population are bound to have little or no impact. Rather, it is important to develop different programs for different profiles. In addition, some programs will be much more expensive than others, with much lower placement rates. For each program, selecting the "right" candidates implies excluding a wide range of applicants. For instance, Harambee, an organization that trains and places vulnerable youth in South Africa, only accepts around 10 percent of the initial pool of applicants.

Profiling also happens in the informal sector—we simply may not call it so. Hardy and McCasland (2015), for instance, study the market for informal apprenticeships in Ghana and argue that the requirement of posting a bond to start the apprenticeship is a way for employers to learn about the candidate's motivation and potential productivity. These asymmetries of information not only support the need for profiling, but also generate a space for public intervention. In Ghana, the bond prevents capital-constrained candidates from applying for apprenticeships. Developing other tools to screen candidates for motivation and productivity (such as time-consuming assessment tests) can thus improve the matching.

and evaluation will be needed, but, based on existing evidence and current vulnerabilities, it is possible to begin identifying programs that may work better than others. Based on the magnitude of some of the skills and employment gaps, three broad groups of programs may be worth further experimentation, evaluation, and investment: adult literacy programs, programs to improve the productivity of the self-employed, and programs to support informal apprenticeships (figure 5.10).

Figure 5.10 Mapping Employment and Vulnerabilities to Programs

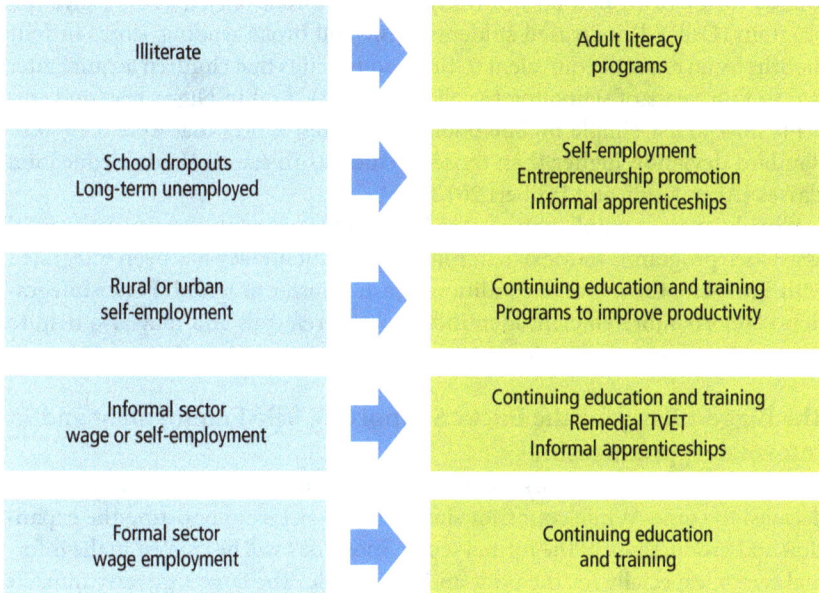

Illiterate	➡	Adult literacy programs
School dropouts Long-term unemployed	➡	Self-employment Entrepreneurship promotion Informal apprenticeships
Rural or urban self-employment	➡	Continuing education and training Programs to improve productivity
Informal sector wage or self-employment	➡	Continuing education and training Remedial TVET Informal apprenticeships
Formal sector wage employment	➡	Continuing education and training

Note: TVET = technical and vocational education and training.

Experiment and Expand with a New Generation of Adult Literacy Programs

Existing adult literacy programs have had modest impacts, especially in shifting people's reading ability from decoding to comprehension. But modest impacts are not a reason to abandon them. More than 300 million people are illiterate throughout the continent, a handicap that is severely affecting their ability to improve their earning opportunities. Research about *how* adults learn differently needs to be included in the design of a new generation of adult literacy programs, which considers andragogy and people's constraints and incentives, and new approaches need to be piloted and evaluated to improve the success rate.

Because little is known, however, it may be advisable to go back to the drawing board and start small (but in many places), until further evidence emerges on the best way to teach adults basic literacy and numeracy skills. However, starting small should not be a pretext for inaction: rather, it should be an incentive to implement as many innovative pilots as possible in the next years.

There is also great potential to improve the effectiveness (and costs) of adult learning by experimenting with new technologies. Combining standard teaching with distant learning with mobile phones, for instance, is a promising avenue. In Los Angeles, an innovative mobile phone–based adult education program (Cell-Ed) increased students' basic and broad reading scores in four months by an amount equivalent to the reading skills that children acquire after two to four years of schooling (Ksoll et al. 2014). And in Niger, teaching students how to use simple mobile phones led to test scores that were 0.19–0.26 standard deviation higher than those of students in standard adult education classes (Aker, Ksoll, and Lybbert 2012).

Finally, there is ample potential to better integrate adult literacy with social assistance programs. In Mexico, for instance, adult literacy has been integrated with Prospera, the national conditional cash transfer program. Better integration supports more efficient identification and referrals and may also help to improve take-up and retention rates.

The Biggest Bang for the Buck? Supporting Self-Employment and Informal Apprenticeships

The vast majority of the working population in Africa will remain informal for decades to come. While countries should not desist from boosting the expansion and productivity of the formal sector, most jobs will be created in the informal sector, especially for the poor and vulnerable. The largest poverty impacts will therefore reside in boosting the employability and productivity of informal sector workers. Rather than trying to formalize workers or the training of workers, the focus should be on seeking effective ways to improve the productivity of workers independent of their formality status. In fact, most attempts to put a formal structure on top of informal activity have led to poor results. A more promising generation of programs is doing the opposite—accepting the informal nature of most jobs and training agreements and focusing on improving the quality of training.

Concretely speaking, three types of programs are beginning to show results and are worth further investigation. The first type consists of comprehensive programs to improve agricultural productivity in rural areas (figure 5.11). As discussed, these programs consist of a mix of extension, livelihood, and cash

Figure 5.11 How to Support Informal Sector Productivity and Employability: A Skills Perspective

Rural areas	Urban areas
Improving agricultural productivity	Entrepreneurship programs	Support to informal apprenticeships

support, and the scaling up of pilots is showing promising results, although ample space remains to experiment with different designs to improve cost-effectiveness. These programs may be most appropriate for countries that are lagging in transformation and that employ most of their workforce in agriculture.

The second type consists of programs that train new and existing small entrepreneurs in business skills and help them to address some of the capital constraints they may be facing. Such programs can be implemented in both rural and urban areas and are also showing interesting results. The main challenge with entrepreneurship programs is their cost (particularly if they also support beneficiaries with start-up capital) and the extent to which they are scalable. Beneficiaries of these programs often are active in a narrow set of fields, such as hairdressing or car repair. Accordingly, while small pilots may show promising returns, if too many people become active in these fields, they may soon face decreasing returns (that is, there can be only so many hairdressers before earnings start to fall). The challenge going forward is therefore to expand the reach of these programs to new and promising activities. It is also vital to link training to broader aggregate demand, for instance, by linking the training provided to small firms to the needs of larger enterprises in the economy. These programs are appropriate in most African countries, but particularly in those that are lagging in transformation.

In implementing entrepreneurship and livelihood programs, attention should also be paid to institutional arrangements and the need to avoid excessive fragmentation. Many NGOs support livelihood and entrepreneurship programs; even within government, programs similar in nature are often implemented by various ministries, such as the ministries of youth, community development, and agriculture. To some extent, diversification allows for greater experimentation and adaptation to the local context and profile of beneficiaries. But excessive fragmentation may also lead to inefficiencies, such as heterogeneities in the coverage of specific geographic areas or profiles of beneficiaries, and higher administrative costs. The adoption of national education and social protection strategies is beginning to address some of these inefficiencies; nevertheless, the agencies in charge often do not have the financial means and institutional power to play an effective coordinating role.

Finally, a promising area of intervention consists of programs supporting informal apprenticeships. These programs typically provide master craftsmen with incentives to improve the quality of their training and apprentices with incentives to complement OJT with classroom training, without the ambition of integrating these training efforts in the formal TVET stream. While such programs have been implemented in various forms throughout the continent, very few of them have been implemented on a large scale.

Two interesting examples are elements of Kenya's Youth Employment and Opportunities Project and Ghana's National Apprenticeship Programme.

In Kenya, the project targets youths who are without jobs and have experienced extended spells of unemployment or who are currently working in vulnerable jobs. It provides three months of training and three months of internship experience in both the formal and informal sectors; for OJT in the informal sector, it supports the training of master craftsmen to improve the quality of their teaching. In a subsequent phase, the project also aims to provide selected individuals with seed capital to start their own businesses. In Ghana, the National Apprenticeship Programme, based on the traditional apprenticeship model common across West Africa, is offering master craftsmen a financial incentive by paying them a bonus if their apprentices perform better in a skills assessment at the end of the training. A formal evaluation of the Ghanaian program is ongoing, but evaluation of similar programs targeting the formal sector suggest that they have the potential to become effective tools to improve productivity (Hicks et al. 2011). Given the magnitude of informal apprenticeship arrangements in most African countries, it is worth investing more in the implementation, experimentation, and evaluation of these programs.

Continuing Education and Training: Proceed with Caution

Formal sector firms in Africa do, on average, provide their workers with limited opportunities to obtain continuing education and training, and one could easily conclude that there is scope for incentivizing continuing education. However, it is necessary to understand first the reasons why many formal firms underinvest in training. On the one hand, to the extent that firms do not use cutting-edge technologies, training the formal sector workforce without addressing the technology side of the challenge may deliver only modest results. On the other hand, if the underlying reasons for low investment levels relate to credit constraints or high staff turnover, the rationale for public interventions becomes stronger. In countries that are more advanced in transformation but lagging in reforms, policy makers should pay greater attention to creating the appropriate policy environment for OJT to take place.

Juggling Harsh Policy Trade-offs

The realm of remedial and continuing education and training is a place where the harsh policy trade-offs discussed in chapter 1 may be difficult to solve. The trade-offs lie between skills building aimed primarily at increasing aggregate productivity and skills building aimed at improving livelihoods, between addressing the skills needs of today versus addressing the foundational skills needs of tomorrow, and between investing in today's generation of workers and investing in tomorrow's workers.

Among the large numbers of youths and working-age adults in need of skills upgrading, two distinct groups need different interventions. The first (significantly smaller) group consists of higher-skill workers in sectors of the economy that are growing and productive: for these workers, continuing education and OJT play an important role in allowing for technology upgrades and productivity growth. At the same time, the majority of workers in Africa are either poor or at risk of falling into poverty, unemployed or underemployed, and active in low-productivity jobs. For these workers, providing remedial education and training is an effective poverty alleviation and inclusion strategy aiming to improve their modest earnings, but having little impact on productivity growth overall. The presence of these two distinct groups of workers also highlights the complexity of choosing between investing in skills for the future (through continuing education and OJT), which may not have immediate poverty impacts, and investing in skills for the present (through remedial education and training), which may help to alleviate poverty but contribute little to productivity growth. Policy makers need to be cognizant of these trade-offs in choosing the right mix of programs and balancing the needs for productivity and inclusion.

Notes

1. Only the most recent Enterprise Survey data are considered for each country, from 2009 onward. In some countries where the survey was conducted in 2009, only manufacturing firms were asked questions about training, so the related statistics should be interpreted as referring to manufacturing only for Brazil, Burkina Faso, Cabo Verde, Chad, Eritrea, Fiji, the Federated States of Micronesia, Niger, Samoa, and Tonga.
2. Literacy is defined as the skills of (1) "recording information of some kind in some code understood by the person making the record and possibly by other persons in some more or less permanent form and (2) decoding the information so recorded." Similarly, numeracy is defined as "the skill of using and recording numbers and numerical operations for a variety of purposes" (Oxenham 2002).

References

Abadzi, Helen. 2006. *Efficient Learning for the Poor: Insights from the Frontier of Cognitive Neuroscience.* Directions in Development Series. Washington, DC: World Bank.

Acemoglu, Daron. 1998. "Why Do New Technologies Complement Skills? Directed Technical Change and Wage Inequality." *Quarterly Journal of Economics* 113 (4): 1055–89.

Acemoglu, Daron, and Fabrizio Zilbotti. 1999. "Productivity Differences." NBER Working Paper 6879, National Bureau of Economic Research, Cambridge, MA.

Adam, Susanna. 1995. *Competence Utilization and Transfer in Informal Sector Production and Service Trades in Ibadan/Nigeria.* Bremer Afrika-Studien 16. Münster: Lit.

Adams, Arvil, Sara Johansson, and Setareh Razmara, eds. 2013. *Improving Skills Development in the Informal Sector: Strategies for Sub-Saharan Africa.* Directions in Development Series. Washington, DC: World Bank.

Adoho, Franck, Shubha Chakravarty, Dala T. Korkoyah Jr., Mattias Lundberg, and Afia Tasneem. 2014. "The Impact of an Adolescent Girls Employment Program: The EPAG Project in Liberia." Policy Research Working Paper 6832, World Bank, Washington, DC. http://papers.ssrn.com/sol3/papers.cfm?abstract_id=2420245.

Aggarwal, Ashwani, and Christine Hofmann. 2010. "A Study on Informal Apprenticeship in Malawi." Employment Report, International Labour Organization, Geneva. http://www.ilo.org/wcmsp5/groups/public/---ed_emp/documents/publication/wcms _151254.pdf.

Aitchison, John, and Hassana Alidou. 2009. "The State and Development of Adult Learning and Education in Subsaharan Africa: Regional Synthesis Report." UNESCO Institute for Lifelong Learning, Hamburg, Germany.

Aker, Jenny C., Christopher Ksoll, and Travis J. Lybbert. 2012. "Can Mobile Phones Improve Learning? Evidence from a Field Experiment in Niger." *American Economic Journal: Applied Economics* 4 (4): 94–120.

Aker, Jenny, and Melita Sawyer. 2017. "Adult Learning in Sub-Saharan Africa: What Do and Don't We Know?" Tufts University, Medford, MA.

Alibhai, Salman, Niklas Buehren, and Sreelakshmi Papineni. 2016. "From Learning to Earning: An Impact Evaluation of the Digital Opportunity Trust (DOT) Entrepreneurship Training." Africa Gender Innovation Lab, World Bank, Washington, DC.

Almeida, Rita, Jere Behrman, and David Robalino. 2012. *The Right Skills for the Job? Rethinking Training Policies for Workers.* Human Development Perspectives Series. Washington, DC: World Bank. http://www-wds.worldbank.org/external/default /WDSContentServer/WDSP/IB/2012/07/11/000333038_20120711021256/Rendered /PDF/709080PUB0EPI0067869B09780821387146.pdf.

Anderson, Stephen J., Rajesh Chandy, and Bilal Zia. 2016. "Pathways to Profits: Identifying Separate Channels of Small Firm Growth through Business Training." Policy Research Working Paper, World Bank, Washington, DC.

Aubery, Frédéric, John Giles, and David Sahn. 2016. "Do Apprenticeships Provide Skills Beyond the Master's Trade? Evidence on Apprenticeships, Skills, and the Transition to Work in Senegal." Working Paper 256, Cornell University, Ithaca, NY.

Bandiera, Oriana, Robin Burgess, Narayan Das, Selim Gulesci, Imran Rasul, and Munshi Sulaiman. 2013. *Can Basic Entrepreneurship Transform the Economic Lives of the Poor?* London: International Growth Centre.

Banerjee, Abhijit, Esther Duflo, Nathanael Goldberg, Dean Karlan, Robert Osei, William Parienté, Jeremy Shapiro, Bram Thuysbaert, and Christopher Udry. 2015. "A Multifaceted Program Causes Lasting Progress for the Very Poor: Evidence from Six Countries." *Science* 348 (6236): 1260799.

Barron, John M., Mark C. Berger, and Dan A. Black. 1997. "How Well Do We Measure Training?" *Journal of Labor Economics* 15 (3): 507–28.

Bartel, Ann P., and Nachum Sicherman. 1993. "Technological Change and Retirement Decisions of Older Workers." *Journal of Labor Economics* 11 (1, pt. 1): 162–83.

Beneke de Sanfeliú, Margarita. 2014. "Evaluación de impacto del Programa de Apoyo Temporal al Ingreso (PATI)." Centro de Investigación y Estadísticas de FUSADES, La Libertad, El Salvador.

Berge, Lars Ivar Oppedal, Kjetil Bjorvatn, and Bertil Tungodden. 2015. "Human and Financial Capital for Microenterprise Development: Short-Term and Long-Term Evidence from a Field Experiment in Tanzania." *Management Science* 61 (4): 707–22.

Bertrand, Marianne, Bruno Crépon, Alicia Marguerie, and Patrick Premand. 2017. "Contemporaneous and Post-Program Impacts of a Public Works Program: Evidence from Côte d'Ivoire." Working Paper, World Bank, Washington, DC.

Blattman, Christopher, and Stefan Dercon. 2016. "Occupational Choice in Early Industrializing Societies: Experimental Evidence on the Income and Health Effects of Industrial and Entrepreneurial Work." IZA Discussion Paper, Institute of Labor Economics, Bonn.

Blattman, Christopher, Nathan Fiala, and Sebastian Martinez. 2014. "Generating Skilled Self-Employment in Developing Countries: Experimental Evidence from Uganda." *Quarterly Journal of Economics* 129 (2): 697–752.

Bloom, Nicholas, Benn Eifert, Aprajit Mahajan, David McKenzie, and John Roberts. 2013. "Does Management Matter? Evidence from India." *Quarterly Journal of Economics* 128 (1): 1–51.

Campos, Francisco, Michael Frese, Markus Goldstein, Leonardo Iacovone, Hillary Johnson, David McKenzie, and Mona Mensmann. 2016. "Personality vs. Practices in the Making of an Entrepreneur: Experimental Evidence from Togo." Draft paper for the 2017 Centre for the Study of African Economies (CSAE) conference "Economic Development in Africa," Oxford, UK, March 19–21.

Chakravarty, Shubha, Smita Das, and Julia Vaillant. 2017. "Gender and Youth Employment in Sub-Saharan Africa: A Review of Constraints and Effective Interventions." Policy Research Working Paper 8245, World Bank Group, Washington, DC.

Cole, Shawn A., and A. Nilesh Fernando. 2012. "The Value of Advice: Evidence from Mobile Phone-Based Agricultural Extension." Harvard Business School Finance Working Paper 13-047, Harvard Business School, Cambridge, MA.

Collier, Paul, and Jan Willem Gunning. 1999. "Why Has Africa Grown Slowly?" *Journal of Economic Perspectives* 13 (3): 3–22.

Cromley, Jennifer G. 2005. "Metacognition, Cognitive Strategy Instruction, and Reading in Adult Literacy." *Review of Adult Learning and Literacy* 5 (7): 187–220.

Darvas, Peter, and Robert Palmer. 2014. *Demand and Supply of Skills in Ghana: How Can Training Programs Improve Employment and Productivity?* Washington, DC: World Bank.

Davodoun, Complan Cyr. 2011. *Apprentissages dans l'artisanat au Benin.* Cotonou: Editions Ruisseaux d'Afrique.

Dehaene, Stanislas, Felipe Pegado, Lucia W. Braga, Paulo Ventura, Gilberto Nunes Filho, Antoinette Jobert, Ghislaine Dehaene-Lambertz, Régine Kolinsky, José Morais, and Laurent Cohen. 2010. "How Learning to Read Changes the Cortical Networks for Vision and Language." *Science* 330 (6009): 1359–64. http://www.ncbi.nlm.nih.gov /pubmed/21071632.

Escobal, Javier, and Carmen Ponce. 2015. "Combining Social Protection with Economic Opportunities in Rural Peru: Haku Wiñay." *Policy in Focus* 12 (2): 22–25.

Fafchamps, Marcel. 1996. "The Enforcement of Commercial Contracts in Ghana." *World Development* 24 (3): 427–48.

———. 2003. *Market Institutions in Sub-Saharan Africa: Theory and Evidence.* Cambridge, MA: MIT Press.

Franz, Jutta. 2016. "Apprenticeship Training in Africa." Background paper for this report, World Bank, Washington, DC.

Giné, Xavier, and Ghazala Mansuri. 2011. "Money or Ideas ? A Field Experiment on Constraints to Entrepreneurship in Rural Pakistan." Policy Research Working Paper 6959, World Bank, Washington, DC. http://www-wds.worldbank.org/servlet /WDSContentServer/WDSP/IB/2014/06/30/000158349_20140630163715/Rendered /PDF/WPS6959.pdf.

Goldin, Nichole, and Matthew Hobson with Peter Glick, Mattias Lundberg, and Susana Puerto. 2015. *Toward Solutions for Youth Employment: A 2015 Baseline Report.* Solutions for Youth Employment (S4YE) Coalition. https://www.ilo.org/employment /areas/youth-employment/WCMS_413826/lang--en/index.htm.

González-Velosa, Carolina, Laura Ripani, and David Rosas Shady. 2012. "How Can Job Opportunities for Young People in Latin America Be Improved?" IDB Technical Note IDB-TN-345, Inter-American Development Bank, Washington, DC. http://publica tions.iadb.org/handle/11319/5539.

Goyal, Aparajita, and John Nash. 2017. *Reaping Richer Returns: Public Spending Priorities for African Agriculture Productivity Growth.* Africa Development Forum. Washington, DC: World Bank.

Gunning, Jan Willem, Arne Bigsten, Paul Collier, Stefan Dercon, Marcel Fafchamps, Bernard Gauthier, Abena Oduro, Catherine Pattillo, Måns Söderbom, Francis Teal, and A. Zeufack. 2003. "Credit Constraints in Manufacturing Enterprises in Africa." *Journal of African Economies* 12 (1): 110–25.

Hardy, Morgan, and Jamie McCasland. 2015. "Are Small Firms Labor Constrained? Experimental Evidence from Ghana." Department of Economics, University of Notre Dame, South Bend, IN. https://economics.nd.edu/assets/217472/.

Hayes, Elisabeth, and Daniele D. Flannery. 2000. *Women as Learners: The Significance of Gender in Adult Learning.* Jossey-Bass Higher and Adult Education Series. Hoboken, NJ: Jossey-Bass.

Heckman, James J., Lance Lochner, and Christopher Taber. 1998. "Explaining Rising Wage Inequality: Explorations with a Dynamic General Equilibrium Model of Labor Earnings with Heterogeneous Agents." *Review of Economic Dynamics* 1 (1): 1–58.

Hicks, Joan Hamory, Michael Kremer, Isaac Mbiti, and Edward Miguel. 2011. "Vocational Education Voucher Delivery and Labor Market Returns: A Randomized Evaluation among Kenyan Youth." World Bank, Washington, DC.

Hoare, Carol. 2006. *Handbook of Adult Development and Learning.* Oxford, UK: Oxford University Press.

Honorati, Maddalena. 2015. "The Impact of Private Sector Internship and Training on Urban Youth in Kenya." Policy Research Working Paper 7404, World Bank, Washington, DC.

Honorati, Maddalena, and Yoonyoung Cho. 2013. "Entrepreneurship Programs in Developing Countries: A Meta Regression Analysis." *Labor Economics* 28 (June): 110–30.

Horne, Richard, Sameer Khatiwada, and Ste Kuhn. 2016. *World Employment and Social Outlook: Trends 2016.* Geneva: ILO.

ILO (International Labour Organization). Various years. School-to-Work Transition Survey. Geneva: ILO. http://www.ilo.org/employment/areas/youth-employment /work-for-youth/WCMS_191853/lang--en/index.htm.

ISTARN (Informal Sector Training and Resources Network). 1999. *Adding Value Manuals.* Manual 1: *Is a TAP (Traditional Apprenticeship Programme) an Option for You?* Manual 2: *How to Set up and Run a TAP (Traditional Apprenticeship Programme).* Harare: ISTARN, German Technical Cooperation Agency.

Johanson, Richard. 2009. "A Review of National Training Funds." Social Protection Discussion Paper, World Bank, Washington, DC. http://siteresources.worldbank.org /SOCIALPROTECTION/Resources/SP-Discussion-papers/Labor-Market-DP /0922.pdf.

Johanson, Richard, and Theogene Gakuba. 2011. "Rwanda: Training for the Informal Sector." Unpublished paper, Africa Department, World Bank, Washington, DC.

Kluve, Jochen, Susana Puerto, David Robalino, Jose Manuel Romero, Friederike Rother, Jonathan Stöterau, Felix Weidenkaff, and Marc Witte. 2017. "Interventions to Improve Labour Market Outcomes of Youth: A Systematic Review of Training, Entrepreneurship Promotion, Employment Services, and Subsidized Employment Interventions." Campbell Systematic Review 2017-12-04. Campbell Collaboration, Oslo. https://www .campbellcollaboration.org/library/improving-youth-labour-market-outcomes.html.

Knowland, Victoria C. P., and Michael S. C. Thomas. 2014. "Educating the Adult Brain: How the Neuroscience of Learning Can Inform Educational Policy." *International Review of Education* 60 (1): 99–122.

Ksoll, Christopher, Jenny Aker, Danielle Miller, Karla C. Perez-Mendoza, and Susan L. Smalley. 2014. "Learning without Teachers? A Randomized Experiment of a Mobile Phone-Based Adult Education Program in Los Angeles." Working Paper 368, Center for Global Development, Washington, DC.

McCandliss, Bruce D., Laurent Cohen, and Stanislas Dehaene. 2003. "The Visual Word Form Area: Expertise for Reading in the Fusiform Gyrus." *Trends in Cognitive Sciences* 7 (7): 293–99.

McKay, Veronica. 2015. "Measuring and Monitoring in the South African Kha Ri Gude Mass Literacy Campaign." *International Review of Education* 61 (3): 365–97.

McKenzie, David, and Susana Puerto. 2017. "Business Training for Female Microenterprise Owners in Kenya Grew Their Firms without Harming Their Competitors." Finance and PSD Impact 42, World Bank, Washington, DC.

McKenzie, David, and Christopher Woodruff. 2013. "What Are We Learning from Business Training and Entrepreneurship Evaluations around the Developing World?" *World Bank Research Observer* 29 (1): 48–82.

Oxenham, John. 2002. "Skills and Literacy Training for Better Livelihoods: A Review of Approaches and Experiences." Africa Region Findings and Good Practice Infobrief 209, World Bank, Washington, DC.

Paterson, Andrew, and Jacques L. Du Toit. 2005. "Uneven South African Private Enterprise Training: The National Skills Survey of 2003." *Journal of Vocational Education and Training* 57 (4): 477–97.

Perotti, Valeria. 2017. "Training, Skills, and Firm Productivity in Formal African Firms." Background paper for this report, World Bank, Washington, DC.

Puerta, Maria Laura Sanchez, and Mathilde Perinet. 2016. *Kenya Jobs for Youth*. Report 101685-KE. Washington, DC: World Bank, Social Protection and Labor Global Practice Africa Region.

Rodrik, Dani. 2016. "Premature Deindustrialization." *Journal of Economic Growth* 21 (1): 1–33.

Rosholm, Michael, Helena Skyt Nielsen, and Andrew Dabalen. 2007. "Evaluation of Training in African Enterprises." *Journal of Development Economics* 84 (1): 310–29.

Royer, James M., Helen Abadzi, and Jules Kinda. 2004. "The Impact of Phonological-Awareness and Rapid-Reading Training on the Reading Skills of Adolescent and Adult Neoliterates." *International Review of Education* 50 (1): 53–71.

Sekkat, Khalid. 2011. "Firm Sponsored Training and Productivity in Morocco." *Journal of Development Studies* 47 (9): 1391–409.

UNESCO (United Nations Educational, Scientific, and Cultural Organization). 2015. *EFA Global Monitoring Report 2015: Regional Overview; Sub-Saharan Africa*. Paris: UNESCO.

Valerio, Alexandra, Maria Laura Sanchez Puerta, Namrata Tognatta, and Sebastian Monroy-Taborda. 2016. "Are There Skills Payoffs in Low- and Middle-Income Countries?" Policy Research Working Paper 7879, World Bank, Washington, DC.

Valerio, Alexandria, Viviana Roseth, and Omar Arias. 2016. "Improving Workforce Skills: The Role of Training." Background paper for this report, World Bank, Washington, DC.

van den Ban, Anne W., and H. Stuart Hawkins. 1996. *Agricultural Extension*. Hoboken, NJ: Blackwell Science Ltd.

Walther, Richard, and Ewa Filipiak. 2008. *Towards a Renewal of Apprenticeship in West Africa. Enhancing the Professional Integration of Young People*. Paris: Agence Française de Développement.

Wellard, Kate, Jenny Rafanomezana, Mahara Nyirenda, Misaki Okotel, and Vincent Subbey. 2013. "A Review of Community Extension Approaches to Innovation for Improved Livelihoods in Ghana, Uganda, and Malawi." *Journal of Agricultural Education and Extension* 19 (1): 21–35.

World Bank. 2007. *World Development Report 2008: Agriculture for Development*. Washington, DC: World Bank.

———. Various years. ASPIRE (Atlas of Social Protection Indicators of Resilience and Equity) database. Washington, DC: World Bank, Social Protection and Jobs Global Practice.

———. Various years. Enterprise Surveys database. Washington, DC: World Bank.

www.ingramcontent.com/pod-product-compliance
Lightning Source LLC
Chambersburg PA
CBHW060136280326
41932CB00012B/1538